Design Research Foundations

The goal of the series is to provide a platform for publishing state of the art research on foundational issues in design and its applications in industry and society. Suitable topics range from methodological issues in design research to philosophical reflections on the specificities of design rather than actual design work or empirical cases only. The definition of design behind the series is inclusive. In terms of disciplines, it ranges from engineering to architecture. In terms of design work, it ranges from conceptual issues in design through design experiments and prototypes to evaluative studies of design and its foundations.

Proposals should include:

A proposal form, as can be found on this page
A short synopsis of the work or the introduction chapter
The proposed Table of Contents
The CV of the lead author(s)
If available: one sample chapter

We aim to make a first decision within 1 month of submission. In case of a positive first decision the work will be provisionally contracted: the final decision about publication will depend upon the result of the anonymous peer review of the complete manuscript. The series editors aim to have the complete work peer-reviewed within 3 months of submission.

The series discourages the submission of manuscripts that contain reprints of previous published material and/or manuscripts that are below 150 pages/75,000 words.

For inquiries and submission of proposals authors can contact the series editors, Pieter Vermaas via: p.e.vermaas@tudelft.nl; or Ilpo Koskinen via: ilpo.koskinen@polyu.edu.hk

More information about this series at http://www.springer.com/series/13775

Thomas Fischer • Christiane M. Herr
Editors

Design Cybernetics

Navigating the New

Springer

Editors
Thomas Fischer
Department of Architecture
Xi'an Jiaotong-Liverpool University
Suzhou, Jiangsu Province, China

Christiane M. Herr
Department of Architecture
Xi'an Jiaotong-Liverpool University
Suzhou, Jiangsu Province, China

ISSN 2366-4622 ISSN 2366-4630 (electronic)
Design Research Foundations
ISBN 978-3-030-18556-5 ISBN 978-3-030-18557-2 (eBook)
https://doi.org/10.1007/978-3-030-18557-2

This Springer imprint is published by the registered company Springer Nature Switzerland AG.
The registered company address is: Gewerbestrasse 11, 6330 Cham, Switzerland

Foreword
Ranulph's Heritage: Design Cybernetics

Most people will initially perceive design and cybernetics as two very separate fields, but as will become clear from this book, both fields have a lot to offer to each other. The work of Ranulph Glanville has enormously contributed to making researchers understand the potential and mutual value. In fact, Ranulph inspired many designers with concepts from cybernetics, and, by doing so, he learned from them to sharpen his ideas of cybernetics and then brought these back to cyberneticians. This book captures Ranulph's heritage and develops a foundational layer for research in architecture, design and arts (the creative disciplines). In doing so, it establishes the field of *design cybernetics*. As such, this book should be warmly welcomed as a valuable and relevant continuation of what Ranulph and others have been working on for a while.

(Second-order) cybernetics has developed into a meta-field which studies systems and develops overarching principles. It takes a constructivist perspective and seriously values the observer being part of the system. This is a fundamental concept connecting to the recent shifts in science which more and more recognise the value of the specific and subjective position of the researcher-observer. It is the position in which the researchers in architecture, design and arts undertake their endeavours. Fundamental is the understanding that the researcher-observer is part of the system and not an observer who is neutral and external to the system he/she is researching. It also embraces the subjective position of the designer in all his/her work. To value the specificity and the potential of such experiences is very much in line with the way venturous practitioners research, not by trying to establish objective observations but to construct knowledge from the personal and specific observations and actions.

A further relevant quality which resides in cybernetics is that it is interested in opening up possibilities and choice; this is something many designers and artists value and are looking for as well. Furthermore, many designer-researchers do not fully understand their knowledge processes, how our understanding comes into being and how their research develops. The concept of conversation reflection, and sketching as a way of a conversation with the self will help us in explaining their underlying cognitive processes.

I first met Ranulph Glanville at the eCAADe Conference 1995 in Palermo. Adam Jakimowicz (from TU Bialystok, Poland) introduced me to him in the lobby of a hotel, and he immediately made a strong impression on me. We did have a little bit of small talk, he made a couple of funny comments, and it soon became clear he was a special person. He was interested in learning from people, and it turned out that he was interested in how one could use digital systems in unconventional ways to let the computer surprise you. This perspective was interesting and refreshing in a community where technical possibilities and developments were high on the agenda and the main focus.

Some years later, he visited my family and playfully interacted with my children. He did it in such a way they became interested in learning from him (even though there were huge language barriers as they were still very young). He told stories and anecdotes, at the same time connecting to their interests and asking questions in such a way their thinking was stimulated, hence opening their view on the world and what was going on. I understood that this was his way of probing and testing and exploring the world in a playful way, educating others and helping them to learn and, at the same time, improving and learning himself. It was his way of living and behaving. In his genuinely cybernetic way of living, Ranulph acted on everything which and everyone who entered his range of attention. This happened playfully and enjoyably. He always tried to learn and to help others gain insight and make them learn. He tried to bring delight, to push borders and trigger innovation.

Only much later on, I learned Ranulph was an expert in cybernetics, a field which was at that time completely unknown to me. The field is also mostly unknown to architects and designers, although it includes many relevant concepts for them. Ranulph was educated in architecture and received his degree from the Architectural Association (AA) School in London. During his final year, he spent most of his time working with Gordon Pask and soon began contributing to developing cybernetics. Later on, he further developed and became a proponent of second-order cybernetics.

Having interacted with Ranulph Glanville for many years (and having spent some time during the holidays with him and his "Mrs. wife", the wonderful Aartje Hulstein), I feel privileged to write the Foreword for this book, *Design Cybernetics: Navigating the New*. Having experienced the value of Ranulph's work and cybernetics in general to research in architecture, design and arts, it is wonderful to see how cybernetics and the creative disciplines are brought together in this book.

Although he may have gained more recognition in the field of cybernetics, his impact on research in architecture, design and arts should not be undervalued. To develop his ideas, he found a fertile context supporting and contributing to the development of the PhD programmes at RMIT,[1] Sint-Lucas School of Architecture

[1]Van Schaik, Leon and Anna Johnson. 2011. *By Practice, BY invitation: Design practice research in architecture and design at RMIT, 1986–2011*. Melbourne: onepointsixone. http://www.blurb.com/books/3599320-the-pink-book

(KU Leuven)[2] and the RCA (Royal College of Arts, London).[3] He talked to PhD candidates and helped and inspired them. He did so by asking questions and trying to help to explicate their ways of developing knowledge. He was a fan of Samuel Beckett's phrase "Fail, fail again, fail better". At the same time, his work in these schools and how he inspired and positively impacted on the doctoral candidates prove the value cybernetic thinking brings to architecture, design, and arts. Consequently, I am convinced this book will further Ranulph's heritage into future research endeavours. Through his cybernetic way of looking for surprise and his interest in every phenomenon, Ranulph helped designers to explicate and value the qualities in what they are doing. It is this attitude, not imposing any specific method but looking for the interesting and inspiring, valuing the observations and the experiences, as a subjective observer within a system or activity, which helps to develop a fertile research context in the creative disciplines. It is this attitude which is part of a cybernetic way of looking and experiencing the world that is of paramount relevance for the creative disciplines. Moreover, it is this position which is explained, clarified and explicated in this book. The book helps the reader to develop a deeper understanding of key concepts of cybernetics which may help to develop the research of venturous practitioners and creative researchers.

Research in the field of the creative disciplines has been developing enormously during the last three decades, partly because of pressure from governments, partly because of the Bologna declaration and partly because schools see the benefit in developing research. This is reflected in a growing number of prominent PhD programmes, academic conferences and research projects, especially artistic research, research by design and creative practice research value building on the vast (usually tacit) knowledge residing in creative processes and practices.

Although momentum has been gained and there is much developing and wonderful PhD projects have been completed, many researchers find challenges in their school and university contexts to argue the value of their undertakings. As they position themselves as designers and researchers, it is obvious they take a very different perspective than the positivist one. It is in this context that this book, *Design Cybernetics: Navigating the New*, becomes useful. It provides a background and context to explain the knowledge processes in the creative disciplines. Furthermore, it shows that what is happening in these disciplines should not be seen as something special but as something which is very much in line with what is happening in other disciplines. Cybernetics comes in very useful here. Cybernetics and this book bring a position where it is natural to position oneself as a researcher within the system one is observing. It also values a constructivist approach. It is this fundamental position which is crucial to further the creative disciplines in their research endeavours, and it is cybernetics and this book which bring the arguments and the foundation, a crucial

[2] Verbeke, Johan. 2016. Ranulph and Sint-Lucas. *In Ranulph Glanville. Art architecture cybernetics design. London and the 1960s*, eds. Marianne Ertl, Werner Korn, and Albert Müller, 33–44. Vienna: edition echoraum.

[3] https://vimeo.com/131408983

and highly needed open and inclusive perspective on knowledge and how to extract it from our experiences and undertakings. Hence, this book is highly needed and timely as it will allow in consolidating and building further on the explorative work of the past years.

To make these statements more tangible for the reader, I will introduce two short examples. Occam's razor[4] is a very well-known concept, the idea of simplicity (which is also connected to beauty and aesthetics) bringing the best explanation for a phenomenon. Designers usually deal with a mess and a multitude of issues, all brought together in wicked problems. While architects, designers and artists are inclined to work towards solving the big complex problems, Occam's razor helps us to focus on the simple but powerful aspects which bring understanding and delight. It has helped researchers to suddenly understand what was the important issue they were dealing with.

Ashby's law of requisite variety[5] is very relevant for architects and designers. At the moment in time where we begin to understand that it is impossible to control cities, Ashby's law makes researchers understand they should not aim for trying to control societal development with more and more sophisticated systems, but they should aim for allowing possibilities within a certain range. This is very relevant in architecture and urban design, especially when discussing smart cities.

The authors of the chapters in this book have been active in the domain for many years, some more in cybernetics while others more from the design perspective. They bring a wide range of experiences, and this is one of the qualities of this book. The wide range of contributions, from a more historical background and theoretical chapters to design perspectives, contributes to a stimulating experience for the reader. Consequently, researchers in cybernetics as well as in design and practice will find valuable insight in this book.

In line with the above perspective, this book will be a great reading for (a) cyberneticians as they can learn from the use of concepts in design – it will bring these concepts into reality – and (b) researchers in architecture, design and arts as they will find concepts and theories which shine new light on their work. It will especially bring explorative and innovative perspectives on what research has to offer to researchers in the creative disciplines. It will help researchers struggling to find ways forward by offering paths to pursue in doing what brings delight.

The book is an entertaining and inspiring collection of chapters. These range from more historical to more connected to design research as is very well explained in the Preface. The book is interesting as it gives the reader, either a researcher in design or his/her supervisor, a meta-level perspective which will help to frame the research. Furthermore, it will provide a range of concepts and perspectives which will help them explain how knowledge comes into being and how processes bring value. The book is worth reading and studying as it offers researchers ways to find confidence in how they position themselves in academia.

---

[4]"Entities must not be multiplied beyond necessity" being one of the popular formulations.

[5]The degree of control of a system is proportional to the amount of information available.

The book can be seen as a sincere effort by a group of excellent researchers to bridge the gap between cybernetics and architecture, design and arts in establishing a transdisciplinary field of design cybernetics. It can be expected that in the future, design cybernetics will impact on both cybernetics and the creative disciplines. Consequently, it will contribute to opening the understanding of what research in these fields is for more possibilities and variety. I am convinced this is the start of a great new development.

Aarhus/Elewijt
July 2017

Prof. Dr. Johan Verbeke[6]

[6]Editor's note: Johan Verbeke unexpectedly passed away on Sunday, August 6, 2017, at the age of 55, shortly after contributing the Foreword to this volume.

Preface

The convergence of design and cybernetics continues to be a major undertaking spanning several decades and disciplines and involving numerous contributors. Of these, nobody has contributed to the establishment of design cybernetics as much as Ranulph Glanville (shown with his wife, Aartje Hulstein, in Fig. 1). Having been introduced to cybernetics by Gordon Pask while studying at the Architectural Association in London in the 1960s, Glanville spent the following decades bringing design and cybernetics together in various ways, developing an explicitly cybernetic theory of design between the 1970s and late 2014.

Fig. 1 Aartje Hulstein and Ranulph Glanville upon receiving the American Society for cybernetics' joint 2014 special award at the Clarion Collection Hotel Savoy in Oslo on the 17th of October 2014

Milestones by which Glanville helped establish design cybernetics (besides his numerous writings, presentations, thesis supervisions and so on) include his guest-editing of a 2007 special double issue of the journal *Kybernetes* on the subject of cybernetics and design; his chairing of the 2010 conference of the American Society for Cybernetics titled "Cybernetics: Art, Design, Mathematics" at Rensselaer Polytechnic Institute in Troy, NY; the publication of his *The Black Boox* trilogy with edition echoraum in Vienna in 2009, 2013 and 2014; as well as his keynote lecture titled *How design and cybernetics reflect each other* at the Third Relating Systems Thinking and Design Symposium in Oslo in October of 2014. Now, over a decade after the *Kybernetes* special issue, this volume brings together another collection of articles on design cybernetics with an emphasis on design research, including a reprint of the paper Glanville himself contributed to the 2007 *Kybernetes* issue.

Involved in several postgraduate programmes including RMIT University, the RCA and KU Leuven, Glanville travelled extensively and described himself as a faculty member of the "University of 747". Many who encountered Glanville in these predominantly architectural contexts, including several authors contributing to this volume, adopted design cybernetics as integral parts of their approaches to research. The roots at the Architectural Association and Glanville's impact in leading postgraduate architectural programmes contributed to the close connections between design cybernetics and architecture in recent decades.

The initiative to produce this volume originated during a breakfast conversation at the Scandic Hotel Potsdamer Platz in Berlin during the 2015 conference of the International Society for the Systems Sciences (ISSS), half a year after Glanville's death, when seven of us, all mid-career academics, resolved to celebrate Glanville's design cybernetics with an edited collection of our Glanville-inspired work. Our group soon grew to include more representatives of a new generation of design cyberneticians engaged in the advancement of design cybernetics in a range of fields, extending well beyond our group's earlier architectural centre of gravity. Once we had the opportunity to propose this volume for inclusion in Springer's Design Research Foundations series, we followed the series editors' encouragement to also seek contributions from eminent design cyberneticians. The volume then grew to its present form and now offers a comprehensive cross-section of work undertaken in design cybernetics.

The 16 chapters presented here offer readers a multitude of perspectives on the field of design cybernetics, ranging across architecture, interior lighting studies, product design, embedded systems, design pedagogy, design theory, social transformation design, enquiry theory, art and poetics as well as theatre and acting. We hope this variety will offer suitable entry points to design cybernetics for readers from a similarly broad range of backgrounds. Readers will identify overlaps and intersections as well as differences and contrasts between the contributions included here. We believe these reflect the subjective appropriation and appreciation of concepts described by radical constructivism, a close relative of second-order cybernetics. This plurality of perspectives and voices, we hope, will illuminate and contextualise design cybernetics in ways that are accessible to readers from various design-related backgrounds. Furthermore, we offer any differences readers may identify between the following contributions as invitations to engage with design cybernetics, to participate and to contribute to the field's further development.

We open this collection with an introduction to design cybernetics, tracing the development of both design research and cybernetics since World War II to realisations of the limits of control, and on to the second-order cybernetic conception of design as an open-ended, conversational and ethical process.

In a reprint of his 2007 *Kybernetes* article, Ranulph Glanville establishes design and cybernetics as complementary arms of each other. Presenting cybernetics as a theory for design, and design as cybernetics in practice, Glanville notes that both cybernetics and design imply the same ethical qualities, which stand in contrast to qualities associated with traditional scientific research. Glanville makes the case that scientific research is a subset of design.

Liss C. Werner illuminates design cybernetics from the perspective of its origins in conversation theory, developed by the British cybernetician, Gordon Pask.

Approaching design as conversation, Hugh Dubberly and Paul Pangaro offer a second-order cybernetic framing of *both* the means (process) and the ends (outcomes) of designing and present "second-order design" as creating possibilities for others to have conversations.

Delfina Fantini van Ditmar critically examines and questions the embedded epistemology of the Internet of Things (IoT), which she refers to as the algorithmic paradigm, when applied to human activities in "smart" homes.

In a thoroughly updated version of a 2007 paper, Klaus Krippendorff reciprocally connects cybernetics and design and contrasts both with what the sciences do. After developing cybernetic epistemologies that constructively embrace the practices of design, he applies cybernetics to the emergence of artefacts in interactions between organisms and their environments, associating cybernetic epistemology with the evolution of sensory-motor coordinations, not of things, and finally develops a cybernetics of human-centred design.

Based on Glanville's observation that design and research are fundamentally related and that design methods may be applied across domains, Ted Krueger and Ute C. Besenecker present a case study of the perceptual effects of alternate contemporary lighting technologies at an architectural scale to show how designers/researchers can approach this kind of investigation from a design-cybernetic perspective.

Christiane M. Herr introduces radical constructivist theory in the context of design cybernetics and illustrates how its approach to learning complements and extends the conversational perspective on designing and reviews implications of radical constructivist epistemology for design research and design education.

Highlighting some prevalent features of contemporary devised theatre practice, Tom Scholte develops parallels between Halprin's *RSVP cycles* and Glanville's cybernetic conception of design in which lack of control, transcomputable complexity and under-specification of the problems investigated become virtues that propel us on a conversational forward search in which we must "act in order to understand" while bound by a deep ethical commitment to the autonomy of others.

Ben Sweeting reviews the intimate relationship between cybernetics and design in terms of their shared concerns with conversational interaction, drawing on the work of Ranulph Glanville and Gordon Pask.

Michael Hohl argues that design educators and design students may learn from cultural traditions of the Polynesian Voyaging Society and from its "Eight Elements of Education", explaining that this source of informal knowledge, combined with modern means to communicate and to collaborate, can lead to new, more empathetic, ethical and environmentally aware ways of designing.

Timothy Jachna draws on second-order cybernetic principles and concepts, particularly those associated with Pask's conversation theory and subsequent work inspired by and derived from it, to propose a conceptual basis for articulating modalities of designing with others.

Taking uncertainty and limited understanding as fundamental, Claudia Westermann argues that any activity is a design activity and presents second-order cybernetics as a basis for design poetics.

Thomas Fischer presents a *theory of (and for) enquiry* to show postgraduate and PhD design researchers and their supervisors how the challenge of defending their work may be approached where thesis examinations continue to adhere to tenets of (natural) science – not by creating inscrutable emulsions between design and scientific research but by concatenating and nesting multiple modes of design research.

Larry Richards describes cybernetics as a way of thinking about ways of thinking and, from the cybernetic vocabulary of choice and autonomy, develops an ethics for social transformation in which violence is not an alternative or, at least, is an alternative of last resort.

Wolfgang Jonas then presents a summarising and reflecting chapter in which he contextualises and critiques the positions offered in the preceding contributions. He identifies the further development and strengthening of design cybernetics as an urgent task ahead of us, to ensure its continuation in the harsh and unfriendly context of digitised global capitalism.

With this collection, we address cybernetically inclined designers and design researchers, and we hope to demonstrate the rigour, quality and potential of design cybernetics, not only in its formal manifestations but, first and foremost, in its aesthetic and ethical manifestations in the wider sphere of human judgement and values. As the easier-to-grasp first-order cybernetic subset of control engineering has taken the world by storm, the more-challenging-to-grasp second-order cybernetics of design spreads at a slower rate. This calls for an accommodating design cybernetic agenda of simplification and of exemplification. The present volume, we hope, will serve as a stepping stone in that agenda.

Finally, we acknowledge the valuable support we received while editing this volume, in particular from the editors of Springer's Design Research Foundations series, Clementine Thurgood, Ilpo Koskinen and Pieter E. Vermaas. For the permission to reprint Ranulph Glanville's article Try again. Fail again. Fail better, we thank Emerald, who published it in *Kybernetes* 36(9/10) on pages 1173–1206. As this article has subsequently also been published in volume II (pages 253–292) of Ranulph Glanville's *The Black Boox* trilogy with edition echoraum in Vienna, we are also indebted to Aartje Hulstein as well as to Albert Müller of the Department of Contemporary History at the University of Vienna for their reprint permission and for their kind advice. We also thank the Gordon Pask Archive in Vienna for their valuable advice and support.

Suzhou, China
January 30, 2019

Thomas Fischer
Christiane M. Herr

Contents

Contributors

Ute C. Besenecker Raumseele, West Warwick, RI, USA

Delfina Fantini van Ditmar Royal College of Art, Kensington Gore, London, UK

Hugh Dubberly Dubberly Design Office, San Francisco, CA, USA

Thomas Fischer Department of Architecture, Xi'an Jiaotong-Liverpool University, Suzhou, Jiangsu Province, China

Ranulph Glanville is deceased

Christiane M. Herr Department of Architecture, Xi'an Jiaotong-Liverpool University, Suzhou, Jiangsu Province, China

Michael Hohl Faculty of Design, Anhalt University of Applied Sciences, Dessau-Roßlau, Germany

Timothy Jachna College of Design, Architecture, Art and Planning, University of Cincinnati, Cincinnati, OH, USA

Wolfgang Jonas Braunschweig University of Art, Braunschweig, Germany

Klaus Krippendorff The Annenberg School for Communication, University of Pennsylvania, Philadelphia, PA, USA

Ted Krueger School of Architecture, Greene Building 212, Rensselaer Polytechnic Institute, Troy, NY, USA

Paul Pangaro Human-Computer Interaction Institute, Carnegie Mellon University, Pittsburgh, PA, USA

Laurence D. Richards Indiana University East, Richmond, IN, USA

Tom Scholte Department of Theatre and Film, University of British Columbia, Vancouver, BC, Canada

Ben Sweeting School of Architecture and Design, University of Brighton, Brighton, UK

Liss C. Werner Institute of Architecture, Technical University of Berlin, Berlin, Germany

Claudia Westermann Department of Architecture, Xi'an Jiaotong-Liverpool University, Suzhou, Jiangsu Province, China

Acronyms

AA	Architectural Association
AMG	Architecture Machine Group
AI	Artificial Intelligence
ASC	American Society for Cybernetics
BCL	Biological Computer Laboratory
CT	Conversation Theory
DRS	Design Research Society
DoD	Department of Defense
EMPAC	The Curtis R. Priem Experimental Media and Performing Arts Center
GPA	Gordon Pask Archive
HCD	Human-Centred Design
HCI	Human-Computer Interaction
ICA	Institute of Contemporary Arts, London
IoT	Internet of Things
ISSS	International Society for the Systems Sciences
KU	Catholic University of Leuven
MIT	Massachusetts Institute of Technology
NASA	National Aeronautics and Space Administration
NTM	Non-trivial Machine
PVS	Polynesian Voyaging Society
RCA	Royal College of Art
RIBA	Royal Institute of British Architects
RMIT	Royal Melbourne Institute of Technology
SD	Systems Dynamics
SoC	Second-Order Cybernetics
STS	Science and Technology Studies
TM	Trivial Machine

Chapter 1
An Introduction to Design Cybernetics

Thomas Fischer and Christiane M. Herr

Abstract Since it ascended in the mid-twentieth century on the basis of technical and scientific advances made during World War II, cybernetics has influenced design theory and research. It was appreciated by its originators primarily as a theoretical framework and as a common language to bridge disciplinary boundaries, but soon found more prominent applications in goal-oriented control engineering. Since around 1970, it developed a reflective, more philosophical, and less control-focused perspective referred to as second-order cybernetics. This perspective recognises circular causality, non-determinism, the subjective observer and other concepts avoided by natural science. In this way, it offers an approach to self-organising systems that negotiate their own goals in open-ended processes – in other words: design. As an introduction to design cybernetics, this chapter outlines the development of cybernetics from a technical engineering discipline to a design-philosophical perspective.

Keywords Cybernetics · Control · Communication · Design · History

1.1 Introduction

Cybernetics has come a long way since it was widely associated with the mechanistic feedback loops that engineers establish in thermostats, guided missiles and other control systems. Over the past half century, it has expanded its scope far beyond the technical systems and computational formality with which it has stereotypically been identified. Today, it also encompasses fields more closely concerned with human being: biology, management, social science, anthropology, education, therapy and, recently, design. Cybernetics offers an abstract philosophical approach to design as a creative epistemic practice. Unlike other disciplines, design is more to cybernetics

T. Fischer (✉) · C. M. Herr
Department of Architecture, Xi'an Jiaotong-Liverpool University, Suzhou, Jiangsu Province, China
e-mail: thomas.fischer@xjtlu.edu.cn; christiane.herr@xjtlu.edu.cn

T. Fischer, C. M. Herr (eds.), *Design Cybernetics*, Design Research Foundations,
https://doi.org/10.1007/978-3-030-18557-2_1

than merely an application field and has been described as cybernetics in practice (see page 25 in this volume). The purpose of this chapter is to contextualise design cybernetics by showing how a field that gained initial prominence for control engineering has come to offer itself as an approach to the doings of curious, creative, and ethical humans. Our discussion of this development begins around the time of World War II and addresses historical parallels and philosophical connections between cybernetics and design research.

1.2 World War II and the Rise of the Systems Traditions

Well before the outbreak of World War II, Norbert Wiener, who would come to be known as the "father of cybernetics" [9], had a ground-breaking insight. He realised that there is a notable difference between the "strong" electrical currents of power systems and the "weak" currents "that were transforming the sounds and sights of the Roaring Twenties" [9, p. 65]. He saw that electrical currents (as well as radio waves) in communication and control systems could be arbitrarily weak, as long as they performed their signalling function. After World War II broke out in Europe, Wiener and his collaborators Arturo Rosenblueth and Julian Bigelow had another profound insight: Since ancient Greece, Western thought had banned circular causality due to its inconvenient potential to produce paradox conditions, which conventional logic cannot resolve. The team realised, however, that certain systems, such as the metabolisms of higher organisms, "purposefully" respond to the effects of their own actions in circularly-causal ways [63]. Circular causality, while still posing a logical conundrum, could in practice no longer be ignored. With these insights, Wiener grasped key intellectual and technological transformations of his time. More than other military conflicts before, World War II would be shaped by insights into signals and causality, and hence unfolded not only as a war of power and force but also as one of communication and control. The Nazi regime for its part owed much of its rise to power to new means of communication, albeit along linearised relationships. Having placed affordable radio receivers in German homes and thereby established a one-directional propaganda dissemination network, the regime had, to a large extent, replaced social mutualism with hierarchical authoritarian structures.

Wiener sought to contribute to the war effort in the area of defence technology [24, p. 228]. Together with Bigelow, he attempted to develop an anti-aircraft artillery system that would predict the trajectories of attacking bombers and aim its projectiles "ahead of" the aircraft to achieve hits by the time fired projectiles reached their altitudes [9, pp. 110ff.]. Their system displayed a "positively uncanny" ability to predict aircraft trajectories across a few seconds. Over the required longer time spans, however, the system offered no operational benefits when compared with existing methods, and was therefore never applied in battle [9, pp. 120–123]. The Germans, meanwhile, incorporated internal guidance systems into airborne weapons such as the *Fritz X* and the *V-1* flying bombs. Using gyroscopes as attitude sensors, this approach had been pioneered decades earlier in the *Whitehead Torpedo*. It is based on circularly-causal self-regulation and what cyberneticians refer to as "negative feedback": Once a goal is set and a path to this goal is plotted, a system can be set up with a self-correcting cyclic signalling structure between motor output and sensory input called a "feedback loop" to regulate its movement continuously along this path. By minimising departures of its actual path from the plotted path, the so-called "error", such a system ensures its eventual arrival at its set goal.

When *V-1* flying bombs were launched across the English Channel, they encountered defence systems with negative feedback loops of their own in the form of automated radar tracking stations and projectiles containing proximity fuses: an unprecedented clash of autonomous weapons with little human interference [59, pp. 39–42]. When the successor of the *V-1*, the much faster *V-2* rocket, was used to attack London, the British managed to impose error-amplifying "positive feedback"[1] [49] on the missiles' goal-seeking negative feedback control by having double agents feed false impact locations back to the Germans, resulting in subsequent missiles being aimed away from their densely populated target areas, which is believed to have saved many lives [50, pp. 262ff.].

Other pioneering developments of World War II occurred in the fields of cryptography and cryptoanalysis, with key contributions from Alan Turing in the UK and Claude Shannon in the US. Also having worked on the above-mentioned anti-aircraft challenge [6], Shannon developed his signal analysis work into his well-known *Mathematical Theory of Communication* [66] (sometimes also referred to as *Communication Theory* or *Information Theory*). In this effort, Shannon was tutored by Wiener, and benefitted in particular from the statistical methods Wiener had developed for the anti-aircraft project [46, p. 31].

The rise of authoritarianism in Germany, Italy and Japan prompted the establishment of the Committee for National Morale in the US. Advising the President on matters of propaganda and public morale, the committee developed strategies to prevent the re-emergence of authoritarianism. It explained the National Socialist psyche with a separation of emotion from reason, with emotions being amplified, and reason being muted by mass-mediated propaganda. This view would soon inspire new kinds of media that allow individuals to freely make their own, emotionally grounded as well as rationally informed choices [71, pp. 64–65]. Members of democratic societies were not to be constrained from above, but to be free and guided by internal values. Government thus found itself in the paradoxical challenge to mandate from outside what must rise from within.

After the War, the relevance of control and circularly-causal feedback systems did not fade. When a small group of academics met to discuss cerebral inhibition, Bigelow's presentation of the work he had undertaken with Rosenblueth and Wiener on purposeful, circularly-causal systems caused much excitement. This prompted

[1] The terms "negative feedback" and "positive feedback" are also used less formally to describe discouraging and encouraging comments. Since not all encouraging comments are error-amplifying, and not all discouraging comments are error-reducing, the informal and the cybernetic uses of the two terms are different.

a series of further meetings on the subject between 1946 and 1953, with a core group and a changing cast of invited guests from a wide range of disciplines. Sponsored by the Josiah Macy, Jr. Foundation, this series of meetings is commonly referred to as the Macy Conferences [55]. Besides Wiener and his two collaborators, the core participants included neurophysiologists Warren McCulloch and Walter Pitts, mathematician John von Neumann, physicist Heinz von Foerster as well as anthropologists and Committee for National Morale alumni Margaret Mead and Gregory Bateson. The participants of the Macy Conferences overcame the jargons of their various subject areas and developed a common new language to explore their shared interest in circularly-causal feedback systems [51, p. 2]. In this way, the Macy Conferences became the cradle for what is today known as inter- and transdisciplinarity.

Mead had practised circular causality already in the 1920s during field work in the South Pacific. Mead rejected the scientific imperative of linearly-causal, "objectively" removed observation and became probably the first American to conduct anthropological research as a participant-observer [67, p. 268]. Independently from Mead, Wiener had rejected the notion of the objective observer and described observation as active participation in an article he published during his tenure as a visiting professor at Tsinghua University in Beijing between 1935 and 1936 [77].

The role of the observer became a contentious issue during one of the Macy meetings when the invited British cybernetician W. Ross Ashby presented his *Homeostat* – a configuration of four interconnected boxes. Each of the boxes had a movable indicator. When an experimenter moved one or more of these indicators away from their neutral position, the indicators on the remaining boxes would compensate by moving in proportional opposite ways, thus maintaining a stable overall average, comparable to the ways in which organisms maintain glucose levels and body temperatures. Ashby described the *Homeostat* in terms of the relationship between organism and environment. When Bigelow and other attendants asked where the boundary between organism and environment was drawn in the *Homeostat*, Ashby caused frustration by not committing to any particular boundary line between the four devices and the experimenter [55, p. 593; 59, p. 57]. Two years later he wrote [2, p. 39]:

> As the organism and its environment are to be treated as a single system, the dividing line between "organism" and "environment" becomes partly conceptual, and to that extent arbitrary.

Taking this view, Ashby agreed with Mead's and Wiener's views on observer-dependency. He also anticipated a shift in how the term "system", central to cybernetics and its wider family of systems traditions, would come to be understood. The etymological roots of the term system (in the Greek συν = with, together, and ἵστημι = cause to stand, set up) point towards "putting together", which is conceptually juxtaposed to the reductionist tendency of science to "take things apart" [7, p. 9]. After early systems theorists described systems in objective terms as "sets of elements standing in interrelation" [73, p. 38], cyberneticians would eventually describe systems in subjective terms as distinctions drawn by observers when deciding what is relevant in their observations. According to this more recent view, system boundaries are projected through the act of observation and negotiable, rather than found properties of observed configurations [21, p. 37].

Wiener published a seminal book [78] titled *Cybernetics; or, control and communication in the animal and the machine* in 1948. The title of the book *Cybernetics* was adopted by the participants of the Macy Conferences as the name of their field, and its subtitle "control and communication in the animal and the machine" became a prominent definition of cybernetics, amongst many others that were be proposed subsequently. Wiener derived the term cybernetics from the Greek adjective describing steersmanship κυβερνητικός [23, p. 15], which is also the root of the word government. Despite its success and its wide distribution, the suitability of this book to serve as the foundation for the new field has eventually been called into question. Glanville [39, p. 32] argues that Wiener made a "massive tactical error" by publishing *Cybernetics* first, followed by his subsequent and more philosophical book titled *The Human Use of Human Beings* [79]. The technical and mathematical nature of *Cybernetics* led to cybernetics being widely perceived as a technical engineering subject. Had the more philosophical *The Human Use of Human Beings* been published first, or, as Glanville speculates elsewhere [34, p. 1385], had Gregory Bateson, rather than Norbert Wiener, authored cybernetics' first book, the field might today be appreciated more appropriately not as a mostly technical subject, but as one concerned primarily with living human beings.

In the UK, Ashby helped formalise "control" by introducing *variety* as a measure of the number of states a system may assume. Ashby noted in his personal journal [1, p. 4312] at the time:

> I want to get away from the Shannon method of entropies [and] averaging over infinitely long messages; I want something I can count.

Ashby explained that traffic lights, with their three signalling lamps red, amber and green, each with the two states *on* and *off* have a combined *potential variety* of eight states. In their traffic control application, however, only an *actual variety* of four states is used – the combination red and green, for example, is not used. The difference between potential and actual variety is *constraint* [3, pp. 121ff.; 44, p. 6]. Ashby also recognised that reliable control requires particular conditions to be met within feedback loops, expressed in his *Law of Requisite Variety* [3, pp. 202ff.]: *the variety of the controller must be equal or greater than the variety of the controlled.*[2]

As the world bifurcated into the "Eastern bloc" and the "Western bloc", and engaged in the Cold War, cybernetics was again setting the tone. Conflict was now as much an academic challenge as it was a political and military one. Academics,

[2]Ashby's law has later been refined with *Glanville's Corollary of Ashby's Law of Requisite Variety* [37, p. 121] according to which the variety on both sides of a control loop must be exactly equal. Any "excess" states on one side that are not matched by the respective other side are irrelevant or a possible source of ambiguity in the relationship between them. For effective control to take place, such excess states must hence either be hidden, suppressed or lumped together, or they must be matched by amplifying the variety on the lacking side. See also [20].

most notably cybernetician John von Neumann, developed "game theory" – a mathematical approach to model competition between rational decision-makers. Conflict, be it in the form of an arms race or in the form of all-out violence, was now understood in terms of positive feedback with the potential to escalate disastrously if not curtailed. The nuclear weapons and rocket technologies of the past war developed to ensure "mutually assured destruction" of both sides of the Iron Curtain. Both the Soviet and the US sides had captured large portions of the research centre that had been in charge of German rocket development during World War II. Now, the Space Race emerged as a symbolic battleground where escalation would amplify innovation rather than immediate violence. The Soviets made fast progress early on in this race, and, with its launch of the first Earth satellites, left the West in "Sputnik Shock".

Sputnik's beeping radio signals and night-time visibility made Americans question their assumed scientific, technological and educational superiority. The perceived "missile gap" and the anxieties it caused prompted a wave of soul-searching with repercussions throughout the US. Following a few years of "space age" optimism, American scientists and engineers lost confidence in the country's creative edge [11, p. 1], and policy-makers as well as the general public questioned the standards and methods of the US education system. The US had fallen behind in a competition that could arise because both sides adopted scientific development and technological progress for the benefit of their populations as their central tenets. This allowed them to agree on how to disagree and provided shared terms and standards by which to measure and compare national achievements. As the US fell behind Soviet achievements, President Kennedy committed in 1961 to send men to the Moon and back by the end of the decade. In doing so, not only did he frame the race as a goal-directed governance challenge to be addressed in terms of path-goal management theory, using the systems engineering approach; he also drew a finishing line, which had so far been missing in the Space Race. The location of this finishing line and the technical challenges it implied re-framed the race as a long-term development challenge biased towards the strengths of the US side. In effect, President Kennedy had taken care of the "difficulty facing every systems designer [which] is in determining the overall system specification, or 'statement of objectives'" [10, p. 140].

Pioneered in early ballistic missile development, the *systems engineering* approach (systems approach for short) was adopted across NASA's entire Lunar Programme. A somewhat distant relative of cybernetics in the systems traditions family, systems engineering adheres to scientific reductionism as well as to linearly-causal utilitarianism. With a technical focus on pre-specification, rationalisation and optimisation, systems engineering is inherently compatible not only with the modularity of systems for space exploration such as staged rockets and space station assemblies, but also with the hierarchical organisational management structures in charge of their production and operation. Allowing spacecraft, for example, to be divided and subdivided into systems and subsystems for propulsion, communication, navigation and guidance, life support, and others, this approach is based on the presumption that once each subsystem satisfies its respective sub-objectives, then overall objectives are satisfied once all subsystems are integrated into the whole [8, pp. 6ff.].

1.3 The Limits of Control, Instrumentalism, and Design Methods

Soon after World War II, technological innovation, organisational management, mission operations and international conflict were all approached in terms of strategic governance. Increasingly, cybernetics was seen as a theory not only to describe control, but also to purposefully exert control. An ideological rift appeared around the issues of ethics and instrumentalism. While many hailed the coming age of industrial automation, for example, it was again Wiener who warned of the impending demise of the common worker [78, p. 28]. This ethical rift is epitomised by the juxtaposition between Norbert Wiener and John von Neumann, two outstanding mathematicians and founding members of the new field of cybernetics [42]. While Wiener remained absent from the Manhattan Project,[3] objected to the secrecy involved in war research and detested the use of nuclear weapons on civilian populations [9, pp. 126–127], von Neumann took on a leading role in the Manhattan Project, was a member of the committee that selected Hiroshima and Nagasaki as nuclear attack targets and advocated a nuclear first-strike policy against the Soviet Union.[4]

In the post-war years, challenges of various kinds were assumed to be purposefully manageable with scientific and systemic methods. The "Sputnik Shock" spurred the development of "creativity techniques" and soon, systemic methodology and management were applied to innovation and design [11, p. 1]. An early cybernetic overture to creativity was prompted when Wiener was invited to write a book on the philosophy of invention. In a manuscript he wrote in response, but abandoned in 1954 in favour of other projects, Wiener explained that "the really fundamental and seminal idea is to a large extent a lucky and unpredictable accident.", and he rejected the notion of invention being rationally determinable [80, pp. 25, 116]:

> The most critical stage of invention [. . .] is the change in intellectual climate which produces and is produced by a new idea. This may be of untold value to the community, but in the essence of things it is not subject to actuarial work.

[3]The secret effort to develop the first nuclear weapons during World War II, which enlisted a workforce up to 130,000 strong.

[4]The second-order cybernetics that would emerge in the 1970s, and the design cybernetics that developed within second-order cybernetics, would commit itself to the non-instrumentalist side of this rift. Concerned with learning rather than with bending the other to one's will, second-order cybernetics seeks the (co-)construction of understanding via conversation. This more recent development will be discussed in greater detail below.

Wiener also likened the serendipitous occurrence of new ideas to the occurrence of lightning strikes. Due to their sporadic nature, he argued, conditions favourable and unfavourable to both lightning strikes and to new ideas can be understood and harnessed to either promote or suppress them [80, pp. 58–59]. Invention, in this view, can be nurtured but not controlled or triggered deterministically. Yet other precursors of today's design cybernetics can be identified in Wiener's work [18]. His definition of feedback as "the property of being able to adjust future conduct by past performance" [79, p. 33] anticipates Simon's later description of designers as anyone "who devises courses of action aimed at changing existing situations into preferred ones" [68, p. 111] as well as Rittel and Webber's [62, p. 165] description of problems (i.e. design challenges) "as discrepancies between the state of affairs as it is and the state as it ought to be".

Wiener's work also foreshadowed the design-cybernetic future in more metaphorical, philosophical ways. The wartime anti-aircraft system he developed with Bigelow integrated two kinds of causality described by Aristotle [74, p. 298]: *causa efficiens* (explanatory description: "because of...") and *causa finalis* (control: "in order to..."). These two kinds of causality correspond to the descriptive agenda of natural science on the one hand and the prescriptive, intervening agendas of engineering and design on the other hand. Simon explains: "The natural sciences are concerned with how things are [...] Design, on the other hand, is concerned with how things ought to be, with devising artefacts to attain goals" [68, pp. 132–133].

If there was one defining moment when the spark of cybernetic theory jumped to the field of design, then it was the moment when design theory adopted Ashby's notions of variety and constraint. Curiously, this moment occurred twice and largely independently when both Gordon Pask in the UK [53] and Horst Rittel in Germany [58] found inspiration in Ashby's work. Rittel soon described the design process as involving "the generation of variety, and the reduction of variety" [58, p. 107]. These two operations are today often referred to as simply "diverging" and "converging" stages of design [15, p. 34], as shown in design process models such as the double-diamond model [14].

In the 1950s and 1960s, there was a desire to "scientise" design [11, p. 1; 36, p. 89]. Buckminster Fuller declared a "World Design Science Decade" beginning in 1965 [22]. The first Conference on Design Methods was held in London in 1962 [70] and ushered in the design methods movement, a decade-long academic attempt to rationalise and scientise design. In the following year, Rittel moved from the Hochschule für Gestaltung in Ulm to the University of California, Berkeley where he became a key proponent of the design methods movement. He later remembered:

> [I]n the beginning, outsiders from architecture, engineering, and business heard about the methods of the systems approach and thought that if it were possible to deal with such complicated things as the NASA programmes then why couldn't we deal with a simple thing like a house in the same way? Shouldn't we actually look at every building as a mission-oriented design object? [61, p. 318]

Within a decade, however, the design methods movement had run its course and faced rejection by many, including some of its early proponents [11, pp. 1–2], who by now recognised prescriptive methodology as antithetical to the idea of design. Jones, one of the early proponents and later opponents of the movement, explained:

> Methodology should not be a fixed track to a fixed destination, but a conversation about everything that could be made to happen. The language of the conversation must bridge the logical gap between past and future, but in doing so it should not limit the variety of possible futures that are discussed nor should it force the choice of a future that is unfree. [45, p. 73]

The notion that with suitable methods and technologies systems could reliably be predicted and controlled had been abandoned in other fields also, most notably in ecology [12]. Following the failure and abandonment of the design methods movement, design research assumed a less instructive and more reflexive posture, which Rittel refers to as "design methods of the second generation" [60]. This transition occurred, maybe not coincidentally, in parallel with the expansion from first-order to second-order cybernetics, which will be discussed in the following section.

1.4 First-Order to Second-Order Cybernetics

Despite its Cold-War-era reputation as a science of deterministic, instrumentalist control technology, we argue that those who initiated the field had different motives. Mead's work as a participant-researcher as well as Wiener's early recognition of the role of the observer, circular causality and non-determinability show that cybernetics was, in its origins, much more reflexive than the general perception and application of cybernetics around the mid-twentieth century suggest. To illustrate this further, let us consider Fig. 1.1, which shows Norbert Wiener with *Palomilla*, a robot he helped develop at MIT in the late 1940s.

Equipped with sensors, circuitry and motors, *Palomilla* navigated spaces "purposefully" in relation to light sources, somewhat as insects do. Unfamiliar with Wiener's biography, one could read Fig. 1.1 as showing an MIT mathematician-engineer automating a vehicle in an effort that would one day find application in robotic vacuum cleaners, self-driving cars and unmanned battlefield drones. While such systems indeed have some of their origins in Wiener's work, we propose a different reading of this image, which, we argue, is more consistent with Wiener's broader body of work as well as with the ethos of design cybernetics. We suggest that Wiener was less interested in *Palomilla* with regards to instrumental utility, and more as a metaphor for his own epistemic navigation, which, in his 1936 article on the role of the observer, he depicted as follows [77, p. 315–316]:

> The practicing mathematician knows very well that mathematics as a living investigation is inductive and experimental, whatever it may be when stuffed and mounted in text-books. When I want an auxiliary function to do a definite job, I try one after another, finding the first too big here, the second too small there, until by grace of luck and a familiarity with the habits of the species, I come on an exact fit. Nine-tenths of the possibilities are eliminated on the basis of a general feeling for the situation before it comes to a matter of any real deductive logic whatever. The tenth suggestion slips into place in a way which convinces an

Fig. 1.1 Norbert Wiener with tricycle robot *Palomilla*

old hand that there is something in it – it resolves the difficulties at just the right points, but not so readily as to excite suspicions of a sheer blunder. Once the key will go into the lock, and the bolt begins to show signs of turning, it is a matter of mere filework and oil to get a perfect fit.

Alongside this passage, consider another picture of *Palomilla*, shown in Fig. 1.2. It shows a long-exposure photograph of *Palomilla* navigating spaces. The robot's glowing vacuum tubes have traced zigzagging, forward-searching lines that, like tracks in the sand, tell a story of its path and its operative logic. We argue that the path of light in Fig. 1.2 relates to *Palomilla's* movements in space in much the same way as Wiener's above account relates to his practice as a mathematician. They are tracks left behind by ephemeral processes, recorded to invite others to read, to relate to their own forward-looking searches [56, p. 18], and to engage in speculations towards yet better metaphors and understandings of how we venture into and navigate the as-yet unknown. In this way, *Palomilla* is not just the great-grandmother of today's *Roomba* vacuum-cleaners, but a rudimentary embodied theory developed to account for the processes by which *Roomba* vacuum-cleaners, as well as other things and processes, come into being – a "machine for showing" [43], an epistemic reflection, and a great-grandmother of design cybernetics.

As a "practicing mathematician", Wiener remained largely committed to the representationalist paradigm until his death in 1964. He did not live to see the self-reflection he hinted at emerge as an explicit grounding for his discipline. It was chiefly Heinz von Foerster who would articulate a performative cybernetics that applies to itself and whose content matches its form [19, pp. 128–129]: second-order

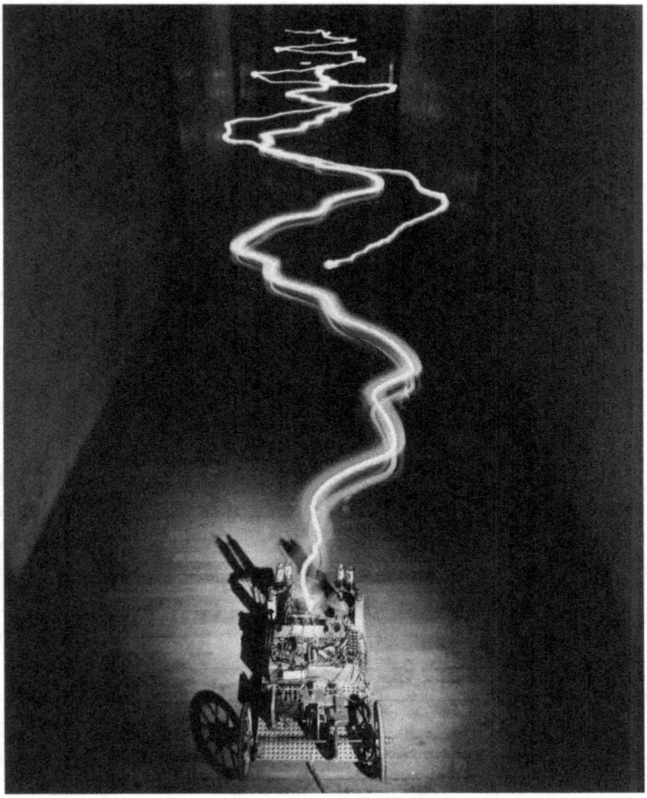

Fig. 1.2 Long-exposure photograph showing a path explored by *Palomilla*

cybernetics.[5] Later, when asked how second-order cybernetics "came upon" him, von Foerster attributed its initiation to Margaret Mead and her 1968 address to the American Society for Cybernetics (ASC) [74, p. 302]. In this speech, which Mead retrospectively titled *Cybernetics of Cybernetics*, she challenged the ASC to apply cybernetic insights and techniques to its own organisation and operation [51].

Recognising the role of the observer and circular causality, von Foerster explained that any description or theory must account for who observes and describes, as well as for their describing and theorising [74, p. 247]. To those who adopt it, this approach is a research attitude, an ethical position guided by internal responsibility, and, ultimately, an aesthetic desire. Von Foerster's second-order cybernetic conception

[5]Contrary to an occasional misconception, the term second-order cybernetics expresses a qualitative appreciation of cybernetics' applicability to itself rather than a quantitative assessment of nested levels or recursion depth in particular circumstances. The identification of additional layers of reflection therefore does not constitute the discovery of cybernetics of third, fourth, nth orders.

of ethics is based on the subjective responsibility of the *self*, as defined by his/her systemic boundaries. Based on the view that "... freedom always exists. *At each and every moment, I can decide who I am*", von Foerster explains that choices of actions are made *within*, and that, therefore, responsibility also lies *within*. The alternative is externally motivated action, the basis of authoritarianism, and the rejection of personal responsibility as observed in the Nuremberg trials: "I had no choice. I was merely following orders!" [57, p. 19]. Von Foerster, accordingly, distinguishes ethics from morals. In this view, (linearly) instructing others what to think and what to do ("though shalt...", "though shalt not...") constitutes morals, whereas ethics is (circularly) addressed to oneself ("I shall...", "I shall not..."). Ethics, therefore, cannot become explicit, but manifests itself in action [74, pp. 287–304]. To help propagate the requisite freedom, von Foerster proposes his Constructivist Ethical Imperative: "I shall act always so as to increase the total number of choices" [74, p. 282].

Throughout much of the 1960s, cybernetics, and von Foerster's Biological Computer Laboratory (BCL) in particular, had benefited from research funds offered by the U.S. Department of Defense (DoD) for the advancement of computing technology. This changed when the Mansfield Amendment to the Defense Procurement Authorization Act of 1970 restricted DoD support to basic research "with a direct and apparent relationship to a specific military function or operation", which ethically-oriented cyberneticians, first and foremost von Foerster himself, were not prepared to offer. Others, in particular in AI, responded with bold promises – often based on technical concepts that originated in cybernetics – with battlefield applicability of research outcomes, and hence enjoyed generous support. Although this Pentagon policy was later relaxed, its redirection of funding strengthened AI research at MIT, Stanford University and elsewhere, and is seen as a cause of the closure of the BCL in 1974 as well as of von Foerster's retirement in 1976 [52, pp. 296–297; 72].

The transition from first-order to second-order cybernetics was less a shift than it was an expansion. Cybernetics as a control engineering subject can be understood as a constrained subset of cybernetics as a broader, more general ethos, much in the way that Newton's mechanics continues to have its place within the mechanics of Einstein [38] (see also page 37 in this volume.). Amongst other systems-oriented research traditions, this broader, more recent form of cybernetics has been found to deviate most radically from assumptions underlying conventional empirical science by acknowledging "holism", context, relationships, circular causality, non-determinability, the subjective observer, and self-organisation [13].

To illustrate non-determinability and observer-dependency as consequences of circular causality, von Foerster introduced two automata named the trivial machine (TM) and the non-trivial machine (NTM) [17, pp. 1381–1382; 74, pp. 309–313; 33, pp. 98–101]. Both machines are thought experiments rather than proposals for technical implementation. They both have an input as well as an output channel, but different internal mechanisms for translating inputs into outputs. The TM predictably

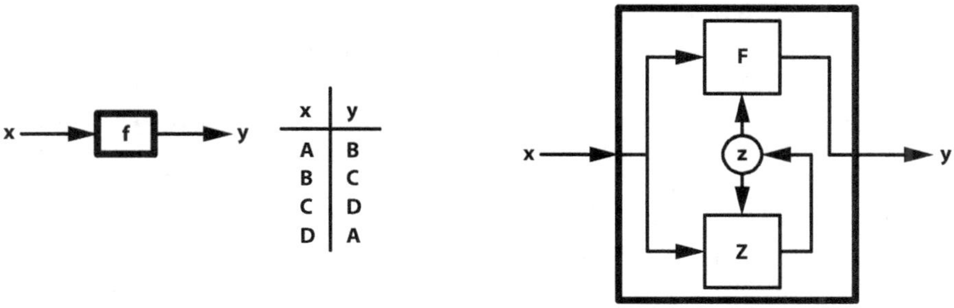

Fig. 1.3 Trivial machine with assignment table (left) and non-trivial machine (right), redrawn from von Foerster [74, pp. 310–311]

translates inputs into corresponding outputs, so that an external observer can, after a period of observation, establish clear relationships between possible inputs and resulting outputs, for example in the form of an "assignment table" as shown on the left of Fig. 1.3. A complete assignment table is a reliable model for predicting the TM's output responses to given inputs, regardless of how long the machine has been in operation. The NTM, in contrast, contains means to memorise a machine state (labelled z on the right of Fig. 1.3). This state is not only affected by each input-output translation; it also co-determines the outputs of subsequent translations.

This results in vast numbers of changing input-output mappings. The NTM's history of operations can be said to leave traces in the machine, which in effect turns it into a different machine with each of its input-output translations. Von Foerster approaches the challenge of determining both machines from the perspective of an external observer who, without insight into their inner workings, must construct a mental model of their inner workings – to "whiten" a "black box" in Glanville's [25] terms. This is straightforward with the TM and practically impossible with the NTM [74, p. 312]. Such failure to understand and to predict observed systems can be desirable and delightful, since this is the source of magic and wonder [33; 74, pp. 325–338]. Von Foerster used the juxtaposition of his two machines to distinguish trivial input-output systems from non-trivial ones. Non-trivial systems, including humans, are equipped with memory and circular pathways by which outputs of earlier operations can re-enter as input of subsequent operations, thus affecting themselves through their interactions in ways that are difficult to predict. Using *mechanisms* to question cultural preoccupations with mechanistic cause-and-effect relationships was and remains a cunning rhetorical move. To avoid misconceptions, however, it must be stressed that mechanistic cybernetic metaphors for biological and social systems are nothing more than metaphors. The likening of the NTM to the human mind is not to imply that the mind is like a mechanism, or that mechanisms can act in the ways that human minds do. This analogy is merely to show that with the recognition of circularly-causal re-entry and memory comes an appreciation of non-determinability encountered in simple mechanisms as well as in humans.

One context in which von Foerster referred to the distinction between triviality and non-triviality was his critique of educational institutions that approach children as trivial systems by training them to reliably produce known answers to old questions [74, p. 196]. In this context, he also used an alternative illustration of non-triviality: a school child who, in response to the question "How much is two times two?" replies "Green!" and is therefore reprimanded and "trivialised" until she produces the expected answer "four". The child's spontaneous display of novelty, i.e. the transcendence of expected variety, captures the kind of creative moment Wiener likened to lightning strikes. While the principles at work in such moments remain unaccounted for in von Foerster's descriptions of the NTM, they are explained in Conversation Theory, which will be outlined in the following section.

1.5 Conversation and Design

Jones was not the only design researcher who described the design process as a "conversation". Design researchers within and beyond design cybernetics have since recognised the cyclical structure of the design process by describing it as an "argumentative" "conspiracy", characterised by a "symmetry of ignorance" [61, pp. 320, 325, 327], as "dialectical" [41], as "discursive" [40, p. 166], as a "dialogue" [65, p. 68] or "dialogical" [69, pp. 41ff.], and as "negotiation" [47, pp. 269–271].

A theory that does justice to this cyclical structure of the design process must depart from the linear structures that characterise formal Western logic and Shannon's Communication Theory [66]. Pask's *Conversation Theory* (see [54, p. 424] and Chap. 3 in this volume) offers such a structure. Conversation Theory explains epistemic processes, i.e. processes through which we come to know – as we do in learning, designing and researching. It is a radical constructivist theory [64, p. 347] based on circular exchanges. It does not conceive of "knowledge" as a storable and transferrable commodity, but of knowing and coming to know as subjectively performed processes. Sometimes perceived as impenetrable, Pask's body of work has been made more accessible and was further developed by his students Ranulph Glanville, Paul Pangaro (see Chaps. 2 and 4 in this volume) and Scott [64].

In contrast to Shannon's linear conveyance of symbols from a sender to a receiver along a linear channel that is subject to the distorting effects of noise, Conversation Theory describes a circularly-causal practice in time between two or more conversants. Following the desire to explain more with less (*Occam's razor*), Conversation Theory is commonly illustrated and explained using two conversants only: a subjective *self* with an *other*.[6] It is possible that both roles may occur within one person who may conduct a conversation with an imagined *other*, or in groups larger than two, with multiple individuals possibly acting as one. A key challenge in modelling such human exchanges is that meaning is private. Shannon's

[6]The *self*/*other* distinction used here is equivalent to that between *I* and *other* used by some authors.

Communication Theory recognises this challenge by explicitly excluding meaning from its concerns. Conversation Theory addresses it by describing a process in which conversants pursue mutual concordance of ideas through comparing and rephrasing in time. This process unfolds until the conversants assume that their respective understandings are close enough to allow conversing further *as if* meanings were held in common and *as if* they were dealing with the same matter [28]. When they reach no such concordance, then conversants must agree to disagree. This process is portrayed in Fig. 1.4.

Much day-to-day conversation is conducted between individuals "getting on the same page", aligning and synchronising ideas and understandings by reducing "error" through negative feedback. Some conversations, however, also amplify differences in understanding to challenge prior notions and to amplify variety in the *other*, inspiring new ideas by harnessing "error" through positive feedback. These two conversation modes reflect how design processes both "converge" and "diverge" and how designers can both fulfil expectations reliably (say with regards to schedules, budgets, regulations) and defy expectations surprisingly (say by inventing, speculating, challenging). A designing *self* may engage conversationally with various kinds of *others*. The *other* may be, for example, a person, an imagined person, a physical model, a pen and sketching paper, or a piece of technology, as shown in Fig. 1.5.

What qualifies such engagements as conversations is the *self*'s readiness not only to affect the *other*, but also to be affected by the *other* in a circularly-causal manner. A designer may, for example, put marks onto sketching paper (affecting the *other*) and then, maybe looking at the sketch sideways, discover something that was not expressed intentionally, and take that idea on board in the creative process (being affected by the *other*). Fantini and Glanville [16] point to the importance of this openness by emphasising the role of "listening" (applied metaphorically to all modes of perception). Von Foerster, along similar lines, proposes his Hermeneutic Principle: "It's the listener, not the speaker, who determines the meaning of an utterance" [75, p. 353]. Complementing this principle, he also proposes his Aesthetical Imperative: "If you desire to see, learn how to act" [74, p. 303]. As the Latin root of the word conversation suggests (*conversare* = to turn together, i.e. to dance), designing, in this view, unfolds as a feedback loop of affecting and being affected, of articulation and listening, or, more generally, of acting and understanding, with a negotiable goal. This characterisation, we believe, is an adequate definition for *designing* – for design cybernetics in general and for this volume in particular.

Conversation Theory is, according to Scott [64, p. 345], a "pioneering achievement in modelling cognition as an evolutionary, self-organising process". This portrayal highlights a crucial characteristic of conversation: it is a *process* performed *in time*. As such, conversation stands in contrast to some tenets of Western, and in particular natural-scientific reasoning. Feedback and conversation run contrary to the formal logic by which we evaluate declarative statements and conclude in terms of "truth" or "falsity". For millennia, Western logicians have shunned circular causality in order to avoid the paradox conditions they can give rise to. Statements like "This is a lie." are simply forbidden [48, pp. 37–41] in

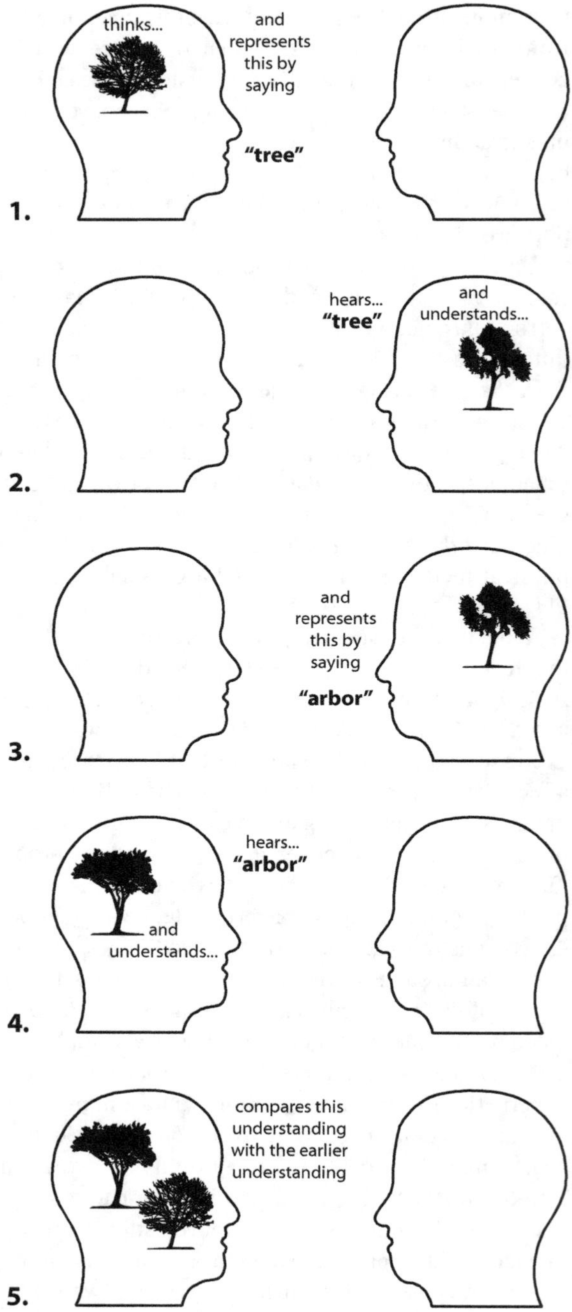

Fig. 1.4 Achieving close-enough understandings through conversation, as described by Gordon Pask and Glanville for example in [35, pp. 378–384] (see also p. 41 in this volume.). In an encounter between a *self* and an *other*, (1.) one expresses a thought. The other (2.) perceives the expression, forms a corresponding understanding and (3.) expresses it in their own words. This is (4.) perceived by the first who forms a corresponding understanding. If (5.) this understanding and the initial thought are close enough, then the other's understanding is deemed to be similar enough to believe that the understanding is shared. If not, then they repeat the process until either they agree, or they agree to disagree

Fig. 1.5 Designing as described by Glanville [31, p. 88], unfolding as a conversation between a *self* and various possible kinds of *other*, such as a pen and paper, a person, an imagined person, computer soft- and hardware, physical models and so on. The crucial requirement is for the *self* to allow the *other* to "speak back" and to accommodate the unexpected so that *self* affects *other*, and *other* affects *self*. Avoiding requisite variety, both get partially "out of control" in a mix of positive and negative feedback, thus conversing along non-determinable trajectories to arrive at previously unknown destinations

conventional formal reasoning. This is because formal logic is *atemporal* [5, p. 117] and because, according to the principle of the excluded middle, a statement cannot be both *true* and *false*. Cybernetics, in contrast, recognises temporal process. A thermostatic heater, for example, can be both *on* and *off* in temporal alternation. What appears to be paradox from the perspective of formal logic plays out as a straightforward oscillation from the cybernetic perspective. The temporal structures recognised by cybernetics can furthermore produce desirable dynamics, such as sustained self-stabilisation (as can be observed in technical control systems) and spontaneous novelty (as can be observed in conversation). The purpose of many cybernetic feedback loops is precisely *not* to "conclude", but to keep going. This is one of the obstacles to doing justice to the performative nature of designing in the rational language of academic research.

"Conversational cycles" [31, p. 88; 37, pp. 428ff.] unfold "out of control" [27] in the way everyday conversations develop in unpredictable directions, leading to unexpected thoughts and new ideas. Neither requiring nor aiming for requisite variety, the conceptual grasps (variety) of both conversants are different, with the conversation itself interactively generating new variety at some times, and reducing variety at other times, taking conversants to what was previously unknown (at least subjectively) rather than prodding them to known goals. While technical control systems are limited by the variety available on the controlling side, conversations are unlimited. In conversations, variety may (and commonly does) differ from conversant to conversant. It is itself variable and subject to the conversations it shapes. Error, differences and misunderstandings between *self* and *other* are valued as possible sources of insight and inspiration, and not necessarily corrected or avoided.

Even the digital computer, conventionally thought of as a logical machine that translates given input into output with perfectly determined precision, makes for a conversant if approached accordingly. This is because computational processes, unfolding in time, allow for circularly-causal human-computer interaction. Bateson [4, p. 317] observes: "The computer is only an arc of a larger circuit which always includes a man and an environment [. . .]." Glanville [26, pp. 100, 102] exemplifies this with a digital surrealist technique: A poet may close her eyes and randomly type into her computer's text processor, which will then highlight this material as misspelled. The poet may then select her preferred words and phrases from the spell-checker's suggestions to interactively construct poetry. What is achieved in this way is achieved by, and between, both *self* and *other*: "Betweenness is the source of interaction and is also its mode and its site" [32, p. 4]. In this design-cybernetic view, media are appreciated for not being determinable [30, p. 48], while error, noise and misunderstanding are valued because "[t]he imprecision we experience [. . .] may lead to [. . .] novelty" [28, p. 449]. Glanville [29, p. 4] likens the relationship between such conversational design processes and their outcomes to turning wheels and the tracks they leave behind.

1.6 Summary: Adjustments Towards a New Perspective

Cybernetics can be defined, in a broad sense, as *the study of processes in which states of affairs are adjusted with reference to other states of affairs.*[7] We have laid out in this chapter how cybernetics, applying to itself, performed a number of self-adjustments since World War II and expanded from a technical control theory to an abstract philosophical approach to design as a creative epistemic practice.

One of these adjustments is the recognition of circular causality (A affects B, and B affects A) as it plays out in self-regulating feedback mechanisms including thermostats and missile guidance systems. Another adjustment is the realisation that objects of observation cannot be separated from the act of observing and that the observing human finds herself as a subjectively participating part of the object of interest. Along with this re-orientation from the objective external view to the subjective view from within comes an adjustment away from the notion of objective reality to the notion of subjectively constructed realities. Another adjustment is that from an interest in static descriptions to an interest in dynamic processes. Instead of producing descriptions in the form of conclusive declarative statements, expressed as atemporal statements in terms of truth and falsity, cybernetics, concerned with adaptive processes, is based in time. Yet another adjustment is the one from determinability to non-determinability. In simple mechanistic systems, effects may be determined from preceding causes. With increasing numbers of "moving parts" affecting each other in circularly-causal ways, the consequences of actions are not likely to be predictable. A further adjustment is the realisation that cybernetic principles often apply recursively across various scales.

Each of these adjustments constitutes, on the one hand, a departure from ideals of natural science, and, on the other hand, an approximation of design as it is appreciated by many designers. Besides these adjustments, there is also continuity in the expansion from first-order to second-order cybernetics. Much of the early control engineering terminology turns out to be suitable to describe aspects of processes that are out-of-control: *feedback*, *variety*, *requisite variety*, *constraint*, *error*, and so on. We argue that to those who were most closely associated with early cybernetics, and to second-order cyberneticians, cybernetics is an ethos. The ethical ambition of design cybernetics in particular is to increase total numbers of choices. The aesthetic ambition of design cybernetics is delight, be it through magic and wonder or through insight. Both ambitions apply to the design process, to design outcomes, as well as to design research. Design cybernetics aims to foster rigour that is independent from adopted procedures, and therefore offers no methodology. In essence, it seeks to avoid the exercise of restrictive control over the *other*, while pursuing increased numbers of choices and delight in the interactions between our individual and collective *selves*.

---

[7]This is a paraphrasing of a definition offered by Whitaker [76, Part 6/6, 4:31min–4:48min].

References

1. Ashby, W. R. (1952). Journal 17, Barnwood House, Gloucester. Available at: http://www.ashby.de/rossashby.info/journal/page/4312.html. Accessed 19 Jan 2019.
2. Ashby, W. R. (1954). *Design for a brain.* New York: Wiley.
3. Ashby, W. R. (1956). *An introduction to cybernetics.* New York: St. Martin's Press.
4. Bateson, G. (1972). *Steps to an ecology of mind.* New York: Ballantine Books.
5. Bateson, G. (1979). *Mind and nature. A necessary unity.* New York: E. P. Dutton.
6. Blackman, R. B., Bode, H. W., & Shannon, C. E. (1946). Data smoothing and prediction in firecontrol systems. In *Summary Technical Report, Div. 7, National Defense Research Committee, Vol. 1, Gunfire Control* (pp. 71–159, 166–167). Washington, DC: National Defense Research Committee.
7. Beer, S., Blohm, H., & Suzuki, D. (1985). *Pebbles to computers. The thread.* New York: Oxford University Press.
8. Churchman, C. W. (1979). *The systems approach. Revised and updated.* New York: Dell.
9. Conway, F., & Siegelman, J. (2005). *Dark hero of the information age. In search of Norbert Wiener the father of cybernetics.* New York: Basic Books.
10. Cross, N. (1977). *The automated architect.* London: Pion.
11. Cross, N. (2007). Forty years of design research. *Design Studies, 28*(1), 1–4.
12. Curtis, A. (2011). *The use and abuse of vegetational concepts.* All watched over by machines of loving grace, Episode 2. London: BBC. Available at: https://vimeo.com/groups/96331/videos/80799352. Accessed 19 Jan 2019.
13. Dent, E. B., & Umpleby, S. P. (1998). Underlying assumptions of several traditions in system theory and cybernetics. In R. Trappl (Ed.), *Cybernetics and systems'98* (pp. 513–518). Vienna: Austrian Society for Cybernetic Studies.
14. Design Council. (2007). *Design council eleven lessons. Managing design in eleven global brands. A study of the design process.* London: Design Council.
15. Dubberly, H. (1995). Managing complex design projects. *Communication Arts* 30–36. http://www.dubberly.com/wp-content/uploads/2008/06/ddo_article_managingdesignprojects.pdf
16. Fantini van Ditmar, D., & Glanville, R. (2013). Listening: Proceedings of the ASC conference 2011. *Cybernetics & Human Knowing, 20*(1/2), 5–11.
17. Fischer, T. (2013). Enigmatic mechanisms in defense of the capability to have new ideas. *Kybernetes, 42*(9/10), 1374–1386.
18. Fischer, T. (2015). Wiener's prefiguring of a cybernetic design theory. *IEEE Technology and Society Magazine, 34*(3), 52–59.
19. Fischer, T. (2015). Designing together. *Cybernetics & Human Knowing, 22*(2/3), 127–140.
20. Fischer, T. (2019). Transcomputability, (Glanville's corollary of) Ashby's law of requisite variety, and epistemic processes. *Kybernetes*, *48*(4), 793–804.
21. Fischer, T., & Richards, L. D. (2017). From goal-oriented to constraint-oriented design: The cybernetic intersection of design theory and systems theory. *Leonardo, 50*(1), 36–41.
22. Fuller, R. B. (1968). *Operating manual for spaceship Earth.* New York: Pocket Books.
23. Gage, S. (2007). The boat/helmsman. *Technoetic Arts: A Journal of Speculative Research, 5*(1), 15–24.
24. Galison, P. (1994). The ontology of the enemy: Norbert Wiener and the cybernetic vision. *Critical Inquiry, 21*(1), 228–266.
25. Glanville, R. (1982). Inside every white box there are two black boxes trying to get out. *Behavioral Science, 27*(1), 1–11.
26. Glanville, R. (1994). Variety in design. *Systems Research, 11*(3), 95–103.
27. Glanville, R. (2002). On being out of control. Available at: http://www.mom.arq.ufmg.br/mom/arq_interface/3a_aula/on_being_out_of_control.pdf. Accessed 19 Jan 2019.
28. Glanville, R. (1996). Communication without coding. *Modern Language Notes, 111*(3), 441–462.

29. Glanville, R. (1997). A ship without a rudder. In R. Glanville & G. de Zeeuw (Eds.), *Problems of excavating cybernetics and systems* (pp. 131–142). Southsea: BKS+. Available at: https://www.univie.ac.at/constructivism/papers/glanville/glanville95-ship.pdf. Accessed 19 Jan 2019.
30. Glanville, R. (1997). The value when cybernetics is added to CAAD. In N. Koenraad et al. (Eds.), *The Added Value of Computer Aided Design. AVOCAAD First International Conference* (pp. 39–56). Brussels: HWK Sint-Lucas.
31. Glanville, R. (1999). Researching design and designing research. *Design Issues, 15*(2), 80–91.
32. Glanville, R. (2000). The value of being unmanageable: Variety and creativity in cyberspace. In H. Eichmann, J. Hochgerner, & F. Nahrada (Eds.), *Netzwerke* (pp. 27–40). Vienna: Falter Verlag.
33. Glanville, R. (2003). Machines of wonder and elephants that float through air: A valedictory understanding of understanding understanding. *Cybernetics & Human Knowing, 10*(3/4), 91–101.
34. Glanville, R. (2004). The purpose of second-order cybernetics. *Kybernetes, 33*(9/10), 1379–1386.
35. Glanville, R. (2007). Grounding difference. In A. Müller & K. H. Müller (Eds.), *An unfinished revolution? Heinz von Foerster and the biological computer laboratory 1958–1976* (pp. 361–406). Vienna: edition echoraum.
36. Glanville, R. (2007). Designing complexity. *Performance Improvement Quarterly, 20*(2), 75–96.
37. Glanville, R. (2009). *The black boox Vol. III. 39 steps.* Vienna: edition echoraum.
38. Glanville, R. (2012). Second order cybernetics. *The black boox – Vol. I. Cybernetic circles* (pp. 175–207). Vienna: edition echoraum. Previously published In F. Parra-Luna (Ed.), *Encyclopedia of life support systems, systems science and cybernetics Vol. III.* Oxford: EoLSS Publishers. Available at: http://www.eolss.net/sample-chapters/c02/e6-46-03-03.pdf. Accessed 19 Jan 2019.
39. Glanville, R. (2012). Radical constructivism = second-order cybernetics. *Cybernetics & Human Knowing, 19*(4), 27–42.
40. Goel, V. (1995). *Sketches of thought.* Cambridge: MIT Press.
41. Goldschmidt, G. (1991). The dialectics of sketching. *Creativity Research Journal, 4*(2), 123–143.
42. Heims, S. J. (1980). *John von Neumann and Norbert Wiener. From mathematics to the technologies of life and death.* Cambridge: MIT Press.
43. Herr, C. M., & Fischer, T. (2013). Systems for showing and repurposing: A second-order cybernetic reflection on some cellular automata projects. *Journal of Mathematics and System Science, 3*(4), 201–216.
44. Heylighen, F., & Joslyn, C. (2001). Cybernetics and second-order cybernetics. In R. A. Meyers (Ed.), *Encyclopedia of physical science & technology* (3rd ed.). New York: Academic.
45. Jones, J. C. (Ed.). (1992). *Design methods.* New York: Van Nostrand Reinhold.
46. Kline, R. R. (2015). *The cybernetics moment. Or why we call our age the information age.* Baltimore: Johns Hopkins University Press.
47. Lawson, B. (2005). *How designers think* (4th ed.). Amsterdam: Architectural Press.
48. Lynn, S. (2001). *The dream of reality. Heinz von Foerster's constructivism* (2nd ed.). New York: Springer.
49. Maruyama, M. (1963). The second cybernetics: Deviation-amplifying mutual causal processes. *American Scientist, 5*(2), 164–179.
50. Macintyre, B. (2007). *Agent zigzag. A true story of Nazi espionage, love and betrayal.* New York: Harmony Books.
51. Mead, M. (1968). Cybernetics of cybernetics. In H. von Foerster, J. D. White, L. J. Peterson, & J. K. Russell (Eds.), *Purposive systems* (pp. 1–11). New York: Spartan.
52. Müller, A. (2007). A brief history of the BCL: Heinz von Foerster and the biological computer laboratory. In A. Müller & K. H. Müller (Eds.), *An unfinished revolution? Heinz von Foerster and the Biological Computer Laboratory/BCL, 1958–1976* (pp. 277–302). Vienna: edition echoraum.

53. Pask, G. (1961). *An approach to cybernetics.* London: Hutchinson & Co.
54. Pask, G. (1976). *Conversation theory. Applications in education and epistemology.* Amsterdam: Elsevier.
55. Pias, K. (2003). *Cybernetics | the Macy-conferences 1946–1953.* Zürich-Berlin: Diaphanes.
56. Pickering, A. (2011). *The cybernetic brain: Sketches of another future*. Chicago: University of Chicago Press.
57. Pörksen, B. (2004). *The certainty of uncertainty.* Exeter: Imprint Academic.
58. Protzen, J.-P., & Harris, D. J. (2010). *The universe of design: Horst Rittel's theories of design and planning.* London: Routledge.
59. Rid, T. (2016). *Rise of the machines. A cybernetic history.* New York: Norton.
60. Rittel, H. W. J. (1972). On the planning crisis: Systems analysis of the 'first and second generations'. *Bedrifts Økonomen, 8*, 390–396.
61. Rittel, H. W. J. (1984). Second-generation design methods. In N. Cross (Ed.), *Developments in design methodology* (pp. 317–327). Chichester: Wiley.
62. Rittel, H. W. J., & Webber, M. M. (1973). Dilemmas in a general theory of planning. *Policy Sciences, 4*(2), 155–169.
63. Rosenblueth, A., Wiener, N., & Bigelow, J. (1943). Behavior, purpose and teleology. *Philosophy of Science, 10*, 18–24.
64. Scott, B. (2001). Gordon Pask's conversation theory: A domain independent constructivist model of human knowing. *Foundations of Science, 6*(4), 343–360.
65. Schön, D. (1983). *The reflective practitioner. How professionals think in action.* New York: Basic Books.
66. Shannon, C. E. (1948). A mathematical theory of communication. *The Bell System Technical Journal, 27*(3/4), 379–423, 623–656.
67. Silverman, S. (2005). The United States. In B. Fredrik, A. Gingrich, R. Parkin, & S. Silverman (Eds.), *One discipline, four ways: British, German, French, and American anthropology* (pp. 255–347). Chicago: University of Chicago Press.
68. Simon, H. A. (1996). *Sciences of the artificial* (3rd ed.). Cambridge: MIT Press.
69. Snodgrass, A., & Coyne, R. (2006). *Interpretation in architecture.* London: Routledge.
70. Thornley, D. G., & Jones, J. C. (Eds.). (1963). *Conference on design methods.* Oxford: Pergamon Press.
71. Turner, F. (2012). *The Family of Man* and the politics of attention in Cold War America. *Public Culture, 24*(1), 55–84.
72. Umpleby, S. (2003). Heinz von Foerster and the mansfield amendment. *Cybernetics and Human Knowing, 10*(3/4), 187–190.
73. von Bertalanffy, L. (1968). *General system theory. Foundations, development, applications.* New York: George Braziller.
74. von Foerster, H. (2003). *Understanding understanding. Essays on cybernetics and cognition.* New York: Springer.
75. von Glasersfeld, E. (2007). The constructivist view of communication. In A. Müller & K. Müller (Eds.), *An unfinished revolution? Heinz von Foerster and the Biological Computer Laboratory/BCL 1958–1976* (pp. 351–360). Vienna: edition echoraum.
76. Whitaker, R. (2011). From Rosenblueth to Richmond. In *Tutorial Delivered at the 2011 Annual Conference of the American Society for Cybernetics in Richmond.* Available at: https://www.youtube.com/playlist?list=PL242A1FFCF353DC66. Accessed 19 Jan 2019.
77. Wiener, N. (1936). The role of the observer. *Philosophy of Science, 3*(3), 307–319.
78. Wiener, N. (1948). *Cybernetics; Or, control and communication in the animal and the machine.* Cambridge: MIT Press.
79. Wiener, N. (1954). *The human use of human beings. Cybernetics and society.* New York: Doubleday.
80. Wiener, N. (1993). *Invention: The care and feeding of ideas.* Cambridge: MIT Press.

Thomas Fischer is a design researcher, epistemologist and cybernetician. He is a Professor and Director of Research at the Department of Architecture at XJTLU in Suzhou, China. Thomas is also a Visiting Associate Professor at the School of Design at The Hong Kong Polytechnic University. He is a Fellow of the Design Research Society and received the American Society for Cybernetics' Warren McCulloch Award. Thomas holds a PhD in Education from the University of Kassel in Germany and a PhD in Architecture and Design from RMIT University in Australia. His research is focused on epistemological issues of design computing, design cybernetics, and digital media.

Christiane M. Herr is an architectural researcher and educator focusing on the areas of structural design, digitally supported design, radical constructivism, design pedagogy and traditional Chinese approaches to creative thinking. Christiane is a Senior Associate Professor at Xi'an Jiaotong-Liverpool University in China, where she directs the Master of Architectural Design as well as the Bachelor of Architectural Engineering programmes. Christiane is President of the Association for Computer Aided Design Research in Asia and a member of the executive board of the American Society for Cybernetics.

Chapter 2
Try Again. Fail Again. Fail Better: The Cybernetics in Design and the Design in Cybernetics

Ranulph Glanville

Abstract Purpose – The purpose of this paper is to explore the two subjects cybernetics and design, in order to establish and demonstrate a relationship between them. It is held that the two subjects can be considered complementary arms of each other.

Design/method/approach – The two subjects are each characterised so that the author's interpretation is explicit and those who know one subject but not the other are briefed. Cybernetics is examined in terms of both classical (first order) cybernetics, and the more consistent second order cybernetics, which is the cybernetics used in this argument. The paper develops by a comparative analysis of the two subjects, and exploring analogies between the two at several levels.

Findings – A design approach is characterised and validated; and contrasted to a scientific approach. The analogies that are proposed are shown to hold. Cybernetics is presented as theory for design, design as cybernetics in practice. Consequent findings, for instance that both cybernetics and design imply the same ethical qualities, are presented. The criteria for the evaluation of cybernetic/design actions are derived and contrasted to those associated with a traditional, scientific approach.

Research limitations/implications – The research implications of the paper are that, where research involves design, the criteria against which it can be judged are far more Popperian than might be imagined. Such research will satisfy the condition of adequacy, rather than correctness. A secondary outcome concerning research is that, whereas science is concerned with what is (characterised through the development of knowledge of (what is)), design (and by implication other subjects primarily concerned with action) is concerned with knowledge for (acting).

Ranulph Glanville (1946–2014).

The title "Try again. Fail again. Fail better." is taken from Samuel Beckett's 1984 novel *"Worstward Ho"* [3] published by the Grove Press in New York. In my view, it captures the conversational act at the heart of designing which is the central focus of this paper.

T. Fischer, C. M. Herr (eds.), *Design Cybernetics*, Design Research Foundations,
https://doi.org/10.1007/978-3-030-18557-2_2

Practical implications – The theoretical validity of second order cybernetics is used to justify and give proper place to design, as an activity. Thus, the approach designers use is validated as complementary to, and placed on an equal par with, other approaches. This brings design, as an approach, into the realm of the acceptable. The criteria for the assessment of design work are shown to be different to those appropriate in other, more traditionally acceptable, approaches.

Originality/value – For approximately 40 years, there have been claims that cybernetics and design share much in common. This was originally expressed through communication criteria, and by the use of classical cybernetic approaches as methods for use in designing. This paper argues a much closer relationship between cybernetics and design, through consideration of developments in cybernetics not available 40 years ago (second order cybernetics) and through examining the activity at the heart of the design act: whereas many earlier attempts have been concerned with research that is much more about assessment, prescription and proscription. The paper develops a base for other work interested in exploring any possible relationships between cybernetics and design, and thus provides background for this special issue.

Keywords Analogy · Circularity · Conversation · Cybernetics · Design · Novelty

2.1 Introduction

Because this special double issue of *Kybernetes*.[1] pursues the intersection of two fields, cybernetics and design, there may be readers who are not familiar with one field or the other. Furthermore, both fields may often be presented in an almost bewildering variety of ways some of which appear to contradict others. It seemed that there was, therefore, a need for an introduction to each field. I present this in the first half of the paper, although I do not attempt a field survey (which would be beyond what is possible in this issue).

Approaches to design cover a wide range. The word design has roots in drawing and in designation. It is used as both a noun and a verb (the preferred use in this paper). There is a long history in the way the word "design" came into English, but studies of the activity are relatively recent. I will distinguish three streams here. Herbert Simon [49] thought of design as a complex but essentially mechanical action (and saw much of how designers actually design as a shortcoming rather than a

[1]Editors' note: This chapter has previously been published as the lead paper for a special journal issue on the theme of cybernetics and design, which Ranulph Glanville compiled and edited, in *Kybernetes* 36(9/10):1173–1206. It was subsequently re-published in Glanville, Ranulph. 2014. *The black boox vol. II. Living in cybernetic circles*, 253–292. Vienna: edition echoraum. Reprinted here with minor changes and with kind permission by Emerald as well as by edition echoraum. Ranulph Glanville opened the initial version of this chapter with the explanation that it is made up of two halves, and should, in effect, be seen as two papers in one.

strength – if he saw it at all). His approach can be typified by the notion of generating a set of alternatives which might be assessed against criteria (assuming the criteria can be specified). In contrast, Horst Rittel [45] posited the concept of "wicked problems" as a central feature of designing, while Henrik Gedenryd [8] (with whom I share most sympathy) investigated the relationship between designing and cognition and pointed out that much design research had been concerned with what researchers thought designers should do, whereas he (and I) are more interested in what they do.

Approaches to cybernetics are equally wide ranging. The classical presentation of the subject, deriving from Wiener [56] and the Macy Conferences [40], is of control, feedback, communication, circular causality. This approach takes various forms, with applications in hard engineering to management, law and so on. Social systems soften the approach, but the radical and contrasting variant is second order cybernetics: the cybernetics of observing (rather than observed) systems, as von Foerster [54] described it. Second order cybernetics grew out of Margaret Mead's [35] advocacy of the examination of cybernetic ideas and institutions using cybernetic principles and understandings. Second order cybernetics is thus recursive, constructive and very consistent! My own position in each field (in radical disagreement with many other authors in the issue[2]) is as follows.

2.1.1 Design

I value what designers actually do: the act that is at the centre of designing, the heart of the design act that is the source of its distinctiveness, and of the creativity, the novelty, with which design is associated. So I take it that the act of designing is a worthwhile act in its own right, and a proper focus for research. Indeed, designing may be so worthwhile that it may not need improvement: and improvement may not be possible. Unlike some of my colleagues, I consider the attempt to force design to be scientific to be ludicrous – for several reasons, including that the whole point of design is that it is design. Design is a way of acting, a way of thinking, and I have argued that design (as I understand it) is the act at the centre of the Piagetian development of the constant objects with which, Piaget claimed, we populate the world we create from the experience we live in. In fact, rather than benefitting from ways in which other areas might be applied to design, it may be it is design that has more to offer to other areas.

[2]Editors' note: *Kybernetes*, 36(9/10).

2.1.2 Cybernetics

Cybernetics is a way of thinking that bridges perception, cognition and living-in-the-stream-of-experience (the involvement of the observer), which gives important value to interaction and what we hold between ourselves and others – whether animate or inanimate. It is concerned with circular causality and the wish to control in a beneficial manner. It comes from a mechanical metaphor for the animate, which is now partnered by an animate metaphor for the mechanical. While it can be of great use in its traditional business of modelling control systems (and hence in control engineering), for me its interest lies in the significance given to the involved observer and the consequent individuality of and responsibility for his/her actions. My position lies at the radical extreme of second order cybernetics and is unrecognisable to some others in the field.

2.1.3 A Sketch of the Argument

If the first half of this paper is concerned with an exposition of the understandings of cybernetics and design that I argue from, the second half of the paper is concerned with the development of a series of analogies that show how design and cybernetics are so closely related, at least in my exploration of them (which reflects my interests in them). The reason for composing this issue of *Kybernetes* is to (where possible) explore the relationship between cybernetics and design. In the last half of the paper I present the analogies I have developed that allow me to claim that cybernetics can act as the theoretical arm of design, while design acts as the practical (active) arm of cybernetics.

This paper works with these particular interpretations of design and cybernetics. Many disagree with these interpretations, and the analogies I build. However, my purpose is not to show I am right and others are wrong, but that something may be held between cybernetics and design that is worth considering, thus bringing them together.

Some may say my way of considering design is hopelessly imprecise, that design should be more like science, etc. I reply that if design is more like science, why should we bother with design at all (to repeat myself: the whole point of design is that it is design)? It is the difference that makes design interesting and gives it its value, allowing us to have more than one way of acting, more than one set of values. In my opinion, those who cannot see this should think twice before speaking: it is assertive and wishful thinking to claim that because you cannot see something, no one else can and that your blindness should be taken as universally shared. I say this as a scientist as well as a designer.

There will also be those who claim this approach is romantic. But it is not romantic to accept that not everything can be defined and computed, or that there are ways of working that do not depend on such definition: and it is not romantic to value criteria and qualities other than the strictly measurable, or to accept that reality is as we make it. And, for that matter, what is wrong with romantic?

2.2 Cybernetics and Design: Introduction

2.2.1 Why Should We Think There Is a Connection

The notion that cybernetics and design might have something to tell each other is not new. The history, over the last 60 years, of both has served to bring them together on several occasions and has shown striking parallels in their histories. For instance, in its early days, when technological optimism was at its height, cybernetics was seen as the subject that would help realise this optimistic view. At the same time, design (particularly in the form of architecture[3]) was seen as being unscientific (and hence theoretically inadequate) and began the search it has pursued ever since to find a theory that it could import that would make it properly scientific. Cybernetics (and its near cousin, Systems Theory)[4] was seen as a likely candidate.

In the late 1950s, there was a profound and serious attempt to turn design into a scientific activity, to rationalise it.[5] This approach originated at the Hochschule für Gestaltung in Ulm, and found as one of its sources of strength the "new" science of cybernetics, which was at the time, in the way in which we humans look for the universal answer, ambitiously promoted as a new science that would allow us to solve all our problems. It was, therefore, obviously significant for design.

At the turn of the 1960s into the 1970s the movement towards explicit scientific rationality as the sole generator of objective design "solutions" (the term is redolent of science) began to wane, and, at about the same time, thinkers in cybernetics began to investigate the paradox that the way cybernetic systems were discussed failed to reflect the nature of cybernetic systems[6]: Cybernetic systems were presented using the traditional scientific device of the detached observer, even though they spoke of systems in which the observer (the sensor) is anything but detached: that's the point of feedback![7]

[3]Architects tend to believe they do not belong in the same category as designers. From my point of view (and even though I was educated as an architect and teach architecture), architects design like all other designers, and in this paper I use the verb design for the activity of all designers, including architects.

[4]Systems Theory and Cybernetics are closely related. As Charles François [7] says: "Cybernetics is obviously the dynamic complement of systemics [*sic*]."

[5]The Oxford Conference in the mid 1950s derailed architectural education for some decades by imposing an inappropriate and clumsy pseudo scientism on the teaching of the subject.

[6]See Margaret Mead's [35] paper, Cybernetics of Cybernetics.

[7]It is difficult to appreciate just how revolutionary feedback, circularity, purpose and intention were in science in 1943.

So at the time that design was retreating from the design methods approach (as so clearly indicated in what I see as the brave volte face of J. Christopher Jones [30] in the 1980 revised edition of his classic, *Design Methods*, in which Jones completely rethought the approach used in the earlier version of the book), cybernetics was also becoming less traditionally scientific, for it began talking of the observing system as well as the observed, of the observer in the system rather than the observer of the system.

The change in cybernetics has scarcely been noticed by many in the field, for a number of reasons I will not go into here, and many approaches, from post modern theory to complexity studies and cognitive science, have suffered from having to re-invent a wheel cybernetics had already invented. Indeed, cybernetic developments are still arguably far ahead of much research in these fields, because cybernetics understood the change in the role of the observer to be so radical that it required a complete re-think[8] one example of which is Ernst von Glasersfeld's (e.g., [52]) development of a form of constructivist philosophy known as radical constructivism.[9]

The change in design was much more apparent both to and in the field. The regular importing into design (and specially architecture) of theories and modes of argument/vocabulary from other fields became absolutely apparent in, for instance, the various "critical" and "theoretical" accounts of Jencks, who has led (at least in populist consciousness) the import into architecture of several "foreign" theories.

The theories associated with Jencks and others, which continue to dominate much theoretical discourse in design, are theories concerned with the individuality of perception and understanding, which can also be thought of as the unpredictability of the process of design (and its outcome). As cybernetics moved into a study of systems that include the observer rather than standing independent of him/her, design became more quirkily based in the individual as opposed to a general, single "style" of the period – or, rather, it formed schools which followed theories that recognised the presence of the individual (the observer) in such a manner that these theories came to be expressed, literally, as styles – that is, as ready made algorithms that simplify the contexts in which we work so that many (design) decisions are already made.

Both cybernetics and design thus accepted the inescapable presence of the observer, who must therefore be understood as active – an actor.[10] It is bizarre that, with this parallel between the two fields, design did not recognise the developments in cybernetic thinking (which became known as second order cybernetics) but

[8]Karl Müller has recently published a study in which he shows that the developments von Foerster made in second order cybernetics amount to a radical and revolutionary research programme [36].

[9]For a critical exposition of von Glasersfeld's work, see the recent festschrift edited by Glanville and Riegler [29].

[10]I owe my dawning understanding of the importance and workings of actors to my long association with Gerard de Zeeuw. For a critical exposition of certain central themes in de Zeeuw's work, see the festschrift edited by myself [16].

took to the earlier, less active version of cybernetics,[11] for this newer cybernetics is specifically concerned with understanding systems in which the outcome is unpredictable and individual, and the observer is always present and never ignorable. Nor did cyberneticians generally reach out to design – or, rather, they were all-too-often only prepared to understand design in the manner of so many importers of the word, as a problem solving activity that lives in the world of the complex-yet-definable.

There was one cybernetician, however, who did reach out to design: Gordon Pask. Already in the 1960s Pask had understood there were close parallels to be explored between cybernetics and design. In 1969 [37] he brought his nascent insights into the processes of conversation to the world of design in a paper in which he explored the relationship between the architect and the client. Pask's outreach was long-term and committed: he worked with arguably the most radical architect of the second half of the Twentieth Century, Cedric Price, and he taught in architecture schools, particularly London's Architectural Association School. And he created art works and environments. In the world of art and design he is perhaps best known for his "Colloquy of Mobiles" at the Cybernetic Serendipity Exhibition of 1968 [43], but his design of learning environments is probably more important.

More important, still, is the connection to design of his students. At one stage I calculated that of twelve successful doctoral students at Brunel University, eight were architects and six came from the Architectural Association. I was one of those six students. This is an extraordinary accretion of architects who realised that cybernetics had something special to offer them. What is interesting about this cohort is that they were students of Pask at exactly the time when cybernetics began exploring its basic paradox: that it had talked about systems with an involved observer from a position in which the observer of these systems was not involved.[12]

Pask died in 1996. The link between cybernetics and design was obscured at that time. Today there is a revival of designers' interest in cybernetics. However, most designers who pursue this interest do so – as has been noted – in ignorance of the developments in cybernetic understanding since 1970, which is perhaps the last time designers looked to cybernetics. In a bizarre twist, the result is that designers may be moving back towards an inappropriate determinism which they are seeking to prop up (and mechanise) with ancient cybernetic arguments.

[11]It is, indeed, stranger that even now, when there seems to be a reawakening of an interest amongst designers and artists in cybernetics, that they are still looking at the older version of cybernetics which is far less relevant to their concerns than second order cybernetics – as we will find out over the course of this paper.

[12]There are other personal connections, two of whom participated in the special issue of *Kybernetes* on the theme of cybernetics and design. Paul Pangaro comes from drama and studied with Pask, sharing with Pask an appreciation of the importance of drama. He now teaches design. The architect Stephen Gage worked with Pask both as a student (I recently saw Pask's diary for 1967 – the year I met him – which was full of appointments with Gage) and later as a teacher and practitioner. He even contemplated studying with Pask for a PhD.

I believe I have shown above that there are parallels between design and cybernetics: in the sorts of approaches they used at various times, and in the sensitivity to the involvement of the active observer. In this paper I shall explore these parallels, specially using the conceptual framework of second order cybernetics, particularly in the form of Conversation Theory – the second order cybernetic account of communication. In doing so I hope not only to demonstrate there is an important connection(s) between the two fields, but also that more recent cybernetic thinking offers particular relevance and value to designers. In my mind, the homomorphism between the two is such that, as I said in my introduction, I am prepared to claim cybernetics is the theory of design and design is the action of cybernetics.

But before I can do that, I need to introduce cyberneticians to design (as I intend it in this paper) and designers to cybernetics (in its recent guise).

2.2.1.1 Design for Cyberneticians

What is meant by design, in the context of this paper?[13]

Before I go into this question, I should re-assert that there is much disagreement and debate in design and design research over this question, and about whether there is a design process and, if so, how to characterise it. The descriptions I give are my descriptions and reflect my belief, experience and understanding. I believe that most designers, and many researchers who are sensitive to what designers do, will recognise what I describe. I base this statement less on the literature than on personal experience and discussion with many designers and students over a long period.

Let me start with some negatives. By design, I do not mean problem solving, or even a way of facing complexity (though design does that well, as we shall see). I do not refer to an object, the result of a design process, or even a process, itself also the result of a design process.

Design, in this paper, is an activity that is often carried out in the face of very complex (and conflicting) requirements. We may deal with many of these requirements (functions to be accommodated and other factors) through logical procedures: for instance, an optimal sequence of rooms in the layout of a building may be created using simple network theory.

Yet the interest of designers is generally to create the new. They wish to bring delight to the user (and to themselves as designers), while finding a form that can house the requirements in a manner that is satisfactory, by the creation of something

[13]My original design education was in architecture (and musical composition), and I have taught design, mainly in architecture, all my professional life. When reading an overview of approaches to design, it is often important to keep in mind the design discipline that the author comes from. There are differences in, for instance, beliefs about optimum outcomes that vary from very ill-defined areas such as architecture, to more proscribed areas such as industrial design. This paper is no place to explore this, but it is mentioned in Krippendorff [32]. Regardless of these differences, the activity of holding a conversation with oneself is central to all.

new.[14] Sometimes, convenience may even be traded off for added delight: we will on occasion accept the less convenient in order to have the more beautiful. And sometimes the process of bringing all the requirements into a new form leads to a new way of accommodating the requirements that transcends traditional logical procedure, at which point a novel type of arrangement may appear.

What I refer to is design as a verb, not as a noun. The verb, design, indicates a particular process that constitutes the design activity, a particular and relatively little studied process which I maintain is at the heart of design, the whole undertaking generally being included under the one name. I am not talking about evaluation of the outcome of the process, or of situating that outcome within some schema. This process can be thought of as a conversation held mostly (but not exclusively) with the self. In the most common traditional version, the conversation consists of making a mark with a pencil on paper (equivalent to talking, in a verbal conversation), and then looking at it to see what the mark suggests (equivalent to listening) and, consequently, modifying the drawing. The process goes on and on in a potentially endless circle. Reasons for stopping are that the outcome is good enough or that it fails. As an initial process it may have little or no intention: it's just a sketch or (to downplay the action) a doodle. But the sketch/doodle suggests a form and that is explored, playfully, and requirements are gradually assimilated into the design as form is brought into being.

It is apparent that this design process is based around the actions of the designer: to talk of this process as if the designer were not present in it is, clearly, impossible – for there would be no process. It is therefore assumed that whenever this design process is discussed, the process includes the designer.

It is this process of conversation, primarily held with the self (but also with others in, for instance, an office), that indicates a cybernetic process at work: for conversation is perhaps the epitome of second order cybernetic systems.[15] And, like any conversation, it is open and can take us to places we did not expect to be, thus introducing novelty. In looking at the sketch, we see it in ways other than we saw it when we drew it: viewing is an exploratory and constructive act. As I was instructed as a student: "Learn to think with your pencil!".

In this manner, sketching, the central source of creative design action, can thus be described and explained as and by means of a primary second order cybernetic system – the circle of conversation. And, although this is not all of design, it is a, if not the, key activity at the heart of design: so cybernetics supports design and design supports cybernetics, in a further second order, conversational, cybernetic circle! Design may be thought of as an inductive process, where science is deductive.

[14]The earliest, and still arguably the best, definition of architecture was by the Roman architect and writer, Vitruvius, who called for "firmnesse, comodotie and delight" (in the translation by Sir Henry Wootton [57]): in today's terms, being well-built, functional and delightful.

[15]I have argued that Pask's study of conversation epitomises truly interactive systems [11, 22]. Interactive systems may include those systems in which the observer acts. I have also argued that those entities that persist through the action of self observing, which I call Objects, provide a form for inhabitants of a universe, the entry to which is through observation and being observed [9].

Science has problems when it tries to be inductive: design shows a way (and a change in legitimate expectations) by which we may act inductively.

2.2.1.1.1 Design and the Ill-Defined

The design activity (design as verb) that I have described grows what may later be seen as a unique solution to an ill-defined and under-specified set of problems – some so under-specified that they should not even be considered problems. The lack of definition has many sources. In a sense, what is at the centre of design is scarcely concerned with problems, at least as we have come to think of them. We can think of designing leading to an outcome which can be seen as a solution that defines the problem(s), in contrast to the way we normally think of a problem leading inexorably to the solution. This does not mean that designers fail to "solve" what are quite conventional "problems", but that what makes their work and their approach unique is not this aspect.

This is one reason design is not and cannot be scientific, in the sense of recent Anglo Saxon use of that word. Design is not a science, but, I have argued, science is a specially and particularly limited form of design [12, 15]. No scientific experiment just happens, no theory exists without a reworking of the knowledge associated with it (a point made by Popper (who called himself a constructivist) in *"Conjectures and Refutations"* [42]); more extremely, still, I have argued that the processes of mentation which Piaget argues are at the centre of our thinking are properly considered as design acts, and therefore design is the primary human activity [26].

And when we come to specify the problems a design outcome has been designed to accommodate, we find that these problems are very complex indeed, that their interrelationships lead quickly to vast complexity and to those areas of problem space that the great cybernetician Ross Ashby referred to as the transcomputable: there is simply not enough physical stuff for us to even dream of computing, exhaustively, logically driven solutions, which makes design an effective approach to complexity – for design is not so consequent upon a problem statement, which will often enter into the realm of the transcomputable [2].

2.2.1.1.2 A Very Brief History of (the Word) Design

The use of the word design in English is recent, and until it acquired its application to what have also been called the applied arts, its meaning was not what it is now. The origins of the noun are in the Italian disegno, to draw.[16] But this verb apparently follows another route, coming into English (according to the *Oxford Dictionary of the American Language*) from a Latin root: designare, to designate (via French désigner): this dual route is particularly poignant when thinking of the command

[16]This is the use made by the architect Inigo Jones in his annotations of Palladio's Five Books.

"Draw a distinction!" with which George Spencer Brown starts his book, *Laws of Form* [50]. This book had a major influence on cybernetic thinking, and reminds us that every line we draw also designates, bringing the two understandings together in another way.

The intention in using the word design, and the activity it designates, has also changed. But the recent adoption of the word design in areas that have nothing to do with the traditional, central activity I have indicated in my view weakens the concept. Design has become a buzz word appropriated by many fields where, according to my interpretation, it scarcely belongs: it has been colonised. My intention in using it relates to the conversational activity I have described above, and not the post-colonial.

There are two more points to make.

Firstly, as stated above, design always involves the designer. That is, of course, nothing more than an assertion of a grammatical rule: verbs have subjects. But it is important because it shows in another way that design, with its active agent, the designer, fits in with cybernetics (particularly of the second order), which considers circular systems in which the observer is understood to be both present and active.

Second: there are no absolute criteria (there is no clear specification: the criteria emerge after the solution has been found and may be seen as being defined by the solution): design outcomes can only be validated as being good enough (the phrase introduced earlier), not by being best. In fact, it is often difficult to determine that one design outcome is better than another simply because there is no shared standard against which to evaluate. This may be a great, though unexpected extra benefit, difficult for many to appreciate.

2.2.1.2 Cybernetics for Designers

Cybernetics is apparently a modern science, though the origin of its name is old Greek (meaning helmsman) and the word has been in occasional use for a long time.

Its modern use is generally taken to originate with Norbert Wiener, whose eponymous 1948 book, *"Cybernetics"*, was subtitled *Control and Communication in the Animal and the Machine.* However, what is perhaps a better definition is the title of a series of working conferences, "Circular Causal and Feedback Mechanisms in Biological and Social Systems", funded by the Josiah Macy Jr Foundation in New York (1942, 1946–52) and attended by Wiener, amongst others (including Gregory Bateson and Margaret Mead). The name cybernetics was, after the publication of Wiener's book, taken as summarising the theme of the Macy Conferences by the conference secretary, Heinz von Foerster.

The word control, in English usage, has two rather different meanings. Probably the more common is restrictive control, where the controller limits the controlled according to his/her whim. This sort of control is essentially aggressive and destructive, e.g., dictatorial.

The other, Wiener's intended use, is enabling control. This sort of control talks of the benefits of controlled movement in achieving aims: the purpose of enabling control is not to restrict, but to guide towards better performance. Being in control:

so that a skier is in control as (s)he speeds down a mountain responding to all the arbitrary surprises in the slope without falling.

Control implies two further things. Firstly, some goal or intention. In Wiener's (and colleagues') first proto cybernetic paper [46] he and his fellow authors talk of teleology: purposive or intentional action. This was a brave move at a time when science was particularly preoccupied with the removal of intentionality from its processes and practice.[17] Secondly, control implies some means by which the intention (and the control action) can be communicated to an effector or actor. Wiener's interest in communication largely concerned capacity, and he is the (unacknowledged) precursor of Shannon and Weaver's [48] *Mathematical Theory of Communication*, commonly known as Information Theory.[18] The question arises as to what constitutes control in a system that enables rather than restricts. This was defined by Ashby [1] in his Law of Requisite Variety. Variety is a measure of the number of states a system either might or does take. In order not to restrict behaviour, Ashby's Law tells us, the system that is to control must have at least as many states as the system to be controlled. That is, the controller must have the Requisite Variety for control not to be, in principle, restrictive.

A simple example of a cybernetic system is a domestic heating system. This consists, in essence, of two elements: the sensor and a space served by a heat source. The situation in the room being heated can be described (assuming some goal temperature) using only two states: it is too hot or it is too cold. The controller (sensor) needs, thus, only to have two states, which can be easily achieved with a (heat sensitive) on/off switch. The Requisite Variety is two, the controller (sensor) may have many more states, but they are optional (and unlikely to be of much use).

2.2.1.2.1 First Order Cybernetics

The sensor in the thermostatic system (strictly speaking, the whole system, maintaining a constant room temperature, is thermally static) observes[19] the room's thermal conditions, distinguishing them into one of two groups (too hot, too cold) that effect one of two actions (respectively, turn heat source off, turn heat source on). The need for this constant monitoring is based on a pragmatic consideration itself as novel and daring as reference to intention: the notion that error is, in itself, neither bad nor good, but endemic – it cannot be eliminated. The cybernetic system

[17]The difficulty of intentionality is specially associated with social sciences. While it is not difficult to consider systems made of so-called inert matter as intention-free, it is much harder to avoid intention when we examine animate systems, such as people. The "Hawthorne Effect", in which the subjects in a study change their expectations in line with changes in experimental conditions (what is considered an acceptable light level in a factory increases as the light level of a work place is increased) has been well known since the 1930s.

[18]See Conway and Siegelman's [6] biography of Wiener, *"Dark Hero of the Information Age"*.

[19]The term "observe" is used in its scientific sense, rather than to more pictorial visual sense of the everyday.

constantly drives to achieve its goal. Some attain this and come to a stop, some enter a cycle around the goal as a fixed point, while others pursue a goal that itself moves, so they are always playing catch-up. Consider the primary cybernetic metaphor of the helmsman: any sailor will attest that simply pointing the rudder will not get you where you want – you have to constantly trim and adjust until you arrive. The difference, in cybernetic terms, between the helmsman of a boat and the thermostatic sensor, is that the helmsman hopes his boat will arrive and stop, whereas the heating system will not achieve this: it goes on forever seeking the desired room temperature in a perpetual loop that merely keeps it adequately near that temperature because error is endemic. (In fact, careful consideration shows it is error that drives the system!)

Even in this simplest of systems (the thermostat), control is effected through a feedback loop, and the sensor is active: it turns the heat source on and off. However, the behaviour of the sensor, itself, is controlled, in turn, by the room heated by the heat source. We will return to this point in the next section: what is relevant, here, is that the (organisational) form of control is circular – as is the causality. The temperature in the room drops below the goal temperature causing the sensor to switch, sending a message to the heat source, which causes it to provide more heat. The heat source provides heat until the temperature in the room exceeds the goal temperature causing the sensor to switch, sending a message to the heat source, which causes it to stop providing heat, and so on, *ad infinitum*. In fact, we can describe this system as having three goals: the overriding one of maintaining a specified steady temperature, which is made up of two subsidiary ones; to gain heat when below the specified temperature, and to lose heat when above it.

I used the word cause in order to point, in this feedback loop, to the concept of circular causality (remember the Macy definition of cybernetics). This is another radical concept. The aim of traditional science has been to get rid of circularity, yet here is a subject (Wiener, in his book title, was careful not to call it a science, though many have since appended the word as can be seen in earlier usage in this paper) that lives in circularity and turns cause into a circular mechanism: herein lies the radical (and brave) novelty.

In fact, some (I among them) have claimed that circular causality is the norm and the linear causality science espouses is a special case with very weak feedback, so weak that it is insignificant. Subjects such as chaos theory and its precursor catastrophe theory show us what happens when we consider that we may ignore the insignificant. My point is that circular causality is the more general case, with linear causality as a specific limitation; just as Einstein's mechanics is the more general case while Newton's mechanics is specifically limited. This doesn't stop Newton's mechanics from being very powerful and very beautiful: the Americans flew to the moon using Newton's mechanics rather than Einstein's.

A legitimate question arises in relation to the nature of control in circular systems: which element controls and which is controlled? In the thermostat example, the sensor switches on the heat source, but the heat source then switches the sensor off. Control is neither in one element nor the other, but between them, shared. It would seem that the general convention is to call that which uses little energy the controller, as if we were dealing with an energetic (and hence physical) system. This was Wiener's position. I believe he was wrong: cybernetics is not focussed on the physical world, but the informational. Which element we call controller and which controlled is arbitrary and our choice, should we chose to make it.

2.2.1.2.2 First to Second Order Cybernetics

In Sect. 2.2.1 I outlined the shift from first to second order cybernetics. In a system such as the typically cybernetic one of the thermostat, the sensor (the part of the system that was traditionally thought of as controlling) is not only an observer of the system (it observes the two states – too hot and too cold), but also an observer (actor) in the system. It causes changes in the states of the heat source and, hence, through the action of the heat source (turn off, turn on) the room, in turn, changes the state of the sensor. The sensor, in this description, is an example of an involved and active observer. In cybernetic systems such an observer is the norm.

Margaret Mead's 1968 paper (commissioned by Heinz von Foerster) has already been mentioned. In it she asked why cyberneticians did not treat their own systems (in this case exemplified by the American Society for Cybernetics) as a cybernetic system: why not treat a cybernetics society through cybernetics, itself. Hence the title of her paper, "The Cybernetics of Cybernetics" that also came to be called the New Cybernetics and, more commonly, Second Order Cybernetics. We can generalise from her request: why not treat cybernetic systems through cybernetic understandings and insights?

A way of summarising what makes cybernetic systems different from (I have earlier argued more general than) traditional ones is circularity. Circularity is embodied in the role of the observer in cybernetic systems: the observer cannot be inactive, or there would be no system.

The question, in discussing and treating cybernetic systems, becomes why, if we are going to treat cybernetic systems cybernetically, do we not treat our examination of them in a similar manner, recognising that the observer even in the conventional scientific arrangement can only be remote and detached through a carefully structured deceit. In actuality, the observer is always present, always active in several ways (for instance, setting up experiments, choosing variables, arranging outcomes in the body of knowledge). Consistency demands that we treat the observer of the cybernetic system in the same way that we treat the observer in the cybernetic system; and the observer in the cybernetic system must be active (to effect change), so the observer of the system should be treated as active, in just the same way. The observer, in second order cybernetics, is in the system he/she is describing just as (when, for instance, describing the thermostatic system) the sensor in that system is understood as an observer in the system. We have observers of observers that are observing (their) observing: another cybernetic recursion. There is, nevertheless, still an irony. In order to talk about the observer in a second order cybernetic system, I have taken the position of an observer of rather than an observer in. This is a consequence of this sort of description. The observer in requires an act of sharing of exactly the sort that happens within a conversation. It can happen in a performance, in a lecture (a special type of performance): we become observers in when we live in experience rather than describing it. For a designer this may be summarised as experiencing total involvement in the act, often thought of as being lost in it.

2.2.1.2.3 Subject and Metasubject

Cybernetics is one of those rare subjects (another being mathematics) which, while being a distinct field worthy of consideration in its own right, is also a subject that casts light upon other subjects. It is an abstract subject which has often been applied to enhance our understanding of other subjects. In its incarnation as second order cybernetics it is both its own subject and its own metasubject. Design is another such subject: a subject in its own right, that can cast light to other subjects, and which, I have argued, needs to be studied in the light of its own criteria, as a design equivalent of second order cybernetics: the (recursive) cybernetics of cybernetics and the (recursive) design of design [17]. Cybernetics talks of structure and form, leaving emotion and meaning to the observer's interpretation and insertion. It may be thought of as providing possible structures within which it is possible to construct the individual meanings and emotions we chose. It does not negate such deeply human areas, but supports structures that in turn support our freedom to enjoy them, leading to another form of second order recursion: the support of support.

2.2.1.2.4 Circularity

As stated in the Macy Conference theme, the central and distinctive feature of cybernetic systems, in contrast with the more traditional systems of science, is circularity: cybernetic systems are circular, whereas scientific systems have traditionally aimed at being linear.

When we look at the cybernetic circle, one key point becomes clear: that the circle is organisational, it is the form. The experience, the passage around this circle, is a spiral. That is, the passage acquires history, and, at least for the cognisant observer, there is a process of learning, of change. On each iteration we act, collecting the history of the iterations in an ever enrichening spiral. We do not experience the same spot (twice), for although the spot may appear the same at least in terms of location, we are not. As Heracleitus tells us, "Upon those who step into the same rivers different and ever different waters flow down". This is another way of expressing what we have been calling recursion.

2.2.1.2.4.1 Autopoiesis, Eigen Forms and Objects

Second order cybernetics has developed several very particular circular systems. The most famous of these is the Autopoietic system of Varela, Maturana and Uribe [51]. Autopoiesis (literally, self-creation or self-production) is a process described thus:

> An autopoietic machine is a machine organized (defined as a unity) as a network of processes of production (transformation and destruction) of components which: (i) through their interactions and transformations continuously regenerate and realize the network of processes (relations) that produced them; and (ii) constitute it (the machine) as a concrete unity in space in which they (the components) exist by specifying the topological domain of its realization as such a network.
> [. . .] the space defined by an autopoietic system is self-contained and cannot be described by using dimensions that define another space. When we refer to our interactions with a concrete autopoietic system, however, we project this system on the space of our manipulations and make a description of this projection. [34]

A second is von Foerster's Eigen forms. This is not the term he used, but one I use as an umbrella term to include Eigen structures, Eigen functions, Eigen objects, Eigen behaviours and Eigen values – terms he did use. Von Foerster wrote of objects – tokens for Eigen behaviours – and talks of recursive functions which arrive at a stable and self-reproducing value. Recursion is the act of continuously repeating a process, applying it to the earlier output (consequence) of that same process. Eigen forms provide a model for how, by a process of repeated action (such as observing) we can arrive at a stable and fixed outcome. Von Foerster [55] used this as a model for the establishment of those stable entities Piaget referred to in his conservation of objects.

A third, less familiar circular system, contemporaneous with autopoietic systems and predating Eigen forms is what I have called an "Object". An Object is a self-referential entity (which maintains its form through (circular) action on and in itself). It provides a structure or form for entities that are observable. If entities are to be observable, that is to inhabit a universe of observation, the question is how they come to be in the universe in order to be observable (by others). The answer provided by Objects is that they must (be assumed to) observe themselves. The great advantage of this form is that Objects, being observed by others, will always reflect the individuality of those others. There are other advantages that come with the package, such as the generation (as opposed to the assumption) of a logic[20] [9, 13].

2.2.1.2.4.2 *Conversation as the Essential Second Order Cybernetic Paradigm*

To these systems we must add Pask's Conversations. The word conversation was chosen by Pask [38] because it is everyday, and refers to a common experience and form of communication. Conversation involves us listening and talking to each other, in an essentially circular form.

Pask analysed the basic mechanism of conversation to get a grip on the bare bones, the structure. This is in contrast to those who consider the meaning of elements in a conversation, or the emotional content and such like. Cybernetics is concerned with mechanism (the machine of Wiener's subtitle) and with structure/form: this allows

[20]It is not claimed that Objects exist in any physical sense, but that they can act as an explanation, a structure that permits.

enormous freedom in, for instance, emotional interpretation because the structure supports many such interpretations. The purpose of building such a structure, at least for some cyberneticians, is to permit and support such freedom.

Pask's conversational structures required at least two participants, the first of which presented some understanding (of some topic) to the second. The second took this presentation and built his/her own understanding of the first participant's understanding, presenting this understanding of an understanding in turn to the first participant. The first participant then makes an understanding of (the presentation of) the second participant's understanding of (the presentation of) the first participant's understanding, thus comparing his/her original understanding with the new understanding developed via the second participant's understanding. If these two understandings are close enough, the first participant can believe the second participant has made an understanding that is, at least operationally, similar to his/her original one. Of course, we may never claim the understandings of the two participants are the same. No meaning, no understanding is sent from one participant to the other: the meanings we acquire as we build understandings are ours alone. This is an enormous strength of the conversational model of communication.[21]

Pask evolved his Conversation Theory in the context of learning. Pask may be considered the first to develop machines that learnt, and which took part in a shared learning environment with learners. His conversations were originally intended to permit learners to study the ordered topics of a subject in a manner, and developing understandings, that suited each learner. The conversations were held over the topics of a vast "entailment mesh" of topics that constitute a subject, and also in the process of testing understandings developed by means of a thoroughly conversational process – teachback.

Conversation is the fourth essential circular cybernetic system that embodies the features of second order cybernetics. As Pask describes it, the conversation is the basic form of genuine interaction: and it is this which makes it so important, such a good model for design.

2.2.1.3 The Interesting Conjunction

In Sect. 2.2.1.1 I showed something of the conversational character of the process I maintain is at the centre of designing. This parallel is at the heart of the argument in this paper, that cybernetics and design are parallel activities.

It is the circularity of conversation that is at the heart of this parallel. The circular second order cybernetic systems mentioned in sections "Circularity" and "Autopoiesis, Eigen Forms and Objects" also have something to show us about

[21] A traditional view is that, to take part in a conversation, we need coded (and hence meaningful) communication. I argue the opposite. We can have no code that we share and interpret without a conversation, by which we can establish that we will set up a code. Thus, for me, conversation is the essential communicational mechanism.

design. In particular, von Foerster's Eigen forms and my Objects provide strong theoretical support for aspects of the central design process, enriching the support provided by Pask's conversations.

But earlier, first order cybernetics still has something to contribute. I do not refer to the old parallel that helped sustain the Design Methods movement, but to the working of Ashby's Law of Requisite Variety. I shall start the in depth examination of the parallels between cybernetics and design with what this Law can tell us about creativity.

2.3 Body of Argument

2.3.1 Cybernetics, Design and Determinism

Cybernetics was born at about the time that design became recognised as a way of acting, yet seen to be somehow lacking. This led, in architecture, to the development of design science and attempts to show that design could be carried out in a completely rational and logical manner – that is, scientifically. This is not the place to explore how this was attempted or the source of what I believe is its inevitable failure. Cybernetics was seen as a major weapon in the arsenal used in the attempt to produce a rational design process, within a determinist framework. This was not surprising, for cybernetics was correctly understood to be concerned with mechanism. What has changed in cybernetics since those days is how that mechanism is seen (Wiener's metaphor of the animal as the machine has in some respects reversed in second order cybernetics so that the machine is often seen through the metaphor of the animal).

There is, however, one first order cybernetics example of an understanding of design that continues to have great relevance and power, and that concerns Ashby's Law (of Requisite Variety).

2.3.1.1 Variety and Design

As recounted, variety is a measure devised by W. Ross Ashby to help us understand the (cybernetic) controllability of a system, and Ashby's Law of Requisite Variety states the conditions necessary for effective cybernetic control: that the controlling system has at least as much variety as the system to be controlled. (For a second order system, in which which element is recognised as the controller and which the controlled is essentially arbitrary, each controlling the other, the variety clearly can only be the same. Second order cybernetics originated at the end of Ashby's career and was not formulated before he died, so he never had the need to reconsider his Law.)

In this part of the paper we will examine how Ashby's Law can illuminate the activity of design.

2.3.1.1.1 Animal and Machine

Cybernetics, especially in its original version, dealt with definable examples which it determined, modelled and then controlled (in the cybernetic sense). It was concerned with clear-cut states. Being able to define states and their causal relationships is one way of describing classical physics (especially mechanics), and abstracting it to this level is one reason cybernetics is (like maths) both a subject and a meta-subject at the one time. This assumption is essentially the assumption in Louis Sullivan's dictum, sloganised by the Modern Movement in design as "Form follows function," and was one reason design methods and first order cybernetics were such natural bed fellows: for both wished (to quote Wiener's subtitle) to use the machine as the metaphor for the animal.

2.3.1.1.2 The Undefinable

Ashby, himself, pointed to one of the main problems of problem definition that are significant in design. In his "Remarks at a Panel" Ashby [2] explains that there is a limit to the computing capacity of even the most powerful conceivable systems. These derive from the finite size and life of the universe as we understand it. Beyond this limit we reach the transcomputable. Because the (literally) astronomically vast universe is nevertheless finite, there is a limit to what may (theoretically) have been computed in it. Ashby shows that this limit can very quickly be exceeded. Even relatively simple problems such as computing, exhaustively, the possible states of a light matrix of 20 by 20 light bulbs exceeds the computability limit Ashby derives, using both his own argument, and the argument developed by Hans J. Bremermann. These arguments tell us that problems very rapidly become transcomputable. Design almost always faces a situation where it has so many interrelated variables (assuming this concept is appropriate to design) that the problems it deals with are essentially transcomputable.

But it is questionable whether the concept of a variable (and thus a measurable unit) is relevant in design. In Sect. 2.2.1.1, I explained that designers are interested in the new: the new is, by definition, not something that is inherent in the existing (so it cannot, in the original sense of the word, be predicted and thus does not depend on a notion such as "variable").[22] It may be seen as connected, and even rational, after the event, but before the event it can only be thought of as what, in Chaos Theory, would be a sort of discontinuity. The new is, by definition, outside the predictable (at least until it is created, when it may be accounted for).

Furthermore, as any designer will attest, for all but the very simplest jobs (and perhaps even for them) it is extraordinarily difficult to specify precisely what is needed or wanted, and within whatever specification can be produced there will be conflicts and inconsistencies. I have explored this aspect in a recent paper on design

[22]This is also why it does not emerge, at least in any historical sense of the word.

and complexity [28] and will not take it further here except to draw to the reader's attention the lack of experience most of us have in specifying – except in the crudest terms – what we want of a house (to use an architectural example). How do we describe the experience we seek? Do we, in specifying a wc, also take into account that this is the one room (in most houses) where privacy is guaranteed, so that it may serve, for instance, the function of a retreat? Or how do we get light into a kitchen from east, south and west (so that it's sunny all day, in the northern hemisphere) when the kitchen has to fit in with other rooms that also demand light and view – the kitchen being the most used room in a house?

These factors render it impossible to expect to adequately and accurately define a design problem.

2.3.1.1.3 Definability and Variety

Ashby's arguments about limits and transcomputability were introduced at the start of the previous section. Ashby's Law of Requisite Variety states that, for any system to be controlled, or, to use one of the two other cybernetic synonyms, managed (the other is regulated)[23] the variety (number of states) in the controller must exceed the variety in the system to be controlled. But if the variety of the controlled system is transcomputable, it is in principle inconceivable that we can compute enough states to be able to control it. This happens in principle, as has been reported, in surprisingly simple systems. Thus, the aspiration to model, to control (without restricting) the performance of many systems is unrealistic. This is profoundly shocking to most of us, and takes some getting used to.

Of course, this doesn't stop us trying, but we use strategies that belie the problem. Ashby also states (in the same paper) "The systems theorist may thus be defined as a man, with resources not possibly exceeding 10^{100}, who faces problems and processes that go vastly beyond this size" – an explicit recognition of the difficulty. The tactics we use to alleviate this essential problem lie in how we define the context in which we chose the states according to some (often unspoken) notion of relevance or appropriateness; or by transforming what we do to the notion of control so it becomes control-as-restricting. Both of these strategies work, but one intentionally restricts, while the other also finds a way of redefining variety so that it becomes manageable. As Ashby tells us in this quote:

> Systems theory ... will be founded, essentially, on the science of simplification ... The systems theorist of the future, I suggest, must be an expert in how to simplify.

[23]A reminder: the cybernetic notion of control is distinct from the popular notion. In popular use, control is often connected with restriction. Cybernetic control is enabling: it helps us towards some aim. Another way of saying this is that cybernetic control is concerned with effectiveness, as in Stafford Beer's definition of cybernetics as effective management.

2.3.1.1.4 Being Out of Control, Unmanageability, and Creativity

It is therefore possible to describe design problems as essentially unmanageable, in the two senses that:

(1) variables may not be relevant and, even if they are,
(2) such variables are often incomplete, contradictory and define problems that exceed the transcomputable.

In general, when we use the word unmanageable, we indicate a negative. But here it is positive. This is why:

A common idea of how we should be in our world is to be in control – that is, to manage. We use this "control" language extensively. It is useful to be in control! Drivers who are not in control, for instance, may be an enormous danger.[24] But being in control means defining, in some sense, the range of what will be considered, that is, the range of the possible. In effect, when I am in control I restrict the world to what I can imagine or permit: I define possible and desirable states; I impose my order. But, doing this, I necessarily restrict: not in the sense of the limiting control practised by, for instance, dictators; but in the sense that I support a predetermination of what-is and what-might-be, and aim towards specified – and therefore predetermined – goals.

Let me give an example of the way this sort of control restricts. If I go to a restaurant with a group of friends, and it is always I who chooses the restaurant, we will only go to restaurants that I choose; and choosing the restaurants reflects my taste and knowledge (or, perhaps better, ignorance), which can be seen as a limitation, a sort of filter that reflects only what I already know. If, however, I let others choose the restaurant, I will often go to a restaurant I did not know, thus finding new (to me) restaurants. I can regard these introductions as gifts from my friends, increasing the range of my experience, knowledge and choosables, even if I decide a particular, new-to-me restaurant is bad. (Often, of course, I find great new delights.)

My contention is that the restaurant situation provides a good illustration of the operation of the Law of Requisite Variety. The great benefit of not having enough variety to control a system is that, if I give up trying to control rather than being annoyed that I cannot, I can discover many possibilities I would have excluded if I had insisted on being in control. These possibilities are unexpected, outside my frame of reference, in a word, novel. This is akin to giving up control of the choice of restaurant, letting others introduce new possibilities. If you want to use the concepts and measure of variety, you can easily set up situations in which the variety to be controlled is vastly greater than any variety you might ever have access to and so you cannot possibly control the situation, except restrictively. Stopping trying to find enough variety to control means accepting the vastly greater variety in the now

[24]Contrast this to drivers in, for instance, Egypt, who appear to be completely out of control but are actually very much in control: the control is, however, localised in each driver, rather than in a large system.

out-of-control element while all those possibilities you would have excluded are no longer excluded, and, to take a cliché, the world is your oyster.

Not restricting what you will consider to what you know already opens you up to experiencing the vast unknown; and in that you are likely to encounter what is to you the new.[25]

2.3.2 *Design as Done*

Research in design can be seen to fall into two categories (see, for instance, Gedenryd [8]). The first and largest is that in which design is investigated through perspectives and methods imported from or associated with other subjects. For example, the history of design examines the outcome of designing through the perspectives and values of history; while this may give interesting insights, it can be argued that this research misses the central concerns of design, treating design as material to be subjected to investigation by and according to the aims and values of the imported discipline. The same can be said for design science, cultural studies and so on. Many researchers believe this is the only way to progress, implicitly suggesting that design is lacking a viable approach of its own and, therefore, needs to import one. These approaches bring their own insights but, I hold, recognise little value in design's own approaches.[26] There is also slight consideration of the appropriateness of the imported theory [18] but, of course, bringing in that which may not be obviously appropriate can lead (as in the argument about Ashby's Law) to benefits.

The second category is research that searches for the presence of a design approach in designing. I have argued in support of this position for nearly 30 years (starting with [15]). I believe design is a way of acting which has great (and largely unrecognised) power and potential, and that researching this will tell us not only a lot about design, but will also give us insights into "different" ways of acting, and can cast a different light on other fields. Therefore, I will proceed in this paper by extending the earlier exploration of design as it is done, in a form of conversation.

2.3.2.1 Design as a Conversation with the Self (and with Others)

The idea that the central act in designing is a form of (Paskian) cybernetic conversation held with oneself has already been introduced.

It is a common experience that, having drawn something, we look at it later and see in it a different something that was not part of what we were thinking about as we drew it. This experience is at the heart of designing. There are two factors that are central:

---

[25]This is one way to increase creative potential. It is not the only way! [10, 14].

[26]See the 1958 Oxford Conference on Architectural Education.

(1) we look and then we draw
(2) we see something new, not previously intended

The first is the basic mechanism that allows the circle which is the form of a design conversation. When I participate in the more familiar verbal conversation, speaking, I expect that my conversational partner will listen, and then, in turn, speak. My conversational partner, speaking, expects that I will listen, and then (completing the conversational circle) speak. For a conversation to take place, each participant must switch roles from being a listener to being a speaker (note how listening precedes speaking). It is not enough to speak, or to listen: what is at the heart of a conversation is the switch. This switch happens within each participant (I speak, I listen), but also between participants: I speak, my conversational partner listens; my conversational partner speaks, I listen. For a design conversation, substitute draw for speak, view for listen.

This is how, when I am my own conversational partner as is commonly the case in design, I can hold a conversation with myself: instead of the drawer/speaker and viewer/listener being identified with two different participants, we understand them as roles, which can be embodied in one participant (by role switching) and even, between groups. This is a basic quality Pask requires for participants in a conversation.[27] (The conversational model also allows the same process to operate between different individuals. It can, thus, also support the familiar social dimension of design – exactly as in the account of a conversation just given.)

The second comes from the first. A basic assumption of a conversation is that participants do not transmit or share meanings (this is one of the ways conversation theory is more powerful, and more accurately represents experience, than information theory). It is in this difference that novelty can be seen to arise: indeed, it cannot but arise. Thus, the aspect of the design process seen as conversation (novelty) can be understood not simply as an aim of the designer that some would count an irresponsible whim, but as unavoidable and necessary.

Why? Because if we construct our meanings differently, we cannot assume our individual understandings will be the same. Therefore, every time my conversational partner expresses back to me his/her understanding, I must assume it will be in some way different from mine.[28] Every utterance I make (whether spoken, gestured or drawn) will return from my conversational partner as different, and my test for understanding is, to put it tersely, whether I can adequately bring together what I hear with what I said. (This is the basis of Krippendorff's *"Semantic Turn"* [31], although, surprisingly, he fails to recognise Pask's pioneering work.)

The difference between the two views comes from the distinctiveness not of the body embodying, but of the cognising entity: that is, the distinction in role between

[27] Pask calls such participants p-individuals: p is for psychological (and not, as many have suggested, Pask). In Pask's account, they are embodied in m-individuals (m is for mechanical).

[28] Unless the tendency of language to make uniform flattens out difference. This is why repeating back the statement of the other cannot indicate an understanding, in a conversation, but only an ability to imitate sounds.

speaker and listener, drawer and viewer, regardless of whether they are taken to be in one or several physical bodies. It is the role that makes the difference, and it is the change between roles that allows the conversation with the self: for it matters not whether Pask's p-individuals are situated in one body or many, or even between members of a group of bodies.

To return to the argument about variety made in Sect. 2.3.1 to section "Definability and Variety", the conversation is one way in which the variety of the "repertoire" of the designer can be increased.

The process of the design conversation with the self opens another important possibility, that of accommodating more and more functions. This process is akin to Piaget's accommodation in the construction of constant objects and will be discussed below. The point, here, is that iteration of the circle of conversation allows, on each cycle, the addition of more functions and requirements to be accommodated into the design outcome. These can lead to failure, or they can lead to development. Their assimilation and accommodation doesn't always have to be perfect: the requirement is that they fit in well enough. This is, I have argued, a major part of how design handles what, in other fields, would be called complexity.

There is, in this account, one mechanism that is at the centre of design. This mechanism implies that difference (and hence both the development of design, and the unavoidable potential of novelty) is inevitable; and that conversational partners can exist, equally, in one person or in a group. The circle of the design conversation can be used as a way of increasing "complexity'', assimilating or accommodating ever more functions.

2.3.2.1.1 Trying, Failing and Re-Starting

There are several further features of conversation that grow out of this account and which are also familiar in designing.

The first of these is the importance (and value) of failure. It is conceivable (and everyone reading will know the experience) that we cannot communicate in some conversations. There are times when we cannot complete the conversational circle. Under these circumstances, we have to give up. In Pask's terms, we agree to disagree, after which we can try to begin again. The same often holds in the central process of design. The conversation with the self may end up somewhere where the result is non-viable or even aesthetically unacceptable. It may also be that the conversational process cannot accommodate a particular enrichment of functions, with the result that the designer has to reject what has so far been developed and start again. Designers are all too familiar with this need!

It has been said of design that the most important ability of a designer is to throw away an old idea that isn't working, and start again. This is a regular experience for the designer. In design, there is nothing negative about failure. In this sense, we have another analogy with cybernetics – possibly the first study to take error on board as a fact of life rather than something to bemoan and curse. Cybernetic systems exist because error is endemic.

2.3.2.1.1.1 Popper and Piaget

The activity that is design can be seen as proto-scientific. Taking Popper's characterisation of science as conjectures, tested thoroughly in an attempt (finally assumed to be successful) to refute them [42], we have a circular activity of improvement and enrichment which fits well to the characterisation, above, of the design conversation.[29]

Furthermore, I have argued [26] the process Piaget describes in which we take experience, and, breaking it into parts, create (recurring) patterns and consistencies between them – leading us to consider that which recurs as constant or conserved – what we come to treat as an object with an independent existence in a separate world, but which we learn about and know in experience. In this manner, Piaget [39] tells us, we come to construct our realities. Of course, sometimes our constructions do not manage to sustain themselves and we have to reject them in favour of new assemblages of constructed patterns of repetition, which we take to be new objects in our (re-constructed) reality. And sometimes we have to modify or expand a constant object to accommodate new experiences. All these ways of behaving are strongly analogous to the way we work with the circle of the design conversation.

2.3.2.1.1.2 Conversation and Objects: Autonomy and Eigen Values

The three other examples of second order cybernetic system that have been mentioned can be seen to represent a behaviour or characteristic of the central design conversation, the conversation with the self.[30]

The first is the autonomy of the autopoietic system. An autopoietic system is one that in the first place generates, and then maintains itself within an environment. It was invented as an explanation of the process of living, by Humberto Maturana, and developed into its full form with Francisco Varela and Ricardo Uribe. It is the best known second order cybernetic system. While the authors of the notion of autopoiesis have never, to my knowledge, explored in detail how their systems come into being (it is a definitional point that they do so), they nevertheless create the conditions to create themselves, and they continue to generate themselves in their environments. We can say this is their purpose. But this is what designers do in the design process: they create the conditions in which the design outcome can come into being and continue to generate itself – that is, continuing the design act leads to an outcome that remains constant (at least in the designer's eye),[31] although detail may be enriched. In this respect, the process of designing can go on in principle forever, and, in essence, when we chose to stop designing is generally a personal and

[29]Keep in mind, however, that science is deductive whereas one intention of design is to be inductive, transcending deduction.

[30]The concept of constancy, here, refers to maintaining an identity. It is a tricky concept and I will not try to further elaborate here.

[31]For references, see section "Autopoiesis, Eigen Forms and Objects".

arbitrary decision.[32] What is important is that, when we have finished designing we have produced an outcome that maintains itself, as it were, independently of us (even if we still have influence) for no matter what we do it remains essentially unchanging, continuing to regenerate itself: in this manner it appears as an autonomous outcome, that is "organisationally closed". Thus, our designs are like our children, which grow to become their own persons.

The second is von Foerster's Eigen forms. Von Foerster is interested in certain types of process that, no matter where you start, always end up, and then continue to be, at the same place. Eigen functions that produce Eigen objects are (mathematical) recursive functions that stabilise on particular values. Von Foerster developed them as a mathematical example that mimics the (cognitive) process which Piaget describes for the construction of his constant objects. Von Foerster's Eigen forms give a rigourous mathematical demonstration of a process by which a system can operate on its own output, treating it as input, and arrive at a self-reproducing value. They model the process of coming into being, and continuing to be.

Von Foerster called the particular systems that behaved in this way Eigen objects. Earlier, I had also used the word Object (but with an initial capital letter), to refer to supposed structures of inhabitants of universes of observation – in other words, structures which might support all the different views made by different observers, which, nevertheless, can be thought of as observations of the same object. Von Foerster referred to this work as a calculus for Piaget's notion of object constancy. The significant aspect of Objects is that, in order to become members of the universe of observation, they are argued to "observe themselves"[33] by taking two alternating roles: (self) observing and (self) observed, between which they are assumed to switch in a continuing circle. In this manner, they switch in the way that the designer in a design conversation does, and there is a strong analogy between the design conversation process and the process by which an Object continues to be in a universe of observation. A universe of observation is, of course, the universe of (radical) constructivism: the experience lies in the observing from which we may postulate and live by/in an external reality made up of objects. These experiences come from observation tagged onto what I call Objects.

Thus, it may be argued that the design conversation is not only built out of Pask conversations, but is reflected in major elements of at least 3 other prime second order cybernetic systems: Maturana, Varela and Uribe's autopoietic systems; von Foerster's Eigen forms; and my own Objects.

[32] I am not yet certain, myself, whether the progress by which the autopoietic system generates itself is in a manner similar to the progress of the design process.

[33] The term "observe" is again used in the scientific, rather than the visual sense.

2.3.2.2 Conversation as Design

We might, after the accounts above of how design activity can be seen as a prime example of second order cybernetics, ask how this cybernetics can be seen as a design activity.

We can consider a conversation as being like wandering in the country; perhaps in a wood, maybe carrying a hamper for a picnic.

As we talk, we follow paths that, to someone else, will almost certainly seem arbitrary. Even talking around a topic we will move away in a manner that is both unpredictable and seemingly without purpose. We will end up somewhere, and will decide that this is a good place to stop.

Swap the word "walk" for the word "talk", and the word "topic" for the phrase "feature in the landscape", and the similarity is clear. The place where we end up is the place where we "decide to have our picnic". Arriving at this point, we can make sense of our journey: we can explain the trip and give it purpose. The word we use for this sort of walking is wandering: designing and conversation are both like wandering.

This is the process of design translated once more. We do not really know where we are going, when we design, but when we arrive we know that we have arrived, and can make sense of the progress. This is not to deny the importance of those aspects of design that we can treat as specifiable and which we can solve (in the traditional sense), but to recognise and allow the central act that makes (almost stumbles on) the new without quite knowing how or why, and can then explain this, by means of explaining the route taken, as a seemingly sensible (even logical) path. This account is, however, not a purposive problem solving activity. It is a post-rationalisation, an explanation after the event.

In our post-rationalised explanations, we often refer to the path we have trodden as a design: and thus we treat the outcome of a primary cybernetic event (a conversation) as design. What we do is to design an explanation that makes our activity seem purposive and logically directed: we use the word design in its meaning as intentional, as goal orientated, and therefore as cybernetic.

2.3.2.2.1 Arriving and Stopping

And what are the criteria by which, after the event, we may explain the choices we make? Certainly neither truth nor utility, in any ordinary sense. Perhaps the concept of beauty fits in here? If so, we have re-established the importance of beauty as a guiding criterion, in a world where we have come to prefer to measure utility. And we are judging the cybernetic act by criteria normally used for such acts.

How do we know we've arrived? Through a feeling of "all-rightness", a sense that this is "just right". This is an intuitive condition, an act of recognition and resolution rather than of a problem solved. We may be able to account for it after the event, but at the time, and to us and the involved deciders, it satisfies our intuition and our sense of OK-ness. This reminds us that designers do not seek the perfect solution, but one that is good enough. They do this not through lack of rigour, but by recognising that the area in which they work is ill-defined: and perfection, therefore, is unattainable. Design brings with it the concept of adequacy as a means of evaluation, rather than perfection. This is a recognition and accommodation of the presence of error – that core aspect of cybernetics. Nevertheless, there are outcomes that are so special and which work so well and so transcend inconvenience that we may indeed consider them perfect: such outcomes occur when by some magic the disparate elements and functions to be fitted together are somehow magnificently accommodated by the form that arises: when the designer is "on a roll."

2.3.2.2.2 Shaping and Forming: Not Designing an Outcome

Perhaps one of the most interesting differences between first and second order cybernetics lies in the manner in which they deal with purpose as internal or external. For a first order cybernetic system, purpose is associated with a goal external to the system: the system is then steered towards the goal, giving rise to the cybernetic metaphor of the helmsman for which the subject was named. The goal, seen as outside the system, gives motivation,[34] but also allows the observer, again outside the system, to examine it in a "quasi-objective" manner. Thus the external goal is associated with the external observer (the observer of) [19].

When the observer is in the system, as in second order cybernetics, the goal that the observer sees the system move towards must also be within the system.

The system with the observer in it has a different quality to the system as the observer of it observes it. We can, as observers of the system, talk of a stable system (as in the thermostat). When, however, we consider a system with an observer in it, and we are that observer, we may be perfectly stable from our point of view, while to an external observer of us we may appear to veer all over the place. Continuity of being, of maintaining our stability, lies within the system (in terms of Objects, and hence the self-conversation at the heart of design, in the switching between observer and observed within the circle that is the system). Viewed against some external goal by an external observer, all may appear different. We cannot, of course, see within the second order system from outside in the same way as we can from within. There is a problem with second order cybernetic systems, indicated earlier yet rarely recognised, that most descriptions of them are from a first order position. To create the second order description, the observers of need to enter in and become observers in. This is, in my experience, where the power of performance enters.[35] But it is also

[34]In a sense, purpose in a cybernetic system can be thought of as arising from the attempt to unite system and goal.

[35]I refer to the power of, for instance, the lecture-as-theatre. Theatrical events (which, by definition, are performed events) have a presence and ability to both convince and involve the audience. The power of performance in the context of explaining second order cybernetics is that the observer (audience member) is no longer left only to appreciate, intellectually, the explanation, but is sucked into the experience of the explanation: they become part of a second order cybernetic system. The immediate effect is often of knowing something powerful has happened but not being sure what it was.

the power of the design conversation, where we, within, become (to the outsider) lost: what we do is incomprehensible and often beyond the scope of the best attempts at explanation. Think of what happens when you try to observe a conversation from outside, as opposed to being part of it.

A system, perfectly stable within, may appear erratic when viewed from without. That is the lesson of, for instance, ageing, of erratic behaviour, and of the design act.

2.3.2.2.3 Stopping and Starting Again

A further, also previously mentioned, feature of design is that of stopping and restarting. This characteristic is not particular or exclusive to activities known by the term design: for instance, it is inherent in much recent theory of science, such as Popper [42] and (in a different manner) Kuhn [33]. It is familiar in many activities, of which conversation is the cybernetic example used above, as it is also familiar in the act of wandering that was used to illustrate the path of a conversation – and an act of design. But if this stop-reject-restart course of action is widely familiar, we might argue that this is an example of how design thinking is (unknowingly) in far more general use than in just those areas known as design. Note, this is not, however, the same point as the point about non-designerly research into design.

This is, then, an argument for design as a primary way of thinking and acting, and from this we get notions such as management as a design activity (see for instance [5]). Indeed, several bodies have set themselves up to bring design thinking into "non-design" areas, for instance the Centre for Design at RMIT University, Melbourne. The observation in this section reflects a specialised application of the argument I made that the concepts Piaget argues for can best be understood as ways of designing [26].

2.3.2.3 Being Out of Control

Let us return briefly to that other cybernetic stream we have pursued: the concept of unmanageability; that is, the outcome already discussed of Ashby's Law of Requisite Variety. Unmanageability comes about when we try to control the uncontrollable.

In section "Being Out of Control, Unmanageability, and Creativity" the argument was made that being out of control does not have to be a bad thing: it can be seen as offering more options than we could, ourselves, imagine. Thus it is a way of increasing our creativity because we have access to (for instance) ideas which would otherwise not have come to our minds.[36]

[36]The concept of creativity being used here is associated with novelty. How the novel may be made is important. The position taken here may seem to those who believe in the romantic depiction of the troubled creative genius to be too easy, but will be recognised by others as close to the way many people recognised (by their peers) as creative account for the way their novel ideas come into being.

It will be noticed that much of what has since been described in this paper in the form of the (design) conversation, can work only because we do not control. A conversation controlled by one participant is not a conversation. The point of conversation is that others bring what you do not. Restricting your response and the conversation to what you know is to destroy the conversation. It follows that design operates in a world in which Ashby's Law is not utilised. It is not that the Law is wrong: it is that this is a (second order) cybernetic activity to which the Law does not apply.

The same holds with the wandering metaphor. The point of wandering – its power – and the pleasure in it, is to follow your nose, to get lost, not to plan, to avoid the dominance of "efficiency".[37]

Both wandering and conversation gain their strength and effect because they epitomise systems to which Ashby's Law of Requisite Variety is not applied. They are acts in which we are out of control – our lives have become unmanageable.

2.3.2.4 Complexity

Complexity is often taken to be a major area of concern. Let me repeat a quote from Ashby used earlier. In the same paper in which he discusses the transcomputable, Ashby states:

> Systems theory ... will be founded, essentially, on the science of simplification ... The systems theorist of the future, I suggest, must be an expert in how to simplify.

However, complexity is not a simple and unalterable property of phenomena. Consider what may be understood under the label "London": we can think of the amazingly complex organism made up of an almost unimaginable set of interrelated parts with a complexity measure that vastly exceeds Bremermann's transcomputability limit; or we can think of a very simple, unitary whole. The complexity we see in phenomena depends on what we want to see, our purpose, the context and so on.

Designers, by definition, are faced with situations generally seen to be of great complexity and ambiguity. But the circular process they go through leads to what may be seen, in the end, to be simple outcomes. Some (including some designers) may claim they are complex. But that complexity lies in what is embodied and contained in the outcome: the outcome itself is more often than not simple and,

[37]Contrarily, the outcome of this wandering (designing) activity often transcends what we could have imagined without wandering, in a manner that leads to improvements in "efficiency" while also promoting qualities such as delight.

indeed, simplicity is a frequently used criterion of success. The Italian designer Bruno Munari is quoted on the walls of the Design Museum in London, thus:

> Progress means simplifying, not complicating.

Simplifying is not to be confused with over-simplification: what Munari points to (as does this paper) is a process by which complex requirements can be brought together within one, unified, unitary form. The complex requirements are dealt with (contained) within this form. Rather than try to specify every requirement and every relationship between these requirements, and then find an optimal solution, design starts more-or-less "aimlessly" and gradually constructs an "evolving" form[38] that not only changes, but in doing so accommodates the required functions, often in a novel and surprising manner, where normal relations between functions are enriched or even replaced by new ones that are unexpected, different, and often very good! The accommodation of further requirements within the form, the assimilation of requirements by substantial shifts in that form (including rejection and restarting), and the conversational manner in which this is done (itself leading to developments in the form) all help designers to simplify the complicated (complex) in finding their final form through a recursive, circular action process.

Design brings to complexity an approach that is distinct from complexity science, which can lead to outcomes of great beauty and elegance. And if some functional requirements are less well satisfied than others, the result may be no worse than the complexity scientist achieves, and has the added value of bringing the beauty of the designed form (in this case, usually the form as physical, an object), and on occasion relationships that bring new pleasure and delight. (See [28]).[39]

There is always a question of how to stop in such situations. Again, (second order) cybernetics gives us an answer. Von Foerster's Eigen forms give us recursive, design-like processes which, at a certain point, reproduce themselves. The outcome of an iteration has the same value as the outcome of the previous (and the next) iteration: repeatedly carrying out the process on the output, leads to the generation of the same output (the value of one output is the same as the value of the following output). In design terms, the next iteration of the design conversation leads to no change in the form. When this occurs, the designer has reached a stable outcome, but not necessarily the "best": the criterion best has no relevance in this way of thinking. In practice, designers learn to know when to stop: they develop an intuition that recognises when they have reached a good enough place, just as the wanderer with the picnic hamper recognises when to stop, when (s)he has reached a point where there is no need to go further and (having "arrived") the wandering can be explained

[38]Form, used in design, is strongly associated with shape. Although not completely divorced from mathematical and philosophical usage, it is the shapely quality that is generally referred to in this paper.

[39]There are, however, some who believe that complexity science may be the theoretical arm of design.

as if purposeful in a manner that makes sense of the journey to this place, because of the recognition of arrival: the arrival defines and gives purpose to the journey just as, so often in design, the "solution" defines the "problem".

2.3.3 Criteria and Conditions: From Cybernetics to Design

In the above we have already indicated one condition that derives from this understanding of design and cybernetics: that the notion of "best" (in the sense of finding the optimal solution) is scarcely applicable and has little or no relevance in design. The appropriate criterion is not best, but good enough. A design should satisfy the specifiable requirements. It should lead to the creation of a special object or process that is new. The criterion of being best (or even being better) cannot be applied in any absolute manner because there is no strict scale and no basis for strict comparison, and because the so-called problem is, for many reasons already explored, undefinable. It may, of course, turn out that one design is judged better than another, perhaps because it's more in tune with popular taste, or because it's better marketed, but these are criteria of a different sort.

Notions such as optimisation, and other similar efficiency measures are scarcely appropriate to the outcomes of a design act: and the act, itself, is scarcely optimisable. What makes a designer effective is luck, guided by experience, intuition, talent and judgement. The fact that this will not appeal to those who follow a more mechanistic and realist approach does not mean they should be excluded: indeed, it is the argument of this paper that they cannot be avoided and so should be welcomed.

Nor is the more practical outcome necessarily to be preferred to the less practical, for one outcome may be deemed preferable to another simply because of the novelty and/or beauty of its form, or for some other apparently arbitrary reason such as marketing success.

This is not to argue against functional adequacy, or sound fabrication: it is to say that the criteria by which we may value design outcomes are open, variable, chosen (optional), and not absolute. I can, of course, say that one knife, for instance, is better than another according to many criteria, but I cannot be insistent on the superiority of these criteria. Consider the success of knives with toothed, serrated edges: they never need sharpening, but they are never sharp. Against the functional criterion of sharpness, they fail. But against the criterion of staying as sharp as they were, they succeed. The resulting outcome of a design process is the outcome, and that is all.

A particularly attractive consequence of this is the responsibility the designer must accept for what (s)he has designed. The process of design is begun by the designer, the conversation is largely private, the designer drawing to him/herself. The outcome of the process is different in each case: design leads not to the best, but to a large variety of different outcomes, giving choice. The design process may be terminated when it reaches a self-reproducing (stable) state: but further judgements about it, and even about when to stop, are not judgements of absolute rightness or truth, but of honest recognition and beauty.

2.3.3.1 Ideals of Behaviour Brought from Cybernetics and Design (Ethics)

There are certain behavioural consequences of this way of working. These are seen in the environments in which designers practice. While designers may be almost paranoidly secretive about their ideas with outsiders, in a team they are remarkably open and generally willing to listen to comments and accept suggestions for improvements.

Consider the nature of the design conversation: for it to operate there has to be a listener (viewer). To listen requires an open mind and generosity. Without these, we cannot listen (as a creative act) and we do not participate. To design means to be able to see the possibilities not that we already have in mind, but that appear given to us by the other: to do this, we need an open mind (for a closed mind blinds us to (the value of) what the other says); and generosity (of heart) to welcome it as at least worth listening to, and potentially of more value to us than what we had thought of.[40]

Together with accepting responsibility (and acting responsibly) these are amongst those qualities we seem to hold as the most humanly and ethically desirable in ourselves. While we do admire, on occasion, the quality of ruthlessness, or we talk with either admiration or quiet resignation of competition, winning and the survival of the fittest (in which we profoundly misunderstand Darwin) and the lean, mean machine, it would nevertheless seem that we do admire people who are generous, open-minded and accept responsibility. Indeed, in today's world of approaching ecological disaster it is these qualities rather than those of selfish and self-centred competition that will save us, if we are to save ourselves. Design, in this account, is a way of acting that reflects and requires these more admired qualities; in contrast to that sort of problem solving which attempts to turn the world into an ever more efficient machine.

What does this offer us, from the side of design, for cybernetics? I have recently argued [20, 23] that cybernetics (at least, second order cybernetics) has ethical implications that exactly match those listed above: cybernetic systems work if we accept responsibility, and act generously, with an open mind.[41]

This is hardly surprising, for the point of this paper has been to claim the central design act is an essentially second order cybernetic conversation: and it is the conversation in each that implies such decent qualities!

2.3.4 Epistemology

Design is, I have argued [25], the quintessential constructive activity. Designers, by definition, construct (new) realities. Epistemologically, this places design in a

[40]I am using the conventional, realist short-hand, in this example.

[41]These qualities are not the only ones I argue for, but are the most relevant here.

sensitive position. Clearly, there is an aspect to design (in how it has been discussed here) that is close to philosophical solipsism/idealism, as opposed to realism. But the position argued is not idealist. Constructivism proposes a philosophical position that accepts the essential undecidability of questions of the nature of the world when we posit that we are removed from (our experience of) such a world. In effect, it denies that we can remove ourselves from our own acts of observing, and thus it questions what we can know of a world from which the observer is excluded. It is not idealist, it is not realist, it asserts we cannot resolve the difference between these two polarities and must chose, therefore, either one or the other (as we wish, to suit our purposes and convenience, and not necessarily with any great consistency); or we may chose to "sit on the fence" and refuse to decide. In the extreme, some few will chose not to sit on the fence, but to make sure the fence is maintained and valued for what it is.

Designers work within a constructivist framework [26]. This is clear in the literal sense that they construct (or, in the physical world, cause to be constructed) new artefacts, outcomes of the design process. The assumption of the desirability (and inevitability) of novelty in itself presupposed the notion of construction. But at a less literal level, designers also work within a similarly constructivist framework. To understand this we need to return to the primary act at the heart of designing, the conversation with the self.

A conversation is a mechanism to contain a constructivist act. No meanings are passed, rather, they are made by the participants. They are constructed, and the presence of the constructors is always acknowledged. Each participant makes his/her own understanding of what they believe their conversational partner means, and re-state them to that partner. Each compares their own understandings before and after conversational interchanges, to confirm adequate similarity in these personally held understandings. The conversation (as developed by Pask) is a basic second order cybernetic activity: the conversationalist is always involved, is always in the conversation, rather than, as a traditional observer would be, talking about it.[42] So conversation, as expressed in Pask's Conversation Theory, is both a quintessentially second order activity, and a constructivist one. But it is also at the heart of design. If the heart of design can be understood as cybernetic and constructivist, design is, itself, a constructivist activity – in terms of its philosophical position.

The epistemology appropriate to the act of design is constructivist and the analysis is second order cybernetic. In fact, design is perhaps the most universal and widespread of all second order cybernetic activities. And it is one of the oldest: in terms of both human development (Piaget) and of the history of known, conscious human activities.

[42] A fuller account of conversation theory would include a discussion of the concurrent levels of a conversation: the contextual level of the substrate, and the critical level of the meta-conversation, including an explanation of how the conversation can switch levels so that, for instance, it may ascend to the meta-conversational level. At that point, the meta-conversational level becomes the level of the conversation (we talk about how we talk about conversation, for instance), with a new (meta-)meta-level above this. And so on, recursively and in either direction. See [11], a summary of Pask's work (especially Conversation Theory), with extensive references to his work.

2.3.4.1 Knowledge Of and Knowledge For

There is one final epistemological aspect, which concerns the type of knowledge that both design and second order cybernetics work with and construct [21, 27].

The word Design, as we have discussed it, is intended as a verb; it is an activity, leading to an outcome which (in other contexts) is also called design – in this case used in the form of a noun. In this paper I have generally tried to avoid the use of the word as a noun.

The sort of knowledge that science gives us, through the observer of the system, is knowledge of the system. This sort of knowledge helps us understand, in a very particular way, what is.[43] This is passive, neutral, leading to no action on and creating no change in the world – as good science should. An important aim in disengaging the observer is to leave the world neutral and untouched. The concern is to produce knowledge of the world, as we find it.

But the purpose of designers is to change the world. They are concerned with action on the world that is intended to change it – to create the new. They are not observers of the world, but observers in the world, and hence actors. Designers need knowledge for acting. And, in a sense, the process at the heart of design, generating those actions, can be said to generate this knowledge for acting on the world as we make it.

These – knowledge of and knowledge for – are very different sorts of knowledge, reflecting differences in understandings of knowledge (and intelligence) that stem back to at least Aristotle, which has been built on in recent studies by, for instance, Polyani [41] (tacit knowledge) and Schön [47] (reflective knowledge).[44]

There is a rarely questioned orthodoxy, that if we understand better, we can act better. This is taken as self-evident, yet seems untested and may be flawed. For instance, being able to predict the heat loss of a proposed building does not much help a designer. Unless the designer is very lucky, all (s)he learns is that (s)he has got it wrong. Knowledge of has traditionally been converted to knowledge for by means of a sort of transfer knowledge that is the special area of technology. Technology, consisting in large part of what we refer to as engineering, converts knowledge of into knowledge for.

However, designers look for a direct knowledge for. Often, knowledge of simply gets in the way. Second order cybernetics is the field that constructs knowledge for action in the sense that it is always concerned, not so much with knowledge, as with knowing, with knowledge that is generated by and concerned with action and the actor: with observer-involved knowledge for.

---

[43] I am using the conventional, realist short-hand in this description.

[44] There is a whole body of work on design knowledge. The work of the two cited scholars is often considered essential. This paper is not the place to explore design knowledge in detail.

2.4 Conclusions

2.4.1 *The Interesting Conjunction*

In writing this paper I have had two intentions. The first has been to show that there is an interesting conjunction between the two subjects, cybernetics and design. To argue this point I have characterised the understanding I have of each field, and introduced a number of qualities which are central to each and can be seen to be similar. In this way, the sympathy and empathy of each subject to the other, and their mutual relevance, was introduced.

2.4.2 *Conversational Circularity: The Analogy Between Cybernetics and Design*

The second intention was to demonstrate a strict analogy between cybernetics and design. In the case of cybernetics, circularity is present from the first attempts to characterise the subject of the Macy Conferences, and the general interest in that circularity in cybernetics, to the point where it is understood to be the key characteristic of the subject. We can go so far as to insist that cybernetics studies circular systems and their consequences, even taking this as a definition, should we want.

One such circular (cybernetic) system around which the argument was developed is Pask's conversation; and the workings of the Paskian conversation were explored in this paper.

In the case of design, the central act of designers is claimed to be a form of conversation that takes place largely with the self, via paper and pencil.[45] This central act is argued to be circular, and the workings of this circularity are explored – in part as a way of introducing novelty. (There are many other aspects to design, but they are taken to be secondary.)

Further examples of circular systems are explored for their presence in design, and qualities of design are sought in cybernetics. The implications of these further parallels are explored in, for instance, understandings of ethical considerations.

The crucial analogy of this paper is drawn around the centrality to each subject of circularity, in the guise of a conversation (usually held with the self). The central analogy between cybernetics and design is argued to exist in circularity as embodied in a conversation.

---

[45] Of course, nowadays paper and pencil are not always used. Here the phrase is used as a token for all media in which a sketching type of activity takes place. The change of media may, however, lead to significant changes in how we sketch and what outcome we may expect, possibly modifying the design act, in consequence.

References

1. Ashby, W. R. (1956). *An introduction to cybernetics*. New York: St. Martin's Press.
2. Ashby, W. R. (1964). Introductory remarks at a panel discussion. In M. D. Mesarovic (Ed.), *Views in general systems theory*. Chichester: Wiley. Reprinted in G. Klir (Ed.). (1991). *Facets of systems science* (pp. 507–510). New York: Plenum Press.
3. Beckett, S. (1984). *Worstward ho*. New York: Grove Press.
4. Bremermann, H. J. (1977). Complexity and transcomputability. In R. Duncan & M. Weston-Smith (Ed.), *The encyclopedia of ignorance* (pp. 167–174). Oxford: Pergamon.
5. Boland, R. J., Collopy, F., & van Patter, G. K. (2005). *Next design leadership institute*. New York. Available via DIALOG. http://nextd.org. Accessed 14 Apr 2007.
6. Conway, F., & Siegelman, J. (2005). *Dark hero of the information age. In search of Norbert Wiener the father of cybernetics*. New York: Basic Books.
7. François, C. (2006). The observer reobserved. In R. Trappl (Ed.), *Cybernetics and systems* (pp. 87–90). Vienna: ÖSGK.
8. Gedenryd, H. (1998). How designers work. Making sense of authentic cognitive activities. In *Lund University cognitive studies, 75*. Lund: Jabe Offset AB. Available via Web archive: https://archive.org/details/HowDesignersWork-MakingSenseOfAuthenticCognitiveActivity. Accessed 14 Apr 2007.
9. Glanville, R. (1975). *A cybernetic development of theories of epistemology and observation, with reference to space and time, as seen in architecture, also known as: The object of objects, the point of points – or something about things*. PhD Thesis (unpublished). London: Brunel University.
10. Glanville, R. (1994). Variety in design. *Systems Research, 11*(3), 95–103.
11. Glanville, R. (1997). Gordon pask. In: ISSS luminaries section. Available via ISSS at the Web archive: https://web.archive.org/web/20120308140245/http://isss.org/projects/gordon_pask. Accessed 11 Apr 2017.
12. Glanville, R. (1999). Researching design and designing research. *Design Issues, 15*(2), 80–91.
13. Glanville, R. (1999). Acts between and between acts. In R. Ascott (Ed.), *Reframing consciousness* (pp. 11–16). Exeter: Intellect.
14. Glanville, R. (2000). The value of being unmanageable: Variety and creativity in CyberSpace. In H. Eichmann, J. Hochgerner, & F. Nahrada (Eds.), *Netzwerke. Proceedings of Global Village '97 Conference* (pp. 521–531). Vienna: Falter Verlag.
15. Glanville, R. (2002). Why design research? In R. Jacques & J. A. Powell (Eds.), *Design: Science: Method* (pp. 86–94). Guildford: Westbury House.
16. Glanville, R. (2002). Gerard de Zeeuw—a Festschrift. Special Issue *Systems Research and Behavioural Science, 19*(2), 1–9.
17. Glanville, R. (2003). An irregular dodekahedron and a lemon yellow Citroën. In L. van Schaik (Ed.), *The practice of practice* (pp. 258–265). Melbourne: RMIT Press.
18. Glanville, R. (2004). Appropriate theory. In D. Durling, A. De Bono, & J. Redmond (Eds.), *Proceedings of the Future Ground Conference 2004* (pp. 88–99). Melbourne: Monash University Press.
19. Glanville, R. (2004). The purpose of second order cybernetics. *Kybernetes, 33*(9/10), 1379–1386.
20. Glanville, R. (2004). Desirable ethics. *Cybernetics and Human Knowing, 11*(2), 77–88.
21. Glanville, R. (2005). A (cybernetic) musing: Certain propositions concerning prepositions. *Cybernetics and Human Knowing, 12*(3), 87–85.
22. Glanville, R. (2005). Lernen ist Interaktion: Gordon Pask's 'An approach to cybernetics'. In D. Baecker (Ed.), *Schlüsselwerke der Systemtheorie* (pp. 75–94). Wiesbaden: Verlag für Sozialwissenschaften. Republished in English as Glanville, R. (2007). An approach to cybernetics (Gordon Pask 1961). In R. Glanville & K. Müller (Eds.), *Gordon Pask, philosopher mechanic: An introduction to the cybernetician's cybernetician* (pp. 13–27). Vienna: Edition Echoraum.

23. Glanville, R. (2005). Cybernetics. In C. Mitcham (Ed.), *Encyclopedia of science, technology, and ethics* (pp. 455–458). Woodbridge: Macmillan Reference USA.
24. Glanville, R. (2005). Knowledge and design in the era of second-order cybernetics. In *Keynote Address at the Many Interpretations and Applications of Cybernetics, Annual Conference of the American Society for Cybernetics*, Washington DC, 27–30 Oct 2005.
25. Glanville, R. (2006). Construction and design. *Constructivist Foundations, 1*(3), 103–110.
26. Glanville, R. (2006). Design and mentation: Piaget's constant objects. *The Radical Designist* zero issue. Available at: http://asc-cybernetics.org/systems_papers/Design_and_Mentation.pdf. Accessed 14 Apr 2007.
27. Glanville, R. (2007). Design prepositions. In M. Belderbos & J. Verbeke (Eds.), *The unthinkable doctorate* (pp. 115–126). Brussels: Sint Lucas.
28. Glanville, R. (2007). Designing complexity. *Performance Improvement Quarterly, 21*(2), 75–96.
29. Glanville, R., & A. Riegler (Eds.). (2007). Ernst von Glasersfeld, a Festschrift. *Constructivist Foundations, 2*, (2/3). Available via the Web archive: https://web.archive.org/web/20170201050449/http://www.univie.ac.at/constructivism/journal/2/2-3. Accessed 14 Apr 2007.
30. Jones, J. C. (1980). *Design methods*. Chichester: Wiley.
31. Krippendorff, K. (2006). *The semantic turn*. Boca Raton: Taylor and Francis.
32. Krippendorff, K. (2007). The cybernetics of design and the design of cybernetics. *Kybernetes, 36*(9/10), 1381–1392.
33. Kuhn, T. S. (1970). *The structure of scientific revolutions* (2nd ed.). Chicago: Chicago University Press.
34. Maturana, H. R., & Varela, F. J. (1980). *Autopoiesis and cognition* (Boston studies in the philosophy of science, Vol. 42). Dordrecht: D. Reidel Publishing.
35. Mead, M. (1968). The cybernetics of cybernetics. In H. von Foerster et al. (Eds.), *Purposive systems* (pp. 1–11). New York: Spartan Books.
36. Müller, K.-H. (2007). Heinz von Foerster's biological computer laboratory: An unfinished revolution of an unfinished revolution. In A. Müller & K.-H. Müller (Eds.), *An unfinished revolution? Heinz von Foerster and the Biological Computer Laboratory 1958–1976* (pp. 107–123). Vienna: Edition Echoraum.
37. Pask, G. (1969). The architectural relevance of cybernetics. *Architectural Design, 7*(6), 494–496
38. Pask, G. (1975). *Conversation, cognition and learning. A cybernetic theory and methodology*. Amsterdam/New York: Elsevier.
39. Piaget, J. (1955). *The child's construction of reality*. New York: Basic Books.
40. Pias, K. (2003). *Cybernetics – The Macy-conferences 1946–1953*. Zürich-Berlin: Diaphanes.
41. Polanyi, M. (1976). *The tacit dimension*. Garden City: Anchor Books.
42. Popper, K. (1969). *Conjectures & refutations* (3rd ed.). London: Routledge & Kegan Paul.
43. Reichardt, J. (1970). *Cybernetic serendipity*. London: Rapp & Carroll.
44. Reichardt, J. (Ed.). (1971). *Cybernetics, art and ideas*. London: Studio Vista.
45. Rittel, H. W. J., & Webber, M. M. (1984). Planning problems are wicked problems. In N. Cross (Ed.), *Developments in design methodology* (pp. 135–144). Chichester: Wiley.
46. Rosenblueth, A., Wiener, N., & Bigelow, J. (1943). Behavior, purpose and teleology. *Philosophy of Science, 10*, 18–24.
47. Schön, D. (1983). *The reflective practitioner. How professionals think in action*. New York: Basic Books.
48. Shannon, C. E., & Weaver, W. (1949). *The mathematical theory of communication*. Champaign-Urbana: University of Illinois Press.
49. Simon, H. A. (1996). *Sciences of the artificial* (3rd ed.). Cambridge: MIT Press (originally published 1969).
50. Spencer-Brown, G. (1969). *The laws of form*. London: George Allen and Unwin.
51. Varela, F. J., Maturana, H. R., & Uribe, R. B. (1974). Autopoiesis. The organization of living systems, its characterization and a model. *Biosystems, 5*(4), 187–196.
52. von Glasersfeld, E. (1987). *The construction of knowledge*. Salinas: Intersystems Publications.
53. von Foerster, H. (1950). *Cybernetics: Circular causal and feedback mechanisms in biological and social systems. Transactions of the sixth conference*. New York: Josiah Macy Jr. Foundation.

54. von Foerster, H. (1974). *The cybernetics of cybernetics*. Champaign-Urban: Biological Computer Laboratory, University of Illinois. Republished as von Foerster, H. (1995). *Cybernetics of cybernetics or the control of control and the communication of communication* (2nd ed.). Minneapolis: Future Systems.
55. von Foerster, H. (1976). Objects: Tokens for (eigen-)behaviors. *ASC Cybernetics Forum, 8*(3/4), 91–96.
56. Wiener, N. (1948). *Cybernetics; Or, control and communication in the animal and the machine*. Cambridge: MIT Press.
57. Wootton, H. (1968). *The elements of architecture: A facsimile of the first edition*. Charlottesville: Shakespeare Library by the University Press of Virginia (original work published 1624).

Ranulph Glanville gained a Diploma in Architecture from the Architectural Association School, London. This was followed by a PhD in cybernetics. His supervisor was Gordon Pask, and his examiner was Heinz von Foerster. His second PhD was in human learning. His supervisor was Laurie Thomas, and his examiner was Gerard de Zeeuw. In 2006, he was awarded a DSc in cybernetics and design by Brunel University. He has published extensively on architecture, human learning, cybernetics and design, and spent his life teaching around the world, mainly in the area of design, visiting many universities as an "outside insider" on a freelance basis. Glanville held regular posts at the Royal College of Art, London, UK and at the Catholic University of Leuven, Belgium. During the final six years of his life, Glanville was the President of the American Society for Cybernetics. He lived on the south coast of the UK with his wife and muse, Aartje Hulstein. He claimed that his hobby was whichever of his interests he was not currently doing and that he relaxed in the upper cabin of jumbo jets.

Chapter 3
Gordon Pask and the Origins of Design Cybernetics

Liss C. Werner

Abstract This chapter introduces the subject of design cybernetics from the perspective of its origins in Conversation Theory – interweaving descriptions of cybernetic artefacts, cybernetic design concepts, their socio-cultural implications, and their possible consequences for a cybernetic theory for design. Conversation Theory was initially developed by the British cybernetician Gordon Pask, and later by his students Ranulph Glanville and Paul Pangaro. With a view to opening up strands and avenues for design education and design practice, this chapter positions the act of designing as an embodied conversation between designers, the subject matter and the object to be designed. An introduction to cybernetics and design is followed by a discussion of machines developed by Pask, including *Musicolour* and *Colloquy of Mobiles*. The chapter then offers an overview of Pask's Conversation Theory as based on circular causal, interactive, feedback-based epistemological processes. It constructs and explicates a design reality of interaction, learning and design education. Pask explained Conversation Theory rhetorically, arithmetically and graphically. Pask's entailment meshes, n-dimensional cyclical network graphs, describe conversation topics, paths, attributes and partners of interaction. They are examined and related to contemporary digitally driven systems and societies. The chapter concludes by discussing design cybernetics in view of socio-cybernetic ecologies and the shifting paradigm of design authorship.

Keywords Gordon Pask · Design cybernetics · Computation · Feedback · Conversation theory · Musicolour · Colloquy of Mobiles

---

L. C. Werner (✉)
Institute of Architecture, Technical University of Berlin, Berlin, Germany
e-mail: liss.c.werner@tu-berlin.de

T. Fischer, C. M. Herr (eds.), *Design Cybernetics*, Design Research Foundations,
https://doi.org/10.1007/978-3-030-18557-2_3

3.1 Origin and Etymology: What Is Design Cybernetics?

> The cybernetic theory can also claim some explanatory power insofar as it is possible to mimic certain aspects of architectural design by artificial intelligence computer program (provided, incidentally, that the program is able to learn about and from architects and by experimenting in the language of architects, i.e. by exploring plans, material specifications, condensed versions of clients' comments, etc.). – Gordon Pask [20, p. 496]

During the last decade, the term *cybernetics* has regained visibility. Despite its highly interdisciplinary involvement, cybernetics has, until the second half of the twentieth century, been associated with navigation, warfare, electronics and control theory; and, albeit less prominently so, with biology, the social sciences, anthropology, political governance and interaction between humans. The term *cybernetics* appeared in the design context as early as during the 1950s, for example in conjunction with works such as Gordon Pask's *Musicolour* in 1953, and Nicolas Schöffer's *Première tour spatiodynamique, cybernétique et sonore* in 1954.

The term *cybernetics* had been used before the twentieth century. In the fourth century B.C. Plato described the act of regulating a population with reference to helmsmanship using the phrase αρετής κυβερνητικής (i.e. virtue of government). In the early 1800s, André-Marie Ampère referred to *cybernétique* as the art of governing or the science of government. It was Norbert Wiener who popularised the term with his book "Cybernetics: Or Control and Communication in the Animal and the Machine" [43]. Wiener was aware of the term having been used in the context of the Greek meaning 'steersman', but less of its application to politics as promoted by Ampère. He later commented that "until recently, there was no existing word for this complex of ideas, and in order to embrace the whole field by a single term, I felt constrained to invent one. Hence 'Cybernetics,' which derived from the Greek word κυβερνήτης (*kubernē̄tēs*), or 'steersman,' the same Greek word from which we eventually derive our word 'governor'." [44, p. 15] In the 1960s, pioneers in computer art, such as Max Bense (exhibited at the 1968 *Cybernetic Serendipity* exhibition [32] in London), the French-Hungarian media artist Vera Molnar, and the German mathematician Frieder Nake, amongst others, began to explore the relationships between art, design, science and cybernetic principles. Their computer graphics represented rationalised art and described it in formally abstract, rather than figurative ways. Their work explored the continuous process of generative iterations rather than fixed states.

Such early connections can be seen as one origin of design cybernetics. Today, design cybernetics stands as a maturing field in its own right, as a reflective philosophy of acting and understanding [11]. Ranulph Glanville (1946–2014) retraces the intertwined and inevitable relationship between design and cybernetics in his 2007 paper 'Try again. Fail again. Fail better: The cybernetics in design and the design in cybernetics'. The paper was published in a special issue of the journal *Kybernetes* on design cybernetics – edited by Glanville himself – and is reproduced as Chap. 2 of this collection. Glanville describes a) cybernetics as a way of thinking, and b) design as a verb rather than as a noun to describe problem-solving [9, pp. 1173–1174].

The term *cybernetics*, on the one hand, derives from the Greek word *kubernḗtēs* meaning steering, regulating or governing. The term design, on the other hand, stems from the Latin word *designare*, *de-* meaning *from* or *out*, the second syllable *signare* meaning *to mark* or *a mark, a sign*. Hence, *design cybernetics* can be understood as the art, i.e. process of *steering* the *marking* or *signing*, or, as Glanville points out with reference to Spencer-Brown [3], the *drawing* of a distinction [9, p. 1180].[1] *Signare* implies *semiotics*, referring to the theory of signs, originally investigated by Charles Peirce at the end of the nineteenth century. Pierce's theory points towards the relation design and design cybernetics have with human interactions that involve meaning. Signs are codes "carrying information" between communicating senders and receivers. Both need to encode, to decode and to interpret to arrive at a shared understanding of subject matters referred to.[2] The resulting conversational process is dynamic, non-trivial and intrinsically related to the process of designing. To design implies a creation process in which the designer is actively involved and the final result is not clear at the beginning of this process. The designer engages in a circularly-causal conversation (the design process) with the artefact to be manifested. In cybernetic terms, the act of designing implies an involved participant observer initiating a process that eventually results in something unforeseen and new, emergent and unplanned. When this occurs, the system *designer-design* is operating in a second-order cybernetic mode [8]. Varela refers to second-order cybernetics as "the cybernetics of observing systems" [38, p. xviii]. Designing can be defined as an act of self-organisation and con-struction between two or more elements through which their specific properties transform into properties not inherent in the original elements [4, 13].

Since the 1940s, cybernetics has undergone continuous development, and, occasionally, experienced fundamental re-conceptions. Formative discussions of what would eventually coalesce to form the new discipline of cybernetics took place during the *Cerebral Inhibition Meeting* in 1942, and during the *Macy Conferences* between 1946 and 1954, both taking place in New York City. The discipline developed along various milestones including the publication of Ashby's *An Introduction to Cybernetics* [2] and of Maturana and Varela's *Autopoiesis* [35], the formation of *radical constructivism* on the basis of von Glasersfeld's cybernetic interpretation of the work of Piaget and own experiences [40], as well as von Foerster's proclamation of *second-order cybernetics* – a cybernetics that recursively applies to itself [36]. The abstract language of cybernetics applies to all systems regardless of whether they are technical, biological or social in nature. In the second-order context, however, technical interest is less concerned with utilitarian application than with the modelling of cognitive and social processes, typically for purposes of understanding and speculative exploration as they occur, for example, in the subjectively-driven process of designing. To establish a basis for my description of Gordon Pask's cybernetics later in this chapter, I will first explore selected milestones that are particularly relevant to the understanding of cybernetics in general and of design cybernetics in particular.

[1] See also page 34 in this volume.

[2] See Fig. 1.4 in this volume.

(1) The *Macy Conferences* (1946–1954) allowed for initial encounters between researchers from varying disciplines to explore their shared interest in purposeful feedback systems. The intense interdisciplinary exchanges between the hard sciences and the humanities – including anthropology (Margaret Mead and Gregory Bateson), computer science (John von Neumann), neurosciences (Walter Pitts and Warren McCulloch), physics (Heinz von Foerster), psychology (W. Ross Ashby), mathematics and philosophy (Norbert Wiener) – occurred under the conference theme *Circular Causal, and Feedback Mechanisms in Biological and Social Systems*. The sixth Macy Conference was the first one joined by Heinz von Foerster, who suggested to name the field *cybernetics*, based on the title of Wiener's book.

(2) The proposal was adopted [39, pp. 300–301] and the term added to the beginning to the conference theme for subsequent meetings [8, pp. 1380, 1385]. Conversations between the conference attendants, bringing together different ideas, research methods, and partially contradicting definitions, orchestrated a beautiful exuberance of variety, of difference and of possibilities (documented in [30]) – a cybernetic repertoire provided the roots for design cybernetics. Seeing the world and 'listening' to the world in a cybernetic way offers scope for conversation and learning. "Listening", Glanville states, "gives us entry to conversation and thus to the prototypical embodiment of interaction." [7] It provides a basis for conversation and for approaching the world cybernetically.

(3) Ashby's *Introduction to Cybernetics* explains the subject based on the notions of *variety*, *stability* and *equilibrium*, and points out *difference* as a fundamental concept of cybernetics. The mathematician George Spencer-Brown emphasised *difference* as the result of an action, rather than a found state. In his treatise *Laws of Form*, first published in 1969 in the UK, Spencer-Brown establishes as the first law of forms the *drawing of distinction* [3]. This introduces marked space, in which *difference* is established, analogous to the differentiation of an exterior and an interior space from each other by a physical distinction, a wall.

(4) Pask was strongly influenced by Ashby's *An Introduction to Cybernetics* [2], and its predecessor *Design for a Brain* [1] and presented many of the principles developed by Ashby in his 'cybernetic pocket-book' *An Approach to Cybernetics* [19].

(5) The notion of *autopoiesis* was developed by Humberto Maturana, Francesco Varela and Ricardo B. Uribe in 1974 – partly at the Biological Computer Laboratory (BCL), founded by Heinz von Foerster. The cybernetic concept of *autopoiesis* relates to self-organisation and self-creation in biological and social systems. Following Leduc's 1911 *The Mechanism of Life* [15], *autopoiesis* provided a new theory for the concept of all living organisms. Cognition and biology were discussed as intimately coupled. The definition of terms such as *structure*, *organisation* and *system* became crucial for further discussions on the behaviour of systems – linear, spontaneous or random. In 1997, McMullin and Varela revisited the computational modelling of autopoiesis, applying a swarm simulation algorithm they developed at the Santa Fe Institute to program for "realizing dynamic cell-like structures which, on an ongoing basis, produce the conditions for their own maintenance." [16, p. 39].

(6) *Computational autopoiesis* is now used to simulate complex rule-based behavioural formations of large groups of agents, as seen e.g. in swarms of bees, schools of fish or human crowds. The application of multi-agent algorithms entails cybernetics inherently and suggests that "the architect is no longer a designer of discrete objects, matter and space, but a designer of systems with complex components and multi-layered relationships" [42, p. 288]. It suggests a strand of design cybernetics that addresses evolutionary algorithms in the design of ecologies for social systems, e.g., human, animal and robotic [41].

(7) *Second-order cybernetics* was coined and developed by Heinz von Foerster together and alongside with Humberto Maturana, Gordon Pask and, more recently, by Ranulph Glanville and Paul Pangaro, among others. *Second-order cybernetics* acknowledges the observer as actively involved in the observation of, and the conversation with, observed systems as they occur in design processes. Varela [38, p. xviii] distinguishes:

> First order cybernetics: the cybernetics of observed systems;
> Second order cybernetics: the cybernetics of observing systems.

Second-order cybernetics originates in cybernetic research between 1968 and 1975 and theoretically in Margaret Mead's paper *The Cybernetics of Cybernetics* [17]. The paper was "presented as the inaugural keynote address at the founding meeting of the American Society of Cybernetics (ASC), [...] at a point in the history of cybernetics that can be seen, in retrospect, to have been a turning point" [8, p. 1379]. Mead suggests a model of engaging with the world through acting cybernetically: in response to the systems observed, based in feedback, navigating circularly-causal relationships, while aiming for goals, as parts of larger systems. In the context of design cybernetics, design research as the study of the circularly-causal cybernetic process of designing provides a similar second-order level of observation.

3.1.1 From Cybernetic Systems to Design Cybernetics

In his article *The Cybernetics of Design and the Design of Cybernetics* Klaus Krippendorf [14] describes cybernetics as positioned "in the dialectic between science and design", and adds [14, p. 1381]:

> Whereas scientists [...] insist on causal explanations, excluding themselves as causes of the phenomena they explore, designers intend to cause something by their own actions, something that could not result from natural causes, defying causal explanations in effect.

The dialectic Krippendorff describes[3] shows two ways of working and operating that involve the creation of the new within their individual and overlapping domains. In the German-speaking context the architect is officially described as a designing planner. The act of architectural design can be referred to as both *planning* and *design*. In the British and US-American context the architect is identified as a

[3]See page 120 in this volume.

designer and is distinguished from professional planners who operate at larger urban scales. According to Heinz von Foerster, Gordon Pask "distinguishes two orders of analysis. The one in which the observer enters the system by stipulating the *system's* purpose. We may call this a 'first-order stipulation'. In a 'second-order stipulation' the observer enters the system by stipulating *his own* purpose" (see von Foerster's re-phrasing of Pask [21] in [31, p. 186] as well as in the audio recording of [37, 47:50–48:40]).

This difference illuminates two very different ways of designing that also relate to design education. Glanville refers to "[d]esign as a conversation with the self (and with others)". He stresses "that the central act in designing is a form of (Paskian) cybernetic conversation held with oneself" [9, p. 1189]. While the terms and tools underlying *Design Cybernetics* have been developed over the last 50 to 60 years, a central question now may be how to develop it for contemporary demands and developments. Design cybernetics embraces and integrates all kinds of systems featuring interaction and self-organisation – analogue and digital, machinic and human. Its historical origins can be found in a number of places, of which the most significant are listed in the following paragraphs.

In 1953, the architects Charles and Ray Eames illustrated Claude E. Shannon's *Mathematical Theory of Communication* [34] with flowcharts and models, presented in the 23 min long film *A Communications Primer* for IBM and on a promotional flyer a year later [5]. This led to the commission to design the interior of the IBM pavilion at the World Fair in New York 1964–65. The Eames' role was to design interfaces that featured IBM's novel technology inviting the general public to engage with computers.

The Architecture Machine Group (AMG), founded by Nicholas Negroponte and Leon Groisser at MIT in 1967 and absorbed into the MIT Media Lab in 1985, the Biological Computer Laboratory (BCL) at the University of Illinois in Urbana-Champaign (1958–1974), founded and led by Heinz von Foerster, Carnegie Mellon University and the University of California, Berkeley, among others immersed in cybernetic research. Projects developed at MIT and at the BCL were funded through governmental grants to further advanced communication technologies, computer-aided simulations, training systems, intelligent control, command and navigation systems. Designs of ground-breaking adaptive systems included AMG's software *Urban5* for the simulation of urban growth, and *Sketchpad*, a human-machine graphical communication system for designers developed by Ivan Sutherland in 1963, and the BCL's algorithm modelling *autopoiesis*, designed by Uribe and Maturana in 1974. The latter is a predecessor of contemporary algorithms simulating the behaviour of self-organising multi-agent organisations.

In the UK, the cybernetician Gordon Pask designed *Musicolour* (1953) and *The Colloquy of Mobiles* (1968, see Fig. 3.2). As a cybernetics consultant, Pask joined architect Cedric Price and amusement park owner Joan Littlewood in the design of *The Fun Palace* (1964). A decade later, Pask was commissioned as consultant to the design of yet another high-profile manifestation of cybernetics in architecture, the *Generator Project* (1976–1979). *The Fun Palace* proposed an analogue spatial learning system, as part of which Paskian machines provided first steps into architecture driven by a human-machine relationship.

The projects outlined above drew from the notion of feedback, the concepts of causality and recursivity and human participation, and can be regarded as essential ingredients for (design) cybernetics.

Feedback and communication had begun advancing technologies around World War II, and became drivers of the journey from early automation to our contemporary computationally-governed world. The rise of the computer and its distribution beyond the boundaries of computer laboratories and the context of navy, army and universities has offered a wealth of opportunities and applications. To these developments, Gordon Pask has contributed key innovations and theories, which are outlined in the following sections.

3.2 The Cybernetics of Gordon Pask

Gordon Pask (shown in Fig. 3.1) was born in Derbyshire on the 28th of June in 1928. He initially studied mining engineering at Liverpool Polytechnic and geology at Bangor University, before receiving an MA in Natural Sciences from the University of Cambridge in 1952, and being awarded a PhD in psychology from the University of London in 1964, a DSc in cybernetics from the Open University, and an ScD from

Fig. 3.1 1960s Andrew Gordon Speedie Pask. (Source: Department of Contemporary History, University of Vienna: Gordon Pask Archive (GPA), Photo Collection, Box 3, 26–1)

the University of Cambridge in 1995. Pask was strongly influenced by the cybernetic pioneers Norbert Wiener and Ross Ashby. Bernard Scott, a student of Pask, describes how first reading Wiener's (1948) classic *Cybernetics* had an emotional impact on Pask as a young Cambridge medical student. To Pask, who had a diverse background and interests, "the book brought fully to consciousness a sense of unity in nature and man's endeavours that, thus far, had been latent in his own eclecticism. [...] Here was the vision and the final justification for the generalist: the twentieth century version of the Renaissance man was born." [33, p. 327].

Pask characterises man-system interaction, decision-making processes and cybernetic systems as goal-directed. In *Future Prospects of Cybernetics*, Pask outlines in which man-made organisations or disciplines cybernetics could be applied and stresses to reconsider cybernetics in light of man's involvement in a system. Addressing fruitful future directions of cybernetic research in 1976, Pask defines cybernetics as a science, a method, an approach, a characteristic of a (cybernetic) system and a theory [27, p. 3]:

> Although the mathematical theory of engineering Cybernetics is more sophisticated than that of the other branches it is interesting to observe that the theory is underutilised by industry and commerce. [...]. The fact is that in view of the nature of man, society and the economic system automation (computerisation, mechanisation etc.,) is frequently undesirable. In one sense this is disappointing to the professional, in another, it suggests that as a general rule insufficient attention has been given in the past to man machine relationships, cognition and the character of the social organisations in which all Cybernetic systems are ultimately employed. Hence I am inclined to the view that the most exciting and fruitful directions of research are those that involve human beings as part of the system.

Pask was passionate about creating machines that could communicate and interact with their environments as well as their human users by observing, learning and understanding. Apart from Pask designing and building interactive 'intelligent' 'thinking' robots like the *Colloquy of Mobiles*, he also developed learning machines for radar training from the 1960s to the 1980s. Pask integrated principles of computer science and biology with concepts of learning and behaviour. Working in the context of architectural education, Pask understood architecture as a form and as a result of conversation between the architect, the subject to be designed, the client, design tools and so forth and highlighted the intimate relationship between cybernetics and architecture [20, p. 494].

His article, *The Architectural Relevance of Cybernetics*, published in the journal *Architectural Design*, describes a cross-fertilisation between cybernetics and design [20]. It illustrates the application of the novel tool computer programming assisting the architect, to show that design "is a 'cybernetic' method and there are several instances of its application to architecture" [20, p. 494]. He further argues that "architectural designs should have rules for evolution built into them if their growth is to be healthy rather than cancerous. In other words, a responsible architect must be concerned with evolutionary properties; he cannot merely stand back and observe evolution as something that happened to his structure." [20, p. 495]. While holding positions at the Architectural Association in London and the Centre for Systems Research and Applied Epistemology, Concordia University in Montreal,

Pask suggested a unifying theory for architecture based on cybernetics, which he outlined in his note *Towards a unification of Architectural Theories* [28].

Pask's understanding of architecture as a discipline dealing with systems, and architects as designers of dynamic and relational systems gave him a particular position within both architecture and cybernetics. In his 1976 paper *Future Prospects for Cybernetics* he distances himself from a cybernetic concept that merely engages with "*authoritarian or 'automation-like' systems*" [27]. Instead, Pask offers a new, conversational cybernetics in which human and machine interact with each other. Disappointed with the lack of cybernetic applications, Pask envisioned increased attention to "man-machine-relationships, cognition and the character of the social organisations in which all cybernetic systems are ultimately employed." by extending the computer's capability to co-operate with human actors [27, p. 4].

He continued to investigate human learning and the man-machine relationship in conversations between humans and machines. He examined the nature of conversations, how they take place and how conversations can be distinguished from pure information transfer. Pask published a vast number of papers as well as three major books on the subject, *Conversation, Cognition and Learning* [24], *The Cybernetics of Human Learning and Performance* [23] and *Conversation Theory, Applications in Education and Epistemology* [25].

Following on from Pask, Ranulph Glanville developed and established conversation as a central mechanism of design cybernetics further, arguing that "design and cybernetics reflect each other" [12]. In Glanville's approach, conversation underlies novelty generating design processes, such that (design) cybernetics provides a theory for design, whereas design is the action of (design) cybernetics. Glanville's approach is based on Pask's cybernetic models, concepts and his Conversation Theory. Glanville emphasises Pask's pivotal role as a cybernetician reaching out to design: "Already in the 1960s Pask had understood there were close parallels to be explored between cybernetics and design. [...] Pask's *Musicolour* outreach was long-term and committed: he worked with arguably the most radical architect of the second half of the Twentieth Century, Cedric Price." [9, p. 1177][4] Pask's teaching activities at the Architectural Association have significantly increased awareness and interest in cybernetics within architecture: Among his class of twelve doctoral students, eight were indeed architects who "realised that cybernetics had something special to offer them" [9].

3.2.1 *Musicolour: Man-Machine Co-Creation*

Developed in Cambridge in 1953, *Musicolour* was the brainchild of Gordon Pask and his best friend and colleague Robin McKinnon-Wood and the first of Pask's more speculative devices. It interactively exhibited the capability of "learning" by

[4]See page 31 in this volume.

allowing people to freely interact with it. It was a theatrical and jolly creature, an installation, and an orchestra partner, much unlike the seriousness of government-funded devices. The musical colour machine generated changing coloured light through a conversation between musicians and the machine, interfacing auditory input with visual output. It was installed in various theatres featuring the *Musicolour Fantasy-Play "Moon-Music"*. Despite the excitement of its creators, audiences in Llandudno (North Wales), the Valerie Hovenden's Theatre Club in London, the Boltons and the Mecca Locarno on Streatham reacted sparsely to the abstract conversation and changing light show. The music played by one or more musicians was amplified through a filter system and activated the light machine, which reacted to the music by displaying varying visual projections. Musicians then adapted play in reaction to the projections, thus generating feedback to the machine. Around this time, Pask also developed electro-chemical computers, which may have influenced his work on *Musicolour* or possibly even been applied in the computer system for *Musicolour*. Light projections, output by the computer, were projected through coloured filters and acted as input for the musicians. The dynamics of the musician(s)' play then triggered the computer program to adjust its light output. If rhythms and tones played remained the same for a while, the computer would "get bored" and delay activating the electrodes. Subsequently the colour play would show long reaction time, such that the musician(s) would be prompted to innovate and adjust their mode of playing. *Musicolour* essentially acted as a reactive/interactive construct to enable performance architecture in an information environment involving learning. For Pask, the aim of *Musicolour* were primarily the capabilities of this interactive cybernetic machine [22, p. 78]:

> Musicolour was not synaesthesia but the learning capability of the machine. Given a suitable design and a happy choice of visual vocabulary, the performer (being influenced by the visual display) could become involved in a close participant interaction with the system. [...] In this sense the system acted as an extension of the performer with which he could co-operate and achieve effects that he could not achieve on his own.

Since *Musicolour* required a physical space to function as *Musicolour*, it underpinned architecture as an event, as interaction and as a conversation between humans and their environments. It was a "musicon", converging music, architecture, space and information exchange. It pioneered a novel theatrical experience in which the machine became an actor equal to and alongside the musicians, whereas the musicians also became part of Musicolour.

3.2.2 The Colloquy of Mobiles: Computer-Mediated Social Transformation

In 1968, one year before publishing his article titled *The Architectural Relevance of Cybernetics*, Pask was invited to exhibit at the exhibition *Cybernetic Serendipity*. Curated by Jasia Reichardt [32], the exhibition was shown at the ICA London between

August 2nd and October 20th 1968. It focused on the use of computers and the digital in arts, graphic design, generative aesthetics and music. Pask's exhibit *Colloquy of Mobiles* was a further development of *Musicolour* in as far as the electronically controlled mobiles interacted with each other and the audience. It consisted of a large suspended structure with five mobiles, two males and three females, as shown in Fig. 3.2. The structure exceeded human scale and hence extended to the size of an architectural intervention. Each of the five mobiles was equipped with a specific program, mirrors and spotlights and could mechanically rotate. In addition, the bars that supported the mobiles could rotate.

The mobiles both produced and responded to visual and audible signals, resulting in an interplay amongst each other, as well as with exhibition visitors. Their behaviour was, as most of Pask's machines, designed and presented using diagrams, such as relationship diagrams showing physical spatial relationships between objects used. Process diagrams described behaviour as 'what-if' scenarios. Digital programs interpreted the above categories of information and enabled a "competition", conversation between the mobiles. The *Colloquy of Mobiles* simulated the behaviour of a social system through communication, especially that between male and female. In case of inactivity of the male mobiles, they would activate rays of light that eventually hit mirrors on the female fibreglass structures. Once the reflected rays of light hit the light-sensors attached to the male mobiles, they would reach a moment of

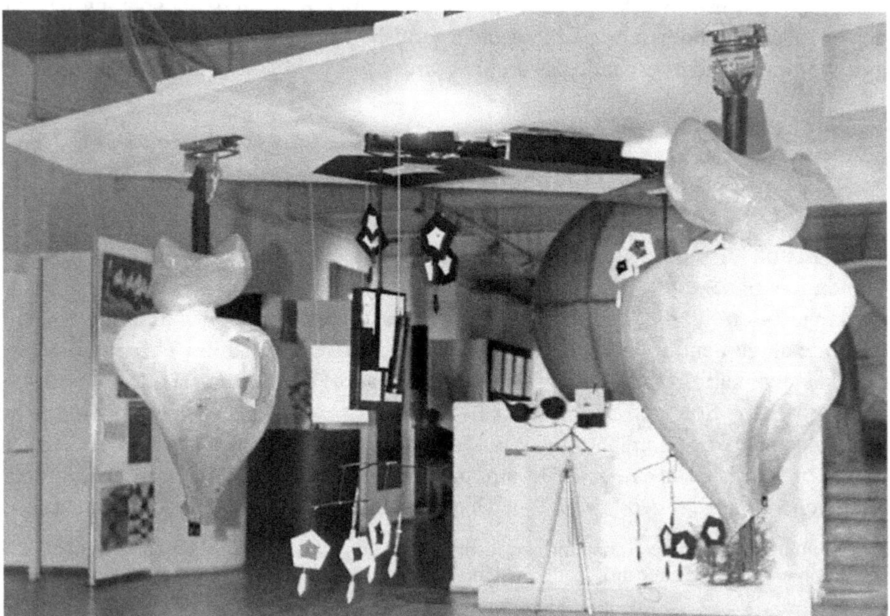

Fig. 3.2 The Colloquy of Mobiles. (Source: Department of Contemporary History, University of Vienna: Gordon Pask Archive (GPA), Photo Collection, Box 2, 17–6)

satisfaction and stop rotating. Based on the concept of learning through conversation the mobiles optimised their relational behaviour over time to decrease the time span until the moment of satisfaction. Visitors could interfere with this process, thus changing the overall interactive dynamics. For Gordon Pask [22, p. 88] the *Colloquy of Mobiles* was

> A socially oriented reactive and adaptive environment. Even in the absence of a human being, entities in the environment communicate with and learn about one another. But a human being can enter the environment and participate; possibly modifying the mode of conversation as a result.

Stephen Gage, a co-organiser of the 2008 exhibition *Pask Present*, emphasises the enduring relevance of the *Colloquy of Mobiles*: "They (the mobiles) had the observer in mind and held the observer in a conversation. It is this aspect of Pask's work that makes him extremely relevant to today's architects. [...] Pask's underlying message reminds us that Architecture is a time-based art."

While Pask's public presentations, exhibitions, lectures and seminars were difficult to understand, his audiences – including architects, students, biologists, computer scientists and yet others – typically left impressed and inspired. What started with Pask's cybernetic machines eventually morphed into the design of larger reactive, cybernetic buildings, spaces and environments. In his work, Pask created the notion of the information environment (IE), environments that could adapt, change, understand and grow, and in which designer and user were linked in complex relationships. Pask's inclusion of the human as an actively shaping part of any environment both demonstrated and established an understanding of architecture as cybernetics and cybernetics as architecture.

3.2.3 Conversation Theory: A Tempting Attempt

This section discusses Gordon Pask's *Conversation Theory* (CT), a theoretical foundation of *design cybernetics*. CT provides a model for how conversational exchanges – circularly-causal interactive process – between conversing entities can generate agreement on meanings as well as learning. Conversation Theory grew out of Pask's realisation that communication in the form of exchanges of coded messages, as proposed by Shannon and Weaver [34], lacked key aspects of conversation as it takes place between human beings. In Pask's CT, conversation starts from diverging points of view that are negotiated among conversing participants until agreements are reached. Pask argued [29, p. 999] that conversation can include communication:

> Communication and conversation are distinct, and they do not always go hand in hand. Suppose that communication is liberally construed as the transmission and transformation of signals. If so, conversation requires at least some communication. But, enigmatically perhaps, very bad communication may admit very good conversation and the existence of a perfect channel is no guarantee that any conversation will take place.

Shannon's model, conceived in 1948, addresses linear one-directional machine to machine communication. It does not address feedback, and excludes questions of meaning. Instead, it utilises statistics for the reconstruction of signals where channels are compromised by noise, or where signals require protection from eavesdropping by means of encryption.

By contrast, Pask's *Conversation Theory* (CT) describes processes of continuous feedback and ongoing learning as a result of exchanges between conversation participants [25]. CT models conversations between individuals. Those include M-individuals (mechanical individuals acting as communication interfaces) and P-individuals (psychological individuals acting as the actual conversation partners, teachers and learners, e.g., A and B). Conversations are enabled through languages such as L-Languages (languages of different knowledge and conversation levels that M-individuals can understand). CT provides an abstract notation for conversations between two or more conversation partners (A and B) on a topic (R), as shown in Fig. 3.3. Through the common understanding of a metalanguage L_0 – such as natural language in the case of human beings – A and B can agree on conversing about the topic R. In Pask's model, a conversation is steered by an external observer who "briefs" the participants about the topic and topic-related terms (e.g. topics related to architecture such as "screed", "damp-proofing" or "surface geometry"). Conversation partners learn about the topic and about each other by conversing, negotiating and eventually agreeing.

The overarching goal of CT is to address processes of creating shared understandings and ongoing learning through a systemic and systematic approach. In Pask's theory, conversations are assumed to be goal driven exchanges, navigated through the conversation partners' states, conditions and contexts. In order to reach the goal of a conversation, participants agree over understandings of a topic by adjusting to each other until either all or some goals are congruent. Other possible outcomes of conversations are that there may be no agreement over the understanding of a topic, or that goals cannot be adjusted sufficiently and the system subdivides into decentralised clusters, which may interact at a later stage. In either case, all actors learn through interacting with each other. Conversation Theory allows open systems and processes, such that systems can interact (converse) with other systems beyond their initial boundaries. The result is an ongoing learning process increasing possibilities and thus, cybernetically speaking, variety. Conversation is the *modus operandi* of and for cybernetic organisation. If we consider the recursivity of conversation in a design process, the concepts of cybernetics and design start overlapping and boundaries between the two become blurred, allowing for links between the two in the form of design cybernetics. By their recursive nature, Paskian conversations can be characterised as design processes of design processes.

In this context, Glanville significantly extended the scope of *Conversation Theory* to include all forms of designing and argued that "design is the action; second-order cybernetics is the explanation" [10]. He observed that agreement was not the most significant outcome of conversations and identified creation of novelty as the central benefit of conversational encounters. Conversations create possibilities through constantly negotiating differences between each conversation partner's

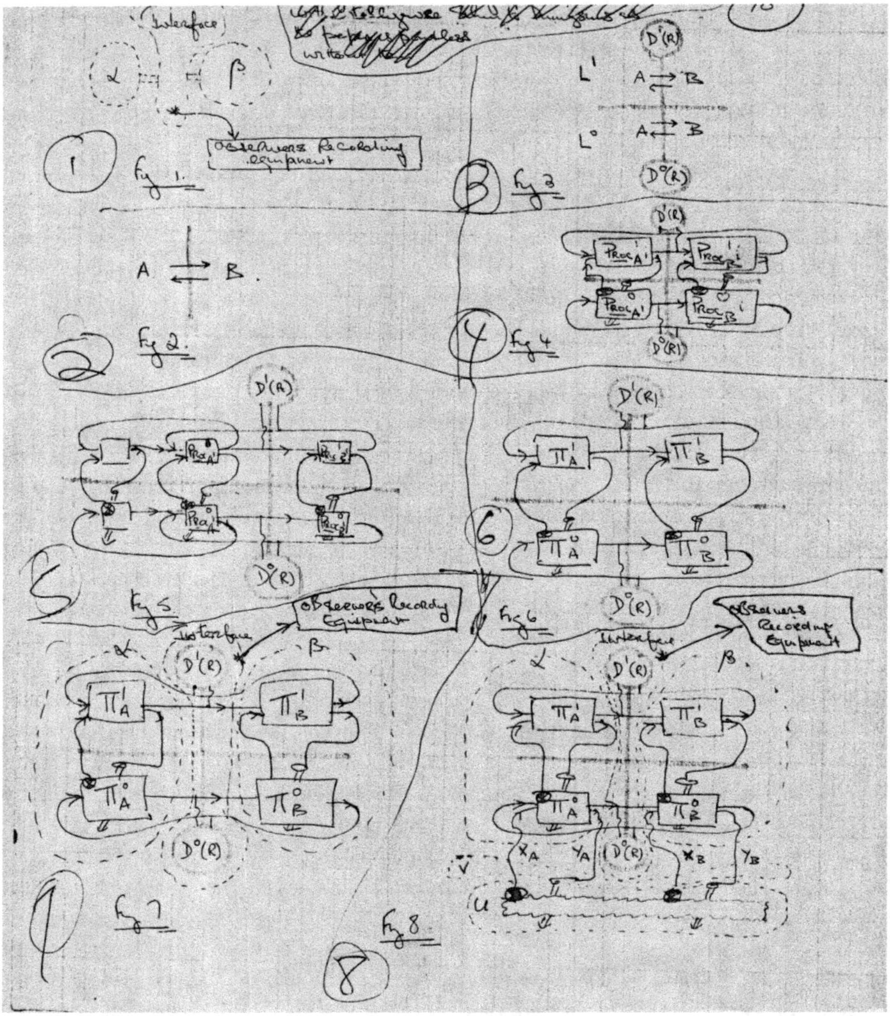

Fig. 3.3 Diagram of Conversation Theory by Gordon Pask. (Source: Department of Contemporary History, University of Vienna: Paul Pangaro's Pask Collection (PPPC), Box IID, Folder 141)

understandings, thereby generating learning in participants. Conversations can be seen as key to processes of learning as well as key to the creation of novel ideas.

Gordon Pask developed a way of capturing conversations in emerging networks of conversational domains in the form of *entailment meshes*. As diagrams and models of conversations, they are extensively discussed in chapter 6 of [25] titled *Conversations with Many Aim Topics* and in chapter 7 of [24] titled *Construction of a General Conversational Domain* of *Conversation, Cognition and Learning*. Pask saw *entailment meshes* as structures showing behaviours similar to biological organisms. They contain nodes, which may contain algorithms to compute the value of this node and its relevance for the next steps of the conversation. Pask applied "pruning" to entailment meshes; in analogy to a technique used in horticulture where branches of plants are cut selectively to direct growth into a desired direction. By pruning entailment meshes, Pask "directed" the conversation.

He expressed *entailment meshes* as diagrams like the one shown in Fig. 3.4, and intertwining toroidal constructs like the one shown in Fig. 3.5, representing conversational syntax and – depending on the dimensions considered – the dynamic and multi-dimensional space a conversation can create.
The diagrams in Fig. 3.4 above show derivations of topics generated by ongoing conversations:

1.1 topic T derived from topic P and topic Q.
1.2 topic T derived from topic P and topic Q, or from topic R and topic S.
1.3 a correspondence, M, between topics F and G, depending upon D and E.
1.4 a shorthand notation for Fig. 3.4. when interpreted to represent an analogy.

Entailment meshes were designed to respond to environmental influences, depending on the conversation topics, attributes and characteristics. New topics emerging through conversations can agglomerate into new regions and further conversations. Translated into contemporary scripting software used in computational architecture and design, we could refer to classes of entities. Conditional expressions, so-called what-if functions, determine which class or which classes a topic belongs to, and hence how it behaves in a conversation. As models representing second-order cybernetic principles, topics observe and are being observed – a topic can have a *perspective*. The concept of *entailment meshes* is powerful in offering a strong

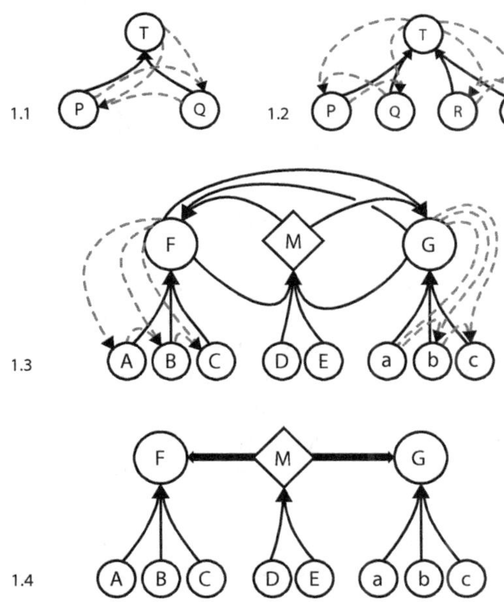

Fig. 3.4 Graphic representation of conversational domains between topics. (Source: [26, p. 17]. Re-drawn by Liss C. Werner, reprinted with permission from John Wiley & Sons, Inc)

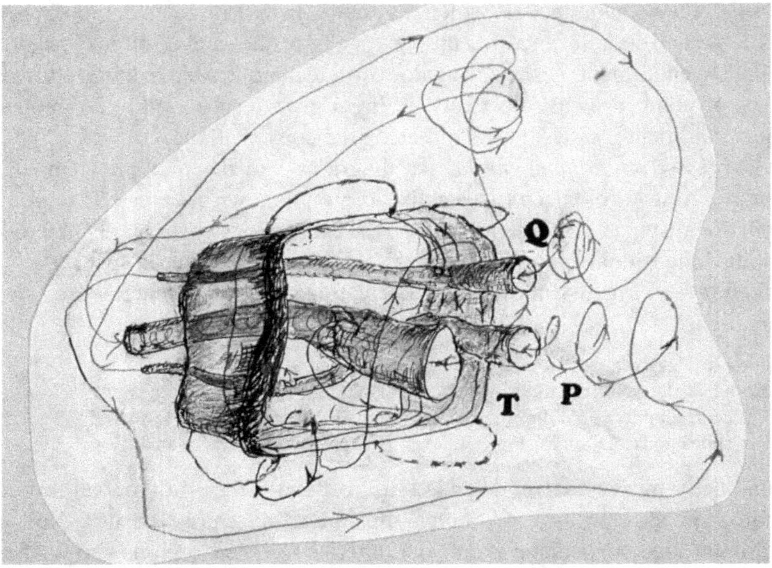

Fig. 3.5 Gordon Pask's drawing of a toroidal representation of conversation domains between topics. (Source: Department of Contemporary History, University of Vienna: Gordon Pask Archive (GPA), Photo Collection, Box 1, 10–3–10)

theoretical guide to multi-dimensional dynamic parametric network structures – found in either materials with complex geometric behaviour triggered by sensorial reception or in the simulation of the morphology of architectural programs through the interaction with different classes of social systems.

3.3 Conclusion

Gordon Pask and Ranulph Glanville took the lead in establishing a cybernetic perspective on architecture and design. In doing so, both, Pask and Glanville conceived of architecture very differently than the conventional understandings of the discipline. In Pask's view, architecture is conversation, and conversation is architecture. A key aspect of Pask's work is his vision of learning environments, which "viewed the human as part of resonance that looped from the human, through the environment or apparatus; back to the human and around again." [18]. Glanville then extended and developed Pask's vision of design activity in a more general sense: cybernetics is design conversation and, conversely, design conversation is cybernetics [9].

Including the human in the loop, and integrating human feedback into "intelligent" digital systems is the next step towards integrated *design cybernetics*. Today, interactive modes of working have become ubiquitous in many fields. Multimedia, social networks and personalised advertising via the Internet are all based on processes of a potentially conversational nature. As a part of the global digital turn, the future may well be shaped by automated artificial forms of conversation.

The digital turn has, on the one hand, empowered large companies to generate floods of data, based on the profiles extracted from digitally connected individuals, using the Internet or other recordable actions. Yet, on the other hand, it has created spaces in which knowledge can be gained, perpetuated, accessed and used. Collective intelligence and collective design processes use decentralised networked databases. In doing so they slowly mutate categorised knowledge domains and offer new opportunities for distributed and parallel forms of conversations across networks and organisations. As a domain may be associated with multiple, changeable categories, entailment meshes may change over time.

In my kind of romantic and at the same time technical understanding I envisage – and it is possible that at the time Gordon Pask did, too – a highly adaptive super-architecture, where matter in space is replaced with bits in time, and atoms amend their structural properties through absorbing bits. The space I envisage is neither material nor virtual, it is both, where thoughts can feed into a cognitive machine of knowledge, a knowledge-manufacturing construct, a kind of Foucaultian *dispositif*, "a system of relations that can be established between these elements." [6]. Data, to feed the machine, may originate from logs of digital activity such as tweets or mobile phone use, as well as from the usage of services such as the frequenting of restaurants, of train stations and of other public transport through apps or via other means of monitoring. *Design cybernetics* in the built environment may harness dynamic data as a "material" for design, and heuristic design strategies may be used to ensure necessary functions. *Architectural mutualism*, a term invented by Pask, describes the "living" together and intertwining of man (individually as well as collectively) and man-made structures:

> A 'functional' building is contrasted with an 'decorative' building; (see categories above) [...] a building cannot be viewed simply in isolation. It is only meaningful as a human environment. It perpetually interacts with its inhabitants, on the one had serving them and on the other controlling their behaviour. In other words structures make sense as parts of larger systems that include human components and the architect is primarily concerned with these larger systems; they (not just the brick and mortar part) are what architects design. – Gordon Pask [20, p. 494]

With the availability and perpetuation of data, the ubiquity of machine learning, the increase in open source platforms and easy access to digital manufacturing in the digital age, the relevance of *design cybernetics* is on the rise. Design processes now – in 2019 – include both, humans and digital machines. We are starting to live in mutual relationships, sharing physical and virtual platforms to participate equally in designing our environments. The idea of *cyberspace*, envisaged in the 1980s as an immaterial realm, has, somewhat ironically, become manifest as a both virtual and material reality: We are physical beings living in a digital world, conversing and learning and teaching with, from and through algorithms and forms. Once a domain belongs to multiple categories it can and does change its relationships to other domains. This happens through situation and time based structural coupling. A relationship between domains – and of the agents that inhabit a domain – entails the exchange of information through communication or conversation, constantly creating new subdomains. One could argue that existing knowledge in novel constellations breeds such 'novel' subdomains. They are either the form of the entailment meshes that constructed them or the entailment meshes themselves. As argued earlier in this chapter, *design cybernetics* encompasses conversations of all kinds, using digital, electronic, analogue devices or a mixture of them. Independent of the choice, design *cybernetics* plays a role in steering the information exchange and cannot be separated from any form of conversation.

I conclude this chapter by raising the issue of authorship. *Design cybernetics* before the digital turn implied a rather controlled design environment dominated by a variety of design languages (styles). *Design cybernetics* post the digital turn dramatically increases the volume of data exchange and conversations, which in turn reduces differences within and between design languages (styles). Individual authorship fractalises and spreads across the grey matter of collective design intelligence. The pressing questions I would like to ask are:

- Can we learn and use *Design Cybernetics* to establish novel design parameters for a man-machine future?
- Can we learn and use *Conversation Theory* to navigate design processes?
- Can we learn and use *Conversation Theory* to navigate research processes in Design Cybernetics?

I think we can.

References

1. Ashby, W. R. (1952). *Design for a brain*. New York: Wiley.
2. Ashby, W. R. (1956). *An introduction to cybernetics*. London: Chapman & Hall.
3. Brown, G. S. (1969). *Laws of form* (1st ed.). London: George Allen & Unwin.
4. Delanda, M. (2011). *Philosophy and simulation: The emergence of synthetic reason*. London/New York: Continuum International Publishing Group.
5. Eames, C., & Eames, R. (1953). *A communications primer*. Directed by Eames, C. A. E., Ray. Available at: https://www.youtube.com/watch?v=byyQtGb3dvA. Accessed 19 Jan 2019.
6. Foucault, M. (1984). Of other spaces: Utopias and heterotopias. *Architecture, Mouvement, Continuité, 5*, 46–49.
7. Glanville, R. (1999). Listen! In G. de Zeeuw, M. Vahl, & E. Mennuti (Eds.), *Problems of participation and connection*. (pp. 425–432). Lincoln: Lincoln Research Centre.
8. Glanville, R. (2004). The purpose of second-order cybernetics. *Kybernetes, 33*(9/10), 1379–1386.
9. Glanville, R. (2007). Try again. Fail again. Fail better: The cybernetics in design and the design in cybernetics. *Kybernetes, 36*(9/10), 1173–1206.
10. Glanville, R. (2012). *The black boox Vol. I. Cybernetic circles*. Vienna: edition echoraum.
11. Glanville, R. (2014). Acting to understand and understanding to act. *Kybernetes, 43*(9/10), 1293–1300.
12. Glanville, R. (2014). How design and cybernetics reflect each other (transcript of keynote presentation). *RSD3. Relating systems thinking and design 2014*. http://systemic-design.net/wp-content/uploads/2014/08/Ranulph_Glanville.pdf. Accessed 19 Jan 2019.

13. Johnson, S. (2001). *Emergence. The connected lives of ants, brains, cities and software*. New York: Scribner.
14. Krippendorff, K. (2007). The cybernetics of design and the design of cybernetics. *Kybernetes, 36*(9/10), 1381–1392.
15. Leduc, S. (1911). *The mechanism of life*. London: William Heinemann.
16. McMullin, B., & Varela, F. J. (1997). Rediscovering computational autopoiesis. In P. Husbands & I. Harvey (Eds.), *Proceedings of the fourth European conference on Artificial Life* (pp. 38–47). Cambridge, MA: MIT Press.
17. Mead, M. (1968). The cybernetics of cybernetics. In H. von Foerster et al. (Eds.), *Purposive systems* (pp. 1–11). New York: Spartan Books.
18. Pangaro, P. (1996). Dandy of cybernetics. *The Guardian* 16 Apr 1996.
19. Pask, G. (1961). *An approach to cybernetics* (3rd ed.). London: Hutchinson & Co.
20. Pask, G. (1969). The architectural relevance of cybernetics. *Architectural Design, 7*(6), 494–496.
21. Pask, G. (1970). The meaning of cybernetics in the behavioural sciences (The cybernetics of behaviour and cognition; extending the meaning of "goal"). In J. Rose (Ed.), *Progress of cybernetics – vol. I* (pp. 15–44). London: Gordon and Breach Science Publishers.
22. Pask, G. (1971). A comment, a case history and a plan. In J. Reichardt (Ed.), *Cybernetics, art, and ideas* (pp. 76–99). Greenwich: New York Graphic Society.
23. Pask, G. (1975). *The cybernetics of human learning and performance. A guide to theory and research*. London: Hutchinson Educational.
24. Pask, G. (1975). *Conversation, cognition and learning*. Amsterdam: Elsevier.
25. Pask, G. (1976). *Conversation theory: Applications in education and epistemology*. Amsterdam: Elsevier.
26. Pask, G. (1976). Conversational techniques in the study and practice of education. *British Journal of Educational Psychology, 46*(1), 12–25.
27. Pask, G. ca. (1976). *Future prospects of cybernetics*. Paper with handwritten notes. Gordon Pask Archive, Department of Contemporary History, University of Vienna.
28. Pask, G. (n.d.) *An initial essay: Towards a unification of architectural theories*. Gordon Pask Archive, Department of Contemporary History, University of Vienna, 4–44–2–8.
29. Pask, G. (1980). The limits of togetherness. In S. H. Lavington (Ed.), *Information processing 80*. (pp. 999–1012). Amsterdam: North Holland Publishing.
30. Pias, C. (Ed.). (2003). *Cybernetics—Kybernetik: The Macy-Conferences 1946–1953. Transactions/Protokolle*. Zürich/Berlin: diaphanes.
31. Ramage, M., & Karen S. (2009). *Systems thinkers*. London: Springer.
32. Reichardt, J. (1970). *Cybernetic serendipity*. London: Rapp & Carroll.
33. Scott, B. (1980). The cybernetics of Gordon Pask, part 1. *International Cybernetics Newsletter* (17), 327–336.
34. Shannon, C. E., & Weaver, W. (1963). *The mathematical theory of communication*. Urbana: University of Illinois Press.
35. Varela, F. J., Humberto, R. M., & Ricardo, B. U. (1974). Autopoiesis. The organization of living systems, its characterization and a model. *Biosystems, 5*(4), 187–196.
36. von Foerster, H. (1974). *The cybernetics of cybernetics*. Champaign-Urban, Biological Computer Laboratory, University of Illinois. Republished as Heinz von Foerster. 1995. *Cybernetics of cybernetics or the control of control and the communication of communication* (2nd ed.). Minneapolis: Future Systems Inc.
37. von Foerster, H. (1977). The curious behavior of complex systems: Lessons from biology. In H. A. Linstone & W. H. Clive Simmonds (Eds.), *Future research. New directions* (pp. 104–113). Reading: Addison-Wesley. An audio recording of this conference presentation is available at: https://soundcloud.com/portland-state-library/pdx-lsta-hs-1553-access. Accessed 19 Jan 2019.
38. von Foerster, H. (1984). *Observing systems* (2nd ed.). Seaside: Intersystems Publications.
39. von Foerster, H. (2003). *Understanding understanding. Essays on cybernetics and cognition*. New York: Springer.

40. von Glasersfeld, E. (1974). Piaget and the radical constructivist epistemology. In C. D. Smock and E. von Glasersfeld (Eds.), *Epistemology and education* (pp. 1–24). Athens: Follow Through Publications.
41. Werner, L. C. (2014). Claryfying the matter: It's not a paradigm shift it's a stage change. In A. T. Estévez (Ed.), *Biodigital and genetic architecture* (pp. 218–233). Barcelona: ESARQ.
42. Werner, L. C. (Ed.). (2014). *[En]Coding architecture: The book*. Pittsburgh: School of Architecture, Carnegie Mellon University.
43. Wiener, N. (1948). *Cybernetics: Or control and communication in the animal and the machine* (1st ed.). Paris: Herman & Cie.
44. Wiener, N. (1989). *The human use of human beings: Cybernetics and society*. London: Free Association Books. First published by Houghton Mifflin, London, 1950.

Liss C. Werner is a registered architect and Assistant Professor at TU Berlin, Institute of Architecture where she founded the CyPhyLab. She is an independent expert for Horizon 2020 proposal evaluations. Werner headed the studio *Codes in the Clouds* at DIA, Dessau 2010–2016, held visiting professorships at Taylor's University and Carnegie Mellon University. She lectures, exhibits and publishes internationally and chaired conferences. She enjoys learning and teaching, creating systems and speculating on new architectures emerging from computation, cyber-physical systems, human-machine relationships and material-intelligence in the era of IoT.

Chapter 4
Cybernetics and Design: Conversations for Action

Hugh Dubberly and Paul Pangaro

Abstract Ranulph Glanville came to believe that cybernetics and design are two sides of the same coin. The authors present their understanding of Glanville and the relationships they see between cybernetics and design. They argue that cybernetics is a necessary foundation for twenty-first century design practice: *If design, then systems*: Due in part to the rise of computing technology and its role in human communications, the domain of design has expanded from giving form to creating systems that support human interactions; thus, systems literacy becomes a necessary foundation for design. *If systems, then cybernetics:* Interaction involves goals, feedback, and learning, the science of which is cybernetics. *If cybernetics, then second-order cybernetics:* Framing wicked problems requires making explicit one's values and viewpoints, accompanied by the responsibility to justify them with explicit arguments; this incorporates subjectivity and the epistemology of second-order cybernetics. *If second-order cybernetics, then conversation:* Design grounded in argumentation requires conversations so that participants may understand, agree, and collaborate on effective action – that is, participants in a design conversation learn together in order to act together. The authors see cybernetics as a way of framing *both* the process of designing *and* the things being designed – both means and ends – not only design-*as*-conversation but also design-*for*-conversation. Second-order cybernetics frames design *as* conversation, and they explicitly frame "second-order design" as creating possibilities for others to have conversations.

Keywords Conversation · Cybernetics · Design · Framing · Glanville · Interaction · Learning · Second-order · Systems · Wicked problems

---

H. Dubberly
Dubberly Design Office, San Francisco, CA, USA
e-mail: hugh@dubberly.com

P. Pangaro (✉)
Human-Computer Interaction Institute, Carnegie Mellon University, Pittsburgh, PA, USA
e-mail: paulpangaro@pangaro.com; ppangaro@andrew.cmu.edu

T. Fischer, C. M. Herr (eds.), *Design Cybernetics*, Design Research Foundations,
https://doi.org/10.1007/978-3-030-18557-2_4

4.1 A Conversation About Conversations-for-Action

This paper began as a conversation with Ranulph Glanville about the relationships between cybernetics and design.

Some background: Glanville studied architecture and taught at the Architectural Association for many years.[1] He also studied with cybernetician Gordon Pask, who developed "Conversation Theory" [33] and was among the first to recognize connections between cybernetics and design. Pask was involved with designers – working with Cedric Price on the Fun Palace, contributing to Nicholas Negroponte's *Soft Architecture Machines* [25], and participating in an early design methods conference. Also, Pask's approach to science and theory might be described as "designerly": he was a "maker" throughout his most prolific period from the 1950s through the 1980s [26], experimenting with "machines for conversation" including, among many others, Musicolour, Self-Adaptive Keyboard Instructor, and Colloquy of Mobiles, [34]. Pask's student Glanville saw the deep connection between cybernetics and design in Pask's work and was among the first to forefront that cybernetics and design are not just connected, they are two sides of the same coin.

This paper is not a review of Glanville's extensive writings, and we may not fully understand his views. However, we would like to report on points he made to us, sometimes quite vehemently – and we would like to comment on the many places where we feel we concur and the few where we do not.

The catalyst for our conversation was Glanville's masterful presentation at the RSD3, Relating Systems Thinking and Design 2014 Symposium in Oslo [15]. Glanville argued that first-order cybernetics, far from being mere mechanics or calculation, provides a necessary alternative to linear causality: it brings us circular causality, critical to understanding and realizing (making) interactive systems that evolve through recursion, learning, and co-evolution. Second-order cybernetics is fundamental to design because it gives us an epistemological framework for designing. Second-order cybernetics moves us from a detached, "objective" pose, where we can duck responsibility, right into the messy middle of things, where we must take responsibility for our actions.

Second-order cybernetics frames design *as* conversation. This creates the conditions for learning together and thus better-directed, more-deliberate actions: hence the second half of our title, "Conversations for Action." And because it is conversation that leads to learning and effective action, the key focus for designers must ultimately be to design *for* conversation.

Sadly, Glanville's passing cut short our conversation with him. We strive to present his views as best we understand them, quoting him when possible. We appreciate his gifts, and we miss him. We invite continued conversation, especially with others who have collaborated with him and who may see his intentions differently. Together let us learn and evolve the field.

[1] An earlier version of this paper first appeared in *Cybernetics and Human Knowing* 22(2–3):73–82. The authors and editors gratefully acknowledge permission to develop this revision based on that original.

4.2 The Context for Cybernetics and Design

To connect design with cybernetics is not new.[2] Both Christopher Alexander (in 1964) [1] and Horst Rittel (in 1965) [36] acknowledge the influence of cybernetician Ross Ashby's *Design for a Brain* (written in 1952) [2]. Rittel notes in his "Universe of Design" lectures, "The explicit view of Ashby is of the designer as regulator." [36, p. 91]. Rittel explains, "Design has been defined as a purposeful and goal seeking activity" [36, p. 124].

Framing the design process as a single feedback loop can be a useful first approximation; it emphasizes several key aspects of the process – iteration; error correction; information flowing from designer through environment and back again; and perhaps even convergence on a goal, as Simon suggested (in 1969), "changing existing situations into preferred ones." [39, p. 111].

Yet, framing the design process as a single feedback loop is a gross simplification. Even simple design situations involve multiple levels of structure, meaning, and goals – nested components and subcomponents, networks of signs (in the semiotic sense), and hierarchies of goals and means for achieving them. While the design process may seek a sort of homeostasis, it is less like the self-regulation of a thermostat and more like autopoiesis, the self-generation of a living organism. Far from being unitary (controlling a single variable, e.g., heat), the system is "fractal," in the sense that feedback loops operate across a range of scales, in the large and in the small, and these feedback loops are connected in a vast web.

Framing the design process as a feedback loop also raises questions at another level. Feedback measures difference from goal. So: Where does the goal come from? Who sets the goal? Who controls the system itself?

What is more: Outside of classes in design schools, very few design situations present with clearly defined goals. Fundamentally, the designer's main challenge is to understand the situation, its constituents, and their context, and from that understanding help facilitate agreement on shared goals. A peculiar aspect of designing is that the process of formulating (and reformulating) goals proceeds not only by explicit discussion of possible goals, but also by making artifacts related to the possible goals. In other words, as designers act to achieve a goal, they often discover the need to change the goal. (Separating goal-formulation from action is also misleading.) Designing requires making goals explicit, otherwise they cannot be examined, critiqued, or improved. This distinguishes design from many other forms of human activity because the "why" – the goals of design – must be transparent so that the intentions and values of the designers are available for review and response, which may come from other designers or from anyone else affected by the outcomes of the design process.

[2]We acknowledge a broader history of associating design and cybernetics but cannot offer a thorough survey here.

Thus we see that connecting design to feedback raises the questions: By what process are goals examined, critiqued, improved? As we will argue below and as Rittel well knew, the answer is: through conversation.

4.3 Conversations for Action

"Action" is inherent in what historian of science Andew Pickering [35] calls the cybernetic ontology – what we might call the "frame" of cybernetics:

> Since Descartes, it comes naturally to us to think of the brain as the home of the mind, and the mind as a centre of knowledge, reason, thought and cognition – the cognitive brain, we could call it. And part of the singularity of the cybernetic ontology was that it had a very different account of the brain. The cybernetic brain was a performative rather than a cognitive organ, understood as geared directly into doing and performance rather than cognition. 'The brain is not a thinking machine,' Ashby wrote in 1948, 'it is an acting machine.' As far as conceptualising the human is concerned, this shift of referent from cognition to performance was a defining aspect of the singularity of cybernetics. – Andrew Pickering [35]

"Design" is what this acting machine "performs'', the process by which it proceeds, the process by which it learns – which is to say, the process by which it understands distinctions; agrees on goals and means; and enacts them – and then, based on the results, iterates with "improved" actions.

For those reasons, we construe design as a conversation for action – that is, as cybernetics. Action may either conserve or change a situation. In other words, design is a conversation about what to conserve and what to change, a conversation about what we value [20]. Both the design process and cybernetic systems involve observing a situation as having some limitations, reflecting on how and why to improve that situation, and acting to improve it. This follows the circular process of observe→reflect→make that is common to the recursive and accumulative process of learning in service of effective action, as is found in science, medicine, biological systems, quality management, and everyday living [10].

We construe cybernetics as a process for understanding [42] as well as a practice for operating in the world that focuses on systems that contain loops that enable the attaining of goals [35]. The term cybernetics comes from Greek roots meaning to pilot or to steer; on moving into Latin it becomes to govern. Some erroneously construe cybernetics to be mechanical. Some even hear in the word "system" the march of jackboots – unthinking, mechanical control. What interests us is quite the opposite – the messy chaos of natural and social systems, which cybernetics can help us begin to understand. We believe there is huge range for variation and possibility while applying the cybernetic frame to designing objects, interactions, services (increasingly driven by data), and more.

We also believe it is a misunderstanding to construe cybernetics as requiring a reductive stance or a focus on engineering. Glanville himself makes the point that Norbert Wiener ought to have published his most famous book *Cybernetics: Communication and Control in the Animal and Machine* after he had published *The*

Human Use of Human Beings – because the former left an imprint of cybernetics as engineering grounded in mathematics, while the latter explains cybernetics as "a way of thinking and a way of being in the world" [15, p. 3]. The flowering of cybernetics in the 1940s came from conversations among a vast range of world-experts from both the hard sciences and the social sciences, who celebrated the field as uniquely focused on a new way of seeing systems [41].

4.4 Connecting Design to Cybernetics and Conversation

The structure of our argument is:

- If design, then systems
- If systems, then cybernetics
- If cybernetics, then second-order cybernetics
- If second-order cybernetics, then conversation

We now traverse that path and offer rationale and implications.

4.4.1 If Design, Then Systems

> [A] building cannot be viewed simply in isolation. It is only meaningful as a human environment. It perpetually interacts with its inhabitants, on the one hand serving them and on the other hand controlling their behavior. In other words structures make sense as parts of larger systems that include human components and the architect is primarily concerned with these larger systems; *they* (not just the bricks and mortar part) are what the architect designs. – Gordon Pask [29, p. 494]

Many of today's design challenges are complex problems, where an appropriate formulation of the situation is neither already agreed-to nor easy-to-characterize. However, through conversations within a design team, an agreeable characterization may be defined (the "problem" formulation) and then tackled by defining actions to improve the situation (the "solution").

The industrial era changed the nature of design from design-for-making (insofar as there were any explicit design steps before making) to design-for-manufacturing. Beginning in the twentieth century, design-for-systems becomes necessary, as evidenced from World War II when operations research as a field of practice and cybernetics as a systems discipline arose [18]. As argued in depth elsewhere [6, 11], designers of digital systems are faced with the challenges of product-service ecologies. (Later we will widen the scope beyond digital and see that design-for-systems still applies.) This new design challenge is often exemplified by the iPod or iPhone, but the same points could be made for any networked device (even the original telegraph). While the user interacts with an iPod as physical device, its software connects to a network of communication systems (internet) and databases (music archive) and marketplaces (music for sale), which has relationships to other actors (social community members, artists) and related aftermarkets. The complications of this system of systems must not be exposed in ways that confuse a user; and the designer must know enough about the system-to-system relationships to produce an effective outcome. Hence, designers must be conversant with this end-to-end mesh of systems in order to design for a tractable set of rich choices from which the user lives her experience.

The rise of design-for-systems has further consequences. Good form-giving is largely table stakes – necessary but not sufficient to ensure the success of new ventures. Beginning in the twentieth century and accelerating in the 21st, new value-creation has moved to the development of systems. The term platform is often invoked [43] in reference to complex, distributed interactions of hardware and software, networks and users, transactions and markets, for which primary examples are Alibaba and Amazon; Facebook and Google; Apple and Samsung [6].[3] Our definition of platform includes the capacity for others to build systems within it, no matter the medium.

Therefore, we wish to distinguish two levels of design: (1) design of things to be used, including tools used to make other things, and (2) the design of situations in which others can create, that is, the design of platforms, including languages. Level 1 we may call first-order design; level 2 we may call second-order design – that is, design-*for*-conversation.

Design for complex problems that bridge product-service ecologies requires new skills:

> Looking at a specific system, recognizing the underlying pattern, and describing the general pattern in terms of the specific system constitutes command of the vocabulary of systems, reading systems, and writing systems – that is, systems literacy. – Hugh Dubberly [7, p. 3]

4.4.2 *If Systems, Then Cybernetics*

> One of the things I should do is try to make a little difference between cybernetics and systems, or see if there is one. – Ranulph Glanville [17, 2'28"]

From the 1960s, The Club of Rome [22] popularized systems dynamics (SD) as a modeling language for complex systems, and since then Donella Meadows' and others' work have brought SD to a wide range of populations, including design students [23]. Conceived as a toolkit for explaining ecologies and economies, the vocabulary of SD – resource stocks and their flows – is well suited to its original application. However, we see limitations in SD for modeling systems for interaction. Meadows only briefly mentions regulation. SD does not clearly differentiate system

[3]The platforms mentioned are grounded in digital technology and therefore incorporate hardware/software infrastructure, but not all platforms are digital (see later example of the Schiphol Airport signage system).

behaviors that are the result of variations in levels (stocks as well as flows of material things) from system behaviors that are the result of feedback (flows of information). Perhaps most limiting is SD's lack of distinction between the effects of changes of levels (for example, an increase in population) and a deliberate act to effect an outcome (for example, a change of course of action as a result of new information, as when a comparator flips action from heating to cooling in a thermostat). Goals require agency, and agency implies actions taken intentionally based on data interpreted as feedback to the system's goals. (Of course we may attribute agency to a mechanical system when it behaves as if it has, see Pask [30].)

Goals and information are about the immaterial aspects of systems while stocks and flows are very much the materiality of them. The originators of cybernetics sought to make a clear distinction between the material and the immaterial. Ashby goes so far as to say "the materiality is irrelevant" [3, p. 1] in order to further distinguish cybernetics as a discipline focused on information in purposive systems. As Glanville states while invoking Ashby, cybernetic systems are "not subject to the laws of physics and energetics, but subject to the laws of information, of messages" [15, p. 4].

Because design involves human beings – what we want and how we might act to get what we want – systems literacy for designers must go beyond SD and incorporate goals and agency. Designers must therefore understand the workings of systems with agency. Cybernetics offers both language and models for understanding and describing such systems.

A cybernetic viewpoint on design also invites (if not demands) consideration of the capacity of a given system to achieve goals (whether imbued by a designer or inherent in the system itself). This of course is the concept of "variety" [3]. When the system is a team of designers, the question need be asked: Do we have the requisite variety to successfully design and construct an outcome that will achieve our goals?[4] This question raises other issues, already raised above: How do these goals arise, and whose are they? To answer requires a shift to second-order.

4.4.3 *If Cybernetics, Then Second-Order Cybernetics*

> I have also developed the analogy between second-order Cybernetics and design so as to give mutual reinforcement to both. Design is the action; second-order Cybernetics is the explanation. – Ranulph Glanville [14, p. 22]

Today's most critical (design) challenges are global in scale and have direct impact on quality of life – and its very existence. They include the future of the climate, water, food, population, health, and social justice. They are characterized as wicked problems [37] because the challenge to be addressed appears irredeemable. Even

[4]For elaboration of design for variety, which is beyond the scope of this paper, see [12].

defining "the problem" is itself elusive, subjective, and controversial. Calling these situations problems is misleading; a better term might be "mess" or "tangle".

What is worse: Wicked situations are impossible to solve fully; rather, we work as hard as we can to minimize their negative effects, but we cannot eradicate them. In part this is because these situations operate across complex systems of systems, with emergent and unpredictable behaviors, including unintended consequences, even when well-intended actions are taken. And furthermore, some of the systems employed are human networks, comprising ecologies of language and conversation, with concomitant ambiguity, conflict, and human defects at play.

In sum, describing a wicked situation so that actions may be identified, whose execution has some likelihood of effectiveness, is a design challenge of great difficulty and greatest importance for our future.

Rather than speaking of "solving" in the context of wicked situations, the convention is to speak of positive change as "taming". Taming wicked situations requires framing – the subjective look at situations from a perspective that is only one possibility of many. Often stakeholders see a wicked situation from very different points of view; finding a new frame – "reframing" – is necessary for progress. The value of one frame above another is guidance to an effective path forward, usually through a frame's power to explain why the system behaves as it appears to behave. This is a form of taming complexity through language [12, 40]. Framing must support objective facts but only by being explicit about the values that forefront some "facts" above others. Fundamentally, it must create an argument for some design approaches above others – the "design rationale". Neither systems dynamics nor first-order cybernetics are enough (emphasis added):

> The systems-approach "of the first generation" is inadequate for dealing with wicked problems. Approaches of the "second generation" should be based on a model of planning as an argumentative process in the course of which **an image of the problem and of the solution emerges gradually among the participants**, as a product of incessant judgment, subjected to critical argument. – Horst Rittel in [37, p. 162]

The shared goal or problem definition emerges from the interactions of the participations as much as the solution does. We interpret this to mean that the problem and its solution are "emergent," in today's jargon – co-emerging as an image, that is, a characterization or (re)framing. Thus Rittel and Webber themselves reframe design-as-problem-solving to design-as-problem-finding or needs-finding. Rittel is important in part because he is among the first to frame design as politics – as discussion and argumentation – as opposed to design-as-art or design-as-science [36, p. 144]. Similarly, Buchanan [4] later framed design as a branch of rhetoric.

Rittel points out that the stance of designer as expert problem-solver is largely a myth. There are few design problems with clear solutions. Design is not objective; it's subjective. It's messy. The designer never stands outside the situation. The designer is always part of the situation – and other stakeholders also have necessary roles to play in the design process.

Thus design becomes centered in an argumentative process that involves "incessant judgment, subjected to critical argument" [37, p. 162]. Rather than existing outside the design situation, judgment and argument appear inside when the stance is that of second-order cybernetics. For the shift from first-order to second-order occurs when the observer – the designer, the modeler, the problem-framer, the participant in design conversations – is aware of her observing.

In sum, design for wicked problems, and the required (re)framing, calls for second-order cybernetics, which makes the role of the observer explicit, which in turn makes explicit the subjective position of every design rationale.[5]

4.4.4 *If Second-Order Cybernetics, Then Conversation*

> Conversation is the bridge between cybernetics and design. – Ranulph Glanville [15, p. 8]

> Design is a circular, conversational process. – Ranulph Glanville [14, p. 22]

Reaching judgments and making arguments are, of course, forms of conversation. Glanville further tightens his assertion about the relationship of design and conversation by stating that conversation is a requirement for design, even when the conversation is with oneself, perhaps just using pencil and paper. (Schön [38] makes a similar point.) There is the person who draws and the (other yet the same) person who looks. The difference between these personae – between making and observing/reflecting – is, in and of itself, a major source of "novelty'', Glanville claims. (We prefer the terms "variation" or "invention". Our position on the role of novelty in design is given below.) Engaging multiple perspectives is a necessary condition for conversation, and without conversation, he writes, "You're not doing design, you're doing problem-solving."[6] Design, instead, is "to do something magical" and "to find 'the new'" [15, p. 10].

With compatible meanings, Rittel, Buchanan, Glanville, Negroponte [24], and Pask [32] describe design as conversation, which can be modeled as two (or more) second-order systems interacting, which in part can be a discussion of goals. We state elsewhere [9] that conversation is required in order to converge on shared goals. To share goals is to agree on (re)framing a situation in order to act together. We see the development of arguments in the course of designing (for or against different ways of framing situations) and the derivation of different choices or actions as the same as conversation. Thus we concur with Glanville's eloquent, albeit general, statements about conversation, cybernetics, and design.

---

[5]For an eloquent exposition of the emergence and practitioners of second-order cybernetics along with a glossary, Glanville [14] is highly recommended.

[6]While we accept the distinction between design and problem-solving, we can imagine typical cases of problem-solving that require conversation. For example, a team might discuss how best to break down a problem into more manageable components. Likewise, much of education involves discussion of strategies for recognizing problem types and appropriate strategies for each type.

However, we find some of Glanville's stated positions to be assertions without an accompanying rationale. For example, he was clear and even adamant that design knowledge is tacit, not explicit. We take this as part of his argument that design knowledge exists only in relation to action. If design is conversation, however, and if conversation is learning – very often, or at least consistently so in relation to design – then is not both the goal and the effect of the design conversation to make its subject explicit? We assert that for the major (design) challenges of today, making design knowledge explicit is a necessity. Form-givers may have the luxury of working alone, but designing systems and designing platforms require teams – and thus goals and methods must be made more explicit so that the resulting artifacts are coherent and actions are coordinated. Just as design is different than problem-solving, making choices in designing is different than making choices in creating a work of art. When designing, fit-to-purpose is the rationale for one choice above another; the question, of course, is do we agree on the purpose? When designing for systems, articulating that rationale is an irreplaceable component of the design conversation that takes place across the individuals, disciplines, and languages that comprise a design team.

A retort might be that a given design conversation is about some specific situation or artifact – not about design. But then, a design conversation about design must be the subject of design education, and we arrive at the same point – making the tacit explicit is a requirement for effective design. Not doing so leaves design stuck in its medieval master-apprentice craft tradition, where change is slow, and innovation is difficult.

But any dive into specifics may lose sight of the universal need for conversations in order to design. Design conversations discuss goals, means, context (itself a conversation, not a state [5]), how-to-frame-the-situation (and who-advocated-for-what-position), what-to-conserve (what-we-value), what-to-try, how-to-evaluate-it, what-happened-when-we-tried, and what-to-try-next.[7]

4.5 The Responsibility of Designers

We have argued that twenty-first-century design requires conversation, as well that (in complete alliance with Glanville) design *is* conversation. When we say "conversation" we mean it explicitly in the second-order sense of recognizing our (subjective) participation in the process of framing and justifying our choices, and therefore our responsibility for it all.

[7]Further work is needed to more carefully dissect and characterize the types of design conversations. One approach suggests that design for innovation requires four broad classes of conversations for these purposes: to agree on goals; to agree on means; to create new language, as required for innovation; and, in an over-arching conversation, to design the conversations required for design, from the perspective of requisite variety [27].

> We human beings can do whatever we imagine if we respect the structural coherence of the domain in which we operate. But we do not have to do all that we imagine, we can choose, and it is there that our behavior as socially conscious human beings matters. – Humberto Maturana [20]

If designers are to be responsible for the process of design, we must seek the most effective tools and methodologies – and to document, evolve, and disseminate them into the community of design and into the world of wicked situations.

Therefore, designers must themselves be responsible for systems literacy as a foundation for design; for working within a second-order epistemology where they take responsibility for their viewpoints; for processes of collaboration through conversation; and for articulating their rationale as an integral part of their process. This has deep implications for the development of new design curricula.

4.6 Implications for Teaching Design

Glanville was influenced by his experience of design methods during his time as a student at the Architectural Association in the 1960s. Perhaps it was in rejection to the "expert stance" of the first generation that he came to prefer to say that design is "at once mysterious and ambiguous" [16].

We agree that when narrowly interpreted in its first-order form, cybernetics as engineering may suggest a sort of problem-solving which accepts or even assumes goals rather than inviting conversation about what our goals should be. But in its second-order form – with subjectivity, values, and responsibility explicit – teaching design as cybernetics is more common sense than straight-jacketed engineering, more about possibility than determinism, more emergent than mechanical. Teaching vocabulary and grammar does not deny poetry. Quite the contrary: A knowledge of vocabulary and grammar, if not a prerequisite, seems at least a more fertile ground for the emergence of poetry, and her sister, delight.

Thus, we argue that "systems" – systems dynamics, first-order cybernetics, second-order cybernetics, and conversation theory – should be a series of courses in all design school programs [8].

The value of teaching systems to designers is that it will help them do better work. It will provide language and models for talking about (and thinking about) the world in which they work, the systems they design, and the process by which they design. It will make them more effective and more efficient. That is, introducing cybernetics to designers will make the design process more "rigorous", in the sense of "stronger" or "more compelling" – *not* more "correct".

4.7 Novelty, Design, and Second-Order Design

> For me, one of the most important things is how to find novelty, and that I don't think can be done by specification or purposeful action, it needs wobbly conversation and deep speculation. After it's found, it can be specified. – Ranulph Glanville [16]

While not presuming too much about Glanville's possible elaborations on the relationship of novelty and design, we want to be clear about ours: Novelty is *not* the primary goal of design. (There is a risk that traditional designers will hear the pursuit of novelty as the pursuit of new form for its own sake.) Like Glanville, we embrace conversations for design, specifically as a way of discovering new goals and new opportunities, as we co-construct our shared frames and persuading arguments. But as yet under-developed in our argument is the role of value and values. Design is a particular set of conversations, which explicitly and implicitly (to oneself alone or with others) embody what we value and what we seek to conserve. Maturana's framing of "possible change" in the context of "what we do not wish to change" is directly useful and actionable:

> Every time a set of elements begins to conserve certain relationships, it opens space for everything to change around the relationships that are conserved. – Humberto Maturana and Ximena Dávila Yáñez [21, p. 77]

Of course we must be aware of what we are conserving, to open the possibility of change. Unstated but what we hear implied in Glanville's position is the notion that the results of design should not be fixed – that is, that designers create possibilities for others to have conversations, to learn, and to act.

This idea is transformational – a paradigm shift. Le Corbusier's publication of *Le Modulor* [19] may be a fulcrum point, the visible signal of the new paradigm. Another signal of the new paradigm was Karl Gerstner's publication of *Designing Programmes* [13], "Instead of solutions for problems, programmes for solutions." (Much earlier, moveable type with its inherent reuse sets the stage for what comes after modernism, even as moveable type creates the revolution of modernism itself.) To single out one example in practice, the Schiphol Airport signage system from 1967 by the Dutch firm Total Design and Benno Wissing is one of the first and most famous examples in practice – creating not a complete system, but a system in which others can create. As a platform for creating – in our terms, a platform for conversations for designing – a signage system is quite limited, but still the outlines are there. The relationship of designer to outcome is changed: The signage system is never completely finished, never completely specified, never completely imagined. It is forever open. "Second-order design" has emerged. Design-*for*-conversation is born.[8]

[8]Chatbots, such as Elisa and her many spawn, e.g., *Mattel*'s Hello Barbie, which follow pre-defined script trees, are not examples of design-for-conversation. Nor are voiced agents, such as Siri and Alexa. Indeed, the current fad for so-called "conversational interfaces" misses the point of conversation [28].

Pask saw this potential and began to explore it through his experimental machines, which sought to engage people in conversations [31]. Influenced by Pask, Negroponte went so far as to imagine an "architecture machine" able to collaborate with designers in designing spaces, physical and virtual, literal and metaphorical. Such a machine embodied design-*as*-conversation to enable design-*for*-conversation. In 1967, the idea of the architecture machine gave rise to a research group co-founded by Negroponte. Amid the convergence of digital content, digital communication, and computing (including the PC revolution), MIT's Architecture Machine Group set the stage for the MIT Media Lab, which opened in 1985 to house an assortment of research directions. Yet, the original idea of the architecture machine was set aside and remains unrealized.

We see design-for-conversation as the emergent space of design for the twenty-first century and aim for it as our goal. Whether designing interactive environments as computational extensions of human agency or new social discourses for governing social change, the goal of second-order design is to facilitate the emergence of conditions in which others can design – to create conditions in which conversations can emerge – and thus to increase the number of choices for all.

> I shall act always so as to increase the total number of choices. – Heinz von Foerster's Ethical Imperative [40, p. 282]

References

1. Alexander, C. (1964). *Notes on the synthesis of form.* Cambridge, MA: Harvard University Press.
2. Ashby, W. R. (1952). *Design for a brain: The origin of adaptive behaviour.* New York: Wiley.
3. Ashby, W. R. (1956). *An introduction to cybernetics*. New York: Wiley.
4. Buchanan, R. (1985). Declaration by design: Rhetoric, argument, and demonstration in design practice. *Design Issues, 2*(1), 4–22. Reprinted In V. Margolin (Ed.), *Design discourse: History, theory, criticism*, 1989 (pp. 91–109). Chicago: The University of Chicago Press.
5. Dourish, P. (2004). What we talk about when we talk about context. *Personal and Ubiquitous Computing, 8*(1), 19–30.
6. Dubberly, H. (2014). The networked platform revolution. Presentation given at IIT Institute for Design, Chicago. Available at: http://presentations.dubberly.com/ID_Networked_Platform.pdf. Accessed 19 Jan 2019.
7. Dubberly, H. (2014). A systems literacy manifesto. Keynote presentation given at relating systems thinking and design RSD3 2014. Published with RSD3 Proceedings. Available at: https://systemic-design.net/wp-content/uploads/2014/08/Hugh_Dubberly_systems_manifesto.pdf. Accessed 19 Jan 2019.
8. Dubberly, H., & Paul, P. (2007). Cybernetics and service-craft: Language for behavior-focused design. *Kybernetes, 36*(9/10), 1153–1157.
9. Dubberly, H., & Pangaro, P. (2009). What is conversation? How do we design for effective conversation? *Interactions Magazine* July/Aug 2009. Available at: http://www.dubberly.com/articles/what-is-conversation.html. Accessed 19 Jan 2019.
10. Dubberly, H., Chung, J., Evenson, S., & Pangaro, P. (2009). A model of the creative process. Report commissioned by Institute for the Creative Process, Alberta College of Art Design, Calgary. Available at: http://www.dubberly.com/concept-maps/creative-process.html. Accessed 19 Jan 2019.

11. Forlizzi, J. (2013). Unpublished manuscript, via personal correspondence with the authors.
12. Geoghegan, M. C., & Pangaro, P. (2009). Design for a self-regenerating organization. *International Journal of General Systems, 38*(2), 155–173.
13. Gerstner, K. (1964). *Designing programmes.* New York: Hastings House.
14. Glanville, R. (2012). Second order cybernetics. *The black boox – vol. I. Cybernetic circles* (pp. 175–207). Vienna: edition echoraum. Previously published In F. Parra-Luna (Ed.), *Encyclopedia of life support systems, systems science and cybernetics – vol. III.* Oxford: EoLSS Publishers. Available at: http://www.pangaro.com/glanville/Glanville-SECOND_ORDER_CYBERNETICS.pdf. Accessed 19 Jan 2019.
15. Glanville, R. (2014). How design and cybernetics reflect each other. Keynote presentation given at relating systems thinking and design RSD3 2014. Published with RSD3 Proceedings. Available at: http://systemic-design.net/wp-content/uploads/2014/08/Ranulph_Glanville.pdf. Accessed 19 Jan 2019.
16. Glanville, R. (2014). Email correspondence with the authors.
17. Glanville, R. (2014). Audio of keynote presentation at *Relating Systems Thinking and Design 2014*. Available at https://www.youtube.com/watch?v=tTN_9mJIWNw. Accessed 19 Jan 2019.
18. Hughes, T. P. (1998). *Rescuing prometheus*. New York: Vintage Books.
19. Le Corbusier. (1948). *Le modulor.* First published in English in 1954, *Le modulor.* Cambridge, MA: MIT Press.
20. Maturana, H. R. (1997). Metadesign. In J. Brouwer & C. Hoekendijk (Eds.), *Technomorphica* (pp. 171–203). Rotterdam: V2 Organisatie. Available at: http://v2.nl/archive/articles/metadesign. Accessed 19 Jan 2019.
21. Maturana, H. R., & Ximena, D. Y. (2013). Systemic and meta-systemic laws. *Interactions Magazine, 20*(3), 76–79.
22. Meadows, D. H., Meadows, D. L., Randers, J., & Behrens III, W. W. (1972). *The limits to growth: A report for the Club of Rome's project on the predicament of mankind.* New York: New American Library.
23. Meadows, D. H., & Wright, D. (2008). *Thinking in systems: A primer*. White River Junction: Chelsea Green Publishing.
24. Negroponte, N. (1970). *The architecture machine*. Cambridge, MA: MIT Press.
25. Negroponte, N. (1975). *Soft architecture machines.* Cambridge, MA: MIT Press.
26. Pangaro, P. (2016). Questions for conversation theory: Conversation theory in one hour. Presentation to the American Society for Cybernetics Annual Conference, Evergreen College, Olympia, Washington, June 2016. Available at: http://pangaro.com/conversation-theory-in-one-hour.html. Accessed 19 Jan 2019.
27. Pangaro, P. (2016). Designing conversations for socially-conscious design. Opening keynote at RSD5 Systemic Design Conference, Toronto, Oct 2016. Available at: http://pangaro.com/rsd5/index.html. Accessed 19 Jan 2019.
28. Pangaro, P. (2017). Conversation is more than interface. Presentation at Interaction 17 Conference. New York: Interaction Design Association. Available at: http://pangaro.com/ixda2017/index.html. Accessed 19 Jan 2019.
29. Pask, G. (1969). The architectural relevance of cybernetics. *Architectural Design, 7*(6), 494–496.
30. Pask, G. (1969). The meaning of cybernetics in the behavioural sciences. Reprinted in *Proceedings of the First International Congress of Cybernetics* (pp. 15–44). London: Gordon and Breach Science Publishers.
31. Pask, G. (1970). A comment, a case history, and a plan. In J. Reichardt (Ed.), *Cybernetic serendipity* (pp. 76–99). London: Rapp and Carroll. Reprinted in J. Reichardt (Ed.), *Cybernetics, art and ideas* (pp. 76–99). London: Studio Vista.
32. Pask, G. (1975). Aspects of machine intelligence. In N. Negroponte (Ed.), *Soft architecture machines* (pp. 6–31). Cambridge, MA: MIT Press.
33. Pask, G. (1976). *Conversation theory: Applications in education and epistemology.* Amsterdam: Elsevier.

34. Pickering, A. (2010). *The cybernetic brain: Sketches of another future.* Chicago: University of Chicago Press.
35. Pickering, A. (2014). Draft for keynote, the next Macy conference: A new synthesis. Prepared for IEEE Conference *Norbert Wiener in the 21st century, Boston*, June 2014. Shared with the authors.
36. Protzen, J.-P., & Harris, D. J. (2010). *The universe of design: Horst Rittel's theories of design and planning.* London: Routledge.
37. Rittel, H. W. J., & Webber, M. M. (1973). Dilemmas in a general theory of planning. *Policy Sciences, 4*(2), 155–169.
38. Schön, D. (1983). *The reflective practitioner. How professionals think in action.* New York: Basic Books.
39. Simon, H. (1969). *The sciences of the artificial.* Cambridge, MA: The MIT Press.
40. von Foerster, H. (1984). Disorder/order: Discovery or invention? In P. Livingston (Ed.), *Disorder and Order: Proceedings of the Stanford Interaction Symposium* (pp. 177–189). Saratoga, Anima Libri. Reprinted in Heinz von Foerster. (2003). *Understanding understanding: Essays on cybernetics and cognition* (pp. 287–304). New York: Springer.
41. von Foerster, H., et al. (Eds.). (1950–1957). *Cybernetics: Circular causal and feedback mechanisms in biological and social systems: Conference transactions.* New York: Josiah Macy, Jr. Foundation.
42. von Glasersfeld, E. (1995). Radical constructivism: A way of knowing and learning. *Studies in Mathematics Education Series: 6.* London: Falmer Press.
43. Yegge, S. (2011). Yegge's rant. Available at: https://plus.google.com/+RipRowan/posts/eVeouesvaVX. Accessed 19 Jan 2019.

Hugh Dubberly is a software, services, and systems designer; design teacher; and author. Since 2000, he has been a partner in Dubberly Design Office, a San Francisco based consultancy. Much of their practice is focused on systems that support health and wellbeing, for clients such as Alere, Amgen, IBM Watson Health, Johnson & Johnson, Lilly, and Robert Wood Johnson Foundation. At Apple in the late 1980s, he managed graphic design and created a series of technology-forecast films. The first, *Knowledge Navigator*, presaged the internet and interaction via mobile devices. At Netscape, he became Vice President of Design with responsibility for Netscape's web presence. He has taught design courses at San Jose State, Art Center, Carnegie-Mellon, Stanford, and Illinois Institute of Technology. He is currently Professor of Practice at Northeastern, where he teaches Design Theory in the MFA IDV program, and an adjunct at CCA, where he teaches Systems in the MDes IxD program. His research focuses on design methods, its history, modeling, systems, and conversation theory. He edited a column "On Modeling" for the Association of Computing Machinery's journal, *Interactions*. In 2012, he was elected to the CHI Academy.

Paul Pangaro is an educator, entrepreneur, and researcher. He is Professor of Practice at Carnegie Mellon and formerly Associate Professor and Chair, Graduate Program in Interaction Design, College for Creative Studies, Detroit. He has taught systems and cybernetics at School for Visual Arts, New York, and at Stanford University. Pangaro's most recent startup is General Cybernetics, Inc., founded to pioneer "conversations with content." His writing and lectures explicate "designing for conversation" from his research and his implementations of software and organizational processes. Paul holds a B.S. from MIT and a PhD from Brunel, where Gordon Pask was his advisor.

Chapter 5
A Circular 'Smart' World

Delfina Fantini van Ditmar

Abstract In the fast-growing Internet of Things (IoT) industry, algorithmic technology promises 'smart' solutions to everyday problems. Drawing on a design research investigation, this chapter questions and critically examines the embedded epistemology of IoT, in the context of what I call the algorithmic paradigm. This examination reconsiders the prevailing epistemology and offers an alternative based on a second-order cybernetics perspective. This alternative recognises the importance of accounting for the role/agency of the observer/designer/user, the circular causality of user behaviour and technology, and the relationality of 'smartness'. To explore the possibility of a shift in perspective from the current algorithmic paradigm to a second-order one, users are approached as experiential, non-linear subjects rather than as probabilistic and linear ones. Outcomes reveal the value of second-order cybernetics as an epistemological stance and a practical approach to research on the design of 'smart' interactions. The methodological framework demonstrates how design research and second-order considerations can work together, asking novel questions to inform disciplines with an interest in IoT interactions, from both a design perspective (the way designers approach their practice) and in terms of broader implications for society.

Keywords 'Smart' · AI · Home · Determinism · Reductionism · Context

5.1 Introduction

As an outcome of the aspiration to extend *intelligence* into devices over the last few decades, there has been an increasing interest in the design and business of 'smart'

D. Fantini van Ditmar (✉)
Royal College of Art, Kensington Gore, London, UK
e-mail: delfina.fantini@network.rca.ac.uk

T. Fischer, C. M. Herr (eds.), *Design Cybernetics*, Design Research Foundations,
https://doi.org/10.1007/978-3-030-18557-2_5

Fig. 5.1 Family Hub Refrigerator (Samsung RF28K9580SG). The interface for 'smart' functions is often a tablet computer attached to the fridge door. With a diagonal of 21.5 inches, the screen of Samsung's Family Hub Refrigerator is of considerable size. It is already possible to see commercial alliances emerging in the domain of 'smart' fridges. In the US, Samsung's Family Hub Refrigerator is already connected to a Mastercard credit card (Groceries™), which is in turn connected to FreshDirect and ShopRite delivery services (Image source: www.samsung.com)

technology.[1] This is reflected in the growing market for the Internet of Things (IoT).[2] IoT technology refers to everyday objects being identifiable, programmable and connected to the Internet. These connected sensor-based objects can send data without human intervention, connect to other objects and respond to the algorithms that govern them.

IoT objects present a new way of interacting with our environment and our body, where the algorithmic processes play a fundamental role. Examples of this include quantified self-movement (e.g., IoT wristbands dealing with physical activity and sleeping patterns), the motto being "self-knowledge through numbers", and 'smart' devices such as thermostats (e.g., *Nest*) or the 'smart' fridge, which *takes care* of our eating habits and claim that it "connects your family" (see Fig. 5.1).

The IoT market also features 'smart' home hubs, such as 'Mother', intended to link data from multiple devices and provide central control. In the shape of a

[1]Throughout this chapter, I question the use of the word 'smart' as a descriptor of devices. Specifically, I contest the implication that it is a commodity that can be stored in a computer, dismissing its significance as a relational concept (both human and algorithm are responsible for the 'smartness' of the interaction). In order to reinforce and highlight the complexity of the word, I will place 'smart' in quotation marks. I will also distinguish lower and upper case – upper case 'SMART' indicates that I am contesting the word in my research projects.

[2]In statistical terms, *Gartner* [5] has estimated that 25 billion connected 'things' will be in use by 2020, while *Cisco* projected that in 2020, 50 billion objects would be connected [2]. The disparity in the figures does not necessarily reflect a downward revision after a three-year gap; rather, it signifies how quickly the field is emerging and the uncertainty that comes with that speed.

Fig. 5.2 An example of Mother's "smartifying everything" marketing campaign (Image © Sen.se 2017, reprinted with permission)

Russian *matryoshka*, this IoT life-coach is characterised by the tagline "Mother knows everything" and by its brand motto "the meaning of life" (see Fig. 5.2).

In the context of networked devices in the domestic space, the way we behave in our homes is subject to increased monitoring and analysis by various companies. Selling and re-selling personal data is becoming increasingly habitual. Data can be resold to insurance companies, advertisers, 'data brokers' and governments, providing unprecedented views into our daily lives.[3]

Connecting an object to the Internet generates a shift in its behaviour and therefore in our relations toward it. As networked objects can now act without human intervention, another potential issue of IoT is misbehaviour or malfunction.[4] From this angle, another relevant issue is around software 'bugs', which have the potential to cause considerable problems.[5]

---

[3]One consequence of this was highlighted in late 2013 when Google sent a letter to the U.S. Securities and Exchange Commission noting, "we and other companies could [soon] be serving ads and other content on refrigerators, car dashboards, thermostats, glasses and watches, to name just a few possibilities" [11].

[4]One example of a misbehaving object was the case of an IoT 'smart' fridge, which was hacked and began spamming its user with junk mail. Due to the integration of the user's Google Calendar with the 'smart' fridge, hackers accessed the network and monitored activity for the username and password linked to Gmail, due to *Samsung*'s failure to secure the fridge software [21]. Cases like this show that such misbehaviour might have nothing to do with the refrigerator's main function, but is solely related to its connectivity to the Internet. This raises the question: How should the law deal with 'smart' IoT objects in cases of inappropriate decisions, and who (or what) is responsible for such decisions?

[5]An example concerns the *Nest* thermostat: in January 2016 a user reported that several such 'smart' thermostats "suffered from a mysterious software bug that drained its battery and sent our home into a chill in the middle of the night" [1]. In response, *Nest*'s co-founder and vice president for engineering blamed a software update, saying: "we had a bug that was introduced in the software update that didn't show up for about two weeks" (ibid.). According to Bilton [1], "[b]uried deep in Nest's 8,000-word service agreement is a section called 'Disputes and Arbitration,' which prohibits customers from suing the company or joining a class-action suit. Instead, disputes are settled through arbitration." In essence, the company is eschewing legal responsibility even for its own possible misbehaviour.

The impact that the advancement of IoT technologies and its algorithmic logic will have on our lives should not be underestimated; it is forecast that IoT will be the largest device market in the world [12]. While successful IoT outcomes can be seen in industry – due to its advantages in optimisation, efficiency, tracking, productivity, resource management and cost reduction, this doesn't mean that when the IoT market, with its commercial agenda, enters the domain of our behaviour and intimate space, such as in the case of the 'smart' home, these parameters are at any point applicable. The 'smart' home has its own dynamics and brings forward a whole new set of concerns.

As Wajcman [28, p. 130] notes, human complexities impose limits on the mechanisation of lives, and technical visions of domestic life are often advanced at the expense of the home as a living practice. This ambition for certainty and predictability, together with algorithmic oversimplifications, relate to Morozov's [20] concept of 'technological solutionism', defined as the tendency of technologists to define problems based on quick, algorithmic solutions, often resulting in fixing a 'non-problem' as a way of dealing simplistically, and hence quickly, with a complex situation. Consequently, 'smart' technology in our intimate space often comes through as simplistic, unnecessary or overly complicated.

In the framework of algorithmic control when applied to the 'smart' home, the complexity and unpredictability of the user's daily life is replaced with technological/numerical determination.[6] IoT's algorithmic logic and the linear causality projected onto the object's 'smart' behaviour create a dominant directionality, which has several socio political implications for the living practice. In this context, besides the business of companies gathering data on our behaviour and the potential benefits of automation, the craving for control in the context of designing algorithmic operations for our everyday environment and living practice can and should be questioned Tony Fadell (Nest's CEO).

During a panel discussion at the Venice Biennale 2014, Tony Fadell, when asked about the values of the technology, replied: "You are always in control. So these products don't take control away from you. All we're doing is we're learning from your habits. So, we're not imposing anything on anyone. In fact, in most cases we're actually just educating and giving you feedback on what your what your abilities are." [3, 17:12min]. Why the urge for control? Glanville [8, p. 68] identifies "at least two reasons we like to exercise control: Wishing to amplify some power [. . .] and the essential centrality of error in our world."This controlling strategy can be seen in IoT's algorithmic approach towards human living, where the *error* of embodied human experience based on a contextual existence is often disregarded. Consequently, it

[6]The term 'user' will be used to describe the human component in a human-IoT interaction. In this chapter it has no commercial bias; 'user' is interpreted as a complex human instead of a passive consumer. Here, complexity is defined as "the quality of being complex', i.e.,"having many varied interrelated parts, patterns, or elements and consequently hard to understand fully", or "marked by an involvement of many parts, aspects, details, notions, and necessitating earnest study or examination to understand or cope with." See George Klir's definition from Webster's Third International Dictionary in the International Encyclopedia of Systems and Cybernetics [4].

seems relevant to reflect about how human attributes and the contingency of our living practice impose limits on the reductionist and controlling algorithmic logic.

Seeing the rapid growth of IoT products based on applying the ruling algorithmic problem-solving 'smart' logic to the living practice, it seems relevant to discuss and question the underlying epistemological approach. By questioning technological 'smartness' as a design issue, it is possible to examine historically how we arrived at this current technological scenario. In this chapter, I will begin by highlighting the influence Artificial Intelligence (AI) has had on the assumptions made in the process of designing current 'smart' technology interactions. In the following section, I will briefly describe the implications of AI and subsequently argue how reconsidering second-order cybernetics as a subject and a way of designing research offers a significant framework for approaching interaction design in future 'smart' technology. I will do this by describing a design research investigation through a case study of 'smart' home interactions.

5.2 AI

The Artificial Intelligence Group was founded in 1958 by John McCarthy and Marvin Minsky at MIT. McCarthy asserts with regards to AI: "The study is to proceed on the basis of the conjecture that every aspect of learning or any other feature of intelligence can in principle be so precisely described that a machine can be made to simulate it." [19, p. 12]. The field of AI, with its interest in human-like computer 'thought', flourished in the 1960s and held a dominant position between 1960 and 1985 [22]. Cognitive science and AI have a tendency to approach the brain and the computer in terms of each other. Cognitive science is an interdisciplinary research field characterised by the understanding of the mind as having comprehensible cognitive processes, in which intelligence and behaviour can be modelled and replicated[7].

Suchman [24, p. 9] notes that in cognitive science and its affiliated disciplines, it is common to find agreement "that cognition is not just potentially *like* computation, it literally *is* computational".[8] According to Pangaro [22], this approach presupposes that knowledge is a commodity that can be stored in a machine, and that consequently for AI, the application of such stored knowledge to the real world constitutes *intelligence*. The technology evolved from the late 1960s, and small 'smart' objects not only began to monitor variables such as room temperature but also began to operate in the domain of our behaviour. Nowadays, IoT devices incorporate a vast

[7]For further discussions of embodiment and the limitations of a cognitivist approach, see, e.g., Maturana [16–18] and Varela [26].

[8]Certainly, there are exceptions. But this is the general trend in the fields of computer and cognitive science, and AI technology.

range of sensors with increased precision; here data is extracted and recombined with large-scale statistical databases.

Regarding the algorithmic decision-making process, there are several strategies for predicting how an individual and its environment will behave; such is the case of machine learning and big data. By using these procedures, 'smart' devices have the potential to make assumptions, judgements, automated decisions and suggestions. Rouvroy [23, p. 2] describes current algorithmic logic as based on infra-individual data and supra-individual patterns, stating that, at any moment, the algorithmic processes call the subject to account for himself.[9]

One consequence of using such AI approaches in digital devices is the reinforcement of an understanding of humans as linear and 'probabilistic beings', which then gets embedded in current commercialised IoT outcomes. This translation into the retail world is reflected in how data is managed by algorithms designed with particular criteria and assumptions derived from a specific idea of 'smartness', which is then applied to our daily interactions. In the context of users interacting with IoT devices in the 'smart' home as a result of AI embedded ideas, I speak of this scenario in conceptual terms as the algorithmic paradigm.[10]

The main difference with the prior technological paradigm is that the previous one was characterised as detached: it was not 'real time'; the speed of the analysis of data was substantially slower and it was delimited, i.e., it had locational limits. It was not 24/7, it was not ubiquitous and, consequently, it did not operate in the domain of behaviour. The algorithmic paradigm is characterised by vastly larger data centres and much greater computational power.

These technological advances came together with the availability of the data in cloud computing technology (i.e., the ubiquity of access to computation). All this then had implications for the quantitative capabilities of trained learning algorithms.

---

[9]Rouvroy [23, p. 11] refers to infra-individual in the algorithmic processes as the digital traces that are extracted below the level of the human, characterising it as "impersonal, disparate, heterogeneous, dividualized facets of daily life and interactions". Supra-individual indicates the idea that data is analysed above the level of the human, as is the case in big data aggregation.

[10]I consider this to be a *paradigm*. Following the use of the term by Kuhn [15], this algorithmic approach within the development of IoT and 'smart' home technology seems to be largely a 'model of reality' for its designers and developers, constituting a scope for what phenomena should be paid attention to and monitored, what questions are considered important to address, and, from an epistemological perspective, what it means to 'know' about reality.

The algorithmic paradigm is distinguished by:

- Representation and modelling of data gathered by the device about a user's daily life, surroundings and body (domain of behaviour).
- Aggregation: The decision making process often includes big data and machine learning strategies to inform the development of predictive algorithms, using advanced analytics to predict probabilistically how an individual is expected to behave in the future.
- Automation in real time: The algorithms have the capacity to control the environment and the potential to change their procedures without informing the user.

Not only does the logic of the algorithmic paradigm have operational repercussions, it also has behavioural implications by being translated into the language that characterises the technological industry. IoT is marked by a discourse that promises that the 'smart' device *knows us, understands us* and *predicts us*. Some products even claim to be *conscious* or, in the case of the *Nest* thermostat, *thoughtful*.

In this 'smart' scenario, algorithms are *learning* more and becoming faster. But what and how are they *learning*? How is the impossibility of translating human life into the machine's 'smartness' being embraced? This is in no way inconsequential. With this in mind, I would like to point out the relevance of second-order cybernetics, a movement that emerged around 1968 from the 'cybernetics movement', which can be traced back to the Macy Conferences (1946–1953) of more than a decade before the emergence of AI.[11] Here, I will illustrate how reconsidering second-order cybernetics principles provides opportunities to rethink 'smart' interactions and will demonstrate their implications for design research in the context of the design of IoT 'smart' interactions.

5.3 Second-Order Cybernetics

In second-order cybernetics, according to Glanville [9, pp. 175, 177], "the role of the observer is appreciated and acknowledged rather than disguised [. . .]. The aim of attaining traditional objectivity is either abandoned/passed over, or what objectivity is and how we might obtain (and value) it is reconsidered."[12] As a result, as Glanville [9,

[11]The relationship between cybernetics and AI is further discussed in Sect. 1.4 in this volume.

[12]The observer in second-order cybernetics refers to the active presence of the provider of the information. Glanville notes that "Second order cybernetics considers (rather than ignores) the observer, studying observing as opposed to observed systems, insisting the observer takes center stage" [9, p. 201]. He goes on: "The observer contributes and, since it is impossible to access what we observe without being an observer, that which is observed is unclear. Is there an object in an external reality? If so, what can we know of it, since our knowing always depends on us, and we can never subtract our presence?"

p. 3] notes, every observation where the indispensable presence of the observer doing the observing is established is autobiographical. With the introduction of the above second-order concepts comes the relevance of acknowledging the observer and its contextualised observations when reflecting upon the idea of personal data gathered and managed by algorithms. In this way, second-order cybernetics principles also make us reflect on how 'smart' interactions could be reframed when thinking in a circular manner.

5.4 Designing Through Second-Order Cybernetics

Along with the theoretical reconsideration of second-order cybernetics come its connection to design, and its implications for design research (for an overview, see Glanville [6, 7, 13, 14]). According to Glanville, "[d]esign is the key to research. Research has to be designed". In the context of research, design is hence best acknowledged "as a way of understanding, acting, looking, and searching" [6, p. 90].

By considering design research as a process that draws attention to the observer and the development not only of objects but also processes, design has the potential to generate novelty and assimilate and accommodate complexity [7, p. 65]. In this sense, design research can be seen as a valuable approach to consider when examining current matters such as designing 'smart' interactions. This is particularly relevant to the design field of 'smart' interactions; as Sweeting [25] states, design research is often concerned with epistemological questions regarding the interrelations of designers, other stakeholders, working methods and the knowledge embedded in what is designed.

With this background, through the development of an design research epistemological journey based on second-order cybernetic principles, I will illustrate how the design research process has the potential to reveal relevant technological issues and propose an alternative way of approaching 'smartness'. To investigate issues of current algorithmic visions of IoT technology, I used as a case study the design of the 'smart' fridge, an IoT device that is related to central human activities.[13]

[13]I consider 'central human activities' as a range of actions (behaviours) which embrace biological activities (e.g., sleeping, eating, physical activities) and which are also related to more ineffable psychological activities such as feeling, motivating, caring, and so on. Perhaps more than anything else, eating habits are illustrative of the complexity and unpredictability of human life, connected as they are to human psychology, personality, culture, budget, the present and history. It is therefore a pertinent subject for reflection on the (possible) issues inherent in the 'smart' home.

5.5 'SMART' Fridge Session (SFS)

To examine the way in which human complexity is translated into an algorithmic logic, during the case study I created a series of active real-time interactions of participants (reflective observers). Through a series of dialogues with a 'smart' device, I was able to observe possible issues emerging from an *intelligent* conversation with an IoT device.

For this, I developed a series of 'SMART' fridge-user interactions which allowed me to analyse the possible issues in embracing human complexity and subjectivity within the algorithms behind the IoT. The interaction consisted of a public engagement event where the 'smart' fridge-user conversation was projected onto a screen so that a broader audience could follow the dialogue.[14] Here the user was instructed to speak with a 'SMART' fridge that formed part of their connected home. So that the user in the project felt embedded in the 'SMART' world, the interactions with the 'SMART' fridge took place through *iMessage*, on an *iPhone*.

In order to investigate the epistemological issues, I developed a dialogue research protocol using two tools which formed the basis for the two sub-projects: *Scripted Dialogues* and *Assigned Roles*. The first, *Scripted Dialogues*, was an interaction between a script that I developed (preset texts) based on a second-order approach and a participant (user). The second, *Assigned Roles* tested the idea of non-neutral aspects of algorithms by assigning roles to participants: one to enact the role of the AI in a 'SMART' fridge, and the other to play the role of the user (see Fig. 5.3).

In the *Scripted Dialogues*, I was interested in exploring the possibility of a shift in perspective from the current algorithmic paradigm to a second-order cybernetics approach, where the user is considered an experiential, non-linear subject rather than a probabilistic and linear one.

In this project I experimented with the script using the following second-order cybernetics concepts: (1) The acknowledgement of human subjectivity (the observer and its observation taken into account); (2) The importance of considering the impact of lived experiences in the present (not as a mathematical accumulation of past history); (3) A systemic understanding; (4) Insights that can only be achieved through conversation; (5) Feedback on the performance of the system itself; (6) Statistical transparency; and, (7) The idea of the user shaping the system.

The idea was that the user was not seen as a mere consumer who receives normative outcomes, but as a subject capable of reflecting on his/her data. With this in mind, I experimented with the creation of a script by considering the user as a reflective observer. I thus avoided the normative and prescriptive strategies that characterise current technology.

During the process of designing the script, I dealt with the following questions: How could I avoid telling the users what to do? How could I possibly make users

[14]The 'SMART' Fridge session was part of 'Off The Wall'; an exhibition held between September 18th and 20th 2015, staged aboard HQS Wellington, a 1933 former military ship moored on the River Thames.

Fig. 5.3 Participants chatting during the interaction at the 'SMART' Fridge Session. London: HQS Wellington, 18th to 20th September 2015

reflect on their data? How could I help users understand the implications of their actions in relation to health, sleeping and fitness, without being normative? How, with all these attempts, could I avoid giving this information to the machine and not have it treated and fed back with the same machine logic I was trying to question?

Even by providing an alternative to normative, linear-causal interaction, the problems of grasping the richness of individual behaviours became evident. An example of the challenge of understanding the particularities of individual behaviour/thinking can be seen in the case of the script's first question: How do you feel today? One participant took this to refer to their particular physical situation (the *'SMART' Fridge Session* taking place on a ship), replying "not fine, I don't like being in a boat". A second participant replied stating her needs ("hungry"), while another replied by applying a metaphor ("sunny").

Through the *Assigned Roles*, I decided to explore the possible issues in capturing subjectivity and the 'non-neutral' aspect of the algorithmic issues in IoT by allowing some participants to play out fictitious roles, and others to embody their everyday professions (see Table 5.1).

People were asked to imagine that they were embedded in the AI of the 'SMART' fridge. I choose several mother roles since mothers take care of our nutrition and influence many of our eating choices later in life (this influence is reflected literally in some current IoT products, e.g., the Mother smart hub). I assigned other roles, such as fashion diva, an authoritarian general, and a mafia Godfather, to test diverse patronising attitudes. I also chose a schizophrenic role to test the possibility of inconsistencies in responses.

Table 5.1 *'SMART' Fridge Session* roles

Professionals playing themselves	Fictitious roles
Interaction designer	Chinese mother
Nutritionist	Italian mother
Programmer/Start-Up CEO	Jewish mother
Banker	Korean mother
Scriptwriter	British mother
User experience designer	The Godfather
	French fashion designer 'diva'
	Authoritarian general
	Coach
	Personal trainer
	Schizophrenic fridge
	Open session

Due to the connection of fridges to health and fitness, I created the roles of a coach and personal trainer. To make this interaction as realistic as possible, in the case of the mother roles (as well as the French diva and the authoritarian general), the actors were participants from those particular cultures. In the case of the professional roles, I involved professionals who will potentially participate in the design of future IoT appliances, including an interaction designer, nutritionist, programmer, banker, and user experience researcher. I also decided to invite a scriptwriter to test storytelling in the interaction.

In order for the 'SMART' fridges to get to know their (oversimplified) users and have material on which to comment, I provided several items from the supermarket (e.g., champagne, broccoli, beer, tortellini, pizza, almond milk, etc.). The users had to select two items each that they usually have in their fridge; this gave the fridge (minimum) information to use during the interaction. Then, the user and the 'SMART' fridge had the opportunity to reflect on what this 'smart' interaction could possibly mean. Through the interaction, it was possible to see how each participant applied a completely different strategy for getting information and keeping the interaction going.

In the *Assigned Roles* I analysed the material through Thematic Analysis; in a second-order manner, I chose the dialogues as the unit of analysis. Through this method, in which the observer was acknowledged, I obtained relevant qualitative data from the dialogues that emerged in the interaction. The main themes that I distinguished were:

i. Control, Power, and 'the 'SMART' limit': In the context of negotiating the power of the machine vis-à-vis the ownership of the appliance, both argued, "I know what I am doing". The 'SMART' fridge claimed that it knew what was better for the user. The user claimed that, as the owner of the appliance, he/she was in control of their own life, making it clear that technology should be subordinate to the user.

Another theme that emerged was the question: at what point is it acceptable for the machine to make judgements and comments about the life and behaviour of the user? As a result of this scenario, it was possible to observe how IoT technology allows us to control our environment; at the same time, it shows how users 'hand over' control to the algorithms behind the technology. These findings reinforce the importance of developing alternative epistemological approaches for future 'smart' technology.[15] Here is an example of an interaction on the location of control:

SF: I know what's best for you.
U: I don't want to need you, I want to buy my own food and choose what I want to eat.

ii. Understanding the 'SMART' world in practice: Communication and the 'SMART' world characterisation.

   a. Communication: In the interaction it was possible to foresee the potential problems which this active machine-user relation could bring, especially when it relates to our own personal metrics (quantified self) or to the home ('smart' home). This was seen on two levels: when the user doesn't expect a particular response or prompt to come from a machine (human-machine relation) and when the 'SMART' fridge uses phrases that don't necessarily relate to the user (language). An issue that emerged from the dialogues was 'figuring out meaning', and the likelihood that the user would reply using metaphors. There were nationality implications based on language and behaviour that showed the personification of a cultural mindset in the machine's responses. The dialogues also revealed that the meaning of a meal goes beyond the food itself; there is an emotional and historical background that can't be reduced to data and suggestions. Here is an example of a communication problem:

   SF: There is nothing wrong with me just caring for your well-being. You can only restore my settings through my input and I won't allow you to do it.
   U: I am going to replace you with an American fridge that won't complain about junk food.

   b. 'SMART' world characterisation: The series of dialogues are an example of people in different roles trying to understand how the 'SMART' world works. Through the interactions it was possible to see how the 'SMART' appliance situates itself with its new technical capabilities. In several dialogues it was possible to see that the users expected the 'SMART' fridge to take care of their lives by using its 'smartness'.

   Another important subject was the allocation of responsibility when outsourcing crucial aspects of our lives to a machine and the issues related to abandoning human agency by relying on a machine. In some cases, the

[15]In the following dialogues, SF refers to 'SMART' Fridge and U refers to user.

user implied that the fridge couldn't be right purely on the basis of it being a 'SMART' fridge with machine credentials and *intelligence*. However, at times the user assumed that the fridge was the one in charge of managing that aspect by asking, "what are you if you are not 'SMART' enough to figure out what I need?" Conversely, the 'SMART' fridge also blamed the user, as if he/she was responsible for ordering products or communicating relevant information. At this point, the issue of transparency of statistical outcomes embedded in suggestions emerged through the conversations. Here are examples of conflicting views on responsibilities:

U: I am hungry, what is there to eat?
SF: There are no vegetables available. You don't eat enough vegetables.
U: Why didn't you order more vegetables, fridge?

SF: We have run out of dessert so I won't give you any.
U: Food is your 'thing', not mine.
SF: Can you buy something healthier next time?

iii. Commercial issues: This aspect of IoT emerged particularly from the real roles, specifically in the case of the programmer and the banker. Both of them incorporated the idea of a commercial food partner being present. The programmer tried to negotiate with payment the destination of the user's data (e.g., the programmer showed the user that, if she paid £5 instead of £30, a commercial partner might be able to re-sell her data). The banker tried to offer more options by pushing additional products, reminding the user of expiry dates, and by bringing commercial 'partners' into the conversation. Also in relation to commercial issues, different approaches to framing the problem emerged as an alternative to the "user-consumer" perspective, as characterised in the programmer and banker dialogues. In contrast to the user-consumer perspective, other roles, such as 'the scriptwriter', embraced the idea of sharing, i.e., the fridge being helpful by not only focusing on consumption, but by also showing empathy to the user and finding non-commercial strategies based on the idea of a community of users. The scriptwriter made the user think about the context (with whom does he live in the house and what are they like) and analyse the narrative of sourced food that he consumes. In this case there was an understanding of the person's situation and resources, which offered an alternative for solving the problem (by buying 'efficient' goods). Here an example of a non-commercial strategy:

SF: Do you live with other people?
U: Yes, one flat mate
SF: Should we think about ways of you both saving time and money? We could do a shared shopping list.

iv. Complexity and variety in people's lives: Our lives are unpredictable and complex, with many systemic implications. As non-linear humans, our psychology, personality, context and history continuously come into play. If on top of this we add the complexity of diet itself (our budget, history and situated context) and embrace the idea that eating is not about optimisation or efficiency, it becomes important to question the reliance on a linear algorithmic approach to manage the complexity and variety of people's lives. Here is an example with an added level of complexity:

SF: What if you slept more?
U: I'd be happier but less interesting.
SF: Can you find a way to manage that? How?
U: I am unbalanced. Nothing is finished. All relationships are pending and unsettled, and I am a neurotic. I don't know how to solve it, can you?

5.6 Reflections

The design research findings provide evidence that the current epistemological stance derived from AI, i.e., the reductionist approach of the algorithmic paradigm embedded in IoT products, presents several problems: the fact that there is an epistemological stance embedded affects people's interactions with the technology, and the specific set of values and way of seeing the world have repercussions in the automation of and communication with the 'smart' system ('smartness' is neither objective nor neutral). Consequently, it seems relevant to rethink the design of 'smart' interactions by reconsidering its epistemological approach.

The investigations highlight issues with the apparently objective algorithmic problem-framing logic behind the 'smart' objects when employing data in a deterministic manner that are isolated from the individuality and subjectivity of the user's behaviour in daily life.[16] This leads not only to a different set of questions, but also to a different way of framing the problem. When 'intelligence' is applied to the technological industry of 'smart' devices, we are reminded of Glanville's reflection when asking Juvenal's question: "who will guard the guard?" or in Glanville's words: "who will control the controller?"; as he then notes, "this is not a question that can be long left unasked: to do so would be a matter of both inconsistency and laziness" [8, p. 66]. By bringing the observer and circularity into the discussion, it became clear that the user should be given responsibility for making sense of his or her own data. Across the dialogues of the *'SMART' Fridge Session*, it was also possible to see how the algorithmic paradigm, which includes big data and machine learning strategies, fails dramatically to capture human diversity and the nuances of our living practice.

[16]It is important to emphasise again that there are risks inherent in providing our personal data to algorithms that have been developed with the strategies of AI machine learning, particularly when this personal data can be sold to companies, commercialised and politicised (e.g., NSA/GCHQ surveillance, *Cambridge Analytica*/*Facebook*'s political influence and *Google*'s perceived omniscience).

The awareness of the differences between AI and second-order cybernetics allowed me to consider the latter as an alternative epistemology for an approach to IoT design. In contrast with the deterministic AI approach, a second-order perspective suggests that, as reflective and contextual humans, our capacities and understanding are still needed and desired. The study demonstrates how design research and second-order cybernetics can be brought together to question 'smart' interactions and to rethink the implications of 'smartifying' our life through algorithmic logic. By valuing the presence (the incorporation) of the observer's observing and by considering that meaning is constructed (it is not available in a world of data-references), a second-order epistemology leads to the acknowledgement of the limitations of 'smart' machines – the 'smart' device is ignorant about the personal aspects of users and the contingencies of their lives. The implications of relying on de-contextualised data in the design of 'smartness' is related to von Foerster's ethical concern with respect to acknowledging the observer: "With the essence of observing [. . .] having been removed, the observer is reduced to a copying machine with the notion of responsibility successfully juggled away." [27, p. 293]. Accordingly, this suggests the importance of rethinking the relevance of the active presence of the user perspective (i.e., the observer) in the equation of the 'smartness' of IoT interactions that engage with humans and their living practice.

While there are several studies in the area of user perspective/experience in the field of human-computer interaction (HCI), together with the growing field of human-centred design (HCD), the contribution of this design research investigation was to bring a second-order perspective to the user and the user's interaction with 'smart' systems rather than to bring a user perspective into the current AI framework.

Since algorithms model the environment to offer 'smart' *solutions*, it is extremely important to be critical and think about the limits and issues of the algorithmic logic in our lives. As the research suggests, it requires a rethinking of the whole system and its embedded epistemology. In addition to the intrinsic algorithmic socio-political issues, these considerations are not included in the development of machine learning, big data or natural language programming. This will not be achieved by continuing the development of 'smart' products in an AI 'smart' fashion, a new perspective is needed. A second-order perspective has the potential to bring novel ways of asking questions that inform the various disciplines shaping the technology, in terms of the conceptual stage of framing IoT technology as well as the broader societal repercussions.

References

1. Bilton, N. (2016). Nest thermostat glitch leaves users in the cold. In *The New York Times*, 14 Jan 2016. Available at: http://www.nytimes.com/2016/01/14/fashion/nest-thermostat-glitch-battery-dies-software-freeze.html. Accessed 19 Jan 2019.
2. Evans, D. (2011). The Internet of Things: How the next evolution of the Internet is changing everything. *Cisco Internet Business Solutions Group (IBSG)*, Apr 2011. Available at: https://www.cisco.com/web/about/ac79/docs/innov/IoT_IBSG_0411FINAL.pdf. Accessed 19 Jan 2019.

3. Fadell, T., & Koolhaas, R. (2014). Elements of architecture, 5000 years of architecture... and now what? Architecture and technology? Interview at the Venice Biennale 2014 – Conversazioni/Talks (Architecture and Technology). Venice Biennale. Available at: https://www.youtube.com/watch?v=dxqFqbAp2Fo. Accessed 19 Jan 2019.
4. François, C. (2004). *International encyclopedia of systems and cybernetics*. Munich: K. G. Saur Verlag.
5. Gartner. (2014). Gartner says 4.9 Billion connected things will be in use in 2015. Press release, 11 Nov 2014. Available at: https://www.gartner.com/en/newsroom/press-releases/2014-11-11-gartner-says-nearly-5-billion-connected-things-will-be-in-use-in-2015. Accessed 19 Jan 2019.
6. Glanville, R. (1999). Researching design and designing research. *Design Issues, 15*(2), 80–91.
7. Glanville, R. (2006). Construction and design. *Constructivist Foundations, 1*(3), 103–110.
8. Glanville, R. (2009). *The black boox vol. III. 39 steps*. Vienna: edition echoraum.
9. Glanville, R. (2012). Second order cybernetics. *The black boox – Vol. I. Cybernetic circles* (pp. 175–207). Vienna: edition echoraum. Previously published In F. Parra-Luna (Ed.), *Encyclopedia of life support systems, systems science and cybernetics – Vol. III*. Oxford: EoLSS Publishers. Available at: http://www.eolss.net/sample-chapters/c02/e6-46-03-03.pdf. Accessed 19 Jan 2019.
10. Glanville, R. (2014). Why design research? In *The black boox, volume II: Living in cybernetic circles* (pp. 111–120). Vienna: edition echoraum.
11. Goodman, M. (2015). Hacked dog, a car that snoops on you and a fridge full of adverts: The perils of the Internet of Things. *The Guardian*, 11 Mar 2015. Available at: http://www.theguardian.com/technology/2015/mar/11/internet-of-things-hacked-online-perils-future. Accessed 19 Jan 2019.
12. Greenough, J. (2014). The 'Internet of Things' will be the world's most massive device market and save companies billions of dollars. *Business Insider*, 18 Nov 2104. Available at: http://uk.businessinsider.com/how-the-internet-of-things-market-will-grow-2014-10. Accessed 19 Jan 2019.
13. Jonas, W. (2007). Research through design through research: A cybernetic model of designing design foundations. *Kybernetes, 36*(9/10), 1362–1380.
14. Jonas, W. (2015). Research through design is more than just a new form of disseminating design outcomes. *Constructivist Foundations, 11*(1), 32–36.
15. Kuhn, T. S. (1962). *The structure of scientific revolution.* Chicago: University of Chicago Press.
16. Maturana, H. R. (1972). Biology of cognition. In H. R. Maturana & F. J. Varela (Eds.), 1980. *Autopoiesis and cognition: The realization of the living*. Dordrecht: D. Reidel Publishing.
17. Maturana, H. R. (1997). Metadesign: Human beings versus machines, or machines as instruments of human designs? Santiago: Instituto Terapia Cognitiva (INTECO). Available at: http://www.digitalcultures.org/Library/Maturana_Metadesign.pdf. Accessed 19 Jan 2019.
18. Maturana, H. R., & Varela, F. J. (1992). *The tree of knowledge: The biological roots of human understanding* (rev. ed.). Boston: Shambala.
19. McCarthy, J., Minsky, M. L., Rochester, N., & Shannon, C. E. (2006). A proposal for the Dartmouth summer research project on Artificial Intelligence, 31 Aug 1955. *AI Magazine, 27*(4), 12–14.
20. Morozov, E. (2013). *To save everything press here: Technology, solutionism and the urge to solve problems that don't exist.* London: Allen Lane.
21. Neagle, C. (2015). Smart refrigerator hack exposes Gmail login credentials. Network World, 26 Aug 2015. Available at: https://www.networkworld.com/article/2976270/smart-refrigerator-hack-exposes-gmail-login-credentials.html. Accessed 23 May 2019.
22. Pangaro, P. (2013). "Getting started" guide to cybernetics. Available at: http://www.pangaro.com/definition-cybernetics.html. Accessed 19 Jan 2019.
23. Rouvroy, A. (2012). The end(s) of critique: Data-behaviourism vs. due-process. Pre-publication version of chapter published In M. Hildebrandt & K. de Vries (Eds.), *Privacy, due process and the computational turn. The philosophy of law meets the philosophy of technology*. New York: Routledge.

24. Suchman, L. (1987). *Plans and situated actions: The problem of human-machine communication*. New York: Cambridge University Press.
25. Sweeting, B. (2016). Design research as a variety of second-order cybernetic practice. *Constructivist Foundations, 11*(3), 572–579.
26. Varela, F. J. (1992). Whence perceptual meaning? A cartography of current ideas. In F. J. Varela & J.-P. Dupuy (Eds.), *Understanding origins: Contemporary views on the origins of life, mind and society* (pp. 235–263). Boston: Kluwer Academic.
27. Von Foerster, H. (2003). *Understanding understanding. Essays on cybernetics and cognition.* New York: Springer.
28. Wajcman, J. (2015). *Pressed for time: The acceleration of life in digital capitalism.* Chicago: University of Chicago Press.

Delfina Fantini van Ditmar, a Tutor and researcher at the Design Products Programme at the Royal College of Art, completed her PhD at the Royal College of Art in Innovation Design Engineering under the supervision of Ranulph Glanville up to his death in 2014. She holds a BA in Biology and accomplished a year of a MFA at Konstfack University in Stockholm. Delfina was awarded the 2011 Heinz von Foerster Award by the American Society for Cybernetics. The incursion with the field of Cybernetics led to her PhD research, and to the thesis entitled The IdIoT. The thesis focuses on questioning and critically analysing the embedded epistemology of Internet of Things (IoT) in the context of the 'smart' home. Her research outcomes highlight the importance of developing a critical approach towards the algorithmic dynamics of our surrounding.

Chapter 6
The Cybernetics of Design and the Design of Cybernetics

Klaus Krippendorff

Abstract This book chapter reciprocally connects cybernetics and design, and contrasts both with what the sciences do. Whereas the sciences aim at understanding, explaining, and theorizing observations, design proposes courses of actions that lead into desirable but currently unobservable futures. Its first section teases out cybernetic epistemologies that constructively embrace the practices of design. Its second section applies cybernetics to the emergence of artifacts in interactions between living organisms and their environments. It grounds cybernetic epistemology in the evolution of sensory-motor coordinations, not of objects. Its third section develops the cybernetics of human-centered design. It suggests that designers cannot escape being part of the very social world into which they intervene. This reflexivity was already evident in the creative conversations in which cybernetics emerged. It is also practiced in design teams. Recognizing designs as proposals means that they have to energize and inform multidisciplinary networks of stakeholders which decide the fate of any design. This section generalizes the concept of user interfaces and acknowledges that designers can at best design affordances for interfaces to emerge, in effect calling for designers to delegate designs to their stakeholders. Its final section turns the cybernetics of design into the design of cybernetics. It draws on the historical shift from a cybernetics of self-organizing systems to a cybernetics of cybernetics, which regards cybernetics as a discourse that brings forth self-governing practices of communication. It concludes that cyberneticians actively shape their discourse, not let it determine what they do.

Editors' note: This chapter is a substantially updated revision of a paper by the same title previously published in *Kybernetes*, 36(9/10):1381–1392.

K. Krippendorff (✉)
The Annenberg School for Communication, University of Pennsylvania, Philadelphia, PA, USA
e-mail: klaus.krippendorff@asc.upenn.edu

T. Fischer, C. M. Herr (eds.), *Design Cybernetics*, Design Research Foundations,
https://doi.org/10.1007/978-3-030-18557-2_6

Keywords Cybernetic/scientific epistemology · Self-organization · Artifacts/observation · Human-centeredness/objectivity · Design ethics · Problem solving/declaring · Possibilities · Delegation of design · Discourse · Stakeholders · Interdisciplinarity

6.1 Cybernetics in the Dialectic Between Science and Design

The mathematician Norbert Wiener [32] coined the word cybernetics, generalizing his work on purposive mechanisms near the end of World War II. At that time several new technologies emerged that seemed to be complex, adaptive, autonomous, and shared a circular form of organization. In retrospect, such forms had a scarce but long history. As early as 400 BC, Heron of Alexandria noted a peculiar mechanism that kept the flame of oil lamps stable. A structurally similar mechanism appeared in James Watt's steam engine, which literally fuelled the industrial revolution. Watt's regulator kept the RPMs of the steam engine stable under varying loads. When Wiener made his proposal, servomechanisms in industry, target-seeking missiles in the military, and problems of coordinating the war effort, not to forget the emerging use of mainframe computers, demanded new vocabularies to understand them. Wiener taught at MIT, a university dedicated to advancing technology. With the enlightenment project still in charge of academia at the time, it was not surprising that Wiener defined cybernetics as a science, the science of control and communication.

All sciences of the enlightenment define their objects of attention with the aim of developing theories and laws that explain them – excluding the inquiring scientist from these explanations. Cybernetics was born during the 1946–1953 Josiah Macy Jr, Foundation conferences on circular causal feedback mechanisms, later renamed on cybernetics. It brought the most cutting edge scientists from various disciplines together to explore the implications of circular causality. The components of mechanisms exhibiting such circularities affect themselves, directly or indirectly, causing the whole system of which they are a part to be to some extent autonomous and self-organizing. Theorizing such systems offered insights in phenomena previously little understood. Participants in this conference found circular causalities in nature, in living organisms, and in society and the exploration of their implications began to challenge numerous orthodoxies of science. However, because mathematics was the preferred way of theorizing such systems, engineers were the first to embrace the proposed science of cybernetics and developed a range of entirely new technologies. Thus, cybernetics gave birth to computation, digitalization, networks, and large systems, all of which we now take for granted.

Inasmuch as design and cybernetics are the focus of this book, it is important to highlight the differences between what scientists cherish and what designers actually do, followed by how cybernetics straddled between them.

- Whereas scientists intend to describe as accurately as possible what was observable, that is, what is known to exists at the time of scientific attention, designers propose something new, something unprecedented, hence not yet observable.

- Whereas scientists celebrate generalizations, abstract theories for example, what designers propose can become real only when working in all of their details, not in the abstract.
- Whereas scientists search for causal explanations of the observable nature, distancing themselves as the causes of the phenomena they explore, designers aim at changing something that could not possibly be explained as resulting from natural causes. The directions that design is taking defies causal explanations.
- Whereas scientists claim to seek knowledge for its own sake, epitomized in value-free theories of the observable universe, designers seek to solve problems or realize better futures. The knowledge that informs design is value-laden.
- Whereas scientific research is re-search, i.e., the repeated and systematic search for generalizable patterns in presently available data, designers inquire about possibilities of realizing something not yet known but worthwhile to live with.
- Whereas scientist assume the position of external observers, spectators and theorists of what has happened, presently exists, and is expected to continue into the future without human intervention, designers assume the position of change agents who seek to retire burdensome presences for more desirable futures.

These contrasts are already telling. Even more troubling is the dominant celebration of the know-what-is knowledge of science as superior to the know-how of professional practices. It relegates designers, engineers, managers, politicians, and teachers, as mere consumers of scientific knowledge. For example, engineering is characterized as merely applying the laws of physics, creating technologies but no new knowledge.

Herbert Simon [23] sought to overcome the disparity of pure versus applied science by proposing a science of the artificial. Unfortunately, his proposal did not go far enough. He defined design as deciding among courses of action to improve systems, and placed problem solving into the center of his project, which limits his science of the artificial to making rational decisions among alternative solutions to presently existing problems.

My conception of design is not limited to improving existing technologies or solving problems by presently established criteria. It includes the proposition of novel practices, startup enterprises, policies, and institutions that are driven by visions of desirable futures, not necessarily informed by presently recognized problems. One of the more daunting aims of design is to make communities aware of being entrapped in conventional constructions and unable to see what is possible. To me design needs to propose ways of escaping conditions of confinement in unworkable conditions, oppression, dictatorships and ideologies [22, 25].

Coming back to cybernetics, W. Ross Ashby adopted a definition of cybernetics that deviated sharply from the enlightenment conception of science. It went beyond the widely shared commitment of cybernetics to attend to the circularities in self-organizing systems by defining:

> Cybernetics as the study of all possible systems (open to energy but closed to information), which is informed (constrained) by what cannot be made, found in nature, or will not survive in interactions with their experimenters [1, p. 2, slightly restated].

He thus placed cybernetics in the circularity of imagining possible systems, designing or realizing some of them, actively exploring what they would do, and experiencing constraints of what cannot be realized. It also routed cybernetics in the notion of information as a constraint on conceivable possibilities, uncertainty reduction if you wish, which has always been at the heart of design.

Much of Ashby's work can be described as an exploration of the epistemological differences between synthesis and observation, between what can be learned from designing systems and what can be learned by observing or using them without knowing their internal structures. He conceptualized the latter as "black boxes," developed a methodology of studying black boxes, and applied it to cognition, the stock market, and other complex systems that one cannot open (like a working brain) or may not want to experiment with (like an economy).

Gregory Bateson [2, pp. 405–416] linked Ashby's "negative explanations" (the acknowledgement of constraints on what can be built or interacted with) to Darwin's theory of evolution (one may not have trouble explaining why a species arrived at its present state, but is unable to predict the evolutionary path it will be taking) but on the level of epistemology. Ashby's cybernetic epistemology encouraged exploring alternative conceptions of any one system as long as interacting with it stayed within the limits of what its environment could afford. Ashby was very deliberate in his own use of language but, unlike Bateson, he was not concerned with social systems involving actors who spoke a language in terms of which they defined their identities, communicated with each other, and created their own social worlds.

The missing attention to language was provided by the anthropologist Margaret Mead. In her remarkable keynote to the 1967 annual conference of the American Society for Cybernetics in Gaithersburg, Maryland, she drew on her experience as an active participant in the above-mentioned Macy Foundation Conferences. She deviated from celebrating Wiener's mathematical abstractions and attention to purposive systems (as stipulated in the conference by this title), by recalling what gave birth to cybernetics. She defined:

> Cybernetics as a language that enables communication across disciplinary specializations and can address complex problems of circular communication that neither discipline can handle on its own [16, p. 2, slightly restated].

Moreover, she observed, much before others realized, that the increased use of the language of cybernetics introduced algorithms in the social, economic, and political segments of society, whose complex implications escaped current ways of understanding them and could endanger how we come to live together. She urged cyberneticians to assume responsibilities for what the use of their language was doing and called for a shift from the cybernetics of machines (à la Wiener) to a:

> Cybernetics of cybernetics, a cybernetics that calls on its practitioners to apply cybernetic principles to the consequences of using cybernetic language in the very society of which they are a part [16, pp. 4–5, summarized].

This was and still is a revolutionary proposal. It acknowledged the importance of language, conversation, or discourse in creating both, cybernetics as a way of talking across disciplines and the complex social realities that resulted from the spread of the cybernetic discourse, in need of cross-disciplinary attention.

Six years later, at a conference I organized, Heinz von Foerster proposed the notion of a "second-order cybernetics." He redefined Mead's *cybernetics of cybernetics* as

> The control of control and the communication of communication [27, 28]

and distinguished between first-order cybernetics as the cybernetics of observed systems and second-order cybernetics as the cybernetics of observing systems. His redefinition played on the logical hierarchy of representations in compliance with Bertrand Russell's Theory of Logical Types [4]. He acknowledged that observations do not exist without observers and insisted that cyberneticians conceive of themselves as part of what they observe. This acknowledgement resonated with Ashby's epistemology. However his definition did not go as far as Ashby, Bateson, and Mead's conceptions by repeatedly insisting that second-order cyberneticians *describe* their observations, including of themselves to other observers, echoed also in Humberto Maturana's biology of cognition [15, p. 28].

I am suggesting that a cybernetics that encourages its practitioners to assume the positions of observers, spectators or theorists, asking them to describe their own experiences, and insisting that "The logic of the world is the logic of the description of the world" [29, p. xvi] is stuck in a representational theory of language that keeps them with one foot in the enlightenment project of science. It focuses on cognition [30] at the expense of the dynamics of social constructions [11]. It does not acknowledge the epistemology of Ashby's dialectic of designing models and experimenting with them within experienced constraints. It does not recognize the constitutive role of linguistic actions that creates the world we know and ourselves. The latter is fundamental to Gregory Bateson, George Spencer-Brown, Francisco Varela, and Louis Kauffman's epistemologies who considered acts of distinguishing as generative of observed differences. And it does not embrace Mead's recommendation to consider cybernetics as a language that introduces complexities into the world which we have difficulties understanding, complexities that cyberneticians need to address.

I am convinced that the limited attention to design cybernetics is due to the hegemony of cyberneticians who celebrate descriptive account of their observations. As Ranulph Glanville recognized: "Design is the action; second-order cybernetics is the explanation" [6, p. 200]. Designers constructively intervene in the world we know. Designers propose actions that bring forth desirable futures, making past observations selectively obsolete and some of their descriptions no longer valid. Design is an undisciplinable profession [13] leading us to unpredictable improvements of forms of life.

Worth mentioning is the School for Designing Society [21] which grew out of ASC. It taught *Doing of Cybernetics* [26], and currently relies on systems and critical theory to actively challenge existing social formations which become fossilized by holding on to a "logic of the world" without action.

Let me proceed to the latter but slowly and start with:

6.2 The Cybernetics of Artifacts

With reference to the biologist Jacob von Uexküll [31], I am suggesting that:

> Worlds arise in the sensory-motor coordinations of organisms in their environment.

This proposition suggests that the worlds known to living species cannot be divorced from what its organisms can sense and what its motor organs can set in motion in the context of other organisms and their surroundings, neither of which are accessible independent of their sensory motor coordinations. All worlds are species-specific. They reside neither in the nervous system of organisms on which the biology of cognition focuses its attention, nor in the physical nature of their environment to which evolutionary biologists see species as adapting. As Bateson repeatedly suggested the units of survival are not species but the relationship of its organisms to their environments. When both are relatively unchanging, their recursive coordinations may converge to stabilities in which the organisms of a species remain fixed. This is the lesson of von Foerster's [29, pp. 273–285] recursive theory of eigen-behaviors, a behavior that is not natural to any one participant but an artifact of the recursive interactions among all constituents involved.

Taking Ashby's epistemology seriously, one needs to add to the above that:

> Sensory-motor coordinations either succeed or fail to be afforded by the circumstances that organisms face.

This proposition suggests that the nature of a species-independent world is principally unknowable. It makes itself known only when coordinations fail. The occasion of failing never reveals its cause. In Ashby's terms, information reduces the space of possibilities, nothing more. Within these constraints, organisms have an enormous freedom to evolve and construct different worlds in the form of sensory-motor coordinations until the expectations they entail fail and coordinations break down. This proposition also chimes with James J. Gibson's [5] ecological approach to visual perception. Gibson suggested that we do not see what is in front of our eyes, as a camera would, but what it affords us to do. As a cybernetician, Ashby considered breakdowns of this kind informative. But for lower level organisms, to which this proposition applies as well, breakdowns may be fatal unless they are able to respond by changing their sensory-motor coordinations before such breakdowns are deadly. Ashby called such behavior ultra-stable, designed a mechanical system that demonstrated this ability, and developed several cybernetic principles after experimenting with it. Bateson, linking Ashby's conception to evolution on the level of epistemology, addressed the properties of such system in ecological terms and Ernst von Glasersfeld's [30] and Stafford Beer's [3] conceptions of the viability of systems chime with this epistemology as well.

This leads to the next proposition:

> Separate artifacts result from distinguishing among sensory-motor coordinations according to their distinct affordances.

It suggests the possibility of organisms to partition their world by drawing distinctions among coordinations that selectively preserve their viability. It is such distinctions that bring forth different artifacts, artifacts that need to be handled by distinct sensory-motor coordinations. Species that fail to distinguish among coordinations in view of their affordances may not be viable for long, for example, when failing to distinguish predators from members of their own species, or in contemporary human terms, when not distinguishing between the use of the gas pedal of a car and its brake, playing with the trigger of a gun whether it is loaded or not, or failing to distinguish nourishing food from poison.

The preceding proposition suggests good reasons for distinguishing among artifact in terms of the sensory-motor coordinations they afford. Whether artifacts emerge during the slow evolution of a species or are proposed by a design office, produced by a factory, and subsequently made use of: artifacts are made. The word "artifact" relates "artificial," "factory" and "facts," the etymology of the latter goes back to the Latin "factum," something manu'*fact*'ured or made. This interpretation is etymologically sound though often ignored by locating artifacts in an objectively available environment.

The cybernetics of artifacts suggests an uncommon but plausible interpretation of the word "object." As a noun, it commonly denotes something existing independent of anyone's attention. However, as a verb, it would be perfectly appropriate to say that the principally unknowable external reality "objects" to sensory-motor coordinations it does not afford. Coincidentally, the German word for object is "Gegenstand," literally meaning something that stands in one's way. All of these interpretations chime with Ashby's epistemology of constraints on Gibson's affordances. It does not deny the existence of an external reality but limits its manifestation to the experience of objections and thereby constraining the freedoms to create artifacts.

Human perception can rarely be divorced from the social use of language. Even Gibson had to talk of affordances by reference to named things. Today, we talk of interfaces in conjunction with using electronic devices. Interfaces are designed to offer users access to namable artifacts known to have been manufactured by others. However, knowing of another origin the artifacts that users face do not provide them insights into their design, how they were manufactured, and how they actually work. In fact, interface designers do everything they can to hide the confusing complexities of mobile phones, computers, wrist watches, websites in what to users surely are Ashby's black boxes.

The reference to interfaces separates the design of what makes sensory-motor coordinations with an artifact affordable from the design of its inner workings. In these terms, the above can be stated as:

> All artifacts manifest themselves in user interfaces.

The notion of interfaces applies to everything knowingly produced elsewhere that humans handle, whether opening or closing a water faucet, driving a car, operating a teller machine, or applying for a job. Artifacts vary considerably in complexity. Filed tax returns interface with a tax authority whose complexity is enormous compared to eating with a spoon, which merely hides its material composition and internal strength from its users.

Again, there never is only one way to interface with artifacts produced by others. What is a screwdriver for a repairman, maybe an ice pick for a bar tender, a lever to pry open a can of paint, or a defensive weapon when under attack. A person who attends the performance of an orchestra for her love of music, may sit next to a reporter who listens in order to write a review for the local newspaper, who in turn may sit next to someone who came to the event to be noticed for the fancy dress worn to the occasion. No artifact is the same for everyone and in all situations. A computer is a prototypical example of an explicitly open system, capable of accepting numerous applications and inviting users to reconfigure its interfaces to suit their needs – without a clue of what is going on inside it.

Talk of interfaces entails using language, and that use opens another dimension of coordination. Ludwig Wittgenstein [33, p, 154] speaks of natural language as consisting of numerous language games. Asking a question and receiving an answer is one language game. To illustrate this conception, Wittgenstein described a builder and his helper talking with each other in the process of constructing a building. Language games are performed when advising someone on how to use an app, praising someone for having succeeded exceptionally well, or explaining why something fell apart.

In such coordinations, it is inevitable that artifacts acquire meanings. When articulated, such meanings maybe shared within a community and enable its members to work together. Meanings may be no more than simple categorical distinctions, names, but could also consist of longer narratives of where and how an artifact was acquired and what it helped someone to do or where it failed. Calling an artifact by one name usually restricts their users' imagination and gives the illusion that everyone would interface with the named artifacts alike. I maintain that humans cannot not attribute meanings to the artifacts they face. Artifacts tend to be approached in terms of the categories learned from others. Whether the meanings assigned to artifacts invite particular uses or prevent users to touch them:

> Humans do not respond to the physical qualities of artifacts but act on what they mean to them [8, p. 51; 9, pp. ix, 47]

To elucidate the reference to physics in this proposition, it should be noted that physics is a discourse whose theories construct an objective universe that excludes human involvement. Biology is another discourse aimed at theorizing living organisms, in Humberto Maturana's case, how organisms maintain their autopoiesis or identity. Engineers, artists, entrepreneurs, and financiers talk among themselves, have their discourses, and may have good reasons to attribute discourse-specific meanings to artifacts that outsiders may consider indistinguishable. I mentioned my preference to call Mead's cybernetics of cybernetics a discourse, one that is, as she insisted, capable of crossing disciplinary boundaries, privileging no one in particular, least of all one that has no place for speakers of discourses, hence dismissing the exclusivity of physics in the above proposition.

The cybernetics of artifacts acknowledges discourse-specific attributions of meanings to artifacts with a common entailment:

> The meanings attributed to artifacts entail expectations of the interfaces they might afford.

This proposition merely articulates Gibson's ecological theory of perception: The meaning attributed to something called a chair is the expectation one could sit on it. The meaning of something perceived as a door is that it can be opened or closed and affords walking from one space to another. The meaning of a car suggests its drivability. A pushbutton invites to be pushed to ring a doorbell, start a car, or vote for a candidate. Evidently, the meanings of artifacts may not only vary individually but also contextually. Meanings are not contained in artifacts, they often originate in language, but when attributed to artifacts, they entail expectations and invitations to interface with them accordingly. An important implication of this proposition is that meanings cannot be designed into products, are not the properties of particular forms, or contained in texts. All user groups tend to have their own repertoires of relating meanings to perceptions and expectations.

In relatively settled discourses, the meanings that their practitioners attribute to the artifacts they typically face tend to result in shared expectations. At home, family members may not even imagine using tableware for anything other than eating. This stereotypy may well be violated by children who are not yet socialized and act on meanings that leads them to interfaces to which adults may object.

But it is also possible that people mistake something for something else and acting on mistaken attributions leads interfaces to break down, minimally frustrating expectations and at worst causing serious harm to someone, self or others. Traffic accidents tend to result from misinterpreting a situation or inattention to what actually mattered. Mistakes made while operating a computer are largely due to wrong attributions of what clicking on an icon means. Advertisers may mislead buyers into believing in a product's value, which may become evident only well after it is sold. It can happen, of course, that artifacts unexpectedly cease to function, disintegrate, wear out, and break apart. Users may be able to recognize signs of such defects and act on them in time to prevent experiencing disasters. Whatever its cause, breakdowns are not entirely preventable, largely because the meanings are not yet interfaces. They are symbolic short-cuts to what can be expected when acted upon. One of the least recognized but most important invention to reduce harmful consequences of breakdowns are computer interfaces that give their users the choice backtracking the steps that got them into trouble and pursue another path.

It is important to note that from a cybernetic perspective, meanings are not referents as conceptualized in semiotics. They are not contained in texts as literary scholars tend to treat them. Nor do they have agency as proposed in Bruno Latour's [14] actor network theory. Meanings serve as clues to interfacing with the world as in Wittgenstein's language games, Bateson's multiple accounts of differences that make a difference, and they are the basis of my *The Semantic Turn* [9].

6.3 The Cybernetics of Human-Centered Design

While I generalize design as constitutive of human being-with others – in Heidegger's terms – in this context, I would add the intent to shape the environments of human practices of living and by implication what we humans desire to be. Stated most simply:

Design activities innovate.

Arguably, design could already be considered evident in the emergence of artifacts as discussed in the previous section. Drawing distinctions among viable sensory-motor coordinations creates differences that were not there to begin with. Species of animals and humans that have lived their evolutionary histories to the present may well regard perceived differences as unalterable, natural, and given properties of their environment. However, I consider design to be a social activity, one that involves the use of language and has been shaping technology and society for as long as human records go.

Design is the source of individual, societal, and cultural viability.

Elsewhere [9], I distinguished everyday design from professional design. Everyday design is the ability of human actors to improve their immediate environment: arranging one's furniture at home, selecting socially appropriate clothes to wear, or identifying oneself, for example, as a child's mother. Everyday design decisions are inevitably coordinated with others by linguistic means. Furniture is bought and its arrangement is justified to and commented on by visitors. Wearing provocative clothes in public is a way to cause conversations among bystanders. Artists may consider their work to be a means of self-expression, but all selves are experienced in contrast with other selves, and as soon as works of art are seen by others, they are categorized, appraised and perhaps sold. By contrast to designing one's own environment, I consider:

Professional designers innovate for the benefit of others, not only for themselves.

All innovations, by definition, are unexpected. They may be contrasted with what is known but cannot be anticipated from precedencies and thus escape scientific theories or explanations. In fact, design undermines scientific predictions wherever it is practiced. Bateson's interpretation of Ashby's cybernetic epistemology as a Darwinian evolution on the level of epistemology applies to innovations as well: In retrospect, it is easy to explain why a technology evolved to its present state, for example what lead to jet airplanes, but almost impossible to say what comes next. Unsurprisingly, scientific efforts to predict technological or cultural developments have mostly failed. Innovations make a difference in the lives of many – not necessarily equally appreciated. In effect, design undermines the certainties on which scientific theories thrive.

Unlike the ideal of the natural sciences, even unlike Wiener's original proposition of cybernetics as a science, but consistent with what Ashby, Mead, Bateson, and von Foerster promoted, professional designers cannot escape being part of the very social system that adopts their innovations. Designers are paid – metaphorically as well as literally – to the extent the innovations they propose are of benefit to those willing to return parts of their gains to their originators.

Unlike traditional craftsmen whose products had to benefit them and their individually known customers, contemporary professional designers work out proposals for something that others will have to realize and benefit from as well. Contemporary design deviates from the ways craftsmen, artists, and celebrity designers worked in at least two ways. First:

> Designs emerge in teams.

It is increasingly recognized that most innovations occur in conversations among participants who respect each other's differences. Conversations are the most efficient evolutionary processes I know of [12]. In conversations, ideas are articulated, developed, or no longer pursued. Conversations coordinate their participants' understanding, not in the sense of sharing cognition as Gordon Pask [17] theorized, converging to truths as suggested in Plato's dialogues, or bringing everyone to comply with a plan of actions as agreed at a board meeting. Recent work by cognitive scientists on how much human beings actually know independent of others concluded that humans can hardly think alone [24]. The eye-opening experiences of participating in the Macy Foundation conferences are what prompted Mead to reflect on how it happened and suggest that a cybernetics of cybernetics acknowledge the creativity of its interdisciplinary proceedings and take advantage of its unique ability to come to grips with the complexities that cybernetics nurtured elsewhere. Although Mead did not mention design, the above proposition suggests that all innovations, perhaps with the exception of what stylist do, form givers aim at, and artists are hired to make appear beautiful, arise in collaborations among people who do not think alike have different expertise and respect each other's participation. Developing information technologies, city planning, solving traffic problems, negotiating legislations, designing a new platform for the Internet, can hardly come to fruition without collaboration among diverse experts.

Second, whereas traditional craftsmen knew their clients, worked with them, and created something they could test together. Since design became professionalized during the industrial revolution, designers have been separated from the current means of production. They have become the proponents of innovations to be realized and of benefit to others. Today's designers consider spaces of possibilities that other people may not be able to think through and propose designs that could become real only when acted upon by others. In whatever form a design leaves a design department or office – drawings, prototypes, specifications, plans of actions, calculations, demonstrations, or presentations – it needs to communicate desirable possibilities to those who have a stake in them.

Stakeholders are individuals or spokespersons for institutions who have an interest in a proposed design. They are capable of articulating their support or opposition to a design and tend to have crucial economic, intellectual, or organizational resources at their disposal to bring it to fruition or prevent it from becoming real. Most importantly they are unlike countable masses of buyers in a market place. They constitute complex networks of diverse interests and abilities to intelligently participate in the realization or opposition to a design. Stakeholders may include engineers, who care for the functionality and manufacturability of a design. They may involve financiers who calculate the short and long term feasibility of financing a project. They may embrace factory workers interested in job security. Regulatory agencies of the government may chime in, checking the adherence to applicable rules and regulations. Market researchers and salespeople may claim a voice. Users and consumers ask what difference an innovation could make in their lives. There are suppliers of needed resources, repair services, environmental activists, politicians, and many more, each with different interests, unlike competencies and various resources needed at different times in the process for a design to make a differences in their stakeholders' lives. Some stakeholders are more influential than others, but no design can come to fruition without the support of collaborating stakeholders:

> The realization of all designs succeed or fail within the networks of their stakeholders.

Successful proposals for a design energize its stakeholders, suggest motivations for forming new or participating in existing institutional arrangements. They tab diverse competencies, and assure that delayed gratifications are worth waiting for. Without getting stakeholders on board of designers' projects, a design cannot make a difference.

Reports suggest that 90% of all designs do not come to fruition. This is due at least in part because of the traditional and still lingering conception of designers as employees of manufacturers whose interests do not extend beyond selling their products in a mass market and of the related conception of designs as specifications to be followed completely in all of its details by employees paid for doing that job. The cybernetic revolution has challenged this top-down conception of industrial production by recognizing stakeholders who have a voice and the resources to act.

It follows that today's designers can hardly claim to be in charge of what happens to their design. The cybernetics of human-centered design recognizes the complexity of stakeholder networks and acknowledge the impossibility of singling out any one over another. For example, the idea of an end-users, frequently invoked by market researchers and consumer society advocates, turns out to be a myth. People who buy a product may not be its users or consumers. Parents buy their children's toys, and the drivers of construction machinery do not buy the machines owned by their employers. Buyers are preceded by complex stakeholder networks that make a sale a possibility. The use of almost any artifacts tends to require complex support networks – think of the roads, gasoline stations, parking spaces, traffic courts, repair places which have evolved in support of automobiles to exist. And when artifacts retire, there are still other stakeholders who claim their share in what can be recycled or has to be removed to protect the environment. All professional designers face complex networks of stakeholders in what they are proposing. Failing to recognize their network structures leaves a design to chance.

From the perspective of the cybernetics of human-centered design, what could possibly motivate the participation of diverse stakeholders in proposed designs? I have argued that design is fundamental to being human and intrinsically motivating any discourse community. To me there is no doubt that engineers are proud when they found a clever solution to a technical problem. Bankers are rewarded by funding a promising project. Sales persons are happy when their buyers are satisfied. And computer users surely are delighted when they manage to expand what they enjoy doing. Cybernetics has opened possibilities not imaginable a decade ago. If professional designers desire their innovations to proceed through a network of its stakeholders, they would have delegate design to those who have expertise that designers may not have. I am suggesting that today:

> Professional designers need to create affordances for their stakeholders to design what they need to realize a proposed design. In effect, professional design needs to delegate design to its stakeholders.

This is not to diminish the role of the design profession. On the contrary, delegating the details of a design to competent stakeholders encourages professional designers to employ a systems perspective similar to that of a cybernetics of cybernetics. They may not be able to control everything that could happen to their proposals but can remain leaders in keeping society and culture viable. The emphasis on planning affordances is important in view of the ethical imperative that:

> While designs will always benefit their supporting stakeholders, they should not harm communities whose members did not have a voice in their development. [7, 9]

Unless it goes nowhere, any design makes unequal differences in the lives of others. Today, the industrial area ideology that mass products benefit everyone alike is just unrealistic, and the idea that design should increase the number of options is equally irresponsible in view of the fact that all artifacts have unintended consequences which designers need to pay attention to. Designers have more control over the affordances of a future artifact than over the meanings that their stakeholders bring to them. On a micro level, containers of medications may have to be designed so that children have difficulties opening them. Guns are harmful in the hands of unqualified individuals which calls on designers to find ways for guns to be used only by their legitimate owners. On a macro level, this ethical imperative questions the design of technologies that limit the viability of communities whose members may not have a clue of how a design could affect them. For example, the design of spyware that can enter a computer unnoticed, the gerrymandering of voting districts that prevents minorities their representation in the government, or laws that limit Internet access to poorer segments of a population.

All of the above exemplifies why the cybernetics of human-centered design cannot surrender to the premises of the enlightenment sciences of describing and extrapolating from current observations of what exists.

> Professional designers need to generate compelling evidence for their proposals to mobilize the stakeholders capable of realizing the possibilities of a design.

The epistemological problem of such evidence is due, not only to the absence of observational data of an envisioned future but also of the impossibility of providing evidence of whether a design would compel stakeholders into action in advance of actually doing so.

The equation of design with making compelling arguments for its realization has been argued by Horst Rittel [18] since the 1970s. It presupposes rigorous inquiries into what could energize the stakeholders needed to bring a design to some kind of fruition. At least four broad categories of such inquiries have been identified [13]: preparatory, methodological, rhetorical, and professional:

- Preparatory: Empirical inquiries into where social and technological possibilities reside for designs to make a difference.
- Methodological: Systematic examinations of current design practices with the aim of establishing reproducible design methods for selecting realistic proposals that could make desirable differences to targeted stakeholder communities, voiceless others, and society and culture at large.
- Rhetorical: Search for persuasive strategies that could enroll the stakeholders of a design into constructive networks capable to bring a design to fruition with the resources at their command. Such strategies may include making design decisions transparent, collaborative, or participatory; providing empirical tests on prototypes, demonstrations, statistical forecasts, and cost/benefit analyses.
- Professional: Improving all discourses of the design profession. This can be accomplished by encouraging contributions to regular publications, supporting design education, and maintaining the competencies of practicing designers to work with stakeholders and in multi-disciplinary teams.

6.4 The Design of Cybernetics (of Cybernetics) as a Discourse

This final section considers cybernetics as an artifact and a proposal to redesign its practices. It began with interdisciplinary explorations of circular causal mechanisms and morphed into what came to be known as cybernetics. In that process, several principles of cybernetics with epistemological implications surfaced and in turn informed the continuing conversations among participants. Cybernetics developed only to a point after which its participants formed their own networks. Internationally recognized academic organizations attracted representatives from diverse disciplines into its discourse. Cybernetics came to be applied outside the orbit of cyberneticians. It shaped an amazing number of socio-technological developments: computation penetrated all spheres of social life, digitalization transformed public communications, automation had already replaced some human labor. Artificial intelligence and robotics continued such replacements by entering scientific practices, corporations, and governments. The Internet globalized businesses, political and cultural divisions, and increased the mobility of population. Undeniably, cybernetics revolutionized how we live today.

At the onset of these vast and unpredictable consequences, Mead's proposal of a cybernetics of cybernetics contained two related recommendations. One was for cyberneticians to expand their attention to include the social consequences of introducing cybernetic mechanisms in society and the other to assume responsibilities for what cybernetics is causing. Although Mead made her proposal half a century ago, her solution for coming to grips with the uncertainties that the unprecedented spread of cybernetics encouraged is still timely. It called for equating cybernetics with a language that not only energized scholars from different disciplines to work together in understanding the complex implications of circular forms of communication but also the transformations of society due to the implementation of cybernetic systems. This is a formidable challenge because of the multiplicity of stakeholders participating in these transformations. However, making that effort with the vocabulary of cybernetic is necessary to realize her invitation to cyberneticians to reflect on the consequences of their own actions, to become self-reflexive, and understand themselves as actors in the very society that cybernetics was transforming.

Following the previous section on the cybernetics of designing artifacts, it should be obvious that Mead proposed a design that the community of cyberneticians could not realize without awareness of what their language did. Consistent with contemporary conceptions, I would call cybernetics not a language but a discourse and I presume Mead would not object. The lack of awareness of the discursive nature of cybernetics at that time was evident in the disconnect between how cybernetics was practiced and how it was published. For example, the proceedings of the Macy Foundation conferences were edited and published. They consisted of several volumes of coherently articulated papers on various topics, hiding the conversations that lead to them. Mead recalled the excitement of participating in these conversations. I have heard similar anecdotes that substantiate her report. To me, conversations are self-organizing circular forms of communication. Everything said responds to what was said previously and elicits further contributions. Conversations collectively converge to something new that resonates with most if not all of its participants. To me, the circular nature of conversations are obvious [12] and should have been recognized by the cyberneticians present. However, the published records reveal none of it. Mead pointed to the enormous ability of the discourse of cybernetics to bridge disciplinary divides and address complex problems that arise in systems involving circular communication, problems that could not be addressed by any one discipline.

To be clear, discourses arise when conversations are limited to a subject matter, unequal competences are respected among its participants, rules of conduct are accepted and discourse-specific artifacts interactively emerge [12]. Physics is a discourse whose trained practitioners construct theories of a universe they cherish. Medicine is a discourse of diseases and physiological injuries that its certified practitioners claim able to address. One can distinguish legal, public, psychanalytic, engineering, and numerous other discourses whose respective practitioners bring forth their own realities. However, the discourse of cybernetics is not as closed as the discourses just mentioned. It does not discipline is practitioners, in fact, it thrives on its interdisciplinarity, on its ability to bring representatives of diverse disciplines into constructive conversations. It addresses in all kinds of circularities. Inasmuch as it is practiced in circular communication and addresses circularities elsewhere, one could say that cybernetic discourse metaphorically extends the circular involvement of its participants to social, natural, and technological systems that semi-autonomously operate in other domains of experiences. However, this reflexivity was not recognized before Mead made her proposal. I suggested later that it is THE defining feature of cybernetics [10].

As a design, the cybernetics of cybernetics has to recognize that language is not merely *about* something – in terms of second-order cybernetics about one's observing – articulations actively change perceptions and actions. In conversations, assertions elicit responses. Declaring bankruptcy has financial implications. Saying "I love you" can define a relationship from within. Notwithstanding herculean efforts by scientists to prevent their theories from being acted on what they claim to be true, when social theories are communicated to those theorized therein or benefitting from them, this renders their validity at the mercy of knowledgeable actors. Social theories either gain validity when believed and enacted or lose it when actively opposed. Social scientists despise self-validating theories, but it is on their circular nature that the cybernetics of design relies. Proposals of a design become real only when acted upon by its stakeholders. To me, the difficulty of predicting the consequences of first- or second-order cybernetic practices is no reason for denying accountability of what they do. Accountability is not possible by a discourse that denies its effects. The design of a cybernetics implies it to be a discourse that is capable of inquiring not only what it unintendedly effects, but also the qualities of the futures that its ideas, proposals, and research could bring forth.

As a discourse, cybernetics needs to embrace Wittgenstein's above-mentioned conception of language games, Richard Rorty's [19, 20] effort to develop a conception of language based on what it does, and Giambattista Vico's 1710 *verum factum* principle [30, pp. 36–38], all of which acknowledge that language constructs realities when acted upon. Mead's conception of a cybernetics of cybernetics is predicated on recognizing that the discourse of cybernetics matters when enacted into mechanical, electronic, organizational, or political systems.

Most scientific discourses grow inside a self-maintained boundary. Physics, for example, has progressed from macro theories of causal mechanisms to atom physics and to quantum theory. Psychology is transforming itself from studying individual human characteristics to a cognitive science. The discourse of cybernetics may also attend to smaller details but its most important source of growth stems from its outward expansion. Recognizing cybernetics as a transformative discourse, Mead's proposal, initially focused on the unintended societal consequences of cybernetics, has to embrace the designs that her cybernetics of cybernetics entails. In this respect the discourse of cybernetics resembles the cybernetics of human-centered design. To make a difference in the worlds of others, designers cannot go home leaving their visions on the drawing board. They have to make their designs communicable and realizable by its stakeholders. It presupposes knowledge of how it could be realized, by whom, its costs and benefit or harm inflicted by what always are interventions, and learn from inquiries of what actually happened – a never ending cycle.

The original conversations during which cybernetics emerged involved cutting edge scientist from diverse academic disciplines. As the discourse of cybernetics spread into other domains with social, economic, organizational and political implications, it gave birth to numerous circular systems not originally imagined. Taking the cybernetics of cybernetics seriously has the effect of roping non-academic stakeholders with diverse expertise and interests into the very discourse that cybernetics had set in motion. Unlike other discourses, the discourse of cybernetics is bound to evolve by expanding into its initially unintended consequences – without an end in sight.

Another way of accounting for the continuous expansion of cybernetic discourse is to observe the growing diversity of explanations for the information that Ashby recognized as constraining the realization of systems with circular forms. The inability of realizing systems in one domain has not always prevented efforts to realize them in others, and to the extent this is so, it has drawn an ever increasing number of different disciplines into the orbit of cybernetics.

On the negative side, the growth of the discourse of cybernetics has enabled numerous sub-disciplines to capitalize on the momentum that cybernetics did and continues to create. They institutionalized themselves as separate disciplines with their own identities. Artificial Intelligence branched off from cybernetics, and so did computer science, robotics, cognitive science, information science, even family systems therapy. Going by different names, catering to different stakeholders, and establishing separate educational programs in universities had the effect of limiting the interdisciplinary core of cybernetics but could not replace it.

To me, the cybernetics of design and the design of cybernetics are projects that continue to fascinate me as one of its stakeholders. This book demonstrates that its ideas are mobilizing many stakeholders for providing possibilities not available otherwise.

References

1. Ashby, W. R. (1956). *An introduction to cybernetics.* London: Chapman and Hall.
2. Bateson, G. (2000). *Steps to an ecology of mind.* Chicago: University of Chicago Press.
3. Beer, S. (1981). *Brain of the firm: The managerial cybernetics of organizations* (2nd ed.). New York: Wiley.
4. Copi, I. M. (1971). *The theory of logical types.* London: Routledge & K. Paul.
5. Gibson, J. J. (1979). *The ecological approach to visual perception.* Boston: Houghton Mifflin.
6. Glanville, R. (2012). Second order cybernetics. *The black boox – Vol. I. Cybernetic circles* (pp. 175–207). Vienna: edition echoraum. Previously published In F. Parra-Luna (Ed.), *Encyclopedia of life support systems, systems science and cybernetics – Vol. III*. Oxford: EoLSS Publishers. Available at: http://www.eolss.net/sample-chapters/c02/e6-46-03-03.pdf. Accessed 19 Jan 2019.
7. Krippendorff, K. (1989). On the ethics of constructing communication. In B. Dervin, L. Grossberg, B. J. O'Keefe, & E. Wartella (Eds.), *Rethinking communication: Paradigm issues* (Vol. I, pp. 66–96). Newbury Park: Sage Publications.
8. Krippendorff, K. (2004). Intrinsic motivation and human-centered design. *Theoretical Issues in Ergonomic Science, 5*(1), 43–72.
9. Krippendorff, K. (2006). *The semantic turn. A new foundation for design.* Boca Raton/New York: Taylor & Francis/CRC Press.
10. Krippendorff, K. (2008). Cybernetics's reflexive turns. *Cybernetics and Human Knowing, 15*(3–4), 173–184.
11. Krippendorff, K. (2008). Towards a radically social constructivism. *Constructivist Foundation, 3*(2), 91–94.

12. Krippendorff, K. (2009). Conversation: Possibilities of its repair and descent into discourse and computation. *Constructivist Foundations, 4*(3), 135–147.
13. Krippendorff, K. (2016). Design, an undisciplinable profession. In G. Joost, K. Bredies, M. Christensen, F. Conradi, & A. Unteidig (Eds.), *Design as research. Positions, arguments, perspectives* (Vol. 124, pp. 197–206). Basel: Birkhäuser Verlag/De Gruyter.
14. Latour, B. (2005). *Reassembling the social. An introduction to actor-network-theory*. New York: Oxford University Press.
15. Maturana, H. R., & Varela, F. J. (1987). *The tree of knowledge. The biological roots of human understanding*. Boston: New Science Library.
16. Mead, M. (1968). The cybernetics of cybernetics. In H. von Foerster, et al. (Eds.), *Purposive systems* (pp. 1–11). New York: Spartan Books.
17. Pask, G. (1975). *Conversation, cognition and learning. A cybernetic theory and methodology*. New York: Elsevier.
18. Protzen, J.-P., & Harris, D. J. (2010). *The universe of design: Horst Rittel's theories of design and planning*. London: Routledge.
19. Rorty, R. (1970). *The linguistic turn: Recent essays in philosophical method.* Chicago: University of Chicago Press.
20. Rorty, R. (1989). *Contingency, irony, and solidarity.* New York: Cambridge University Press.
21. School for Designing a Society, Urbana. Available at: http://www.designingasociety.org. Accessed 19 Jan 2019.
22. Sharp, G. (2010). *From dictatorship to democracy. A conceptual framework for liberation* (4th ed.). East Boston: The Albert Einstein Institute.
23. Simon, H. A. (1969). *The sciences of the artificial*. Cambridge, MA: MIT Press.
24. Sloman, S., & Philip Fernbach, P. (2017). *The knowledge illusion. Why we never think alone*. New York: Riverhead Books.
25. Stolzenberg, G. (1984). Can an inquiry into the foundations of mathematics tell us anything interesting about mind? In P. Watzlawick (Ed.), *The invented reality* (pp. 257–308). New York: W.W. Norton & Company.
26. The School for Designing a Society. (1999). *Doing cybernetics*. Urbana: SDaS.
27. Von Foerster, H. (1974). *The cybernetics of cybernetics*. Champaign-Urban: Biological Computer Laboratory, University of Illinois. Republished as Heinz von Foerster. 1995. *Cybernetics of cybernetics or the control of control and the communication of communication* (2nd ed.). Minneapolis: Future Systems.
28. von Foerster, H. (1979). Cybernetics of cybernetics. In K. Krippendorff (Ed.), *Communication and control in society* (pp. 5–8). New York: Gordon & Breach Science Publishers Ltd.
29. von Foerster, H. (1981). *Observing systems*. Seaside: Intersystems Publications.
30. von Glasersfeld, E. (1995). *Radical constructivism. A way of knowing and learning*. Bristol: Falmer Press.
31. von Uexküll, J. (1957). A stroll through the worlds of animals and men: A picture book of invisible worlds. In C. H. Schiller (Ed.), *Instinctive behavior: The development of a modern concept* (pp. 5–80). New York: International University Press.
32. Wiener, N. (1948). *Cybernetics or control and communication in the animal and the machine*. New York: Wiley.
33. Wittgenstein, L. (1953). *Philosophical investigations*. Oxford: Blackwell.

Klaus Krippendorff, PhD is the Gregory Bateson Term Professor for Cybernetics, Language, and Culture at the University of Pennsylvania's Annenberg School for Communication. He is a Fellow of AAAS, ICA, NIAS (The Netherlands), SSDS (Japan) and others. He has published widely on communication theory, cybernetics, systems theory, social science methodology, and design. He authored several books, most recently: *The Semantic Turn, A New Foundation for Design* (2006) and *Content Analysis* (2004/1980); earlier *Information Theory* (1986); *A Dictionary of Cybernetics* (1986); and edited *Design in the Age of Information*, a Report to NSF (1997).

Chapter 7
Design-Based Research in Relation to Science-Based Research

Ted Krueger and Ute C. Besenecker

Abstract How might a design approach be applied to research? Following Glanville's observation that design and research are fundamentally related and that design methods may be applied across domains, we framed a case study of the perceptual effects of alternate contemporary lighting technologies at an architectural scale to show how a designer/researcher could approach this kind of investigation. Design proceeds in complex domains with incomplete data and open questions. It is often concerned with the singular or unique solution rather than with generalizability. Its products are applied under hybrid and dynamic, rather than controlled, conditions. Rather than work with subjects approximating a general population, informants were recruited with more extensive or diverse experiences than our own. Color perception was investigated in large-scaled installations allowing for locomotion and full visual immersion in a color-field. The effort was not to frame hypotheses for confirmation or refutation but probe the phenomena for insights. Design research methods might be preferred when the nature of the investigation is exploratory or when ecological validity dominates reliability. They might also be useful in situations where significant progress is no longer being made within a particular paradigm by recasting the nature of the inquiry outside the frameworks that presently dominate.

Keywords Design · Science · Methods · Research · Color

T. Krueger (✉)
School of Architecture, Greene Building 212, Rensselaer Polytechnic Institute, Troy, NY, USA
e-mail: krueger@rpi.edu

U. C. Besenecker
Raumseele, West Warwick, RI, USA
e-mail: ute@raumseele.com

T. Fischer, C. M. Herr (eds.), *Design Cybernetics*, Design Research Foundations,
https://doi.org/10.1007/978-3-030-18557-2_7

7.1 Introduction

This paper grew out of an extended conversation about how designers conduct research without necessarily adopting methods from other disciplines, but instead by proceeding in a designerly [5] way. This manner of working was inspired by and indebted to Ranulph Glanville's insights that "[r]esearch [is] a (restricted) design act, rather than design being inadequate research" [7, p. 81] and that "it may be [that] it is design that has more to offer to other areas [of research]" [8, p. 1175].[1] If so, can designerly methods of inquiry be useful not only for design inquiries, but also to interrogate topics that would normally be considered a part of academic research in the social and natural sciences? How would this research move forward? What kinds of differences might it have with traditional inquiry methods? Would it discover new or different insights? Would the results of such investigations integrate better with design practice?

The conversation between the authors on which this paper is based was motivated by the desire to produce a dissertation within a program in 'Architectural Sciences' where the methodological inspiration would come from the first rather than the second term. As such, it was an extended conversation, taking place from 2013 to 2016. Like all conversations, it is difficult to identify the origins of ideas or to assign credit. But in many ways we feel that assigning credit is a failed project from the beginning. Conversation is a method of generating novelty [8, p. 1191][2] and many of the thoughts in this paper arose from within conversations between us. And, a varied and interesting conversation it was.

7.2 Researching Through Design

In an early paper into design research, Frayling [6] identified several different kinds of design research: 'research into art and design', 'research through art and design', and 'research for art and design'. Research into art and design is the territory covered by history, theory and criticism and is situated generally within the practices of the humanities. 'Research for art and design' concerns itself with the gathering of knowledge that supports the activities of artists or designers and is generally undertaken by practitioners in support of their design or artistic activities. It might also include the production of reference materials or their collection into reference volumes and handbooks that are used in practice. It includes the production of knowledge that will be used in support of practice as well as that used in the practicing. The Rensselaer's Graduate Programs in the Architectural Sciences (MS

[1]See page 27 in this volume.

[2]See page 48 in this volume.

and PhD) in which we do our work is intended to produce knowledge in support of design practice and so falls within this group. We know it well.[3]

The remaining type, 'researching through design', is what this paper concerns. However, the examples offered by Frayling, materials research, technology development, and practical experiments in the studio are not our interest in this investigation. In addition, there is an extensive body of work undertaken by designers researching design practice by reflecting on designing. While we have participated in this work and hold it in high regard, that too, is not our subject. Frayling's distinctions are later taken up by Glanville who observes:

> Research through design is research, which explicitly takes on board the nature of design, which is to say research that recognises its source in design, and which uses the insights and understandings of design in its pursuit. These understandings are difficult to formulate: but that, I argue, is part of how design works. [10, p. 321]

So for Glanville, contra Frayling, 'research through design' does not necessarily operate within the field of design practice but is a way of conducting research regardless of the field of inquiry. The research investigation that inspired our conversation about 'design-led research', a dissertation focused on perceptual dimensions of various lighting technologies, was drawn from questions germane to design practice that did not yet have satisfactory answers available within the scientific literature. We observe that Frayling's categories, while presented as clean-cut and mutually exclusive, are not so. While the work presented here makes use of design sensibilities as a research strategy, it hopes eventually to produce insights that will better inform practice. We believe that designers undertaking research that intends to build a structured body of knowledge may well do so in ways that better accommodate design practice than that produced by those who have no understanding or experience of designing.

Taking a weekend workshop on design thinking may well increase one's appreciation for what designers do and how they operate. While it may or may not have a positive influence on business practices, it does not result in one's being able to practice design like an experienced designer, nor to think like one. Design thinking may well be vastly different for different designers and design practices. While we have several decades of design experience, in this paper no general claims are made, rather, we are interested in how the design sensitivities that we do possess might be turned towards problems that are normally considered to be within the domain of science and to interrogate this subject matter using methods that we devise (we design) based on our prior experiences.

We have often experienced difficulty in moving insights from science to design. Some specific examples and reasons are given below. Perhaps this is the case because those outside of design undertake it and so study things that may be tangential to what designers need for their practices. Perhaps the research has been configured

---

[3]Ted Krueger directed this program from 2005–2012. Ute Besenecker undertook her PhD within the program 2013–2016 under his supervision.

to answer questions that arise in other disciplines and so fit into other knowledge structures.

Randall Beer notes that the conceptual frameworks that guide research activity determine the kinds of questions that are asked and the methods used to interrogate them [2]. While he makes his observation about competing approaches to questions within cognitive science, his insight is applicable also to the different disciplinary traditions and strategies that might be brought to bear on a particular questions in other fields. These different traditions will organize knowledge, disseminate, and store it differently. They will structure their questions in diverse ways, and attempt to answer them using distinctive methods. As Beer goes on to note [2], they might also collect dissimilar kinds of evidence and analyze and interpret that evidence differently, perhaps in ways that seem occult from within another disciplinary framework.

7.3 Some Differences in Approach

There is always significant risk in using generalities with disciplines. There is a considerable variation in practices within each discipline, especially when one speaks about individuals. But, it is also the case that individuals self-select and then enter a disciplinary socialization that often has a strong presence in their identity. Many identify themselves as 'architect', or as 'scientist' rather than as an individual practicing architecture or science [12]. Disciplinary culture, values and history are frequently components of this socialization process. Each discipline develops a disciplinary epistemology and world-view that shapes the way it attempts to address problems within its domain.

Design is a separate and legitimate way of knowing. A designerly way of knowing, has a distinct epistemology. Design in its operation as a practice generates knowledge about the products of its activity. It frequently works with and through a team composed of a wide variety of disciplines and interests – sometimes in conflict with one another. It generates understandings about how to proceed in order to solve the problems posed and develop the configurations required. It has techniques for proceeding without complete information and by means of that proceeding to come to know the information that is required.

We authors have both been educated in other disciplines in addition to design and so see these differences in approach from direct experience. But, we also recognize Glanville's observation that design and science are fundamentally related. He notes that all experimental work requires experimental design, the crafting of apparatus, and the iterative improvements and calibrations that are required to get the results to conform to the researchers understandings [7]. We do not see two distinct practices, science and design, but rather a range of possibilities within and between diverse projects. This suggests that there might be a variety of ways to proceed when investigating phenomena and that a diversity of approaches might collectively provide the most robust strategy.

Norman Johnson has studied the role of diversity in complex biological, economic, and social systems. His work provides insights into the role of diversity from a systems dynamics perspective. He notes that the aspects of diversity that are of interest are in terms of function, capability or information, that is, those things that make "unique contributions within the system dynamics" [13]. "Experiential diversity of a group, in both a social and biological context, is related to the varieties of distinct viewpoints that are used to solve a problem" [14]. His studies suggest that there are dynamics to problem formulation and problem solving that operate above the level of the individual at the functioning of the collective and that the effectiveness when measured with respect to the collective is higher in systems with high diversity [14]. So it may well be that collectively our understandings might be more richly developed if a variety of approaches, perspectives and values are accommodated within the research enterprise. Our research attempts to do so from a designer's perspective.

Certainly it is not our objective to assert the superiority of one research methodology over another, but to point out that because results will vary with methods, there is a range of opportunities available from which to choose. It is far more interesting, in our view, to have access to a variety of research methods each of which is capable of yielding different insights into a question or phenomenon than it is to be restricted to a single investigative strategy. In addition, some ways of working may be closer to the sensibility of a particular researcher. There was a time when individual researchers made an effort to become a standard and detached observer. Each subsequent observer made an effort to adopt the same attitude. By so filtering individual difference it was thought that the 'thing itself' might be approached. But if one believes that the 'thing itself' cannot be known, then what we can do together is to understand it from differing viewpoints. Within such an approach, there is ample opportunity for both disciplinary and individual differences. We suggest that investigations within a strictly scientific framework can benefit from other ways of knowledge production that widen the 'search space' and therefore open opportunity for subsequent investigation that would not otherwise be realized within the restricted frameworks of scientific process.

7.4 A Case Study

Below, we briefly sketch the outline of a series of studies that formed a dissertation in the Architectural Sciences so that the reader can make connections between the propositions made about design-led research and an actual research topic. By referring to the research questions one might get a better sense of how a design-trained individual might approach research.

The research project was an effort to understand how different technologies available in lighting practice today affect the way in which color is perceived. There is in color science and engineering the concept of 'metamers', which are equivalent colors rendered by different techniques. For example, one might obtain a particular green color by filtering sunlight through a colored glass, by mixing a pigmented paint, by using monochromatic LEDs, or by alternating white and black at an appropriate frequency. These might all be nominally the same color (as calculated by standard color metrics) and perhaps perceptually be, at first glance, almost indistinguishable, and yet, there may be important differences that are hidden within. Presently, lighting technologies are in transition, driven by new technical developments and the promise of savings in energy and maintenance costs. But, little is known about the perceptual effects and differences that might be obtained when using these various technologies to render and create color. As these technologies shift, are theatrical, artistic, and architectural lighting applications altered? Are there untapped opportunities or limitations that we should consider?

The research topic, as stated here, is deliberately left as open as it was at the beginning of the studies, even though the work outlined for the dissertation has been successfully completed and the degree awarded [3]. The research topic as stated at the onset of the research was in a traditional sense still premature in its structure and definition, and not ready for work to begin. But, many designers are comfortable in moving ahead with incomplete or contradictory information. A significant component of design work is undertaken in order to find, understand, or explore the question at hand. Kirsh and Maglio have used the term 'epistemic' to describe activities that are undertaken in order to 'see what to do,' as distinct from 'pragmatic' activities which are those directly concerned with undertaking and completing the task at hand [15]. The research for the dissertation proceeded without pre-defined experimental protocols in place, but instead sought to investigate color perception with an open attitude. Rather than mastering the subject matter, the effort was to apprentice oneself to it with a willingness to learn, and allow it to 'suggest' the questions that need investigation and the procedures involved.

7.5 Listening to the Phenomena

Pauline Oliveros, experimental musician and composer, contrasts listening and hearing. Hearing operates in an objective world and is amenable to scientific interrogation. Hearing is measurable, as is sound itself, and it's open to physiological interrogation and explanation. Listening, however, is both intentional and attentional. It is simultaneously narrower than hearing, in that one can selectively attend to one conversation out of several simultaneous ones, and wider, in that one can be attuned to multiple non-auditory cues, such as visual location, body language, gesture, and lip-motion that have enormous impact on one's reception. Listening is more difficult to study than hearing, and so has received relatively little attention from the scientific community [20]. In addition, one can argue, that similar distinctions apply between seeing and looking, vision and color science being focused on researching the former.

In *Listening to the Inaudible*, it is argued that listening always involves more than the acoustic dimensions. It is not simply the reception of information. Instead, it is an intentional stance characterized by a willingness to learn from and be open to another.

It might be that what we mean by listening (and looking) has no requirement for sound (and light) whatsoever and can be directed towards any phenomena of interest [19]. Research undertaken in this way does not have as its objective disproving or finding evidence for a specific hypothesis. Researchers may choose to investigate something and attempt to do so with as little predisposition as possible. In this case, an effort is made to put aside preconceived notions, personal, cultural and disciplinary histories, to the extent possible, and to open oneself to the phenomena in question as it presents itself in our experience. This is not an easy thing to do, however. Simon Glynn notes, "Thus the experiences that supposedly form the very bedrock of empirical science are already pre-structured by theories implicit in the very act of perception itself" [11]. Or, as Einstein puts it, "In reality it is the theory that decides what can be observed" (Einstein quoted in [11]). We are interested in the possibility of setting aside prior knowledge and theoretical predispositions and allowing the phenomena to 'teach us what is relevant.' The objective is to become a student of the phenomenon rather than its master, and to thus open oneself to things that are new, unexpected, counter-intuitive, or surprising [4]. Paul Valéry is credited with "seeing is forgetting the name of the thing one sees" [25]. Words carry with them the history of their own use and the deep history and structure of the language in which they are embedded. Tyler argues, for example, that languages having Indo-European roots privilege objects over processes [23]. As language structures and gives expression to thoughts, this subtle bias influences understanding. There is, again, the problem of both excessive generality and the incapacity to capture the fullness of the phenomena. This slippage between language and phenomena holds as well for any form of account that we make of our experiences including mathematical and conceptual models and all manner of description and recording media. It is this cultural baggage that must be set aside in order to apprehend the 'thing' on its own terms.

Researchers face an identical problem as they initiate an investigation into specific phenomena. In fact, it is often exacerbated by the need to do a 'literature review' that is to bring one's understanding up to the current state of knowledge. This tradition is not an empty one. It is necessary in order to avoid duplicating efforts that have already been expended to understand a topic or phenomena. But, it comes at the potential cost of absorbing conventional thought and wisdom on the topic. Certainly a thorough critique of this prior work is advisable, but it is important to understand that existing bodies of knowledge have extensive networks of assumptions already incorporated into them. Many will be unstated agreements between consenting researchers.

But this chapter is not proposing an uninformed research strategy, quite the opposite. The case study dissertation during which these conversations took place was informed by an extensive knowledge of research on vision and color perception. In addition, one of us had a decade of experience in lighting design practices, the other in architectural design. It was these experiences that suggested that designers generate disciplinary-specific knowledge through practice that is held in and disseminated through the social institution of the practice. In contrast to academic culture where the product of work is knowledge disseminated through approved networks, practice has as its objective making designs and placing the resulting products in the world.

The codification of experience into structured observations or theories is not a priority and is not packaged and disseminated to other practices and only rarely through the schools.

In an effort to extract knowledge from practices, a series of interviews were held with a distribution of practitioners. So, in some sense, the compilation of prior work was more comprehensive than that normally included in a more standard scientific approach. The background information for the research was gathered from intentionally diverse sources many of whom came from intellectual traditions in which a standard observer is not privileged. In fact, quite the opposite, insights were solicited directly from the practitioners who's individual observations and experiences were intended to be incorporated within the pragmatics of practice rather into a sharable body of knowledge. These observers were thus cherished for their individual expertise and diversity.

We were influenced by the way second-order cybernetics made a definitive break with the cybernetics that came before by practically and polemically incorporating the observer into the observation. This perspective has supported the development of design-based research methods – objectivity and the standardization of the observer is rejected in favor of a first-person perspective. The researcher and her history are understood to be integral to the process. While the will to move beyond this personal history exists, it is a very difficult thing to accomplish in practice. Others were enlisted to help. Because these others will have different capabilities, histories and perspectives, their insights might provide an effective counter to one's own biases. Research methods that acknowledge and specifically make use of these differences were developed; this perspective was incorporated in order to insure completeness, essential to the research, of representing the 'state of the art' in composing luminous color at architectural-scale. Practitioners were drawn from a distribution of color related practices – researchers into color, artists, lighting designers, fixture designers, color theorists and theater lighting designers were all consulted. The interviews confirmed that a great deal of experience, knowledge and insight was held in design practices, that the nature of this knowledge varied widely and vastly exceeded our own.

7.6 Laboratory Knowledge Versus Practice Knowledge

Not surprisingly, this knowledge also varied significantly from the kinds of knowledge produced in the laboratory. It was immediately apparent that laboratory studies looked at perception in a different way. In particular and perhaps most surprising to us was a relative lack of work that included peripheral vision and the role of bodily movement.

Isolating visual perception from bodily movement is not surprising when one characterizes perception from an information theoretic position, because in this paradigm it is largely irrelevant. But as perceptual theories have increasingly highlighted the role of the body in enactive perception [21] and cognition [24], and as multi-sensory perception comes under scrutiny [16], an active and engaged subject is critical. Certainly, within architectural practices, one assumes a certain degree of mobility and activity as well as awareness of the surrounding space. Knowledge that is developed without regard to motion and peripheral vision lacks the ecological validity that design practice requires.

The knowledge based on practice, however, has a range of other problems. Typically, the sample size is one, the design practitioner, relying on their intimate familiarity and personal motivation to improve their knowledge and thereby their work. Generalizability, when considered, only has to do with the way that a population might respond to design work that incorporates the knowledge of the practitioner. This knowledge is not structured for dissemination, and it may not even be articulated. Instead, it is in the form of a series of experiences held within the practitioner's intuition and expressed as the need arises. It is most often *knowledge for* rather than *knowledge of* [9].

The personal nature of most knowledge held in design practices implies that it may have limited reliability. This classic trade-off in research design is in this case also aligned with disciplinary preferences. This difference also partially explains why the transition from laboratory to practice a difficult one.

7.7 Knowing When Not to Know

We felt that the interviews of design practitioners as a form of 'literature review'–the collection of knowledge and insights drawn from prior work–was quite effective. Designers who had working knowledge of different color mixing technologies, especially those in theater and lighting installations, were knowledgeable of our general research subject and encouraged a closer examination of the topic. For example, some theatrical works developed in the context of filtered broadband (incandescent tungsten) lighting have been converted to LED sources (light mixed from discrete 4–7 color LED spectra) and significant perceptual differences were observed. Some colors and intensities are simply unavailable and this posed problems in converting a lighting design from one system to another. In addition, the designers were aware of the ways that materials react distinctively to metameric light composed of different spectra. These designers have a vast experience and an educated 'eye' for color and its attributes and so were extraordinary sources of information.

The ability of individuals with disparate experience in color to inform the research effort was recognized and employed in later experimental phases. In light of the valuable effect that the earlier-interviewed practitioners had on the structuring of the experiments, it was decided that there remained much to learn from those who were particularly knowledgeable about color. Again, we decided not to presume expertise, rather than selecting 'subjects' for the experiments that approximated the general population, the research was conducted with 'informants' who were invited to participate. We were interested in gathering responses from those who had long experience with color and who may have developed sensitivities or insights far beyond our own.

In this way, we were choosing not to presume that we fully understood the phenomena under investigation, and at the same time to assume that the things we felt confident about might not be widely acknowledged. We attempted to find a research posture that was equivalent to 'forgetting the name of the thing'. We hoped to temporarily suspend our knowledge of what we had absorbed thorough experiences in both academic and professional contexts. This willful *unknowing* [18] was intended to provide opportunity for the expertise and experience of others. We were crafting an opportunity to be surprised [17] by what others might tell us. We were willing to listen.

This approach, however, comes at a cost of generalizability to larger populations, because one cannot claim that the sample tested in the experiments were in any way representative. But we felt that we had more to learn from a distribution of individual expert responses than we would gain by aggregating those responses into a mean or average. Perceptual responses happen to individuals, not to aggregates, and these individual responses each might contain a valuable insight that could easily be lost during the aggregation. We are aware of perceptual studies where those who responses were quite different than the norm, were eliminated from the study, because these 'outliers' did not fit within the researchers' frameworks. Including the responses of the outliers threatened the statistical significance of the project. For our study, which has exploratory rather than explanatory objectives, the individual responses and their range, especially from those who know color well, was judged to be of greater value.

7.8 A More Ecologically Valid Laboratory

One of the limitations of standard laboratory experiments in perception is not conceptual or philosophical, but architectural. In many cases, the laboratories used for perceptual experiments simply aren't large enough to undertake work that comprises a full field of view when the subjects are expected to move freely unencumbered by apparatus. As noted above, contemporary theories of perception often assume that perception and action are intimately related and that research targeted for architectural conditions should assume that the subject is dynamic. This is difficult to accommodate under typical laboratory conditions. Does the space of the laboratory itself influence the kinds of experiments that are considered practical – does it circumscribe the experiments that are done and therefore the kinds of understanding that are created?

Fig. 7.1 Laboratory space used for the described study

The work described here benefitted from a rare opportunity that came in the form of a competitive proposal for a research residency[4] at *The Curtis R. Priem Experimental Media and Performing Arts Center* (EMPAC) at Rensselaer Polytechnic Institute. The remit of the institution is not only as a performance venue but also a platform for research. The residency allowed for the use of a high quality 'black box' studio, $20 \times 15 \times 10$ m in height, effectively making the studio into what may have been the largest laboratory for perceptual experiments available, although for a limited time (see Fig. 7.1). Access to this large controllable environment complete with sophisticated media technologies made an investigation into color perception at an architectural scale feasible. This also allowed for the animated [22] exploration of the experimental apparatus by the informants.

An experimental set-up was created within the 'black box' that shared attributes with both an uncontrolled urban space and a highly controlled laboratory. The enclosure was completely isolated for sound and light and yet permitted, even required, walking from one stimulus condition to another. Participants could view 4.25 m tall curved illuminated panels from afar or walk into them and have their entire field of view awash in a certain luminous color. This locomotion, with its associated head and eye movements and engagement of both foveal and peripheral vision, is much closer to an architectural or urban condition than would be obtained in conventional laboratory studies. The technical systems available in the studio gave a high degree of control over the experimental conditions from an isolated booth (see Fig. 7.2).

[4]Residencies and production funding were supported by the Jaffe Student Production Competition Grant.

Fig. 7.2 Visually isolated lighting control room

The stimuli experienced were like those found in architectural contexts – large painted surfaces with brush texture and small irregularities that cause shadowing. We observed and recorded participants' locomotion, gestures, expressions, and behaviors with the intent of finding both commonalities that might exist and the range of responses that would occur. We believe that design practitioners will find both the commonalities and differences interesting.

The study had to do with metamers produced through a range of lighting technologies – colors that appear similar but are composed of different spectra produced by the technological substrates of the lighting systems compared within the experimental conditions. This resulted in similar but not identical colors. In tightly controlled experimental work, these stimuli would not be considered to be the same. But in this case, the investigation has to do with the color generating ability of the technologies. The fact that, in some cases, the match could not be exact was part of the question as we had formulated it. As an exercise that might inform practice, we retained the pragmatic conditions found in practice for our experimental conditions. We expect that this may not have been acceptable under a different paradigm because the question would have been formulated in a different way. We are also interested in the knowledge that might be obtained through a different ways of framing the question, however, in this study we did pursue that knowledge.

While the subject of this chapter is not the work of the dissertation itself [3], several of its findings are reviewed here in order to illustrate the kinds of observations made using these designerly methods.

It was found that informants could not detect a difference between colored light projected on a white surface and white light on a colored surface when seen from a distance. But those who immersed themselves in the luminous conditions, by walking into the semi-cylindrical spaces could easily tell them apart. This is because the ability to make the distinction does not depend on the luminous surface alone, but also on the way the projected color reacted to another surface, one that was inevitably brought with the perceiver. In this experiment, it was, for example, the pad of white paper used to take notes, or a shirtsleeve, or the hand of the informant that could register the difference between the illumination sources beyond the experimental surface in question. Our use of the 'black box' effectively allowed for the simultaneous conduct of two studies, one distal, approximating a laboratory study investigating color perception under controlled conditions, from an information theoretic perspective, and the other a less controlled 'field' study, approximating an embodied architectural field condition. In the first study we found that the percepts are indistinguishable in observation. In the second study we found that the conditions were perceived as distinct when the informant moved from one condition to the other. Not all of them did.

The informants were remarkably different in their reactions to colors and in their use of the space – in how they interrogate colors with respect to movement. In some of the experimental conditions informants were allowed to move freely in their interaction with the colored surfaces. Some were quickly drawn to immerse themselves, moving in to fill their entire field of vision with the color. Others were reticent, remaining distant, detached, observant, and analytic. One informant when immersed in a color field was moved to tears – clearly, it was an extremely potent experience for them – while another, remaining remote, spoke about the frequency distributions of the colors. One had a background in theater acting, the was other a professional photographer. The correlations are interesting. Perhaps years of experience shapes responses, but as noted above there is likely a degree of self-selection that informs career choices. What we are interested in here by citing briefly these observations, is how certain methodological decisions shape what can be observed and what might become the subjects for additional studies, perhaps, under controlled conditions, of the hypotheses (or intuitions) that support them. The task in this project was not to solve predetermined questions, but to set the conditions and to assume an intentional stance such that these questions could be discovered and perhaps become the subject for additional work.

7.9 What We Have Found

In this paper we have proposed that design research methods might vary significantly from those typically used in science, but that these approaches should not be considered to be in competition. We suggest instead that they are moments on a continuum of various approaches to understanding phenomena. We see research methods to be tactical, chosen for their perceived relation to the task at hand. Design research methods might provide superior tools for exploratory investigations. We believe that design methods might be suitable for research situations where the questions are not tightly scripted, are complex, or perhaps not yet even formed. They might also be useful in situations where significant progress is no longer being made within a particular paradigm and therefore an attempt should be made to recast the nature of the inquiry [1].

Design approaches to research differ from the scientific in the epistemological foundations of the discipline, in the different values placed by each on working with incomplete information, multiple variables, and in the fullness of the phenomena. Designers have a high tolerance for ambiguity and are comfortable in looking for questions as well as answers. Perhaps these disciplinary predispositions are appropriate to certain kinds of research inquiry. Including such research approaches could facilitate complex, multi-disciplinary research tasks, and aid in implementing the findings into application in the field.

References

1. Agre, P. (1995). The soul gained and lost: Artificial intelligence as a philosophical project. *Stanford Humanities Review, 4*(2), 1–19.
2. Beer, R. (2000). Dynamical approaches to cognitive science. *Trends in Cognitive Sciences, 4*(3), 91–99.
3. Besenecker, U. C. (2016). *Beyond appearances: The experience of equivalent colors in architecture*. PhD Dissertation in Architectural Sciences, School of Architecture, Rensselaer Polytechnic Institute.
4. Besenecker, U. C., & Krueger, T. (2015). Luminous color in architecture: Exploring methodologies for design-relevant research. *Enquiry: A Journal for Architectural Research, 12*(1), 35–46.
5. Cross, N. (2001). Designerly ways of knowing. *Design Issues, 17*(3), 49–55.
6. Frayling, C. (1993/1994). Research in art and design. *Royal College of Art Research Papers, 1*(1), 1–5.
7. Glanville, R. (1999). Researching design and designing research. *Design Issues, 15*(2), 80–91.
8. Glanville, R. (2007). Try again. Fail again. Fail better: The cybernetics in design and the design in cybernetics. *Kybernetes, 36*(9/10), 1173–1206.
9. Glanville, R. (2007). Design prepositions. In M. Belderbos & J. Verbeke (Eds.), *The unthinkable doctorate* (pp. 115–126). Brussels: Sint Lucas.
10. Glanville, R. (2009). A (cybernetic) musing: Certain propositions concerning prepositions. In *The black boox vol. III. 39 steps* (pp. 319–329). Vienna: edition echoraum.
11. Glynn, S. (1985). Science and perception as design. *Design Studies, 6*(3), 122–126.
12. Gromala, D. (2016). Pain Matters: Outliers in new tribes and territories. *Digital Creativity, 27*(4), 288–303.
13. Johnson, N. (2000). Importance of diversity: Reconciling natural selection and noncompetitive processes. *Annals of the New York Academy of Sciences, 901*(1), 54–66.
14. Johnson, N., & Dautenhahn, K. (1998). Collective problem solving: Functionality beyond the individual. Los Alamos National Laboratory technical report: LA-UR-98-2227.
15. Kirsh, D., & Maglio, P. (1994). On distinguishing epistemic from pragmatic action. *Cognitive Science, 18*(4), 513–549.
16. Krueger, T. (2006). Nonsense. *Technoetic Arts, 4*(3), 183–191.
17. Krueger, T. (2011). *Designing epistemology*. Doctoral dissertation, RMIT University. Available at: http://researchbank.rmit.edu.au/eserv/rmit:160161/KruegerIII.pdf. Accessed 19 Jan 2019.
18. Krueger, T. (2012). I don't know. In R. Glanville (Ed.), *Trojan Horses: A rattle bag from the 'Cybernetics: Art, design, mathematic—A meta-disciplinary conversation' post-conference workshop* (pp. 39–50). Vienna: edition echoraum.

19. Krueger, T. (2013). Listening to the inaudible. *Cybernetics and Human Knowing, 20*(1/2), 31–38.
20. Oliveros, P., & Krueger, T. (2016). A composer's practice. *Digital Creativity, 27*(4), 282–287.
21. O'Regan, J. K., & Alva, N. (2001). A sensorimotor account of vision and visual consciousness. *Behavioral and Brain Sciences, 24*(05), 939–973.
22. Sheets-Johnstone, M. (2009). Animation: The fundamental, essential, and properly descriptive concept. *Continental Philosophy Review, 42*(3), 375–400.
23. Tyler, S. (1984). The vision quest in the West, or what the mind's eye sees. *Journal of Anthropological Research, 40*(1), 23–40.
24. Varela, F. J., Thompson, E., & Rosch, E. (1991). *The embodied mind. Cognitive science and human experience* (pp. 24–27). Cambridge, MA: MIT Press.
25. Weschler, L. (1982). *Seeing is forgetting the name of the thing one sees: A life of contemporary artist Robert Irwin.* Berkeley: University of California Press.

Ted Krueger is Associate Professor of Architecture at Rensselaer Polytechnic Institute. His doctoral dissertation, "Designing Epistemology", was supervised by Ranulph Glanville and co-supervised by Leon van Schaik at RMIT. He holds a professional Masters of Architecture degree from Columbia University following undergraduate work at the University of Wisconsin-Madison. Krueger's design work and writings have resulted in numerous publications, exhibitions, and lectures on an international basis for the last twenty-five years. He is a member of the editorial board of the British media research journal Digital Creativity and recently guest co-edited its special issue "Creative technologies and innovation: health and well-being".

Ute Besenecker is a design researcher focusing on the impact of lighting on perception, behavior and wellbeing. She is interested in facilitating interdisciplinary collaboration between mixed-methods research, engineering and design application. Her background spans academic human factors research as well as professional practice in lighting design, regulatory policy and architecture. Besenecker holds a PhD in Architectural Sciences from Rensselaer Polytechnic Institute, as well as Master's Degrees in Lighting from the Lighting Research Center at RPI, and in Architecture and Design from Columbia University, from the Leibnitz Universität Hannover, Germany, and from the Polytechnico di Milano, Italy.

Chapter 8
Constructing Cybernetic Thinking, Design, and Education

Christiane M. Herr

Abstract Radical constructivism can be described as the epistemological twin of second-order cybernetics. This chapter presents a close look at radical constructivism, at its implications for design, and at the interrelatedness of epistemology and design in their theoretical as well as in their applied manifestations. The chapter discusses connections between three aspects of design cybernetics: design as a domain of action, cybernetics as its theoretical complement and radical constructivism as an epistemological basis for both. It further outlines implications of radical constructivist thinking for design research and design education.

Keywords Radical constructivism · Epistemology · Design cybernetics · Design research · Design education · Design process · Design conversation

8.1 Introduction

8.1.1 Design as Construction: A Brief Overview

Seeing cybernetics as one side of a coin, Ranulph Glanville placed on some occasions radical constructivism, and on other occasions design on the opposite side of that coin [16, p. 27; 18, p. 11]. Findeli, in turn, related these two possible opposite sides by pointing out that "[radical constructivist] epistemology is, for the time being, the most adequate to describe design's complex epistemological status" [8, p. 2]. We are therefore, in a way, dealing with a three-sided metaphorical coin, with design and cybernetics on two of its sides and radical constructivism on the third side offering an epistemological bridge between the two concerns of our field *Design Cybernetics*. The purpose of this chapter is to explore this bridge.

To position radical constructivist thinking as an integral element of design cybernetics as well as of design research, the following sections gradually weave

C. M. Herr (✉)
Department of Architecture, Xi'an Jiaotong-Liverpool University, Suzhou, Jiangsu Province, China
e-mail: christiane.herr@xjtlu.edu.cn

T. Fischer, C. M. Herr (eds.), *Design Cybernetics*, Design Research Foundations,
https://doi.org/10.1007/978-3-030-18557-2_8

together several strands of thinking. For this purpose, I assume that readers are familiar with design and design research, and begin with a brief outline of key thoughts and developments linking design, design research and design cybernetics before discussing their relationships to radical constructivism. In connecting these three fields, the chapter substantiates Glanville's perspective that conceptual construction can be described not only as underlying all design processes, but as the "most fundamental of human activities, as the way we think and work" [14, p. 107].

Designers tend to focus on their creative processes [17] and typically see the utility of new ideas primarily in their inspirational quality rather than their explanatory capacity. Theory and terminology used in the context of applied design thus often remains vague and evocative, to allow for productive interpretation on the part of designers. The development of design research as a field of enquiry broadened the scope of the discipline to now embrace and integrate specific and applied as well as abstract and analytical aspects of design as both practice and theory. Within the framework of design research, designing is now recognised as a form of enquiry in its own right that generates particular forms of understanding [6]. Design research encompasses both evocative-productive as well as analytical-explanatory modes of thinking, often as oscillating complementary perspectives. The mutual engagement of these two perspectives is regarded as creatively productive, both with regards to thinking and doing.

Design research developed over the course of several decades, eventually transitioning from a science-oriented paradigm to the more design-specific paradigm it is today. While the earlier design methods movement conceived research in design primarily within the broader framework of science [5], later developments started to acknowledge designing as an activity capable of addressing questions beyond the typical scope of science. As Rittel and Webber [41] established in their seminal paper *Dilemmas in a general theory of planning*, the close observation and analysis of design practice leads to the realisation that design tasks and processes are of a particular, "wicked" nature, a characteristic trait that had gone mostly unrecognised and underestimated until described explicitly by Rittel and Webber. Further examination of design processes in the decades since Rittel and Webber first published their observations has yielded more insights into the techniques designers use to address design challenges by employing particular ways of doing, thinking and knowing [2, 4]. More recently, design has been framed within an even larger context: Glanville [13] has argued that design should not be considered a disciplinary subset of science – instead, science should be considered a specific and constrained form of design. Assuming that designing is fundamental to human thinking and doing, how can we describe and communicate about design in a way that is well-defined and makes design thinking and design processes accessible both within and beyond the field of design?

Design cybernetics as introduced in this volume contributes to the development of a conceptual framework that describes design in its own terms, for its own purposes. In the following sections, I give a brief outline of connections between design as a domain of action, cybernetics as its theoretical complement and radical constructivism as an epistemological basis for both. For the sake of brevity, I outline arguments in a condensed form and invite interested readers to further consult key references given for all three fields as well as other chapters in this volume.

8.1.2 The Close Relationships of Design, Cybernetics and Radical Constructivism

Cybernetics as a field of thought emerged from the intense interdisciplinary exchange that took place at the Macy Conferences [36], which were organised between 1946 and 1953 with the aim of bridging various, increasingly specialised and isolated branches of science. At these conferences, scholars from diverse fields including physics, biology, sociology, anthropology, medicine, mathematics and engineering identified and discussed processes and patterns common to the involved disciplines. These observations were made explicit and specific transdisciplinary vocabulary was invented to operationalise the newly developed insights – among these now well-known notions are feedback, stability, black box, variety, constraint and regulation. In his early *Introduction to Cybernetics*, Ashby [1, p. 1] emphasises that cybernetics as a discipline does offer insight into, but is not dependent on or derived from, other branches of science – instead, it has its own foundations. Cybernetics is thus similar to design as a field of scholarly enquiry, which also employs methods and perspectives from various other fields, including the sciences, for its purposes, but is not derived solely from them. Developments in design and cybernetics share yet more parallels, including their adoption, and eventual rejection of, the technical-rationalist approach. In the field of design, this happened in the form of the design methods movement.[1] In cybernetics, a strand of research investigating the consequences of observer involvement in examined systems eventually distanced itself from a more technically focused strand investigating machine intelligence based on science-based methods [33]. The former strand of cybernetics addresses questions broadly relating to living systems and became known as *second-order cybernetics* [54]. Over the past decades, it has developed close links to art and design (see for example [19]). Glanville (see Chap. 2) has characterised the relationship between design and cybernetics as an integral one: cybernetics offers theory for design, whereas design is cybernetics in practice.

Design and cybernetics have in common their interest in process. Ashby [1, p. 1] already characterises cybernetics as a discipline that is less concerned with describing "what is", instead focusing on the question "what does it do?". A similar concern is typical of design, which is primarily concerned with practice, or in cybernetic terms, action [17]. Practice and academic disciplines grounded in applied practice are different from theoretically focused descriptive or predictive science-based disciplines. Schön examined this difference in *The Reflective Practitioner* [42], where he uses examples from a variety of fields, including education and architecture, to illustrate particular modes of knowing, thinking and doing in practice-based disciplines that differ markedly from those typically encountered in fields grounded in technical rationality. Design and cybernetics are both concerned with cyclical processes, in particular those in which observers are not neutral but actively involved,

[1] See pp. 30ff. in this volume.

introducing aims and intentions. While most of applied design practice consists of such processes, they can be challenging to describe and analyse. In order to make explicit, examine and share insights derived from design processes, the question arises how notions such as understanding, creativity, learning or knowledge can be characterised in this particular context? Established frameworks and notions derived from other (especially science-based) disciplines do not adequately capture experiences and observations generated from active engagement in design processes.

The radical constructivist perspective addresses these questions by explaining epistemological processes of coming to understand in a way that integrates well with the perspectives of both design and cybernetics. Similar to design and second-order cybernetics, radical constructivism developed relatively recently. As a consolidated theory, it was introduced under its current name by von Glasersfeld [55], who rooted his argument in thoughts developed in the works of Giambattista Vico, Silvio Ceccato and in particular in Jean Piaget's genetic epistemology [58]. Von Glasersfeld developed radical constructivism in close relationship with cybernetic thought, and proposed it around the same time as von Foerster established second-order cybernetics [54], with the main proponents of both theories knowing each other, developing their thoughts in exchange with each other as well as relying on each other's works. Second-order cybernetics and radical constructivist perspectives complement each other: both describe observers acting within, and making sense of, cyclical processes they are actively engaged in. The respective interests of cybernetics and radical constructivism are however slightly different: where cybernetics focuses more on the description of such processes, radical constructivism pursues epistemological questions regarding the nature of knowing arising from these processes. With both cybernetics and radical constructivism concerned with creating descriptions and theory, it may be easy to see how design forms the active and engaged aspects of these processes.

In the following sections of this chapter, I give a brief introduction and background of radical constructivist theory and examine how a radical constructivist perspective can provide an epistemological grounding for design cybernetics. The chapter concludes with a section discussing implications of radical constructivist thinking for design, design research and design education.

8.2 Radical Constructivism

Against the background of design cybernetics established in the preceding sections, the following sections introduce radical constructivism and examine its links to design understood as enacted conversation. From a radical constructivist perspective, cognitive processes such as learning and coming to understand can be framed as acts of design, such that *all* learning and understanding can be described as grounded in humans' natural ability to design. In the following, I offer a brief introduction and development history of the radical constructivist perspective.

8.2.1 Constructing Understanding: From Vico to Piaget to von Glasersfeld

Radical constructivism is a theory of knowing, perhaps more appropriately a theory of coming to know [57]. While the term "radical constructivism" may be relatively new, related thinking can be dated back at least to the Italian philosopher Giambattista Vico. In 1710, Vico published a treatise on the construction of knowledge claiming that humans can only know what humans have made [59, p. 92]. Vico differentiates the human perspective from that of God, who, unlike humans, can know the world because He made it. Arguments in a similar vein had already been brought forward by the philosophical school of the Sceptics, who had consistently questioned the possibility of matching knowledge with reality. Vico introduced a more precise position: if humans can only understand what the human mind has made, then they can clearly never grasp external reality [59, p. 92]. In effect, Vico's characterisation of the process of developing understanding as a process of active making replaces preconceptions of understanding as making direct representations of a pre-existing external reality, emphasising instead the active, generative capacity of cognition. The cognising subject can now be described as a maker of knowledge instead of the recipient of objective data obtained from an independently existing reality. Vico's arguments were further compounded by Locke, Berkeley [59, p. 93], Kant, and others, who consistently broke with the conventional philosophical belief that human knowledge must in some way provide a representation of an observer–independent material reality. If human knowing is confined to the faculties of human perception, then any understanding or meaning must be constructed based on individual experience.

Extending this line of thinking, Glasersfeld [55] proposed to "reconstruct" in a fundamental way (thus adding the prefix "radical" to the theory) the concept of knowledge, with the aim of further examining the relationship between the cognitive structures humans build up and external "reality". Given that human perception is necessarily constrained to and determined by individual experience, this relationship cannot imply any direct match or correspondence. Precedents for this type of relationship can be found in Darwin's theory of evolution in the concept of fit, and particularly in Piaget's genetic epistemology [58, p. 30]. In his seminal work *La construction du reel chez l'enfant* [35], Piaget presented a model of how the conceptual structure of objects, space, time and causality can be built up to serve as a mental framework for the construction of a coherent experiential reality. Piaget characterised this process succinctly as: "intelligence organizes the world by organizing itself" [35, p. 311]. Further clarifying and developing Piaget's theory, Glasersfeld [57, p. 233] summarises key points of the resulting "radical" constructivism as follows: (1) The function of cognition is adaptive, in the biological sense of the term, tending towards fit or viability, and (2) Cognition serves the subject's organization of the experiential world, not the discovery of an objective ontological reality.

These two key points result in a perspective on cognition that is incompatible with most conventional notions of knowledge as relating to truth and objectivity. Taken seriously, they indicate that we live in, and can only think based on, our experiential worlds. These worlds are neither unchanging nor independent, but "the result of distinctions that generate a physical and a social environment to which, in turn, we adapt as best we can" [57, p. 233]. Piaget describes the cognising subject as abstracting regularities and rules from individual experience, which enable it to avoid disagreeable situations and, to some extent, to generate agreeable ones. Cumulatively, processes of abstracting regularities and rules from experience lead to the construction of mental frameworks that guide behaviours intended to achieve desirable results. This is characterised by Piaget as "assimilation". Over time, such regularities and rules are selected and modified based on how well they fit experiences as well as likely results of actions. If actions do not lead to results anticipated based on existing models of regularities, they can be reconsidered and modified in a process Piaget describes as "accommodation" [57, p. 234]. Accommodation happens when an existing mental model does not lead to adequate results, crating a perturbation leading to either a modification of the action causing the perturbation or to a modification of the abstracted pattern that did not fit what was experienced. In the radical constructivist perspective, processes of accommodation are key to any form of knowing and learning.

8.2.2 Acting in Order to Understand and Understanding in Order to Act: A Design-Based Epistemology

The radical constructivist perspective emphasises action: actions generate experiences, which in turn generate opportunities to construct understanding, which again informs action. In radical constructivist thinking, concepts of "truth" or aiming for a match with a given external reality are replaced by the biological notion of "viability": actions, concepts, and conceptual operations are viable if they fit the purposive or descriptive contexts in which they are used [58, p. 31]. Viable understandings are attained through acting and exploring, to generate experiences and allow construction of understanding. A common preconception is that generally, understanding should precede acting and that theory is superior to practice (which depends on and is justified by theory), with post-rationalisation usually regarded as a shortcoming [17, p. 1294]. In the context of radical constructivism, this preconception seems short-sighted: If acting generates understanding, and understanding, in turn, generates acting, the relationship of acting and doing can be described more appropriately as cyclical. Acting leads to understanding leads to acting. Praxis leads to theory leads to praxis. In this new perspective on the process of understanding, a linearly-causal model is thus replaced by a cycle of mutual influences which, Glanville [17, p. 1294] notes, allows progression in time and the aspiration to improve.

The cyclical nature of this process of coming to understand is a cybernetic one that centres around learning, as learning forms the means by which action is transformed into understanding, and understanding, in turn, is transformed into acting [17, p. 1295]. In a similar manner, Schön's description of "reflective practice" [42] emphasises the interconnected and cyclical relationship of acting and understanding. In Schön's account, reflection is posited as a reflection on action, such that it can be assumed that action forms the starting point of the cycle. In addition, Schön draws attention to the different types of understanding that can be generated during reflective practice: knowing is not limited to explicit theoretical knowing that can be formalised as "knowledge". It can also be inherent in action, adding a "knowing for" to the conventional "knowing of" [17, p. 1295]. This type of knowing is tacit and resists codification or articulation [37]. It also forms a key aspect of knowing and learning as it happens during the process of designing. Design learning encompasses forms of learning exceeding explicit knowing, such as visual understanding (being able to see or recognise without being able to make explicit how this is done) or adopting a new type of aesthetic appreciation [20]. It is not surprising that in his study of reflective practice, Schön focused particularly on designing and design learning, with many case studies deriving from architectural studio education [43, 44].

In summary, the construction of understanding from experience as it is described in radical constructivism is grounded in acting. This implies that learning, understanding and designing are intimately connected in a cybernetic cycle: they all form part of circular conversational processes that generate new insight. Acting leads to experience, which leads to construction of understanding, which leads to learning, which, in turn, leads to acting.

8.3 Constructing Design Cybernetics

Design cybernetics integrates the various relationships and connections outlined above into a coherent field of study. Cybernetics offers a theory of and for design, whereas design forms the practice of cybernetics (see Chap. 2). Design cybernetics extends conversation theory into design contexts and offers an account of how new thoughts can arise from differences in interpretation during the *process of navigating the new*. From the design-cybernetic perspective, design processes can be described as circularly causal conversations, usually held through a medium such as paper and pencil, with an other – or oneself acting as an other – as the conversational partner [13, p. 88]. In a typical design process, designers typically sketch, then look at the sketch anew and differently, see something that was not sketched intentionally, take on that new idea, produce another sketch and so on. The designer affects the sketch, and the sketch affects the designer [9, p. 1012].

Radical constructivist theory complements design cybernetics by providing an epistemological grounding, showing how creativity is inherent in human beings' every interaction with their experiential worlds. It addresses particularly the question of how we construct our individual conceptual worlds and how we come to create abstract concepts and patterns from our experience. Designing is central to the radical constructivist view on the construction of understanding, and radical constructivism in turn offers an epistemological basis for design cybernetics.

In the following, I explore and discuss the implications of the radical constructivist perspective on different aspects of design cybernetics, specifically addressing design practice, research and education. In keeping with the radical constructivist perspective, this is done with the understanding that radical constructivist principles cannot be adopted as an absolute and authoritative "truth" – they can only provide a working hypothesis that may or may not turn out to be viable [57, p. 233].

8.3.1 Radical Constructivism as a Basis for Design Cybernetics

The earlier sections of this chapter have already shown that descriptions of cognitive processes in radical constructivism and descriptions of creative processes in design cybernetics share many similarities and can complement each other. What, then, are the implications of considering radical constructivism in terms of design cybernetics, and design cybernetics in terms of radical constructivism?

Taking the radical constructivist perspective seriously implies that all understanding is constructed in response to individual experience, and that understanding is maintained and revised based on ongoing feedback generated from experience to make sure it remains viable. This process is of a circular, conversational nature, where the conversational "other" is a "reality" that is only accessible in an indirect manner, through constraints and boundaries it imposes on our actions and which we can learn about only through experience. From the perspective of design cybernetics, the construction of new understanding can be described as design process since it happens as part of conversational exchanges, where new ideas emerge through conversation participants' constructive interpretation of others' expressions. Designing thus forms the central cognitive act through which human beings create artefacts as well as thoughts and concepts [14, p. 108].

Already in the first key paper that established – though inadvertently – the notion of "radical constructivism", von Glasersfeld [55, p. 6] explains the process of constructing understanding based on the black box, a cybernetic device [1, p. 86]. A black box is a conceptual tool that allows the mapping of actions in the form of "inputs" to experiences in the form of "outputs", whereby inputs and outputs are not externally given but distinguished depending on intentions and purpose [15]. The inner workings of the black box do not need to be explained or made explicit, what matters is that the relationship between chosen inputs and outputs remains stable enough to predict results of actions in a reasonably reliable manner [55, p. 7]. In this way, viable understandings of an "external world" and our "selves" can be constructed on the basis of input-output relations.

Radical constructivism recognises action or practice as a precondition for generating understanding and learning, mirroring applied designing. In both design cybernetics and radical constructivism, thinking is understood as a process of experimenting with assumptions and experiences in relation to feedback derived from experience. The radical constructivist perspective has yet another implication: If we construct our worlds based on conversational encounters and experience, this also implies that even our making sense of sensory data can be described as inherently constructive. Perception cannot be conceived as a neutral pathway for obtaining data from an observer-independent external reality. Instead, perception itself can be assumed to be naturally generative and a constant source of novelty fuelling creative conversational encounters. It may be argued that human beings cannot help but construct new understanding even in seemingly passive perceptive processes [38]. I thus argue further below that fostering new ways of "seeing" is a key part of design education and forms a considerable part of building up tacit design knowing.

In second-order cybernetics, related discourse has already developed for decades. Von Foerster [53] for example demonstrated the constructive nature of perception with detailed discussions of the characteristics of neurons, which can encode quantities but not qualities, as well as simple experiments such as the ability of visual perception to "fill in" the blind spot existing in all humans' visual field. Emphasising the active, engaged nature of perception, Foerster summarises his discussion by formulating his Aesthetical Imperative: "If you desire to see, learn how to act" [53, p. 227].

A recent related account of the constructive nature of memory has been given by Riegler [39], who also draws on a large body of earlier work on the subject in cybernetics, including the work of von Foerster. In the field of design research, the constructive nature of perception is also increasingly recognised, for example in the work of Suwa [48], who describes constructive perception as a learned but tacit design skill of experienced designers. These developments coincide with growing awareness of constructive (automated) aspects of perception in the field of cognitive science [47, p. 129–134].

8.3.2 A Focus on Acting: Implications for Design Practice

Adopting the radical constructivist perspective does not necessarily affect or change the basic action of designing. It however emphasises the significance of explorative action in design and provides a counterpoint to conventional assumptions that understanding should first be established through theoretical means before it can be applied in design processes. Similarly, the conventional assumption that good research directly leads to good design can be questioned. From a radical constructivist viewpoint, postrationalisation and learning while acting do not appear as somewhat deficient forms of reasoning but as key activities supporting learning during and following design processes [17]. In this sense, understanding is designed and the direct outcome of design processes: from the radical constructivist perspective, design can be considered as the basic cognitive act, the "most fundamental of human activities" [14, p. 107].

While designing as an activity may not change much as a result of adopting the radical constructivist perspective, the theoretical framework offered by radical constructivism and design cybernetics can change the ways in which designers perceive and discuss their activities. Instead of speaking of goal-oriented processes such as "problem solving" or "optimisation" in reference to other fields of study, designers may find it useful to conceive of designing as a way of navigating constraints. Fischer and Richards [10] describe the advantages of this process-oriented perspective and argue that the constraint-oriented approach supports ways of thinking that are not primarily oriented towards goals or achievements but allow for various pathways of exploration. Constraints, in this context, can be perceived not so much as limiting, but as opportunities. Outcomes of constraint-based design processes may even become secondary to the quality of the explorative design process. Designers' focusing on processes of dynamic navigation of constraints also explains Schön's [45, p. 181] observation that designers are not proceeding arbitrarily but tend to establish rules to organize and direct their work. These rules, however, are also found to be "largely implicit, overlapping, diverse, variously applied, contextually dependent, subject to exceptions and to critical modification". These characteristics point to the benefits of a conversational, constraint-oriented rather than a linear, goal-oriented process.

Adopting a design cybernetic approach, Jonas [26, p. 1362] similarly stresses that the core of designing "cannot be found in the axiomatic statements of the formal sciences, nor in the empirical approaches of the natural sciences, nor in the hermeneutic techniques of the humanities". Instead, it can be found in its explorative and novelty-generating conversational nature that allows design to integrate constraints and requirements deriving from artefacts and their human, social and natural contexts. Jonas [26, p. 1362] argues that design, accordingly, could be more consistent in applying its own logic and methods to itself. It is in this spirit that Glanville [12] has argued that science, with its constrained use of constructive-creative thinking, can be considered as a subset of design.

8.3.3 Implications for Design Research

Design research pursues knowing in the context of design, which can take a variety of forms [7, 27]. Of particular concern in design as a practice-based discipline is the integration of action-oriented styles of knowing (Glanville's "knowing for" [17]) with abstract modes of knowing (Glanville's "knowing of" [17]). Design research can be further differentiated according to its specific areas of focus as well as the types of knowing expected to be generated from it. Citing the distinction between "research about", "research for" and "research through" design that was first proposed by Frayling [11], Michel [32, p. 16] argues that the "research through design" approach has special epistemological significance in contemporary design research. Research through design supports at least as much development of application- or action-oriented as formal forms of knowing. More recently, Jonas [28, p. 15] has extended the earlier three forms of design research with "research as design". While Michel [32] clearly separates application-oriented and academic research, it may be argued (especially from a radical constructivist background) that most forms of research involve both aspects, if to different extents. Research through design, as well as research as design, explicitly employ design as research method. In research through design, design provides a pathway to gain both abstract understanding and practical outcomes. Recent descriptions of "constructive design research" [30] for example examine applied research processes realised through the construction of artefacts, but do not link to questions of cognitive construction. In research as design, on the other hand, research approaches themselves are examined as ongoing design processes. Both approaches are relatively new additions to the conventional methodological apparatus of design research and call for new discourse. Research through design provokes the question of how design can be a suitable method for rigorous investigation if it is opportunistic and dynamic in nature? Research as design, on the other hand, raises the question whether, and how explicitly, existing research cultures orchestrate and account for the design processes inherent in their ongoing development. Despite involving much implicit creativity and innovation, these omnipresent processes are rarely if ever made explicit in particular in the context of science-based disciplines.

With its grounding in design processes, research through design is closely related to design cybernetics, and cybernetic terms and notions as discussed in the preceding sections can be used to describe and examine characteristics of research through design. Design research itself can be framed as a form of second-order cybernetic practice, as Sweeting [50, 51] has argued. The radical constructivist perspective reinforces this viewpoint: in particular research through design is a fundamentally constructive process that enacts constructive cognitive processes as described by Glasersfeld [55]. From the perspective of radical constructivism and cybernetics, distinctions made between the different types of design research are less clearly defined, as, being constructed instead of being found in external reality, all involve conversational (design) processes. It may be argued (see [26, 27], Chap. 14 in this volume) that distinctions between them may be more appropriately made from a perspective that considers the relative position and motivation of the observer when deciding how to frame a particular research intention. The radical constructivist perspective can even inform the way in which design research discourse is orchestrated as collective learning, as discussed for example in Sweeting and Hohl's [52] recent account of conversational conferences.

Along the lines of Cross [6], design research may be more adequately considered as a discipline in its own right instead of striving to become more scientific. The radical constructivist perspective strengthens design as an independent field of research, and offers its own, cybernetically informed methods of enquiry and its own forms of rigour. Conceiving design research as a form of both design and construction in the sense of Glanville [14], a key question emerging for further investigation in the future is what constitutes rigour in design research (through design and as design)? How do we construct frameworks that allow us to assess viability of design research outcomes? Fischer (Chap. 14 in this volume) discusses in detail different models for doing design cybernetic PhD research, navigating between formal requirements geared to conventional science-based PhD studies and design cybernetic ways of pursuing research. In this context, it may be helpful to consider similar discourse on the concept of "action research", which has developed for decades, primarily in social science and educational research [31]. Similar to design research, action research was developed to allow researchers to engage directly with the situation under investigation and to allow research outcomes to generate desirable change. Action research is closely related to design research in that it allows researchers to act as involved participant observers who hide neither their values nor their aims when engaging with situations. Depending on situation and context, outcomes of action research consist of both desired change in practice as well as more abstract understanding that may be made explicit to become shareable with others. Similar to design processes, the action research process is modelled as a recursive cycle, which unfolds in time to become a spiral. In close analogy to Schön's characterisation of "reflective practice" [42], each cycle includes action-focused as well as reflective and design-focused stages. Not surprisingly, the development of action research frequently related to simultaneously developing constructivist ideas and approaches, as they can be found in the work of Kolb [29] or Carr and Kemmis [3]. The similarities between action research and practice-based design research are so compelling that Swann [49] has suggested action research could be immediately adopted as a method in design research. Potential crossovers and more mutual awareness between these two related and developing approaches to research may be an agenda for future development for design researchers, as recent studies indicate [46]. Often, however, epistemological implications of constructivist approaches to learning and knowledge are ignored, which, as in Järvinen's approach [25], can lead to the subsumption of action research into rationalist science-oriented approaches to design research.

8.3.4 Constructive Design Education

The radical constructivist viewpoint has significant implications on conceptions of education. From the radical constructivist perspective, understanding cannot be transferred or passively received, it has to be actively built up by learners based on experience [56]. Learning and teaching approaches based on radical constructivist thinking thus focus on offering learners opportunities to engage actively in construction of understanding from experience. Learning is characterised as processes of accommodation in which learners modify existing mental schemata in interaction with their environments [58, p. 65]. This contrasts with the conventional view of education as dispensing given knowledge, with knowledge conceived of as a value-free and objective commodity. From a constructivist perspective, students are best motivated through awareness of the reasons why particular ways of thinking and acting are considered desirable instead of the authority of a claim to objective truth. In design learning through reflection in action, a similar focus on"what works" echoes the radical constructivist perspective: learning and understanding in the context of

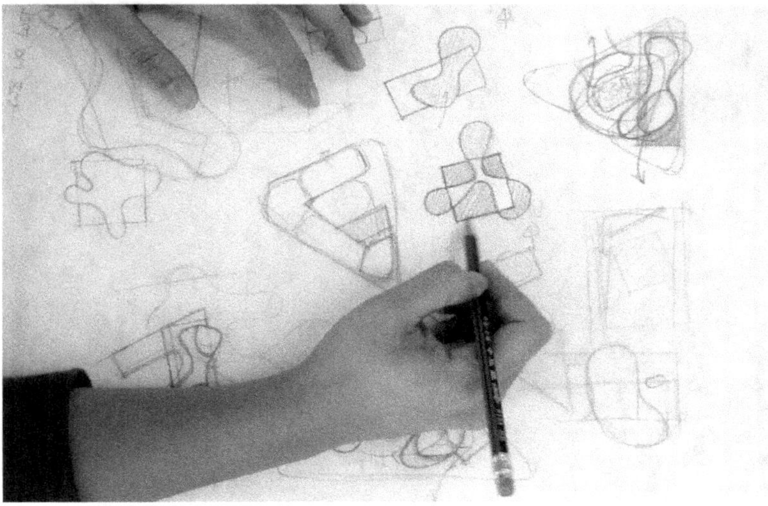

Fig. 8.1 Acting to understand and understanding to act: Cyclic design conversation with pen and paper in the architectural design studio

design-based education are not limited to the abstract and explicit but also include the concrete and tacit [42]. Figures 8.1 and 8.2 illustrate observable aspects of conversational design learning, involving designing both as a means to generate designed artefacts as well as a means to understand. Glanville [17, p. 1297] has differentiated two distinct styles of knowing that support designing: the conventional abstract "knowledge of" and the action-oriented "knowledge for", and argued that while the former is the style of knowledge focused on in conventional research, the latter matters at least as much in action-oriented disciplines such as design.

In educational practice, von Glasersfeld [58] distinguishes teaching from training. Training uses external motivators to elicit desirable behaviours and responses from students, whereas teaching seeks to motivate students intrinsically. Von Glasersfeld emphasises that only intrinsic motivation promotes understanding as students seek to grasp new ideas beyond rote learning. While external motivators such as rewards or grades may quickly generate desired outcomes in exercises of rote memorisation, they do not necessarily lead to individually constructed understanding. Intrinsic motivation can be derived from feelings of satisfaction generated by insight: von Glasersfeld suggests that such self-generated learning engenders a desire for extension and motivates further learning and understanding. Design-based education decidedly relies on student motivation and embraces both "knowledge of" and "knowledge for". This implies that understanding gained during design is not limited to the abstract and explicit and that action is as important as reflection [42, 43].

In addition to motivating learning through perceived usefulness, radical constructivist teaching aims to support students in developing a personal relationship of interest and awareness with a field of study. Among the teaching strategies that

Fig. 8.2 Acting to understand and understanding to act: Cyclic design conversation with physical models in the architectural design studio

may be employed to support these aims (as I have discussed in greater detail in [20] and [22]) are tasks that call for open-ended approaches to address them, and which allow for creativity and diversity in solution proposals. Well-rounded construction of understanding will likely result from processes in which learners try out several different angles and methods to address a given task – which also includes, and even necessitates, repeated failures. Typical tasks preferred in radical constructivist education thus have a strong design component. Conventional rote learning and external motivation do not have to be entirely abandoned but may be seen as complementary offering, establishing socially determined bodies of learning in formal education. Generally, accommodating a plurality of learning and teaching approaches may be most suitable to provide engaging and motivating learning experiences to a variety of individual learning preferences (a recent discussion of various approaches to radical constructivist education is provided in [40]). The radical constructivist perspective also affects approaches to the assessment of learning, which typically focuses on the quality of the process of constructing learning. It may generally be helpful in this context to not assess students directly on the outcomes of their learning, but to develop assessment strategies for the quality of learners' individual reflection and analysis of their own learning experiences.

A cybernetic perspective on learning and teaching grounded in radical constructivist epistemology implies that learning cannot be caused directly by teachers, drawing teachers' attention instead on the creation of learning environments in which desirable changes may be likely to occur [34]. Learning experiences that involve others, in particular peers, can provide motivation and a sense of relevance as well as a more varied and dynamic environment in which understanding can be developed. Such learning environments can include teachers, artifacts, texts, various forms of exchange as well as (even if implicitly) larger social and cultural frameworks. Within the design-oriented disciplines, design learning typically happens in the design studio, where students find an intense and challenging yet open and flexible environment to develop individual understanding in a distinctly action-oriented context. The design studio offers a broad variety of opportunities for constructing understanding individually, all embedded within an intense exchange between learners and their environments to support action alongside reflection. Accordingly, Schön [42, 43] has taken considerable interest in, and examined in detail, design studio learning and teaching in the context of architecture. Many similarities exist between radical constructivist educational approaches and those found in the design studio, which is a core part of design education and well known within, but much less known outside the design-oriented disciplines. Even so, studio design education tends to be clearly separated from other courses, which often adopt more conventional modes of learning and teaching that frame learning as a transaction or a transfer of understanding from teacher to learner. From a radical constructivist viewpoint, design studio learning and teaching approaches could however be extended to offer learners opportunities for lasting high-quality learning beyond the design studio, as I have discussed elsewhere [21, 22].

A final note to conclude this brief discussion of design cybernetic education grounded in a radical constructivist epistemology concerns the relationship of learning and perception that was already raised in Sects. 8.2.2 and 8.3.1. Learning, especially in practice-based disciplines, includes tacit modes of understanding that include learned ways of “seeing”. From a radical constructivist viewpoint, this learned aspect of perception is of considerable interest as it directly impacts the way in which individuals relate to their environments and the types of experiences they are able to derive from these environments as a foundation for their construction of understanding. Discipline-specific ways of seeing cannot be transferred, they have to be cultivated over time, similarly to conceptual worlds in Piaget’s and Glasersfeld’s descriptions [55]. Building up discipline-specific ways of seeing and perceiving arguably form a core aspect of professional knowing, and indirectly, professional identity. If perception can be assumed to be generative, then conversational exchanges based on perception will naturally produce discipline-specific experiences even before explicit cognitive models are formed. In this way, learned forms of perception and appreciation [20] can inspire creative conversational exchanges between individuals and their environments while largely bypassing explicit modes of conceptual knowing.

8.4 Summary and Outlook

In this chapter, I have outlined connections between three aspects of design cybernetics: design as a domain of action, cybernetics as its theoretical complement and radical constructivism as an epistemological basis for both [23]. The act of construction in radical constructivism can be characterised as a form of design, whereas design can be characterised as a form of cognitive construction: they may even be described as essentially the same activity [14, p. 108]. Radical constructivism offers design researchers new vocabulary for and a new epistemological framing of the design process, a "design-based epistemology". Within design cybernetics, radical constructivism links reflection and action in the *process of navigating the new*. Conversely, design cybernetics draws attention to the similarities of conversational design processes and epistemological processes of constructing understanding and so informs radical constructivism [24]. The radical constructivist perspective allows the framing of design, learning and thinking as different aspects of the same process. Taking it seriously has a range of implications that affect design practice, design education as well as design employed as a form of research. Beyond these implications, discussed in more detail in Sect. 8.3, radical constructivism as part of cybernetically informed practice may also have an impact on the ways in which collective learning and researching can be structured, as shown in the recent development of conversational conference formats [52].

Similar to second-order cybernetics, radical constructivism as well as design can be characterised as "a way of thinking and a way of being in the world" [18]. All three are enacted dynamically as parts of processes that involve practice as well as abstract reflection. In this sense, they do not offer bodies of theory readily available for goal-oriented linear application. Instead, these bodies of theory change actions indirectly, by informing observers' perspectives. As part of design cybernetics, radical construcivism supports cyclical processes of navigation that aim for some form of what Glasersfeld has characterised as "fit". This chapter, as this entire volume, offers insights into an ongoing collective design process that aims to develop new understandings as well as new ways of acting in the continuing construction of design cybernetics and design research.

References

1. Ashby, W. R. (1956). *An introduction to cybernetics*. London: Chapman and Hall.
2. Bayazit, N. (2004). Investigating design: A review of forty years of design research. *Design Issues, 20*(1), 16–29.
3. Carr, W., & Kemmis, S. (1986). *Becoming critical: Education, knowledge and action research*. Lewes: Falmer.
4. Cross, N. (1982). Designerly ways of knowing. *Design Studies, 3*(4), 221–227.
5. Cross, N. (Ed.). (1984). *Developements in design methodology*. Chichester/New York: Wiley.
6. Cross, N. (2007). From a design science to a design discipline: Understanding designerly ways of knowing and thinking. In R. Michel (Ed.), *Design research now: Essays and selected projects* (pp. 41–54). Basel: Birkhäuser.
7. Downton, P. (2003). *Design research*. Melbourne: RMIT Press.
8. Findeli, A. (1999). Introduction. *Design Issues, 15*(2), 1–3.
9. Fischer, T. (2011). When is Analog? When is Digital? *Kybernetes, 40*(7/8), 1004–1014.
10. Fischer, T., & Richards, L. D. (2017). From goal-oriented to constraint-oriented design: The cybernetic intersection of design theory and systems theory. *Leonardo, 50*(1), 36–41.

11. Frayling, C. (1993). Research in art and design. *Royal College of Art Research Papers, 1*(1), 1–5.
12. Glanville, R. (1999). Researching design and designing research. *Design Issues, 15*(2), 80–91.
13. Glanville, R. (1999). Listen! In G. de Zeeuw, M. Vahl, & E. Mennuti (Eds.), *Problems of participation and connection* (pp. 425–432). Lincoln: Lincoln Research Centre.
14. Glanville, R. (2006). Construction and design. *Constructivist Foundations, 1*(3), 103–110.
15. Glanville, R. (2007). Grounding difference. In A. Müller & K.-H. Müller (Eds.), *An unfinished revolution? Heinz von Foerster and the biological computer laboratory 1958–1976* (pp. 361–406). Vienna: Edition Echoraum.
16. Glanville, R. (2012). Radical constructivism = second-order cybernetics. *Cybernetics & Human Knowing, 19*(4), 27–47.
17. Glanville, R. (2014). Acting to understand and understanding to act. *Kybernetes, 43*(9/10), 1293–1300.
18. Glanville, R. (2014). How design and cybernetics reflect each other. Keynote Address given at *Relating Systems Thinking and Design RSD3 2014 Symposium: Relating Systems Thinking and Design 3*. Available at: http://systemic-design.net/wp-content/uploads/2014/08/Ranulph_Glanville.pdf. Accessed 19 Jan 2019.
19. Glanville, R., & Sweeting, B. (Eds.). (2011). Cybernetics: Art, design, mathematics – A meta-disciplinary conversation: Papers from the 2010 conference of the American Society for Cybernetics. *Kybernetes, 40*(7/8).
20. Herr, C. M. (2013). Design education between poetry and prose. *Kybernetes, 42*(9/10), 1404–1412.
21. Herr, C. M. (2013). Qualitative structural design education in large cohorts of undergraduate architecture students. *Global Journal of Engineering Education, 15*(2), 96–102.
22. Herr, C. M. (2014). Radical constructivist structural design education for large cohorts of Chinese learners. *Constructivist Foundations, 9*(3), 393–402.
23. Herr, C. M. (2015). The big picture: Relating design, second order cybernetics and radical constructivism. *Cybernetics and Human Knowing, 22*(2/3), 107–114.
24. Herr, C. M. (2016). What can cybernetics learn from design? *Constructivist Foundations, 11*(3), 583–585.
25. Järvinen, P. (2007). Action research is similar to design science. *Quality and Quantity, 41*, 37–54.
26. Jonas, W. (2007). Research through design through research: A cybernetic model of designing design foundations. *Kybernetes, 36*(9/10), 1362–1380.
27. Jonas, W. (Ed.). (2007). *Design research now: Essays and selected projects*. Basel: Birkhäuser.
28. Jonas, W. (2015). Research through design is more than just a new form of disseminating design outcomes. *Constructivist Foundations, 11*(1), 32–36.
29. Kolb, D. A. (1984). *Experiential learning: Experience as the source of learning and development*. Englewood Cliffs: Prentice-Hall.
30. Koskinen, I., Zimmerman, J., Binder, T., Redström, J., & Wensveen, S. (2011). *Design research through practice. From the lab, field, and showroom*. Amsterdam: Morgan Kaufmann.
31. McNiff, J. (2013). *Action research: Principles and practice*. Abingdon: Routledge.
32. Michel, R. (2007). Introduction. In R. Michel (Ed.), *Design research now: Essays and selected projects* (pp. 15–17). Basel: Birkhäuser.
33. Müller, A., & Müller, K. (Eds.). (2007). *An unfinished revolution? Heinz von Foerster and the biological computer laboratory | BCL 1958–1976*. Vienna: Edition Echoraum.
34. Murray, J. (2006). Cybernetic circularity in teaching and learning. *International Journal of Teaching and Learning in Higher Education, 18*(3), 215–221.
35. Piaget, J. (1937). *La construction du reel chez l'enfant*. Neuchatel: Delachaux et Niestle.
36. Pias, C. (2003). *Cybernetics: The Macy conferences 1946–1953. The complete transactions*. Zürich: Diaphanes Verlag.
37. Polanyi, M. (1966). *The tacit dimension*. Garden City: Doubleday & Company.
38. Richards, J., & von Glasersfeld, E. (1979). The control of perception and the construction of reality. *Dialectica, 33*(1), 37–58.

39. Riegler, A. (2005). Constructive memory. *Kybernetes, 34*(1/2), 89–104.
40. Riegler, A., & Steffe, L. P. (2014). What is the teacher trying to teach students if they are all busy constructing their own private worlds? Introduction to the special issue. *Constructivist Foundations, 9*(3), 297–301. Special Issue: Forty Years of Radical Constructivism in Educational Research.
41. Rittel, H. W. J., & Webber, M. M. (1973). Dilemmas in a general theory of planning. *Policy Sciences, 4*, 155–169.
42. Schön, D. A. (1983). *The reflective practitioner: How professionals think in action*. New York: Basic Books.
43. Schön, D. A. (1985). *The design studio: An exploration of its traditions and potentials*. London: RIBA Publications.
44. Schön, D. A. (1988). Toward a marriage of artistry and applied science in the architectural design studio. *Journal of Architectural Education, 41*(4), 4–10.
45. Schön, D. A. (1988). Designing: Rules, types, and worlds. *Design Studies, 9*(3), 181–190.
46. Sein, M. K., Henfridsson, O., Purao, S., Rossi, M., & Lindgren, R. (2011). Action design research. *MIS Quarterly, 35*(1), 37–56.
47. Sternberg, R. J. (2011). *Cognitive psychology* (6th ed.). Belmont: Thomson Wadsworth.
48. Suwa, M. (2003). Constructive perception: Coordinating perception and conception toward acts of problem-finding in a creative experience. *Japanese Psychological Research, 45*(4), 221–234.
49. Swann, C. (2002). Action research and the practice of design. *Design Issues, 18*(2), 46–61.
50. Sweeting, B. (2015). Cybernetics of practice. *Kybernetes, 44*(8/9), 1397–1405.
51. Sweeting, B. (2016). Design research as a variety of second-order cybernetic practice. *Constructivist Foundations, 11*(3), 572–579.
52. Sweeting, B., & Hohl, M. (2015). Exploring alternatives to the traditional conference format: Introduction to the special issue on composing conferences. *Constructivist Foundations, 11*(1), 1–7.
53. von Foerster, H. (1973). On constructing a reality. In W. F. E. Preiser (Ed.), *Environmental design research* (Vol. 2, pp. 35–46). Stroudberg: Dowden, Hutchinson & Ross. Reprinted in: Heinz von Foerster. (2003). *Understanding understanding* (pp. 211–227). New York: Springer.
54. von Foerster, H. (1974). *The cybernetics of cybernetics*. Champaign-Urban: Biological Computer Laboratory, University of Illinois. Republished as Heinz von Foerster. 1995. *Cybernetics of cybernetics or the control of control and the communication of communication* (2nd ed.). Minneapolis: Future Systems Inc.
55. von Glasersfeld, E. (1974). Piaget and the radical constructivist epistemology. In C. D. Smock & E. von Glasersfeld (Eds.), *Epistemology and education* (pp. 1–24). Athens: Follow Through Publications.
56. von Glasersfeld, E. (1989). Cognition, construction of knowledge, and teaching. *Synthesis, 80*(1), 121–140.
57. von Glasersfeld, E. (1991). An exposition of radical constructivism: Why some like it radical. In G. J. Klir (Ed.), *Facets of systems science* (pp. 229–238). New York: Springer.
58. von Glasersfeld, E. (1995). *Radical constructivism*. London: Falmer Press.
59. von Glasersfeld, E. (2007). Aspects of constructivism. Vico, Berkeley, Piaget. In E. von Glasersfeld (Ed.), *Key works in radical constructivism* (pp. 91–99). Sense: Rotterdam.

Christiane M. Herr is an architectural researcher and educator focusing on the areas of structural design, digitally supported design, radical constructivism, design pedagogy and traditional Chinese approaches to creative thinking. Christiane is a Senior Associate Professor at Xi'an Jiaotong-Liverpool University in China, where she directs the Master of Architectural Design as well as the Bachelor of Architectural Engineering programmes. Christiane is President of the Association for Computer Aided Design Research in Asia and a member of the executive board of the American Society for Cybernetics.

Chapter 9
Design Cybernetics Enacted: The RSVP Cycles and Devised Theatre

Tom Scholte

Abstract In the 1960s, environmental designer, Lawrence Halprin, in collaboration with his wife Ann, choreographer and artistic director of the San Francisco Dance Workshop, engaged in an examination of group creative processes in search of a theory outlining their main features. He formalized his findings in the 1968 book, *The RSVP Cycles: Creative Processes in the Human Environment* describing a recursive schema of iteration and evaluation bearing striking resemblances to the conversational conception of second-order cybernetics. Devised Theatre is one of the fields that has been most directly influenced by, and most vividly reflects, the work of the Halprins and will serve as the "research site" for this chapter. Highlighting some prevalent features of contemporary Devised Theatre practice through examples drawn from some of the field's most influential artists, our trip around the cycle will reveal the ways in which the RSVP Cycles reinforce, in a robustly enacted fashion, Ranulph Glanville's cybernetic conception of design in which lack of control, trans-computable complexity, and under-specification of the problems investigated all become virtues that propel us on a conversational forward search in which we must "act in order to understand" while bound by a deep ethical commitment to the autonomy of others.

Keywords Performance · Theater · Collective creation · Conversation · Constraints

9.1 Introduction

In the 1960s, while second-order cybernetics itself was incubating – in Heinz von Foerster's Biological Computer Laboratory (BCL) and elsewhere – architect and environmental designer Lawrence Halprin, in collaboration with his wife Ann,

T. Scholte (✉)
Department of Theatre and Film, University of British Columbia, Vancouver, BC, Canada
e-mail: tom.scholte@ubc.ca

T. Fischer, C. M. Herr (eds.), *Design Cybernetics*, Design Research Foundations,
https://doi.org/10.1007/978-3-030-18557-2_9

choreographer and artistic director of the San Francisco Dance Workshop, was engaged in his own inward examination of group creative processes in search of a theory outlining their main features.

Similar to Glanville, Halprin explicitly rejected "the attempt to make a science out of community design" claiming that "[h]uman community planning cannot ever be a science anymore than politics can rightly be called political science. Science implies codification of knowledge and a drive toward perfectibility none of which are possible or even desirable in human affairs" [18]. This skepticism regarding even the desire for perfect solutions of any kind is echoed in Glanville's admonition that, often, "good enough is better than best" [16] given the reduction of "room for future human action" engendered by a blinkered, single-minded focus on supposedly optimal solutions that risks imposing "an inappropriate order on areas of activity where such order is unachievable" [12, p. 93].

What Halprin did desire was a "means to describe and evoke (creative) processes on *other* than simply a random basis" in the hopes that it "would have meaning not only for (the) field of environmental arts and dance-theatre, but also for all the other arts where the elements of time and activity (particularly of numbers of people) would have meaning and usefulness" [18]. He formalized his findings in the 1968 book, *The RSVP Cycles: Creative Processes in the Human Environment* describing a recursive schema of iteration and evaluation bearing striking resemblances to the conversational conception of second-order cybernetics.

Devised Theatre is one of the fields that has been most directly influenced by, and most vividly reflects, the work of the Halprins and will serve as the "research site" for this chapter. While the majority of Devised Theatre artists currently active may not consciously employ the RSVP Cycles as a design method and may well have never even heard it named, the basic procedural outline of its schema and its core values have essentially been absorbed into the field in various permutations as a kind of "best practice" whose historical origins have become increasingly obscured as the decades have gone by. This is, perhaps, not unlike the absorption of cybernetic principles and practices into cognate fields [20, p. 5] that led von Foerster to claim there was, in fact, no future for cybernetics as a distinct field [14, p. 203].

The precise methods employed by some of the most iconic, influential, and studied companies of North America's "first wave" of Devised Theatre in the 1960s and 70s (*The Living Theatre*, *The Performance Group*) trace their lineage back to the influence of Ann Halprin herself [19, p. 35]. The profound impact of the RSVP Cycles on North America's "second wave" of Devised Theatre in the 1980s had a similar genesis when theatre artist/educator Jacques Lessard returned to his native Quebec City in 1979 after studying with Halprin in San Francisco, and brought with him the guiding principles of the RSVP Cycles as a means of addressing his concern with "a lack of method in devised theatre in Quebec" [8]; adapting them into his own "Repère Cycle" and exploring their application in collaboration with his eventual breakaway disciple, international theatre superstar Robert Lepage.

While the inclusion of performance within the purview of design was certainly not an unusual notion to Glanville and his mentor, Gordon Pask, it is, perhaps, not as widely embraced across the wider design community as is deserved. The descriptions of performance creation that follow aim to correct this trend by re-inscribing a "cybernetic circle" similar to the one underscored by Glanville; one modelled on the cognitive developmental path of babies who instinctively "act in order to understand" rather than the opposite [17, p. 1294].

Taking seriously Gregory Bateson's assertion that the application of two different modes of description to the same phenomenon can yield a particular form of enlightenment [3], this chapter parses Glanville's second-order cybernetic formulation of the design process within the categorical boundaries of Halprin's RSVP Cycles. Highlighting some prevalent features of contemporary Devised Theatre practice through examples drawn from some of the field's most influential artists, our trip around the cycle will reveal the ways in which the RSVP Cycles reinforce, in a robustly enacted fashion, Ranulph Glanville's claim that the cybernetic conception of design, and its procedural, ethical and aesthetic entailments, reflect not simply one among many visions of what the work of designers might look like if it were more thoroughly systematized but, rather, the "mechanism" at the heart of its most successful extant practices "as done" [11, p. 1189].[1]

9.2 Definitions (and Descriptions)

As a result of the vast complexity that it seeks to accommodate, the aesthetic form of much Devised Theatre can be categorized as postdramatic. The term was coined by Hans-Thies Lehmann [22] to describe modes of performance with roots in such early twentieth century avant-garde movements as Dada, Surrealism, and Futurism, as well as the writings of Antonin Artaud [1], which subsequently rose to the fore in the 1960s through such performative phenomena as "happenings" and other experiments often involving John Cage and his associates, and that, to the present day, have been continuously reworked into new methods for decoupling theatre from its traditional grounding in character, plot, and the various conventions of mimesis; all hallmarks of the "dramatic" theatre against which it stands in reaction.

In his "Panorama" of the field, Lehmann provides a description that, while intended to cover one particular sub-genre he dubs the "Scenic Poem," vividly enumerates many of the features distinctive of the postdramatic as a whole.

> In this postdramatic stage space, bodies, gestures, movements, postures, timbre, volume, tempo, and the pitch of voices are torn from their familiar spatio-temporal continuum and newly connected. The stage becomes a complex whole of associative spaces composed like 'absolute poetry.' [...] Texts are combined with the gestures and physicality of the performers. At the same time the fragmentation and collage of different moments of action ensure that instead of the (epic) attention on the course of actions (narrated and played out), the focus is entirely on the presence of the performers and the mutual reflections and analogies. [22, pp. 110–111]

Logically, this mode of performance makes different demands upon its audiences than those made by its dramatic counterpart.

---

[1]See p. 46 in this volume.

> The spectator believes himself to be looking at an unknown 'text' in enigmatic hieroglyphs. The human being, the physical gesture, flesh and glass, matter and space form a purely scenic figuration, the spectator taking on the role of a reader who gathers the human, spatial, tonal signifiers scattered across the stage. [22, p. 111]

While the above description certainly does not reflect all Devised Theatre, or even the work of all the artists discussed in this chapter, in any sort of total manner, it can be very suitably understood as a snap-shot of the extreme end of a spectrum upon which much of it is situated and as a catalogue of features in which much of it partakes in greater or lesser measure.

9.2.1 The Cycle

The four components of Halprin's [18] RSVP Cycles are as follows (italics in original):

R – Resources: what you have to work with. These include human and physical resources *and* their motivation and aims.
S – Scores: describe the process leading to the performance.
V – Valuaction: analyzes the results of action and possible selectivity and decisions. The term "valuaction" is one coined to suggest the action-oriented as well as the decision-oriented aspects of V in the cycle.
P – Performance: the resultant of scores and the "style" of the process.

While the arrangement of the acronym RSVP (the request for a response) was chosen for its elegance in naming an essentially conversational process [18], a typical iteration of the *cycle* would more accurately be expressed, RSPV: the articulation of an inventory of the *resources* available, and desirable, for inclusion in the project, the articulation of a *score* indicating what is to be done with/to the *resources*, the *performance* (implementation) of the Score, and a period of *valuaction* during which the results of the *performance* are evaluated and re-enter the next iteration of the *cycle* as new *resources*, for which a new *score* will be articulated.

9.2.2 Devised Theatre

Devised Theatre is defined by Allison Oddey [26] as follows:

> Devised Theatre can start from anything. It is determined and defined by a group of people who set up an initial framework or structure to explore and experiment with ideas, images, concepts, themes, or specific stimuli that might include music, text, objects, paintings, or movement. A devised theatrical performance originates with the group while making the performance rather than starting from a play text that someone else has written to be interpreted. A devised theatre product is a work that has emerged from and been generated by a group of people working in collaboration. [26]

Even with no further elaboration of the *cycles* at this point, it is probably not difficult to begin to surmise why they should provide such a suitable procedural schema for the type of artistic practice described above and how their iterative execution is well suited to achieve the design cybernetic function of "integrating the parts referred to above into a whole, so that the whole becomes a simple embodiment of what was the complex of requirements, aspirations and aims" [12, p. 80].

Glanville's description of the distillation of complexity into a single artifact (in this case, a performance text) is a particularly apt manner in which to characterize the enterprise of Devised Theatre as defined above. Our journey round the *cycle*, articulating examples of contemporary devising practice as we go, will continue to be grounded in this description.

9.3 Round the Cycle

9.3.1 Resources (and Goals)

The most obvious *resources* found in the description of Devised Theatre above would be the " ideas, images, concepts, themes, or specific stimuli that might include music, text, objects, paintings, or movement"; the group's creative response to which will form the basis of the performance. But we must not forget that the "motivations and aims" of all of the individuals involved in the project must also be articulated and taken into account. This is, in fact, the ethical foundation of the entire schema, as "its purpose is to make procedures and processes visible, to allow for constant communication and ultimately to insure the diversity and pluralism necessary for change and growth" [18, p. 5]. This procedural transparency can be an effective instrument in promoting Glanville's "acceptance and welcoming of opportunity over certainty" and "the notion of leaving room for continuous improvement." It also calls for the "open mind" and "generosity of heart"[2] that help make up Glanville's desirable ethics [12, p. 76; 13].

In design cybernetics, the very notion of "goals" in any traditional sense is deliberately undermined. For Glanville, the second-order cybernetic conception of design is, through "accepting that 'traditional' precision is neither appropriate nor possible" in direct opposition to the "slogan" in modern architecture, attributed to Louis Sullivan, that "form follows function" [12, p. 88]. Given that Devised Theatre emanates from the pluralistic and, at times, contradictory viewpoints of groups rather than the overriding vision of a single author and that it often avowedly resists trafficking in the established conventions of the "well-made play," codified in the nineteenth century by Eugene Scribe and dominant, in various guises, in dramatic theatre to this day, it represents the kind of design opportunity described by Glanville

[2] See page 57 in this volume.

as having "no absolute criteria" and "no clear specification" [11, p. 1180][3]; its very notion of function being wildly underdetermined beyond the technical constraints imposed by budget, venue, composition of the company, and any requirements imposed by the presenter/producer (e.g. length of performance) should this happen to be an entity other than the devising company itself. As a result, any Devised Theatre project demands the kind of, initially, "aimless" cybernetic design strategy defined by Glanville to construct an " 'evolving' form that not only changes but, in doing so accommodates the required functions also, often in a novel and surprising manner." [11, p. 1196].

While it is impossible, and even undesirable, to express the precise nature of desired outcomes, there are still some overarching preferences driving the field of Devised Theatre at large. I will briefly examine some of the recurring and predominant "motivations and aims" immanent to much devising practice, as well as their cybernetic features, by exploring the manner in which their ethical and aesthetic concerns are inseparably interwoven.

One cannot discuss the ethical dimension of second-order cybernetics without confronting Heinz von Foerster's Ethical Imperative: "I shall act always so as to increase the total number of choices" [30, p. 282]. Of equal significance is von Foerster's claim that, when it comes to "undecidable" questions [30, pp. 291ff.], such as the origin of the universe or the existence of God, each of us must take responsibility for our own answers. Glanville expanded upon these notions and included both distinction and autonomy in his list of "cybernetic devices" capable of facilitating the von Foerster inspired ethics he found "desirable" [13, pp. 297–303]. Our autopoeitic nature, through which we create and maintain our bounded existence in a circular process "that continues to organize itself through the process of organizing itself" renders us autonomous within our environment and responsible for the distinctions we draw concerning the boundaries of other things within that environment as well as "the logic they imply." This responsibility entails a complementary sense of mutuality through which the same autonomy is recognized in all other beings we come across. Under such conditions, the assumption of the role of a "privileged observer endowed with authority, who describes and explains reality in the only correct and binding (for everyone) way [. . .]" [25, p. 204] is inherently oppressive and to be resisted in order to avoid what Glanville would call the imposition of "inappropriate order." This notion has implications for both the ethical and aesthetic dimensions of devising.

The term Devised Theatre has evolved, for better and for worse, as a blanket designation for various forms of group performance generation that include older designations such as collective creation. Although the conflation of these terms is not entirely appropriate, it is a fair statement that what we call devising today is a direct descendent of these historically earlier and, now, contemporaneous practices.

The groundswell that was the collective creation movement of the 1960s, of which the Living Theatre is arguably the most iconic example, was explicitly driven by,

[3]See p. 35 in this volume.

among other factors, an ethical concern with the way "theatre can be understood to have a socio-political dimension in terms of the style of organization manifested in its creative processes" [6]. In the words of one of its members, the "violent, polarized society we lived in then demanded new strategies" [6] and the ways in which these strategies functioned to break apart "the hierarchical organization and strict division of labor that plagued both heavy industries and the culture industry" [6], can be seen, as Theodor Shank argues, as "counter-cultural visions of 'the alternative society'" [6]. A strong current of this anti-hierarchical impulse still runs through much devising practice today.

In some contemporary analysis of Devised Theatre [6], as well as the theoretical grounding of some of its practitioners (e.g. Bottoms and Goulish) the philosophy of Gilles Deleuze has played a significant role. One feature of his work, inspired by that of Baruch Spinoza (whom Deleuze dubbed "The Prince of Philosophers") that has drawn considerable attention is the notion of immanence. John Mullarkey describes the philosophical concept of immanence, grounded etymologically in its Latin root, *immanare*, "to dwell within," as "being restricted entirely to some 'inside" existing and acting 'within the physical world." Cull clarifies that Mullarkey's "definition might be formed on the basis of a contrast with the idea of transcendence, where the transcendent is that which 'stands outside or above' the physical world" [6].

The domain of theatrical practice is one where the concepts of immanence versus transcendence "play out" in a more "figural" than "literal" way. This does not, however, blunt the poignancy of their invocation. Leaning on the work of Deleuze scholar, Eugene Holland, Cull frames the traditional function of the dramatic author and/or director in these terms pointing out that "the role of this transcendent figure is to 'guarantee' co-ordination, to impose organization top-down on the chaos of processes." The origin of collaborative and collectively generated Devised Theatre in the 1960s can be understood as a countervailing desire to engage with "immanent modes of organization and creativity [that] allow coordination to emerge bottom-up, and the 'modes and principles of... organization' to come from within the processes themselves, not from outside them" [6]. Again, the implications of this theorization for the practice of Devised Theatre as we have defined it are obvious; as are the resonances with key cyber-systemic concepts echoed in Cull's analysis that The Living Theatre's experimentation might be understood "as an attempt to make what we might call *self-organizing theatre*." This desire to ardently resist the imposition of "inappropriate order" extends beyond the means of production and into the postdramatic aesthetic features that will allow for maximum hermeneutic agency of reception amongst autonomous audience members.

Ric Knowles points out that, by turning from the 'author-ity' of the narrative of the symbolic structure shaped by the imagination of a single author to the 'authenticity' of collective and collaborative creation devising inherently turns "from what Alan Sinfield calls the universal/individual polarity to the historical/social one, where meaning can be contested" [24, p. 89]. As Knowles intimates, the post-modern suspicion of master narratives is deeply woven into much devising practice. The desire for a kind of polyvocality capable of overtly destabilizing the onto-epistemological certainties of any particular observer/author squares nicely with various "imperatives" of second-order cybernetics cited above as well as Larry Richard's subsequent "Anti-communication Imperative": "If you desire the new, compose asynchronicity" by which Richards favors, in the tradition of his mentor Herbert Brün, artistic modes that challenge the use of established and naturalized vocabularies designed to foster convergence of interpretation across observers [28]. When these imperatives are followed, vast complexity is sure to follow.

As soon as we add the "multi-vision (integrating various views, beliefs, life experiences, and attitudes to changing world events) [26] of the individual aesthetic responses of each member of a devising company to the purely "physical" resources enumerated above, we are already faced with a "transcomputable" level of complexity or, to stick with Ashby's definition of the total number of states a system can be in, "variety", in the nascent collaborative system. It is precisely the desire to dance with this variety, rather than programmatically reduce it in the name of control (or even the production of meaning), that is inextricably woven into the fabric of much Devised Theatre practice itself and is spaciously accommodated by the RSVP Cycles. Many directors in the field would likely echo Glanville's assertion that "[t]he great benefit of not having enough variety to control a system is that, if I give up trying to control rather than being annoyed that I cannot, I can discover many possibilities I would have excluded if I had insisted on being in control" [11, p. 1188].[4] Terry O'Conner of the UK's widely celebrated Forced Entertainment echoes this sentiment in the context of a deeply committed devising ensemble that has, through exercising the kind of openness of mind and generosity of heart lauded by Glanville, been willing to tolerate, and even thrive within, the turbulence generated by extreme levels of uncertainty and diversity and have, over a span of more than a decade, evolved mechanisms for, in Bruce Barton's words "mining turbulence" galvanized by an ethical commitment to each other as individuals.

> It's a situation offering the chance to produce work with group of people whose ideas I respect so much, and with whom the working process is so good that I know the result is going to be much greater than what I could do myself. [26].

The postdramatic possibility for expression of transcomputable complexity is, of course, one of the features that have made devising such an appealing alternative to traditional theatre-making for the artists discussed below and allowed them to pose and explore kinds of questions that seem beyond the reach of traditional dramatic theatre. New York's SITI Company began the process that led to their piece, *bobrauschenbergamerica* by simply wondering "[w]hat it would be like [. . .] to create a theater work in the manner of Rauschenberg, not so much about him in any explicit biographical sense, but drawing on his sculptural sense of collage, his use of found objects, his favorite images and motifs, his love of collaboration, his celebratory, often whimsical spirit, and his expansive vision of the USA" [7]. Chicago's now disbanded ensemble, Goat Island, whose published theoretical explication of their own work draws heavily, and overtly, upon Deleuze, began the

[4]See p. 45 in this volume.

creative process culminating in their piece, *When Will the September Roses Bloom? Last Night Was Only a Comedy* with the wildly underdetermined question: "How do you make a repair?" inspired by director Lin Hixson's observation that "today we buy new and discard the old" prompted by her perusal of repair manuals from the 1950's [5]. From this beginning emerged a performance piece featuring "dance/movement sequences, theatrical scenes, and spoken texts" drawn from such Resources as "the history of the teaching of the alphabet in America, the time/space patterns of the fibonacci sequence spiral, the poetry of Paul Celan, the philosophy of Simone Weil, and household repair manuals and diagrams" and that questioned "our place in a damaged world and our aptitude at repairing it." (Goat Island website). The immanent journey from underdetermined question to polyvalent "scenic poem" was facilitated through the strict Performance of recursive, conversational Scores.

9.3.2 Scores (and Doodles and Constraints)

Glanville tells us that "the drawing, sketch or doodle" is "central to the process of design" and that "[t]hese are often made without much purpose." [12, p. 89]. Throughout his corpus, Glanville sings the praises of purposelessness and the "gifts" that it can bring; a position that would seem at odds with the goal-directed preoccupations especially of early cybernetics. It is, however, yet another theoretical commitment shared by Halprin who claimed that "becoming *goal oriented*" is "one of the gravest dangers that we experience" through our tendency to pursue social goods, based on "incontrovertibly 'good ideas,'" by "the most direct means possible" resulting, through an "oversimplified approach [. . .] in the chaos of our cities and the confusion of our politics (or other politics – fascism and communism are clear statements of this approach)" [18]. This aversion to goals has major implications for the Scores that constitute the "initial framework or structure" from which an act of devising must begin.

Halprin opens his book by defining Scores as "*symbolizations of processes* which extend over time" [18, p. 1]. These systems of symbols, including language, "can convey, or guide, or control (as you wish), the interactions between elements such as space, time, rhythm, and sequences, people and their activities and the combinations which result from them" [18]. Beginning with the musical score as the most obvious example Halprin goes on to expand his list of sample scores to include plans for buildings, mathematics, stage directions and dialogue for a play, Navajo sand paintings, the intricacies of urban street systems as well as plans for transportation systems and the configurations of regions, and much more [18]. The most significant feature of any score is its position on a spectrum from "open" to "closed" in terms of the amount of control it exerts; "how much is conveyed of the artist-planner's own intention of what is to happen and to what degree what actually happens and the quality of what actually happens is left to chance; the influences of the passage of time; the variables of unforeseen and unforeseeable events, and to the feedback process which initiates a new score" [18]. The one word directive, "doodle" would obviously sit at the most open end of the scoring spectrum.

Having committed to the creation of the Rauschenberg piece, SITI Company's resident playwright, Charles Mee, began the process with his own equivalent to "doodling": the free-form writing of lists undertaken in a deliberately purposeless fashion; i.e. without an eye to any strategies for the incorporation of any of the listed items into the final piece. The first list, titled, "Stuff in Rauschenberg's Work," included such items as stuffed chickens, roller skates, soldiers in a jeep, and ML King, while the second, titled "Stuff it Makes Me Thing Of" featured, among other phenomena, an automobile racetrack announcer, dialogue from Baywatch, the sound of oil drums being unloaded from a truck, and other seemingly random miscellany bubbling up, uncensored, from Mee's subjective associative responses to the already diffuse materials making up the pastiche that is Rauschenberg's *œuvre* [7]. The items from both lists are integrated gradually into the constraint-based iterative process that follows.

Glanville cogently described the productive centrality of constraints within the second-order cybernetic approach to design identifying the "paralysis" that can overtake the artist/designer when faced with "seemingly limitless variety" [15, p. 56]. As Fischer and Richards explain, the features of a "constraint-based process" can be recognized "not as obstacles to be navigated but as enabling of ideas that would otherwise not be imagined." [9, p. 39]. This notion echoes the sentiments of composer Igor Stravinsky who insisted that "[t]he more constraint one imposes, the more one frees oneself from the chains that shackle the spirit . . . the arbitrariness of the constraint only serves to better the precision of execution" [29, p. 65]. Much devising practice, facing the kind of ill-defined assignments as those named above, makes great use of this advantage.

Through a series of developmental workshops, items on Mee's Rauschenberg lists were explored through SITI Company's "composition" practice developed by artistic director, Anne Bogart. Compositions are short group performances that must contain an assigned number of elements from a list of tropes identified by Bogart as inherently theatrical including 15 seconds of sustained laughter, a moment when everyone on stage is looking up, and a surprise entrance [4]. Added to these lists of assigned elements to be integrated were items from Mee's initial Rauschenberg lists including chicken jokes, prisoners talking about making license plates, and the sound of a car-door slamming. Throughout this iterative process, Mee "warned against rushing to impose conscious or conventional structure on a piece, preferring instead to allow a shape to emerge from the inchoate enthusiasms, anxieties, and other emotional impulses that gave rise to the work." [7, p. 175].

In the case of Goat Island's piece on the nature of repair, director Lin Hixson initiated the devising process with a directive drawing on constraints inherent in one of the resources itself by asking ensemble members to "create a foot phase dance" from a set of "flush tank repair instructions." The second part of the directive was to "Alter Foot Phase Repair Dance with an Al-jabr Operation"; a commonly cited operation in Arab mathematical texts involving "adding equal terms to both sides of an equation so as to 'restore' a quantity which is subtracted from one side by adding it to the other" [5, p. 130]. As we will see in the following section, the journey from these constrained and somewhat "aimless" beginnings to the eventual performance will be accomplished through a conversational process of accretion that is quintessentially cybernetic in nature.

9.3.3 *Performance and Valuaction (and Resources, and Scores and...)*

Conversation is, of course, at the heart of Glanville's design cybernetics. Essential to this mechanism is the "switch" between the modes of talking and listening. They should not, in fact cannot, be carried out simultaneously. The same is true of the phases of Performance and Valuaction in the RSVP Cycles that very deliberately demarcate the execution of the Score from the process of evaluating its outcomes through the lens of the collaborators values and desires and, subsequently, framing those outcomes as new Resources to be further explored through new Scores. For Blake Brooker, of Calgary's One Yellow Rabbit Performance Theatre, the sharp boundaries between the domains of "material generation" and the "period of discernment" that takes place during the "materials survey" are absolutely essential to ensure that the emergent novelty engendered by the accommodation of constraint based Scores is not still-born in the face of the withering forces of self-criticism (Brooker: personal conversation). One cannot doodle freely if one is assessing the quality of the doodle simultaneously and one cannot become a conduit for emergent novelty unless one is free from such ends-focussed judgement that can't help but draw upon past "successes" (of ones' own or of others) as the measure of present achievement.

The devising process as it its carried out by the artists discussed here are structured around conversational mechanisms that instantiate the principles of design cybernetics in robust, embodied ways. Lin Hixson describes Goat Island's process as "a series of directives and responses... I produce a directive. The members of the group present responses to the directive – acts in return. In response to the responses, I produce more directives" [21]. Hixson may seem, at first glance, to be occupying a transcendent position in the ensemble but, as Cull points out, the deliberately poetic nature of her directives, such as "create a shivering homage" avoids "fixed and predetermined concept(s)... to which the performers' responses must correspond" and "allows the final piece to remain surprising, strange, and complex rather than being a representation of her own singular vision." As the iterative cycles continue and new Scores are developed, Performed, and Valuacted "the response creates the directive as much as the other way around" [6].

9.4 Conclusion

The circular, iterative, and gradually ever-more constrained devising processes described above, as well as their positioning within the recursive framework of the RSVP Cycles, push against the "understand in order to act" paradigm underpinning traditional theatrical 'rehearsal to performance' processes in a manner similar to the way in which Glanville's cybernetic conception pushes against the traditional 'process to product' paradigm of design writ large. Through their enactment of a forward search, both also challenge traditional academic models of learning that, as Glanville points out, are similarly based on the admonition that we "understand in order to act."

Through their unfolding history, the RSVP Cycles have managed, in addition to embodying the principles articulated by Ranulph Glanville in his second-order cybernetic theory of design, to embody all three of the design research categories first derived by Herbert Read and subsequently expanded upon by Christopher Frayling: research *into* design, research *for* design, and research *through* design [10]. In search of generalizable principles of successful design activity, Lawrence Halprin examines all manner of extant scores in a project of "research *into* design." His subsequent book, *The RSVP Cycles: Creative Processes in the Human Environment* in which his findings are abstracted and formalized into a suggested method that is, along with case studies of its application, offered to the world, is clearly an artifact of "research *for* design." Finally, the method on offer is employed by Devised Theatre practitioners as an instrument of "research *through* design" in which topics are investigated and questions are asked whose answers are embedded in the result of the design process itself (i.e. the performance).

The creative, novelty-generating procedures of the devising companies described above also embody the "performative ontology" identified by Andrew Pickering as the core of a cybernetic conception of design.

> I have always thought of design along the lines of rational planning – the formulation of a goal and then some sort of intellectual calculation of how to achieve it. Cybernetics, in contrast, points us to a notion of design in the thick of things, plunged into a lively world that we cannot control and that will always surprise us. [27, p. 382].

Pickering also echoes the socio-political dimension of the RSVP-inspired devising examined in this chapter when he speaks of a "levelling of power relations between audiences and artists, a blurring of social roles" [27, p. 384]. Encapsulated in all of this is the rejection of traditional scientific values of "command and control" (in this case, in the guise of a singular author or director) and the belief that the "world can be assimilated" to a "representational schema" [27, p. 24]. Following Martin Heidegger, the world cannot be "enframed" within the subjugating rational vision of a single author but must, rather, be "revealed" through an "open-ended search" embracing ultimate unknowability and turbulence along the way.

> If our usual notion of design entails the formulation of a plan which is then imposed upon matter, the cybernetic approach entailed instead a continuing interaction with materials,

> human and non-human, to explore what might be achieved – what one might call an *evolutionary* approach to design, that necessarily entailed a degree of *respect* for the other. [27, p. 32]

A more apt description of the theatrical devising process would be difficult to find. Interestingly, Pickering also identifies cybernetics as "one of Deleuze and Guattari's nomad sciences that upset established orders" [27, p. 32]. As underscored above, much of the literature in theatre studies places devising on that same list of destabilizing and, ultimately, emancipatory cultural practices.

But, if both the RSVP Cycles and design cybernetics are, as Glanville claimed for his part of this tandem, simply formalizations of what designers actually do, why should it be important to rehearse them yet again in a combined fashion as has been done in this chapter? The reason lies in yet another second-order cybernetic concept; Louis Kauffman's notion of the "reflexive domain." For Kauffman, "a reflexive domain is an abstract description of a conversational domain in which cybernetics can occur." This description is certainly an apt one for the domain of design cybernetics under consideration in this volume. "Each participant in the reflexive domain is also an actor who transforms that domain," according to Kauffman. Description is one of the ways in which this transformation is carried out. In Kauffman's schema, assigning names to processes allows them to "become new elements of the original domain under scrutiny." The power of this process is akin to the moment that an algorithm or procedure is given a name by a computer programmer and becomes a "macro" that is "then on the same level as other original terms in the language" [23]. As any reader with even a passing acquaintance with programming will know, a new "macro" becomes a powerful new tool with which to expedite the pursuit of desirable programming outcomes. In the view of this author, the intrinsic purpose of this volume is, through a similar process of naming and articulating, to elevate the principles of design cybernetics to a comparable level within the reflexive domain of design; ideally, with comparably beneficial effects for the designers of tomorrow. Hopefully, the identification of cybernetic principles within the RSVP Cycles as practiced in the realm of devised theatre has played a helpful role in this endeavour.

References

1. Artaud, A. (1958). *The theater and its double*. New York, NY: Grove Press.
2. Barton, B. (Ed.). (2008). *Collective creation, collaboration and devising*. Toronto: Playwrights Canada Press.
3. Bateson, G. (2002). *Mind and nature: A necessary unity*. Cresskill: Hampton Press.
4. Bogart, A., & Landau, T. (2014). *The viewpoints book: A practical guide to viewpoints and composition*. London: Nick Hern Books.
5. Bottoms, S. J., & Goulish, M. (2007). *Small acts of repair: Performance, ecology, and Goat Island*. London: Routledge.
6. Cull, L. (2015). *Theatres of immanence: Deleuze and the ethics of performance*. New York, NY: Palgrave Macmillan.
7. Cummings, S. T. (2007). *Remaking American theatre: Charles Mee, Anne Bogart, and the SITI Company*. Cambridge, MA: Cambridge University Press.

8. Dundjerović, A. S. (2014). *The theatricality of Robert Lepage*. Montréal: McGill-Queen's University Press.
9. Fischer, T., & Richards, L. D. (2017). From goal-oriented to constraint-oriented design: The cybernetic intersection of design theory and systems theory. *Leonardo, 50*(1), 36–41.
10. Frayling, C. (1993/1994). Research in art and design. *Royal College of Art Research Papers, 1*(1), 1–5.
11. Glanville, R. (2007). Try again. Fail again. Fail better: The cybernetics in design and the design in cybernetics. *Kybernetes* 36(9/10), 1173–1206.
12. Glanville, R. (2007). Designing complexity. *Performance Improvement Quarterly, 20*(2), 75–96.
13. Glanville, R. (2009). *The black boox vol. III. 39 steps*. Vienna: edition echoraum.
14. Glanville, R. (2012). Second order cybernetics. *The black boox – Vol. I. Cybernetic circles* (pp. 175–207). Vienna: edition echoraum. Previously published in: F. Parra-Luna (Ed.), *Encyclopedia of life support systems, systems science and cybernetics – Vol. III*. Oxford: EoLSS Publishers. Available at: http://www.eolss.net/sample-chapters/c02/e6-46-03-03.pdf. Accessed January 19, 2019.
15. Glanville, R. (2014). Cybernetics. Thinking through the technology. In D. P. Arnold (Ed.), *Traditions of systems theory. Major figures and contemporary developments* (pp. 45–77). New York, NY: Routledge.
16. Glanville, R. (2014). *When good enough is better than best*. Available at Youtube: https://www.youtube.com/watch?v=m-8GmlNb6EY. Accessed January 19, 2019.
17. Glanville, R. (2014). Acting to understand and understanding to act. *Kybernetes, 43*(9/10), 1293–1300.
18. Halprin, L. (1968). *The RSVP cycles: Creative processes in the human environment*. New York, NY: Braziller.
19. Heddon, D., & Milling, J. (2006). *Devising performance: A critical history*. New York, NY: Palgrave Macmillan.
20. Heylighen, F., & Joslyn, C. (2001). Cybernetics and second-order cybernetics. In R. A. Meyers (Ed.), *Encyclopedia of physical science & technology* (3rd ed.). New York, NY: Academic.
21. Hixson, L. (2004). Small acts of repair. *Frakcija* (32/35), 02.
22. Lehmann, H.-T. (2006). *Postdramatic theatre*. New York, NY: Routledge.
23. Kauffman, L. H. (2016). Cybernetics, reflexivity and second-order science. *Constructivist Foundations, 11*(3), 489–497.
24. Knowles, R. (2008). The structures of authenticity: Collective and collaborative creations (excerpts). In B. Barton (Ed.), *Collective creation, collaboration and devising* (pp. 89–113). Toronto: Playwrights Canada Press.
25. Matuszek, K. C. (2015). Ontology, reality and construction in Niklas Luhmann's theory. *Constructivist Foundations, 10*(2), 203–210.
26. Oddey, A. (1996). *Devising theatre: A practical and theoretical handbook*. London: Routledge.
27. Pickering, A. (2011). *The cybernetic brain: Sketches of another future*. Chicago, IL: University of Chicago Press.
28. Richards, L. D. (2010). The anticommunication imperative. *Cybernetics and Human Knowing, 17*(1/2), 11–24.
29. Stravinsky, I. (2003). *Poetics of music in the form of six lessons*. Cambridge, MA: Harvard University Press.
30. von Foerster, H. (2003). *Understanding understanding*. New York, NY: Springer.

Tom Scholte is an actor/director/writer for theatre and film who has appeared on professional stages across Canada and whose work has been seen at such film festivals as Sundance, TIFF, Rotterdam, and the Berlinale. His research focuses on cybernetics in the Stanislavski system of acting and Forum Theatre as a modeling facility for the study of complex social systems. He is a Professor in the Department of Theatre and Film at the University of British Columbia teaching acting and directing and is a Research Collaborator with the International Institute for Critical Studies in Improvisation at the University of Guelph.

Chapter 10
Why Design Cybernetics?

Ben Sweeting

Abstract In this chapter I review the intimate relationship between cybernetics and design, drawing on the work of Ranulph Glanville and Gordon Pask. The significance of each of these fields for the other follows from the mutualism between them, such that cybernetics can be understood in terms of design as well as vice versa. The full value of this can be seen in the assistance they offer each other in building support from within. Design may serve as an example for how cybernetics can be practiced *cybernetically*, i.e. in accordance with its own insights and principles. In turn, cybernetics may help design understand itself in its own terms, in contrast to the way that it can become distorted by theories imported from elsewhere. Moreover, this mutualism connects design research to the vast array of topics with which cybernetics is concerned. Recalling its origins as a transdisciplinary project, cybernetics may help mediate diverse concerns within design, while also enabling cybernetic processes in other fields to be explored through the insights and methods of design research.

Keywords Design research · Transdisciplinarity · Cybernetics · Conversation

10.1 Introduction: Cybernetics and Design

In recent years there has been a resurgence of interest in cybernetics amongst designers. It has acted as a point of reference for various contemporary concerns, including the expanding possibilities of technology, the systemic complexity of contemporary design questions, the status of design as a discipline, and the relationship between design and research. These issues recall debates in design during the 1960s and 1970s when cybernetics, which was then a much more prominent discipline, was invoked in relation to the emergence of computing and the study of design methods. There is a rich history of overlap between the two

B. Sweeting (✉)
School of Architecture and Design, University of Brighton, Brighton, UK
e-mail: r.b.sweeting@brighton.ac.uk

T. Fischer, C. M. Herr (eds.), *Design Cybernetics*, Design Research Foundations,
https://doi.org/10.1007/978-3-030-18557-2_10

fields from that earlier period. In particular, the British cyberneticians Ross Ashby and Gordon Pask both engaged directly with design, influencing theorists such as Christopher Alexander, Bruce Archer and Horst Rittel. Pask contributed to the field of architecture, collaborating with Cedric Price and Nicholas Negroponte and influencing the development of interactive architecture through the work of Julia and John Frazer and his own highly original installations.

As Pask notes in the context of architecture, while there are many ways in which designers might "dive into a cybernetic bag of tricks and draw out those that seem appropriate," the two fields "really enjoy a much more intimate relationship" [30, p. 494]. The past decade has seen the connections between cybernetics and design become more apparent,[1] a process that can be credited in large part to the work of Ranulph Glanville. Glanville's efforts to consolidate the relationship between the two fields include his guest-editing of the 2007 *Cybernetics and Design* special double issue of the journal *Kybernetes*, on which I worked as a research assistant [8]. This special issue contained articles by a number of contributors to the present publication [2, 23, 26, 27], as well as Glanville's *Try again. Fail again. Fail better–the Cybernetics in Design and the Design in Cybernetics* [10], which is reprinted here in Chap. 2. Glanville's paper served twin purposes: (1) introducing cyberneticians and designers to each other's discipline and (2) articulating his own understanding of what is shared between them.

The special issue took the form of a survey of different perspectives. The collection was not intended to be definitive, but to open up a further area of research. As Glanville [9, p. 1153] put it in the introduction, the aim was:

> ... to start an exploration which would be as clear and explicit as possible, beginning to develop any relationships that might exist between the two fields of design and cybernetics. The idea was to build the bridges, to find mutualism. [9, p. 1153]

Mutualism was also stressed in the call for papers, which included the following questions:

1. How does cybernetics throw light on design, and lead to developments and improvements in our understanding of and ability to act in design?
2. How does design inform us in our understanding of cybernetics and its potential to parallel and throw light on design?
3. What is the mutualism that may hold between them when questions (1) and (2) are seen as part of the same whole? [9, pp. 1153–1154]

I see the mutualism between design and cybernetics as a way of responding to a question that can be asked of the present volume as a whole: what is it that cybernetics can contribute to design and design research beyond being yet one more vantage point or approach amongst others? Glanville's [15] seminal paper on the relationship between design and research asked a similar question – *Why Design Research?* There, in an argument I briefly summarise below, the importance of design research

[1]The same period has seen a similar deepening of connections between design and the field of systems, which is closely related to cybernetics [24, 25].

is seen to follow from understanding research as a form of design activity (hence the dual meaning of its title, which I echo in the title of this chapter). Similarly, the value of *design cybernetics* follows from the substantial overlaps between the two fields, where cybernetics may be understood in terms of design as well as vice versa. Below, I recount two prominent ways in which this mutualism has been understood. One, put forward by Glanville [10, 11], understands design *activity* as an example of the sort of conversational processes with which cybernetics is concerned. The other, put forward by Pask [30] in the context of architecture, stresses the *outcomes* of design activity, to which cybernetics is relevant in a number of ways. While both Pask and Glanville offer reasons why design cybernetics is worth pursuing, the case for this may be strengthened where their accounts are understood in combination. Taken together, they suggest novel configurations for design research that recall cybernetics' original formation as a radical transdisciplinary project.

10.2 Design and Conversation

Conversational processes are central to both design and cybernetics, and are one way of establishing connections between the two fields. Design is often understood in terms of conversation, such as in Donald Schön's [36, p. 76] characterisation of design as a "reflective conversation with the situation". The interaction present in conversation is a prominent example of the sort of process with which cybernetics is concerned, most notably in the work of Pask [31]. Glanville [10, 11] aligns cybernetics and design by establishing a close analogy between Pask's understanding of conversation and the core design activity of sketching, where designers develop ideas quickly through drawing.

Both conversation and sketching have a circular form, with participants shifting perspective between looking and drawing, listening and speaking. Just as conversation tends to lead places we could not have predicted in advance, so too this aspect of the way designers work helps them create new possibilities. This is crucial for design, given that it is, at heart, a process of transforming existing situations into new ones. The tendency towards the new in a conversation follows from the way that meanings are not transferred between participants. Participants construct their own understanding of the understanding of others, with the process taking the recursive form of "what I think of what you think I think, etc." [5, p. 217]. For instance, if, in a simple conversation between myself and someone else, I begin by presenting some idea, the other participant does not have this transferred directly to them but builds their own understanding of what it is that I mean. They then present what they have understood back to me and, again, I construct my own understanding of their presentation. I can then compare this understanding – what I understand of what they understood – to what I originally meant to communicate (see the diagram given in Glanville [11, p. 432], and Fig. 1.4 in this volume). Even if we continue this process in order to align these understandings, they remain separately constructed. Conversation preserves and is preserved by this difference such that it involves the construction of new understanding at every turn, in contrast to the way coded communication involves the transference of an unchanged message. New ideas are created through this conversational exchange, whether directly from our understanding of the ideas that are shared with us; through misunderstanding, where we see a worthwhile idea in what someone says that was not intended; or where we learn what is implied by our own ideas through understanding how they are interpreted and understood by others.

Similarly to the combination of speaking and listening in conversation, design combines the making of proposals with evaluating and understanding them. The circular process formed by these two aspects is more than one of iterative improvement or optimisation against set goals or criteria. Just as conversation can change course or develop new questions to explore rather than just leading to agreement, designers review and revise not just their proposals but also their understanding of the situation for which these proposals are intended. This can be seen in the characteristic design activity of sketching, which Glanville takes as embodying what is distinctive about design more generally. When sketching, designers simultaneously play the roles of speaker (drawing) and listener (looking), continuously switching between the two. By externalising their thoughts through a medium, designers see more in what they have drawn than they originally intended or understood [10, p. 1189]. This might include new possibilities for proposals or new aspects of the situation that need to be taken into account. While there are many other aspects to design, it is this type of conversational process that makes design so distinctive as an approach to the sort of complex, ill-defined and ambiguous situations that designers encounter, where more conventional forms of problem solving are inapplicable.

10.3 Mutual Support

The commonalities between cybernetics and design are such that they substantially overlap one another. Glanville characterises their relationship as one of mutual support to the extent that "cybernetics is the theory of design and design is the action of cybernetics" [10, p. 1178]. The significance of this mutualism for Glanville can be contextualised by recalling his [6, 15] influential argument about the relationship between design and research. During the period of scientific and technological optimism that followed the Second World War, there was a tendency to see design as something that should be put on rational scientific foundations. As Glanville recounts, this largely failed to recognise what was valuable about design activity itself:

> When Design Research began, say in the 1960s, the eventual success of science was assumed. Already, at the notorious 1956 Oxford Conference, architectural education in the UK (and its sphere of influence) accepted architecture was a second class subject: i.e. not properly scientific. Science (in actuality, technology) was seen as so successful that everything should be scientific: the philosopher's stone! Architects (a significant subdivision of designers)

> were determined to become scientific. The syllabus was changed and design science was invented. Even the Architectural Association School gave over a third of undergraduate time to design science. Prime Minister Wilson and his Government declared the 'White Heat of the Technological Revolution.'
> It was no wonder design was seen not as a discipline in its own right. Design was deficient: effectively, a defective science. It was flawed. But these flaws could be fixed by the proper application of scientific methods. [6, p. 80]

In his *Why Design Research?* paper at the 1980 conference of the Design Research Society [15], later expanded as the journal article *Researching Design and Designing Research* from which the above quotation is taken [6], Glanville made the radical proposal to invert this hierarchy. Rather than seeing design research as one specific form of scientific research, or design as an activity to be corrected by science, Glanville argues that, instead, we can see science as a specific form of design enquiry. This follows from the way that scientific research inevitably involves design activity, for instance in devising and setting up experiments, but not vice versa. This is not to say that designers do not make use of scientific research but that doing so is not essential to what design is, whereas design is a core aspect of conducting research and so science. Design is, it follows, the more general case and, therefore:

> . . . it is inappropriate to require design to be 'scientific': for scientific research is a subset (a restricted form) of design, and we do not generally require the set of a subset to act as the sub subset to that subset any more than we require [that] the basement of [a] building is its attic. [6, pp. 87–88]

Rather than seeing design as something to be corrected by science, we might therefore look to design to inform the practice of scientific research. Indeed, the parallels between design and research are such that Glanville suggests seeing the field of design research as a self-reflexive activity of *researching research* [15, pp. 116–119]. That is, as design is a core part of research, to research design is to inquire into an aspect of research activity itself.[2]

This stands in contrast to the recurring tendency for theories to be imported into design from elsewhere, whether from science or other fields. While there are many benefits to such exchange, there is the risk of what is special about design itself becoming lost or distorted in the process [14]. In arguing that design and cybernetics substantially coincide, Glanville positions them as able to mutually assist each other in building support *from within*. In contrast to the way that designers tend to invoke theory in order to change design practice or to advocate certain approaches to it over others, the value of cybernetics for design is primarily in helping *sustain* and *deepen* those aspects of design activity that are distinctive about it. This is not to say that design should isolate itself, but that it needs to maintain its own identity in engaging with other domains. Indeed, to understand design in cybernetic terms is to do so as a transdisciplinary project (more on this below).

[2] In so doing, Glanville anticipates recent discussions regarding second-order science. See e.g. [29, 38].

Design can, in turn, play a complementary role in supporting cybernetics. At the inaugural conference of the American Society for Cybernetics (ASC), Margaret Mead [28] challenged the ASC to apply the ideas of the field to the organisation of the society itself. Just as what is special about design has sometimes become lost where it is not understood in its own terms, so too what is special about cybernetics is difficult to maintain within the context of conventional science. Glanville took Mead's challenge as a focus of his time as president of the ASC (2009–2014), a theme he addressed in part through developing conversational (i.e. cybernetic) formats for the society's conferences [12, 13, 41, 43]. The principle legacy of Mead's remarks has been the development of second-order cybernetics (the cybernetics of cybernetics) by Heinz von Foerster and others. This has been largely philosophical in orientation, critiquing the exclusion of the observer in conventional approaches to science. Glanville's direct response to the specific context of Mead's challenge offers a more practical interpretation, recognising the importance for cybernetics of conducting itself in accordance with its own ideas and values. Glanville's concern with the relationship between design and cybernetics can be understood as part of this same project, with design contributing an example of how cybernetic ideas may be explored in cybernetic ways.

10.4 Design Cybernetics as a Transdisciplinary Project

Although Glanville's account of the mutuality between design and cybernetics is heavily indebted to Pask (who was his mentor), Pask's [30] own way of establishing the closeness of cybernetics and design takes a different form. While Glanville focuses on parallels between cybernetic and designerly *processes*, and so on the activities of designers, Pask stresses the relevance of cybernetics to the *outcomes* of design activity. Even where these outcomes are physical, such as in architecture, they may also be understood as systemic:

> . . . a building cannot be viewed simply in isolation. It is only meaningful as a human environment. . . In other words structures make sense as parts of larger systems that include human components and the architect is primarily concerned with these larger systems; they (not just the bricks and mortar part) are what architects design. [30, p. 494]

Focusing on architecture, Pask describes the novel and complex challenges that arose during the nineteenth century, with new building typologies such as railway stations leading to questions beyond the scope of previous architectural theory:

> Whereas the pure architecture of the early 1800s had a metalanguage, albeit a restrictive one which discouraged innovation, the new (augmented) architecture had not yet developed one. . . In place of a general theory there were subtheories dealing with isolated facets of the field; for example, theories of materials, of symmetry, of human commitment and responsibility, of craftsmanship and the like. But (it is probably fair to say) these sub-theories developed more or less independently during the late 1800s. [30, p. 494]

A similar tendency to understand architecture piecemeal is recognisable today. This follows in part from the breadth of the discipline. The field of architecture involves the humanities and applied sciences as well as designerly thinking. Moreover, the buildings architects design have consequences that range across all aspects of our lives. There is, therefore, a vast range of perspectives that can be brought to bear on any one architectural question. Depending which aspects one sees as being primary, one might look in very different directions for theoretical support, and it is seldom clear how to mediate between the rival frameworks and agendas that one encounters. While such differences can be productive, not least in the way that they can help sustain conversation (as discussed above), the relations between different aspects and approaches are often fraught or unexplored.[3]

Thus, while interdisciplinarity is often thought about in terms of collaborations across traditional boundaries, there is a similar need for such exchange *within* design fields such as architecture, between different sub-fields and foci. Pask puts cybernetics forward as a possible "underpinning and unifying theory" [30, p. 494] for such a task, a suggestion that recalls cybernetics' origins as a transdisciplinary language. Indeed, the work of cyberneticians has been a point of reference for a diverse array of contemporary issues in architecture and design, including: the digital, networked and interactive technologies that are increasingly a part of both what and how we design, e.g. [3, 4, 16, 34, 37, 42] and Chap. 5 of the present volume; the epistemology of the design process and its relation to research, e.g. [10, 14, 23, 38] and Chaps. 14 and 7; ecological and systemic concerns, e.g. [17, 20, 25, 35]; cognition and spatial experience, e.g. [21, 22]; design education, e.g. [18–20] and Chaps. 8 and 11; and social and ethical considerations, e.g. [1, 33, 40]. While these various invocations of cybernetics have value independently of each other, the potential of design cybernetics as a whole is that diverse areas of action and discourse such as these may be brought into closer relation with each other. This may help mediate between different agendas, as well as allowing for new questions to be asked.

While the ways in which Pask and Glanville connect cybernetics with design pull in different directions, they also complement each other. Glanville's account of the design process is an example of cybernetics informing a specific area of design, giving support to the idea that cybernetics can play a unifying theoretical role. At the same time, the wider relevance of cybernetics that Pask points to can reinforce Glanville's project of understanding and practicing design and cybernetics in their own terms.

Glanville establishes a symmetry between cybernetics and design, such that cybernetics may be understood in terms of design as well as vice versa. Thus, where design looks to aspects of cybernetic insight for support, it can equally be understood as *looking to itself*. As well as helping avoid the risk that design's strengths become distorted in its engagement with other areas of discourse, this symmetry broadens the domain in which designerly thinking can find application. Because cybernetic

[3]Zambelli [44, pp. 107–110] has speculated about a possible root of this tension in the foundation of the RIBA and in eighteenth and nineteenth century disciplinary specialisation more generally.

processes can be understood in terms of design, the insights and methods of design research can be used to explore cybernetic topics in other fields. That is, as well as cybernetics' potential as a transdisciplinary framework *within* design, design may also reach out *through* cybernetics in order to contribute to the vast array of subject areas with which cybernetics, in turn, is engaged. Examples of this include Glanville's understanding of research as a form of design activity [6, 15], and his generalization of this argument in terms of mentation [7]. My own work on design and ethics can also be thought of in this way, with cybernetics enabling design to inform ethical questions as well as vice versa [39, 40].

The relevance of design to cybernetics can be understood in terms of a broader agenda of recovering and enhancing cybernetics as a field. Cybernetics' ability to play a transdisciplinary role comes at the cost of its own tendency towards abstraction. There are therefore limitations to what cybernetics alone can offer in the context of more situated, material, and political issues. These limitations can be countered by emphasising the more tangible qualities of cybernetics itself, such as the experimental devices and installations through which Pask and others developed their ideas [32, 38]. They may also be addressed by developing cybernetics' partnerships with more situated fields, such as its mutualism with design. As such, design cybernetics may be understood *not only* in terms of bringing cybernetic insight to design and design research, *but also* in terms of design's contribution to cybernetics as a transdisciplinary project. The value of this task can be seen in the way that many of the profound and urgent questions we presently face (in design and elsewhere) combine some of the various technological, systemic, and epistemological issues to which cybernetics speaks.

References

1. Cabral Filho, J. S. (2013). The ethical implications of automated computation in design. *Kybernetes, 42*(9/10), 1354–1360.
2. Dubberly, H., & Pangaro, P. (2007). Cybernetics and service-craft: Language for behavior-focused design. *Kybernetes, 36*(9/10), 1301–1317.
3. Fantini van Ditmar, D. (2017). Deconstructing the smart home: AI vs. second-order cybernetics. In L. C. Werner (Ed.), *Cybernetics: State of the art* (pp. 166–173). Berlin: Universitätsverlag der Technischen Universität Berlin.
4. Fantini van Ditmar, D. (2018). Design research: The idiot's role in the 'smart' home. *Diseña, 11*, 122–133.
5. Glanville, R. (1993). Pask: A slight primer. *Systems Research, 10*(3), 213–218.
6. Glanville, R. (1999). Researching design and designing research. *Design Issues, 15*(2), 80–91.
7. Glanville, R. (2006). Design and mentation: Piaget's constant objects. *The Radical Designist* zero issue. Available at: http://asc-cybernetics.org/systems_papers/Design_and_Mentation.pdf. Accessed January 19, 2019.
8. Glanville, R. (2007). Cybernetics and design. *Kybernetes, 36*(9/10). Available at: http://www.emeraldinsight.com/toc/k/36/9%2F10. Accessed January 19, 2019.
9. Glanville, R. (2007). Introduction: Special double issue of Kybernetes on cybernetics and design. *Kybernetes, 36*(9/10), 1153–1157.

10. Glanville, R. (2007). Try again. Fail again. Fail better: The cybernetics in design and the design in cybernetics. *Kybernetes, 36*(9/10), 1173–1206.
11. Glanville, R. (2009). A (cybernetic) musing: Design and cybernetics. In *The black boox, volume III: 39 steps* (pp. 423–425). Vienna: edition echoraum. Reprinted from: *Cybernetics and Human Knowing, 16*(3/4), 175–186.
12. Glanville, R. (2011). Introduction: A conference doing the cybernetics of cybernetics. *Kybernetes, 40*(7/8), 952–963.
13. Glanville, R. (Ed.) (2012). *Trojan horses: A rattle bag from the 'Cybernetics: Art, design, mathematics—A meta-disciplinary conversation' post-conference workshop.* Vienna: edition echoraum.
14. Glanville, R. (2014). Design prepositions. In *The black boox, volume II: Living in cybernetic circles* (pp. 239–252). Vienna: edition echoraum. Reprinted from: Belderbos, M., & Verbeke, J. (Eds.). (2007). *The unthinkable doctorate* (pp. 115–126). Brussels: Sint Lucas.
15. Glanville, R. (2014). Why design research? In *The black boox, volume II: Living in cybernetic circles* (pp. 111–120). Vienna: edition echoraum. Reprinted from: Jacques, R., & Powell, J. A. (Eds.). (1981). *Design, science, method: Proceedings of the 1980 Design Research Society conference* (pp. 86–94). Guildford: Westbury House.
16. Glynn, R. (2008). Conversational environments revisited. In R. Trappl (Ed.), *Cybernetics and systems 2008, proceedings of the 19th European meeting on cybernetics and systems research.* Vienna, Austria: Austrian Society for Cybernetics Studies.
17. Goodbun, J. (2011). Gregory Bateson's ecological aesthetics: An addendum to urban political ecology. *Field, 4*(1), 35–46.
18. Herr, C. M. (2013). Architectural design education between poetry and prose. *Kybernetes, 42*(9/10), 1404–1412.
19. Herr, C. M. (2014). Radical constructivist structural design education for large cohorts of Chinese learners. *Constructivist Foundations, 9*(3), 393–402.
20. Hohl, M. (2015). Living in cybernetics: Polynesian voyaging and ecological literacy as models for design education. *Kybernetes, 44*(8/9), 1262–1273.
21. Jelić, A. (2015). Designing "pre-reflective" architecture: Implications of neurophenomenology for architectural design and thinking. *Ambiances*. Available at: http://ambiances.revues.org/628. Accessed January 19, 2019.
22. Jelić, A., Tieri, G., De Matteis, F., Babiloni, F., & Vecchiato, G. (2016). The enactive approach to architectural experience: A neurophysiological perspective on embodiment, motivation, and affordances. *Frontiers in Psychology, 7*, 481.
23. Jonas, W. (2007). Research through DESIGN through research: A cybernetic model of designing design foundations. *Kybernetes, 36*(9/10), 1362–1380.
24. Jonas, W. (2014). The strengths/limits of systems thinking denote the strengths/limits of practice-based design research. *FORMakademisk, 7*(4), 1–11.
25. Jones, P. H., & Kijima, K. (2018). Systemic design: Theory, methods, and practice. In *Translational systems sciences*. Tokyo: Springer Japan.
26. Krippendorff, K. (2007). The cybernetics of design and the design of cybernetics. *Kybernetes, 36*(9/10), 1381–1392.
27. Krueger, T. (2007). Design and prosthetic perception. *Kybernetes, 36*(9/10), 1393–1405.
28. Mead, M. (1968). The cybernetics of cybernetics. In H. von Foerster, J. D. White, L. J. Peterson, & J. K. Russell (Eds.), *Purposive systems* (pp. 1–11). New York, NY: Spartan Books.
29. Müller, K. H., & Riegler, A. (2014). Second-order science: A vast and largely unexplored science frontier. *Constructivist Foundations, 10*(1), 7–15.
30. Pask, G. (1969). The architectural relevance of cybernetics. *Architectural Design, 7*(6), 494–496.
31. Pask, G. (1976). *Conversation theory: Applications in education and epistemology*. Amsterdam: Elsevier.
32. Pickering, A. (2010). *The cybernetic brain: Sketches of another future*. Chicago, IL: University of Chicago Press.

33. Pratschke, A. (2007). Architecture as a verb: Cybernetics and design processes for the social divide. *Kybernetes, 36*(9/10), 1458–1470.
34. Ramsgard Thomsen, M. (2007). Drawing a live section: Explorations into robotic membranes. *Kybernetes, 36*(9/10), 1471–1485.
35. Rawes, P. (Ed.). (2013). *Relational architectural ecologies: Architecture, nature and subjectivity*. London: Routledge.
36. Schön, D. A. (1991). *The reflective practitioner. How professionals think in action.* Farnham: Arena.
37. Spiller, N. (2002). *Cyber_reader: Critical writings for the digital era*. London: Phaidon Press.
38. Sweeting, B. (2016). Design research as a variety of second-order cybernetic practice. *Constructivist Foundations, 11*(3), 572–579.
39. Sweeting, B. (2019). Applying ethics to itself: Recursive ethical questioning in architecture and second-order cybernetics. *Kybernetes, 48*(4), 805–815.
40. Sweeting, B. (2018). Wicked problems in design and ethics. In P. H. Jones & K. Kijima (Eds.), *Systemic design: Theory, methods, and practice* (Translational systems sciences series). Tokyo: Springer Japan.
41. Sweeting, B., & Hohl, M. (2015). Exploring alternatives to the traditional conference format: Introduction to the special issue on composing conferences. *Constructivist Foundations, 11*(1), 1–7.
42. Werner, L. C. (2017). Cybernetification I: Cybernetics feedback netgraft in architecture. In L. C. Werner (Ed.), *Cybernetics: State of the art* (pp. 58–73). Berlin: Universitätsverlag der Technischen Universität Berlin.
43. Westermann, C. (2010). Cybernetics: Art, design, mathematics—A meta-disciplinary conversation. *Leonardo Reviews Quarterly, 1*(02), 24–26.
44. Zambelli, A. (2016). *Scandalous artefacts: Visual and analogical practice between architecture and archaeology*. PhD Thesis, London: UCL.

Ben Sweeting Ben studied architecture at the University of Cambridge and the Bartlett, UCL. He completed his doctoral research under the supervision of Neil Spiller and Ranulph Glanville, exploring epistemological and ethical questions in relation to architecture and cybernetics. He is a member of the American Society for Cybernetics and a recipient of the society's Heinz von Foerster Award.

Chapter 11
The Polynesian Voyaging Society as a Cybernetic Paradigm for a Design Curriculum

Michael Hohl

Abstract In this chapter, I discuss how design educators and design students may learn from cultural traditions of the Polynesian Voyaging Society, and from its "Eight Elements of Education". I argue that this source of informal knowledge, combined with modern means to communicate and to collaborate can lead to new, more empathetic, ethical, and environmentally aware ways of designing. Developed by Hawaiian educators, and rooted in non-instrument maritime navigation, the "Eight Elements" are centred on traditional Hawaiian values, such as community, responsibility, and living in harmony with all living things. This system of values and practices not only resembles design studio education – it also has a potential to inform it. In this framework, I propose cybernetics as a way of thinking and acting with added dimensions of rigour, critique and reflection. Way-finding across the ocean nurtures acute faculties of observation and of learning environmental patterns. It also requires courage, responsibility, trust, and teamwork. I argue that design curricula can incorporate elements of local traditions such as building practices, materials, language, produce, cooking traditions and customs. Similar to the transition town movement, this can build communities of design students who learn and apply their knowledge in local settings, based upon values such as sustainability, community and awareness of local resources. Design projects thereby transform into "life projects" by accepting the place of study as a home, by designing for local needs, by learning about local traditions and language, and through a commitment to lifelong learning. As such they combine cybernetics and second-order cybernetics.

Keywords Design curricula · Design pedagogy · Reflecting · Feedback · Observing · Theory & practice · Learning from error · Lifelong learning

M. Hohl (✉)
Faculty of Design, Anhalt University of Applied Sciences, Dessau-Roßlau, Germany
e-mail: michael.hohl@hs-anhalt.de

T. Fischer, C. M. Herr (eds.), *Design Cybernetics*, Design Research Foundations,
https://doi.org/10.1007/978-3-030-18557-2_11

11.1 Introduction

He wa'a he moku, he moku he wa'a.[1]

Values of sustainability and harmony with nature and all living things are central to Hawaiian traditional culture, and are embedded in the Hawaiian language. Much of traditional Hawaiian learning takes place in groups, outdoors, either on the ocean, or in particular island habitats. Hawaiians' traditional ways of knowing include local crafts and customs but also an intimate knowledge of local environmental conditions, resources, and the patterns of relationships between flora and fauna, and human influence. My intention is to demonstrate that such practices informing design education, may lead to new ways of designing – and new ways of being – that are more ethically and environmentally aware, integrating aspects of sustainability, community, and consideration of local conditions. While traditions as such might appear too inflexible for the purposes of contemporary learning contexts, cybernetic feedback principles offer possibilities, if necessary, to adapt traditional frameworks through reflection and critique. In such a process, participants construct understanding through acting and observing the effects of their actions. They learn about the environment and use that knowing to reach their goals. They reflect on their goals and actions. Similar to navigating a canoe through a dynamically changing environment, goals are reached by continuously observing and adjusting the course through a process of exploring, designing, playing and learning. Navigator Eric Co writes:

> Traditional navigation is an exercise bound in the metaphysical. Dozens of variables and thousands of observations need to be simultaneously and continuously recorded, collated, processed and used for real-time decision making on a daily basis. All this with very few reference points to confirm the torrential stream of information the navigator perceives. In other words, the navigator cannot act on what they know, but what they think they know. The navigator must envision beyond sight, understand beyond the senses. He must pursue oneness with his surroundings, his environment. [9]

Members of Hawaiian traditional culture did not only learn about their environment, its rules or patterns, but also understood their own impact upon that environment, and how it changed as a result. By re-examining their objectives and values, they adapted to the environment in view of a more sustainable way of life. This understanding still affects Hawaiian language, culture and society as a whole[2] today.

The Polynesian Voyaging Society (PVS), a movement dedicated to instrument-free maritime exploration in the Pacific Ocean, applies cybernetics, steersmanship, not only literally – it also the navigates the continuation of the traditional Polynesian culture it is based on, with an explicit educational framework. Grounded in master-apprentice relationships, this framework bears strong resemblances to Donald

[1]"The canoe is an island, the island is a canoe." – Hawaiian proverb, highlighting that resources are limited and precious, and that people need to work together as a community to succeed.

[2]Humberto Maturana would describe this as "structural coupling" within a "niche" [25].

Schön's [31] design studio model, especially where learners collaborate on projects in small groups, aided by more experienced guides. Parallels between PVS navigation and education, design education and cybernetics relate to practices and theories of exploration, design, play, and learning, amongst others. Albeit largely non-intentional, these parallels are clearly not coincidental, and, I argue, offer interesting opportunities for reflection and cross-pollination.

My own interest in Polynesian navigation reaches back to my final year project at university, where I compared Western instrument-based maritime navigation to traditional, instrument-less Polynesian maritime navigation, which required an acute perception of environmental clues in combination with extensive knowledge of the movement of stars at particular times of the year. Visiting the Hawaiian islands for the first time 15 years after my graduation, Hawaiian culture seemed very much thriving. I met Polynesian navigators and participated in some of their activities. Only after meeting with educators of the PVS, and after reading the *Kamehameha Journal of Education* (see [12]), I realized that the thriving of Hawaiian culture, values and language was due to the reviving efforts of a few individuals who initiated Hawaiian language schools in the 1980s. The people I encountered were the first generation that had attended these schools.

11.2 Design Education

In recent decades, design education – especially that of product designers, graphic designers, interaction designers and architects – had to adapt to an exellerated change. Markets, technologies, consumer needs and expectations all change continuously and become more complex. From designing products that work well and are perceived as aesthetically pleasing, some of today's design curricula additionally consider the application of human-centered design methods, designing with sustainability in mind, and also the design of experiences and services. Furthermore, it is imperative to consider where materials are coming from, under which conditions products are being manufactured, and also what is happening with them once they are discarded. Designers and consumers have become aware of globalization and the distributed negative effects of consumer culture, such as resource depletion and environmental pollution, among others. There also appears to be a growing awareness that Western consumption and lifestyle have effects on a global scale, that the world is a complex system and all things are interconnected; as a result, small actions may have unexpectedly large consequences.

There might be a growing awareness that the world may be too complex a system to be fully understood and responsibly managed, indicating a growing relevance of cybernetics and systems sciences. Perhaps also indicating a shift towards second-order cybernetics: A philosophy of care, values and empathy that offers guidance on how to act responsibly with limited knowledge in dynamic conditions. It also recognizes that individuals perceive the world differently from one another, and that understanding each other's perspectives requires empathy, patience and generosity.

There also appears to be a growing awareness in Western cultures that there is a limited correlation between happiness and increased material wealth above a certain level, and that with a materialistic consumerist lifestyle came a perceived loss of meaning and a desire for a more meaningful and social life. Signs for this might be increasing interest in movements such as minimalist lifestyles (for an example, see [7]), mindfulness meditation, yoga, slow-food and slow-fashion movements, buy-nothing-days, urban gardening and a growing interest in crafts and artisanship, from spoon carving and maker-fairs to repair cafés and food 'foraging'. These might be signs that there is a trend for a more local, more sustainable and less materialistic lifestyle, one that is less career oriented and, instead, focussed on quality of life, social relationships, and open towards a reconsideration of values and priorities.

However, since the beginning of the environmental movement in the 1970s, the negative effects of industrialization and consumer culture have been increasing instead of decreasing on a global scale [13, p. 15]. There appears to be a disconnection between theory and practice, between knowing and taking informed action. Although these might be viewed as the responsibility of policy-makers, designers play a role in the environmental crisis as many of these negative effects are driven by the production, transportation and consumption of consumer goods. Most of these goods, from relatively useful washing machines and refrigerators to relatively less useful fashionable and disposable items, are being designed by educated designers. While design curricula increasingly emphasise designing with sustainability in mind, professional design practice adheres to market principles, with limited regard for environmental sustainability. How do design students cope with the cognitive dissonance between their educational, professional and personal life experiences? How might these be integrated into living designerly, and designing life? What are the implications for design education? Can designing become a lived project, can life be approached as a design project? Might designerly ways of living become part of a political dimension of design?

11.3 The Design Studio Model

Learning to design is not achieved through reading books. Traditionally students learn in a very practical and applied manner, engaging projects with empathy, skill and ingenuity. The design studio model consists of the learners collaboratively working in small groups, organized around projects of simulated practice (see Fig. 11.1). It is not about applying theoretical knowledge to practical problems. Instead, students are asked to act before they know what they need to be doing or learning. It is a hands-on and bottom-up learning approach in which feedback is provided by an experienced designer. Thus, the design process is one of making, reflecting and learning. Making errors, being frustrated and carefully reflecting are part of that learning. Theorizing comes later. Donald Schön notes that the essence of design learning also applies to learners in other fields such as law and medicine: "They are not 'applying' what they have already learned in the classroom but are acquiring, instead, a different order of

Fig. 11.1 The design studio: learning through guided practice

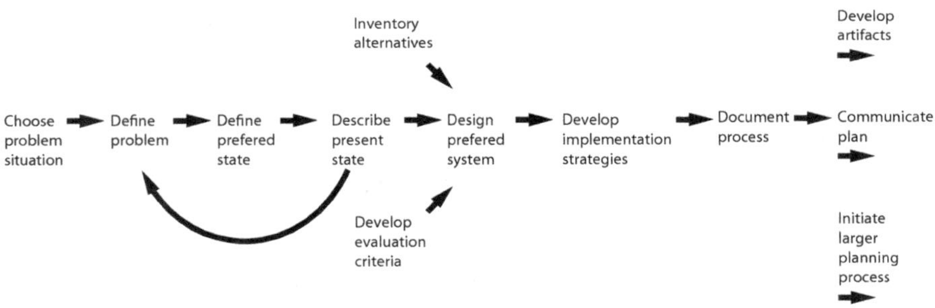

Fig. 11.2 "Comprehensive anticipatory design science" by Buckminster Fuller (1950?). One of many design process models [11, p. 40]

knowing-in-action through exposure to the demonstrations, advice, and criticism of their clinical instructors and their peers." [31, p. 89]. The same can be said about design students. Becoming a designer includes knowing what to do when you do not know what to do.

Design students are often taught to structure the design process sequentially, e.g. to begin by defining the problem, to research its history and context, to look at relevant solutions, and to proceed by empathizing, conceptualizing, ideating, prototyping, implementing, choosing, testing and learning, also with a view to possibly using some of the acquired insights in subsequent iterations (see Fig. 11.2). This pertains to designing artefacts as well as designing processes and services. They learn about marketing theory, design history, design theory, design semantics, inclusive design principles, human psychology and theory of perception – all of which are essential elements of learning to design well.

In a human-centered design approach, this also involves techniques such as interviews or observation, among many others, to better understand how people might use a product or service. It is expected that designers are able to listen to stakeholders with empathy and the intent to understand the perceived "problem" from various "cultural" perspectives. (Even though "listening" is still missing from most curricula). Design professionals might encounter different client-culture with distinct vocabularies several times a year. One client may be a bank, the subsequent one a kitchen utility manufacturer. Due to the scale and complexity of many projects designers very often work together in interdisciplinary teams. Within such teams, designers often perform a function similar to that of a hub of a wheel, a fulcrum connecting the parts that form the system, translating between manufacturers, users, clients, contractors, consultants and other stakeholders. From these responsibilities arises a requirement for designers to learn, with growing experience, to switch between different cultures, languages and viewpoints and, essentially, to listen well – both to what is being said and what is not being said. Engaging a new design project, designers, not knowing in advance what an appropriate outcome might be, may take a research-based approach. The shifting of own and others' perceptions and perspectives is an inherent and continuous part of designing.

However, learning to design with sustainability in mind is taking place in contexts which operate in highly unsustainable manners, especially in industrialized countries. In their everyday experiences, students are surrounded by designs that do not adhere to the standards and values, they are being encouraged to adopt in their educational settings. Designerly values adopted from educators and everyday experience are often separated in a cognitive-dissonant 'value-action gap'. Usually these 'values' focus on principles of designing but may also concern aesthetic qualities and usage. Often these principles are not transferable. They add a dimension of values and design philosophy to an often utilitarian outcome. Think of Mies van de Rohe's "Less is more" or Dieter Rams' "Good design is useful". Bryan Lawson describes these as 'guiding principles' [22, p. 159], adding that "each design problem enables the designer to learn more about the guiding principles and express them ever more clearly" [22, p. 179] (Fig. 11.3).

Klaus Krippendorff writes that competing schools of thought in design had lost their distinctiveness and momentum: "Most educational programs include a little bit of everything in what they offer their students" [21, p. xvi]. With experience, designers learn to design things appropriately, but do they design the appropriate things? Perhaps it is time not only to rethink the values that inform right designing, but also the values expressed in the curriculum? This expands the narrow focus of solving a perceived design problem well, to enquiring into tacitly held beliefs and values of the individual, perhaps inquiring: How might my design affect peoples lives in unintended ways?

Could, for example, the designers of the compelling interfaces of mobile devices have anticipated their effects upon society? When taking a train journey 20 years ago

Fig. 11.3 A word cloud of popular design principles

it would have been considered impolite to not strike up a conversation with the other passengers of the train compartment. Today the opposite might be true: Trying to converse might be considered as intrusive and impolite, as people are engaged with their mobile devices. Who could have anticipated such an effect that took around one generation to change millions of individuals and entire societies? Small influences adding up may have large effects. From an ironic perspective the design brief might have been: What can we do to stop citizens talking to one another? The solution: Let us provide them with headphones and hand-held screens with continuously moving images to keep them entertained and busy. What kind of design principles or theoretical perspectives could consider such future effects? I argue that the necessary principles and theoretical perspectives, in conjunction with designerly values, might be informed by second-order cybernetics.

First-order cybernetics has an undeniable track record of solving technical and industrial problems, and it insinuates that any and all technical problems can be understood completely, and be managed safely – perhaps even at the scale of the entire planet. But, as David Orr argues: "[. . .] the complexity of Earth and its life systems can never be safely managed. The ecology of the top inch of topsoil is still largely unknown, as is its relationship to the larger systems of the biosphere" [28]. Hence, first-order cybernetics has great potential to enable some mechanistic aspects of design strategies, and to implement certain (primarily technical and managerial) aspects of design solutions, but it does not offer an adequate framework from within which to design. This requires other ways of framing.

Second-order cybernetics takes into account the observer, and thereby acknowledges the dimension of subjectivity. This observer is viewed as a part of the system she observes. The consequence being that there is no independent, objective perspective or reality 'out there', that there is no reality independent of an observer, but only different, necessarily confined, perspectives perceived by different observers. We realize that our knowledge will have to remain incomplete. It is impossible to see the whole picture, as this "whole picture" is simply not available. There only ever will be "my perspective" and "your perspective". What is the consequence of this realization and what does that imply for designing?

Such a cybernetic approach to designing would take into account that the perceived design problem does not exist independently in the world, but that it is perceived, invented and 'constructed', by the observing designer. You may find it too warm in here, I may find it too cold. What is the problem? We could open the windows to let cooler air in, or turn down the heating, put on a sweater. All actions entail different advantages and disadvantages. They form a part of a larger system; we expect actions to have consequences, which can be understood, responded to, and controlled in order to arrive at (and to either maintain or re-consider, through a continuation of this process) desired consequences. "Reality," in this view, arises subjectively in the observer through the engagement with what she observes. This "reality" and the observer who constructs it, are parts of each other, and cannot be thought of without one another. Being open to perturbations from within and from outside, this kind of engagement is not only open to error and change, but also inevitably non-determinable, and hence prone to cause unanticipated consequences. Navigating such a system towards desired goals requires, as necessary parts of feedback and learning, an acceptance of uncertainty and of responsibility for one's actions, as well as a set of guiding values. We observe, reflect, learn and theorize.

Linking design education with second-order cybernetics would be based upon an acceptance that the complexity of the world is viewed from a constructed perspective. That the natural and cultural environments consisted of networks, patterns and systems, which are intricately linked, forming a whole. It would affirm that we have different perspectives and thus would inform our interactions by values of generosity, empathy and care. Let us continue with an educational example in which cybernetics of the first order, namely ocean navigation, is used within a larger framework in which it informs the values of a culture. In my view, this is an example of cybernetics and second-order cybernetics beautifully informing each other to form a culture of lived ethics in conscious reflection-in-action.

11.4 Polynesian Cybernetics of Acting and Learning

Like members of other traditional cultures, many traditional Hawaiians had a closer relationship with nature than people living in cities. Over generations their members have distinguished patterns and networks within their ecosystem and learned to adapt to those in creative ways. These patterns include knowledge of flora and fauna in connection with environmental changes, seasonal changes, and human impact. Especially on precarious island habitats, Hawaiians had to know their confined ecosystem intimately, as their well-being was dependent on that knowledge. They were highly perceptive of the systemic dynamics of their environment and recognized minute patterns. On the Hawaiian islands, for example, there were names for the rains in certain areas occurring at particular times of the day (see below). Such experiential knowledge is passed on, often demonstrated, from generation to generation, from senior members of a culture to the younger members. Over time acting became knowing, and knowing acting. The different generations were dependent on one another, as was the future of the community and the ecosystem. Members of such a traditional culture were aware that they had to work together in order to secure their mutual survival.

Another crucial aspect was that the knowledge, acquired over generations, also expressed itself in the language. A distinct vocabulary and its use, reflected the idiosyncrasies of the ecosystem, its flora, fauna, and the patterns of relationships among plants, animals and humans, human actions, values, customs and traditions.

Through the language and its use emerges a culture's shared perception of a reality, a particular way of being in the world and being together. Embedded in the language is the accumulated wisdom and way of being of that culture. Some of this knowledge might be tacit, but it reflects the social sphere, language, actions and traditions. This mutually shared "reality" is intrinsically a social construction, created in a shared effort that spans multiple generations passing on knowledge and a unique perspective upon the world over time.

What may modern societies learn from such an example? What may educators, especially design educators, learn from educational programs that lead to empathy, care for others and the environment, and a sustainable way of life? Especially in view of learning about the patterns and networks of the ecosystem, a curiosity for natural phenomena guided by care and active involvement in the local community - perhaps leading to a more harmonious, sustainable relationship with other beings, the ecological system and the resources shared? Do designers perhaps also need to develop a new culture, a new language?

As a case study, I discuss below the educational framework of the Polynesian Voyaging Society, with particular attention to its "Eight Key Elements of Education," following a look at the specific context in which they are situated.

11.5 The Polynesian Voyaging Society

One organization with an educational program that fosters an awareness of ecosystems is the Polynesian Voyaging Society on the island of Oahu, Hawaii. Central to this program is traditional Polynesian navigation as an inspirational metaphor. Polynesian navigation was the ancient Polynesian practice of navigating the vast pacific ocean without instruments, only using knowledge of the patterns of motion of the sun, moon, stars, swells, wave patterns, clouds and birds as orienting cues to travel vast distances between Polynesian islands.

Hawaiian educators have developed an educational program that has traditional Hawaiian cultural values such as maritime navigation, community and ecology at its centre. In its hands-on approach, learning in small groups on real world problems, and commitment to lifelong learning, critical thinking, evaluating information, among other features, is strongly reminiscent of the design studio model, traditionally used by design educators.

People living on islands are highly aware of the limited nature of their resources and the precarious balance between their natural environment and the cumulative negative effects of unsustainable human actions. In order for their isolated society to survive, Hawaiians had to learn a sustainable way of life. Learning from experience and observing the consequences of actions in a limited and confined ecosystem necessarily lead to an intrinsic understanding of their environment and resulted in a culture that existed sustainably. Jared Diamond argues that a remote island being inhabited for thousands of years was evidence that its culture had succeeded in living sustainably [10]. By this standard, Hawaiian culture, being hundreds of years old, can be said to have achieved such a way of living. Other Pacific islanders were not as successful.

On a larger, planetary scale the experience of being on an isolated island appears to be more difficult to convey. The ‘island earth’ is too large to be identified by us as an island and once unsustainable actions have led to undesired consequences there still remain other places to migrate to.

During colonial history European administrations prohibited the building of long-distance canoes on some Polynesian islands and also banned inter-island travel [23]. Also during colonial rule Hawaiians were prohibited from speaking Hawaiian [26]. As a result the people’s language, knowledge and skills, customs and culture were gradually being lost since the nineteenth century. To learn about Polynesian navigation in the 1970s, navigator Nainoa Thompson had to learn from books, spend hundreds of hours in a planetarium and finally travel to the island of Satawal in distant Micronesia to find a qualified navigator to teach him traditional navigation skills [33]. In 1980 Thompson successfully navigated a long-distance voyaging canoe from Hawaii to Tahiti using only traditional techniques. This voyage inspired a generation of Polynesians and contributed to the renaissance of traditional Hawaiian culture and values. Today this navigation culture is thriving again with many apprentices learning the traditional way of navigating. This change of perspective also affects Hawaiian society as a whole. Navigation is intrinsically linked to Hawaiian culture and inseparable from it, not only leading to acute perceptiveness of natural processes if not to a reverence of nature and all living things, but also fostering reliability, team spirit and responsibility required of those sailing the canoe. How did this culture re-emerge in the modern setting of an industrialized society?

In 1984, the first pre-schools and schools were established teaching in Hawaiian [26, p. 278]. With language and culture being deeply intertwined, the educators wanted not only to teach in Hawaiian but also to convey Hawaiian culture. They began with identifying Hawaiian values they could base their curriculum on: “With the help of Hawaiian resource specialists, we explored those values which continue to influence the daily lives of our children: the values of óhana, or the extended family; the idea of kuleana, or area of responsibility; laulima, or cooperation; íke, knowing or recognizing; and kōkua, or helping” [12]. These schools provide a strong sense of community by conveying Hawaiian language, songs, traditions, culture and values alongside other subjects. As a result a generation has grown up for which the re-established canoe culture is deeply embedded within a rich social framework, part of which consists of speaking Hawaiian, alongside specific rituals, songs, storytelling and gift giving ceremonies that bring different generations together. Central to these traditional customs is also a reverence for the land, the ocean, wildlife and nature, as well as a strong sense of caring, community, and living in peace and harmony among all living beings. Inherent in speaking Hawaiian is expressing these values. Speaking the language implies a very particular way of being in the world.

McGregor writes in this context: "Native Hawaiian ancestors also named the various types of rain and wind of particular districts. The names of places and natural elements not only provide a profound sense of identity with the 'äina or land and natural resources, they also convey a sense of responsibility to provide stewardship of the area where they live" [26, p. 5]. "[This] Native Hawaiian world view is called 'lokahi', or unity, harmony, balance. It refers to the unity, harmony, and balance in the universe between humans, nature, and deities or spiritual life forces. For personal well-being, we need to be in balance with the people around us, and with the natural and spiritual forces of life" [26, p. 2].

By 2014, Hawaiian culture appears to have successfully re-emerged, with traditional navigation and canoe culture as strong symbolic and inspirational values at its centre. Navigating and canoe culture encourage conscious perception of the environment such as the ocean, stars, wind, clouds and wildlife, as well as care for people and natural resources. Additionally it creates a strong sense of community and responsibility. Just as it requires many to build, maintain and navigate a canoe, it takes many volunteers taking part in communal activities such as transporting canoes onto the dry dock (see Fig. 11.4) and maintaining them. On other occasions groups

Fig. 11.4 Moving the *Hōkūle'a* between the dry dock and the ocean is a community effort. Prominently visible: The *Hōkūle'a's* 'second-order' rudder – used to navigate a canoe in the Pacific Ocean, to navigate a traditional culture in a modern world

help clearing trails in the countryside, maintaining shore vegetation or working on the land. For an outsider all these activities may appear to be traditional and timeless while in fact they are not. As communal activities they have only re-emerged since the 1980s as the result of the efforts of a dedicated group of educators.

Polynesian culture appears to have successfully integrated both first-order and second-order cybernetic principles into a lived practice. First-order cybernetics and second-order cybernetics inform each other in a circular relationship: Doing things right and doing the right things.

11.6 The PVS' Eight Key Elements of Education

Its educators have identified eight key elements of education as a part of the PVS' educational program. The origin of these elements emerged from Nainoa Thompson's own reflections upon his personal lifetime learning experiences, as discussed in Speidel and Inn's article 'The Ocean is my Classroom' [33]. These elements are partly based on experiences made in school, but also from insights mixing modern approaches with traditional navigational elements. The primary one being taught by a caring teacher.

1. Vision and Values: "His vision tells [the navigator] where to go; his values tell him why he should go. [. . .] [The vision] embodies a traditional view of the world by which native Hawaiians were able to sustain life in the islands for centuries"
2. Exploration and Challenge: "Add[ing] to existing knowledge through exploration and discovery."
3. Observation and Experience: "While the knowledge we teach includes reading and studying for preparation and orientation, observation and experience are an essential component of mastery."
4. Application and Practice: "We learn most efficiently and effectively by acquiring and applying knowledge to a project or a goal that is meaningful to us, rather than by being asked to memorize knowledge with little or no application."
5. Outcomes: "Real and meaningful outcomes help motivate learning."
6. Culture: "Pride in one's ancestral culture serves as a powerful motivation to acquire and master knowledge. While the knowledge in navigation and crew training includes Western knowledge, the PVS mission has been to recover and perpetuate indigenous knowledge and wisdom and apply it, through practice, in the modern world."
7. Home: Place and Community: "The most relevant, meaningful, and significant context in which learners apply knowledge is the place and community that they are most directly connected to [. . .]"
8. Life-Long Learning: Analyzing information, critical thinking, teamwork, agility and adaptability [29].

While the PVS has several lists around "values" and "themes" concerning education, I consider these 'key elements' most relevant.[3] While they link experiences and values of traditional culture and maritime navigation to modern education, they infer those to other areas of learning. In my view the success of the educational program also demonstrates the value of long-term thinking and having a vision of a desirable future.

Before the success of this distinctly Hawaiian educational program could be evaluated, one generation had to grow up experiencing it. Implicit in this framework are a strong connections to cybernetic ideas, such as the interest in understanding how elements are identified as systems, and the second-order cybernetic interest in how systems relate to values, responsibility and the reflection of one's actions (see also [6]). From this understanding emerges a perspective of the world around us characterized by a web of relationships and interdependence, connectedness taking place within particular contexts. Before I discuss the individual elements of this educational framework in relation to design education, I would like to show its relationship to cybernetics, as well as its similarity to the design studio model.

Similar to the Transition Design Framework [19], second-order cybernetics takes into account how mental images (such as vision or values) can affect the outcomes. It also considers the larger context (exploration, observation), taking on different mental perspectives (culture) and allowing for tensions of paradox and controversy without trying to resolve them quickly (culture). Where I see the strongest relevance to both, cybernetics and design education, are the elements Exploration, Application and Outcomes. Here the learning takes place bottom-up and is learned through doing and reflecting. This explorative, practical approach is also at the heart of the design studio model. Here designing is a collaborative activity, a hands-on experience often with tangible outcomes, involving multiple levels of making and reflecting, receiving feedback by an experienced person.

If we now apply other elements of the PVS framework to design, we might say designers need to learn openness to the expertise of other disciplines, openness to other perspectives and ways of knowing and being, openness to self-organisation and networks, and openness to novelty and change with failures and errors being viewed as learning opportunities (the latter point has been raised explicitly by Glanville[17, p. 10]). Ideally, designers, being educated in these principles, may expand these insights into a cybernetic way of life, a way of continuous learning, questioning and openness for change.

From this perspective, on Hawaii, cybernetics appears to be both a lived practice in the form of traditional instrument-less maritime navigation and an application of the learning of this practice to everyday life. With navigation comes acute perception of the environment, leading to knowing and experience. From this knowing emerged

[3]There are other lists that seek to apply patterns observed in nature to human actions. Among these are Booth Sweeney's "'habits of mind' found in a systems thinker" [5, pp. 3–4], Irwin's "Living System Principles" [18], Stone and Barlow's *Seven lessons for leaders in systems change* [34], and Benyus' *Biomimicry's surprising lessons from nature's engineers* [4].

a highly adapted sustainable way of living off the sea and the land, in harmony with nature and other beings. As such, first-order cybernetics and second-order cybernetics appear to have informed each other in a circular fashion: Doing things right and doing the right things. In this practical approach, the framework reminds of the design studio model. Here, from a cybernetics perspective, human acting becomes human knowing, which again will inform acting in a circular process. In it the observer is a participant, exploring the nature of this circular system, and is concerned with the philosophical, psychological and mechanical examination and understanding of these issues [15, p. 90].

The Polynesian navigators, knowing stars, swells and cloud formations, navigate the canoe and have the responsibility for the other members' well-being. The knowledge of these environmental patterns is coordinated with the actions necessary to navigate the canoe and reach a distant island. At the same time these habits of acute awareness, responsibility, collaboration, care and pattern recognition appear to be transferred to the community and the culture of the fragile island habitat itself. Vision, planning, training, discipline become a way of life [2]. A circular state of lived cybernetics. How might this "framework" inform design education?

11.7 What Can Design Educators Learn from Hawaiian Educators?

Above I have briefly introduced two educational programs: The design studio model, and the elements that inform the Polynesian Voyaging Society's educational program. As Hawaiian culture appears to be thriving today, it is hard to believe that this is actually a renaissance, initiated merely one generation ago. This could serve as an encouragement for design education to include a focus on local conditions, reaching out to the local community, making values explicit, and exploring local history, especially the use of materials, techniques, customs and culture. Even though some of these 'traditional elements' might sound conservative and resistant to learning, change and adaptability, they once stood the test of time and are worth exploring and evaluating. If necessary, they can be adapted and combined with contemporary values, stances and technologies. Design education would be lifted from a limited educational framework into a practice perpetuating culture, a way of being in the world, a life project.

In the following, I discuss those elements which both programs share, and also acknowledge some of the complex interdependencies that arise by combining the diverse concepts. Then I look at those elements of the PVS framework that are absent in design education and how these may be transferred. Let us begin with adapting the 'Eight elements' of the PVS. How might the PVS' elements introduced above inform design education and add to a model for a transition to a design culture that is more local, more environmentally aware, that emphasises acute use of the senses and care? Below I have adapted the original 'Eight elements' presented above to design education:

1. *Vision and Values*: Her vision tells the designer what a desirable future might look like; her values tell her how to design and also that a design might affect culture and nature in complex ways, with implications for the best of the environment, locality and community. This vision is not a fixed goal, but a continuous process, a transition towards a desired state, taking into account complex interdependencies within a dynamic and changing environment. Similar to the metaphorical steersman in cybernetics, it is not only about reaching the (external) goal of making successful landfall, but also to manage the (internal) goal of coordinating actions so that the course is maintained. Every design experience contributes to such a vision [14, 35]. Design curricula are rarely explicit about their values. While designers reflect on concrete design problems and take into account other perspectives via human-centered design principles, reflecting on the implicit values that inform their designing is less often the case. Perhaps students should converse more about values? Design students mostly draw, study or spend time in workshops building models and prototypes. Perhaps discussions and writing essays would aid in becoming more reflective and value conscious? Vision and values also point to the larger, situated context, the society and culture, within which designing takes place. Designers who are experienced in reflection and discussion might also make prolific contributions to public debates.
2. *Exploration and Challenge*: These are an intrinsic part of design education. Designing new solutions is research-based and learned through exploration and being challenged, e.g. by wicked problems [30]. "Problems" do not exist independently in the world, but are perceived as such by observers.
3. *Observation and Experience*: While preparing for a design project includes reading and studying for preparation and orientation, practical experience is at the heart of designing. Also essential to designing a solution for a perceived problem is the ability to observe oneself, others and the environment. Through reflection, such experiences may become deep learning experiences – e.g. as described by Schön through reflection-in-action, and reflecting-on-reflection-in-action [32]. In design education such insights won through reflection are practiced but rarely encouraged or made explicit. Even experienced designers might have difficulties explaining what they do when they design. In general, little attention is given to reflection on observation and experience. Perhaps the pragmatism and goal-oriented attitude young designers are expected to adopt, and exuding an air of confidence and conviction contradicts these reflective states of mind? The design process is often solution-oriented, and less about understanding the process or its phases but producing viable solutions within particular constraints, e.g. such as budget and time-scale. However, it is such reflective attention from which new understanding might emerge. These insights may inform new principles of designing, observing and experiencing and making those insights explicit. It is here where conscious learning is taking place, and design educators should emphasise its importance. Conscious reflection should become habitual for designers.

4. *Application and Practice*: Meaningful goals enable learning as well as testing of knowledge through practice. These also are an intrinsic part of design education as part of the design studio, but might be made more explicit in order to make students aware of the importance of this relationship to learning. By allowing students to acquire their knowledge and experience in meaningful practice, for example, designing for the campus or another local environment, they experience their impact upon their environment and how a design might affect people. This might also lead to understanding the distinction between espoused theory and theory-in-action [1] and a more balanced relationship between theory and practice.
5. *Outcomes*: Design is usually about concrete outcomes and as such intrinsic to designing. Designing a product or service that will actually be used by a community we know may help motivate to design with empathy, realistic conditions and applications in mind.
6. *Culture*: Identify local, historical, cultural contexts, traditions, cooking, crafts, materials, idioms and industries that designers can be inspired by. How can traditional, local skills, customs and techniques inform designing with contemporary applications in mind? Design projects could involve the local community and different generations.
7. *Home-Place and Community*: Living and participating at the place of study, both on and off campus. Learning to design by designing for local context, place and community. What has proven to be relevant here might be adapted to also be relevant within other contexts. This begins with welcoming the first-year students into the community of designers. The place of study should become a home, and not a place of transition. To bond with their new home, students should investigate their new environment and its history. What kind of produce was traditionally grown here? How is consumer refuse recycled? How is the electricity produced? Which watershed do we live in [20]? How may I get involved here and contribute through my design skills? Designers and community members design together for the community. This creates empathy and understanding.
8. *Life-Long Learning*: In a dynamic and rapidly changing world, creativity, critical thinking, teamwork, information literacy, agility, adaptability and other higher-level abilities have become essential for life in general, and for designing in particular. As technologies, tools and methods change or become obsolete, so do needs for particular skills. Higher-level abilities, however, and especially those higher-level abilities though which skills are acquired and evaluated, are of profound long-term value. In this context, a commitment to lifelong learning is a necessity [27].

Are there limits to the extent these principles can be adapted to design education? While designing is both a profession and an academic discipline, the PVS' elements consider the whole of society and how it is affected by actions. Their values are lived, becoming a life mission. Designing typically extends, at best, into the design community or the private home. How might this change? While design as a professional activity is typically bound by contractual agreements, participants of PVS activities are volunteers contributing to shared goals.

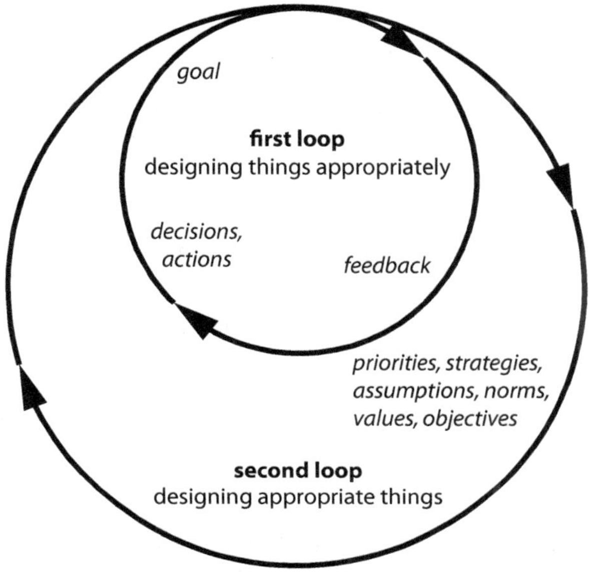

Fig. 11.5 Single-loop and double-loop learning, inspired by [1] and [6, p. 37]

Both the PVS and design education are driven by idealism, empathy and ethics. They share the desire to do a job well, the desire to contribute to a community, as well as the enjoyment of working collaboratively. While the elements "Exploration and challenge," "application and practice," as well as "outcomes" may be regarded as elements already integral, both to designing and explorative research, profound learning happens when these are explicitly communicated in a double-loop learning process [1, 6]. Such a process re-evaluates and re-frames goals, aiding understanding and contributing to a more reflective design community (Fig. 11.5).

In my view the elements "culture," "home" and "lifelong learning" might create the biggest impact for design education. Awareness of local culture, craft, and materials can aid in contributing a local and historical grounding to the idealism and motivation of the designer. They might also result in finding satisfaction in smaller design tasks that make use of local materials, techniques or traditions and benefit local purposes. On the other hand they urge the designer to explicitly make a distinction between how things used to be done, and how and why she is doing them in a different way. In this learning experience they place themselves consciously within a context and a tradition, thus enhancing the scope and grounding. This results in knowledge and techniques which may later be transferred to different contexts. At the same time they might include modern materials, technologies or processes. Designs might also facilitate adopting values that can become habitual cultural practices, such as car-sharing, bicycle-sharing, house-sharing, urban gardening or recycling.

All of the elements above could result in promising new directions for young designers to explore. Adopting some of these principles may lead to profound changes in designing, although these may require time to become visible as they might be subtle and emerge over time through social interactions as well as new designs. A shortcoming here might be the recent implementation of the relatively short 3-year Bachelor's degree resulting in a steep and stressful learning curve for design students. Adding more subjects to the curriculum might prove too demanding. How might some of these elements be implemented?

11.8 Top-Down and Self-Organized

A contradiction appears to arise from the idea of fostering self-organizing processes and the metaphor of a navigator leading the course. In practice, however, this might be not a problem. Most collaborative activities that I participated in on Hawaii had no visible leader and appeared entirely self-organized. To me this was an unfamiliar concept and not without frustration as nobody was able to inform me what we were going to do next. A 'plan' seemed conspicuously absent, although everybody appeared to know their individual role and the desired outcome.

People appeared to be comfortable acting ad hoc, following a fluid and adaptable course. They had a tolerance for paradox and ambiguity, did not rush to resolve problems quickly, very much in the spirit of second-order cybernetics.

Other similarities that design and cybernetics share are that both might be seen as practices of acting and understanding, as well as theoretical perspectives. In both, learning takes place in situated actions. Acting becomes knowing and knowing becomes acting. Both are perspectives that transgress professional or disciplinary boundaries as they may inform a particular perspective upon the world, resulting in a way of being in the world. In that sense both practices might be seen as meta-disciplinary. From a systems thinking perspective this invites critique on the current structure of design education on several levels. For example, learning from nature is rarely a central part of the curriculum. Apart from courses on biomimetics under-graduate students usually do not explicitly learn about systems, networks, or feedback. Perhaps, this would lead to a change of perspective, a "wide-awakefulness" that educator Maxine Greene [24, p. vi] described as a "life project"? Designing does not just entail designing products but how one might organise their kitchen and what kind of food they will be preparing and with whom they share the meal.

All phases of designing involve constructivist elements [16] and working bottom-up as well as top-down simultaneously. Much of this already is implicit in how designers act, yet making this explicit might help to add a reflective and explanatory layer to better understand, analyse and communicate the design experience, leading to design actions that are better grounded and which may be communicated.

What remains yet unresolved is the question of designers interested in designing for sustainability having to cater for the needs of an unsustainable consumption society and an economy that is dependent upon continuous growth. This might require the implementation of education for ecological literacy at schools, educating a new generation of more conscious and discernible consumers, but also economists, decision- and policy-makers.

A 'cybernetic curriculum' would also require teachers to adopt a different style of teaching and a commitment to lifelong learning, one in which theories are either linked to observation and experience, or emerge from those. The question is whether design educators wish themselves to be perceived as learners. The traditional epistemology of the university is about knowledge being conveyed in a one-directional manner from those that know to those who do not know [32]. This would involve a paradigm shift of collaborative learning based on a research approach. And these are only a few of the challenges that should initiate a conversation around design education. As other educational fields, intentionally or unintentional, adopted characteristics of the design studio model (among them law, medicine and the PVS), design educators might learn from educational practices and ideas of those fields, feed those back into design education.

What design education and non-instrumental navigation have in common is that they both are being taught following the Master-apprentice model, a tradition of project-based education and learning-by-doing. For design students this model reaches back to mediaeval guilds, the nineteenth century École des Beaux Arts, and the Bauhaus. For traditional apprentices of non-instrumental navigation this was more based on tradition and ritual, involving also personal relationships. Traditional navigational knowledge, its application and skills involved, were closely guarded and it was expected that students would become leaders and stewards in their own community (Hawaiian Voyaging Traditions, Founders and Teachers, Pius "Mau" Piailug, [3]). Today however this has changed and the knowledge is freely shared, also with members of other communities. In both models an experienced master-practitioner, in the best case also a master-coach, guides the learner through tasks that often involve complex, unique and uncertain conditions [31]. Designers as well as navigators require a strong commitment, carry responsibility, act within a environment of changing constraints and ambiguity, and sometimes need to make decisions intuitively. Students would step-by-step try to solve the given task, while in the process a caring teacher provides critique and feedback, perhaps demonstrating the application of knowledge and skilled activity herself, while making assumptions, strategies and values explicit. Traditional teacher-learner relationships were more hierarchical and authoritative, adhering to customs and traditions such as not criticising the teacher and respecting authority, today's practices are less conservative. This might be especially true in modern environments where the master-apprentice model is challenged and the teacher is a learner herself. Today's navigation students do not have to memorise chants with star positions at particular times of the year, but use pen and paper instead to take notes. They also learn about changing seasons in the planetarium. Contemporary learners learn differently from their predecessors (Hawaiian Voyaging Traditions, Founders and Teachers, Pius "Mau" Piailug [3]).

11.9 Conclusions

Above I have presented how values of traditional Hawaiian culture have been transferred into an educational framework strongly reminiscent of the design studio model. This framework is value-based, encourages teamwork, generosity, a harmonious relationship with nature and other beings, and strives for sustainability. The educators implementing this model had a long-term perspective and in the course of one generation their initiative has lead to a deep societal transformation on the Hawaiian islands. Subsequently, I discussed how elements from their framework – especially "culture," "home" and "lifelong learning" – might make meaningful contributions to design education in view of sustainable design and community experience. Testing those in design education might not only change students' outlook on their profession, but may also affect how they work and live, the values they hold and the communities they build and become part of.

When students study and design with a local culture on mind, this will have an impact on several levels. They may develop a new perspective upon their own culture and its traditions. This can involve to all aspects of life, from architectural patterns, elements and materials, to local culture, communities, produce, cooking and eating customs and many more. By designing for people they know, they engage more deeply with the users of their designs and their own design projects. They learn the local language and its particular perspective upon the world. This conscious awareness also allows for a critical distance. They reflect on what they do and why they are doing it.

By making a home at the place of study, designing for people they know, and an environment they know, they later experience the impact that their design efforts have made. Learning from the impact of a design, also long-term, has hardly been on the agenda of design studios. Design professionals usually move on to the next client and learning from past projects is rarely part of the agenda. Implementing this in the education would create an awareness of the more complex impacts of designing.

Lifelong learning has been on the agenda of various educational studies and it is not a unique insight originating from Hawaiian educators. This requirement is a result of the continuously changing conditions of professional work, often as a result of technology, changes to lifestyles and automation.

Under these changing conditions, design education finds opportunities to self-reflect and adapt on multiple levels. Should students first learn how to design and then learn about complexity, systems and sustainability, or the other way around? Or should the two be intertwined? Learning to design sustainably, and designing to learn sustainably, from the start? As undergraduate degree programs are relatively short, and in many resemble high school timetables more than traditional higher education, any expanded, more comprehensive curriculum would require extending the duration of study. Additionally, *how* designing is being learned would need to change. Such a more comprehensive approach would need to embrace notions of complexity, systems, patterns and networks, and be implemented through project-based learning, interrupted by reflection. It would also include learning from nature –

in accord with a paraphrasing of Clarke's Third Law: "Any sufficiently advanced technology is indistinguishable from nature".

In such an approach, learning would be made explicit through critical reflection and discussions. Attempts would be made to look at problems from broader, systemic perspectives, and impacts of changes over time would be observed and examined to inform subsequent changes. In such an educational setting, the study of second-order cybernetics would, I argue, inspire all involved to consider the perspectives of others, to consider own values, to accept responsibility for own actions, to learn through errors, and to adopt the modest posture of a learner.

By learning about local history, including customs, architecture, produce and cooking traditions, designers would learn that, for example, in the past meat was consumed far less frequently than today, and that lower meat consumption was healthier, both for the individual as for the ecosystem. Such changes in personal, local behaviour would have a global impact.

Designing services and designing for social change can today easier be facilitated through new digital tools. By getting engaged in the local culture, for example building communities through gardening or sharing economies, new design spaces and new economic opportunities open up, mixing high-tech and traditional approaches. This would aid the resilience of local communities and provide transferable knowledge that may be implemented at other places. Incentives might shift from economic and materialistic to social and qualitative domains of life.

These are only a few conclusions I draw from the idea around adding elements of home, culture and lifelong-learning and second-order cybernetics to design education. They are thought of as suggestions to initiate a discussion around the future of the design curriculum.

References

1. Argyris, C., & Schön, D. A. (1974). *Theory in practice. Increasing professional effectiveness.* San Francisco: Jossey-Bass.
2. Baybayan, C. (2000). *From an interview with Chad Baybayan by Sam Low*. Available at: http://archive.hokulea.com/hoonaauao/education_themes.html. Accessed January 19, 2019.
3. Baybayan, C. (2010). *Hawaiian voyaging traditions.Founders and teachers: Pius "Mau" Piailug*. Available at: http://archive.hokulea.com/index/founder_and_teachers/mau.html. Accessed January 19, 2019.
4. Benyus, J. (2007). *Biomimicry's surprising lessons from nature's engineers, Video transcript*. Available at: https://www.ted.com/talks/janine_benyus_shares_nature_s_designs/transcript?language=en. Accessed January 19, 2019.
5. Booth Sweeney, L., & Meadows, D. (1995). *The systems thinking playbook.* Durham: University of New Hampshire.
6. Brand, S. (1976). For God's Sake, Margaret: Conversation with Gregory Bateson and Margaret Mead. *CoEvolutionary Quarterly, 10*, 32–44.
7. Bruno, D. (2010). *The 100 thing challenge: How I got rid of almost everything, remade my life, and regained my soul.* New York, NY: Harper.
8. Capra, F. (1996). *The web of life: A new synthesis of mind and matter.* New York, NY: Anchor Books.

9. Co, E. (2014). *The world is still enormous*. Available at: Hokulea Blog. Available at: http://www.hokulea.com/world-still-enormous. Accessed January 19, 2019.
10. Diamond, J. (2005). *Collapse: How societies choose to fail or survive*. New York, NY: Viking.
11. Dubberly, H. (2004). *How do you design? A compendium of models*. San Francisco, CA: Dubberly Design Office. Available at: http://www.dubberly.com/wp-content/uploads/2008/06/ddo_designprocess.pdf. Accessed January 19, 2019.
12. Fink, G. (1990). The child as a member of a culture. In *Hana hou: Outstanding articles in applied educational research from the Kamehameha Journal of Education* (pp. 117–122). Available at: http://ulukau.org/elib/collect/kamjoe/index/assoc/D0.dir/doc129.pdf. Accessed January 19, 2019.
13. Drexhage, J., & Murphy, D. (2010), *Sustainable development: From Brundtland to Rio 2012, Background paper for the high level panel on global sustainability*. New York, NY: United Nations.
14. Gage, S. (2007). The boat/helmsman. *Technoetic Arts: A Journal of Speculative Research, 5*(1), 15–24.
15. Glanville, R. (1999). Researching design and designing research. *Design Issues, 15*(2), 80–91.
16. Glanville, R. (2006). Construction and design. *Constructivist Foundations, 1*(3), 61–68.
17. Glanville, R. (2014). How design and cybernetics reflect each other (transcript of keynote presentation). *RSD3 Relating systems Thinking and Design 2014*. http://systemic-design.net/wp-content/uploads/2014/08/Ranulph_Glanville.pdf. Accessed January 19, 2019.
18. Irwin, T. (2004). *Extracts: Living systems principles and their relevance to design*, MSc thesis. Devon, UK: Schumacher College.
19. Terry, I. (2015). Transition design: A proposal for a new area of design practice, study, and research. *Design and Culture. The Journal of the Design Studies Forum, 7*(2), 229–246.
20. Kelly, K. (2006). *The big here: 30 questions to elevate your awareness (and literacy) of the greater place in which you live, Blog post*. Available at: http://kk.org/helpwanted/archives/001084.php. Accessed January 19, 2019.
21. Krippendorff, K. (2006). *The semantic turn. A new foundation for design*. Boca Raton, FL: Taylor and Francis.
22. Lawson, B. (2005). *How designers think* (4th ed.). Oxford: Elsevier Architectural Press.
23. Lewis, D. (1994). *We, the navigators: The ancient art of landfinding in the Pacific* (2nd ed.). Honolulu, HI: University of Hawaii Press.
24. Lyons, N. (2010). *Handbook of reflection and reflective enquiry: Mapping a way of knowing for professional reflective enquiry*. New York, NY: Springer.
25. Maturana, H. R. (2002). Autopoiesis, structural coupling and cognition: A history of these and other notions in the biology of cognition. *Cybernetics and Human Knowing, 9*(3/4), 5–34.
26. McGregor, D. (2007). *Nä Kua'äina: Living Hawaiian culture*. Honolulu, HI: University of Hawaii Press.
27. OECD. (2008). *21st century learning: Research, innovation, policy. Directions from recent OECD analysis*. Paris: CERI.
28. Orr, D. W. (1991). What is education for? *In context* 27. Available at: http://www.context.org/iclib/ic27/orr. Accessed January 19, 2019.
29. Polynesian Voyaging Society. (2007). *Key elements of education*. Available: http://pvs.kcc.hawaii.edu/hoonaauao/education_elements.html. Accessed January 19, 2019.
30. Rittel, H. W. J., & Webber, M. M. (1984). Planning problems are wicked problems. In N. Cross (Ed.), *Developments in design methodology* (pp. 135–144). New York, NY: Wiley.
31. Schön, D. (1985). *The design studio: An exploration of its traditions and potentials*. London: RIBA Publications.
32. Schön, D. (1987). *Educating the reflective practitioner*. Transcript available at: http://post.queensu.ca/~russellt/howteach/schon87.htm. Accessed January 19, 2019.
33. Speidel, G. E., & Inn, K. (1994). The ocean is my classroom. *Kamehameha Journal of Education, 5*, 11–23.

34. Stone, M., & Barlow, Z. (2011). *Seven lessons for leaders of systems change.* Available at: https://www.ecoliteracy.org/article/seven-lessons-leaders-systems-change. Accessed January 19, 2019.
35. Sweeting, B. (2015). Cybernetics of practice. *Kybernetes, 44*(8/9), 1397–1405.

Michael Hohl is a designer, educator and researcher, and Professor of Design Theory at Anhalt University of Applied Sciences Dessau, Germany. With a PhD in fine art & computer science, he likes making things, thinking about things, how we do them and how this changes us. He enjoys working with BA, MA and PhD students, from first-year BAs to supervising and mentoring PhD research students from Art, Design and Architecture. He also conducts Research Training Seminars at the Royal College of Art and other institutions. He organises and co-organises conferences, research seminars and guest lectures, co-edits publications and conferences – and is interested in turning these experiences into conversations.

Chapter 12
Designing, Together and Apart

Timothy Jachna

Abstract Designing is a conversational activity. This chapter draws on second-order cybernetic concepts, particularly Pask's Conversation Theory and subsequent work inspired and derived from it, to propose a conceptual basis for articulating various modalities of designing-with-others. This approach unifies different ways in which people and artifacts are linked in processes of designing, from the simple designer-client relationship to people's interactions with designed things, to the ripples of effects of these things, beyond the control and intentions of the designer, once they are out into the world at large. After introducing the concept of conversation as applied to the processes of design, the chapter explores the detailed anatomy of such conversations with reference to a model of conversations by Dubberly and Pangaro, drawing on Pask's concept of the conversation. Other cybernetic scholars, notably Krippendorff, are cited to demonstrate that the "statements" exchanged in the course of design conversations consist of both verbal and written utterances and the diverse range of artifacts produced in the course of the design process. The chapter then applies these concepts and perspectives to discuss different levels of design conversations, from those that take place within *teams* of designers working on a project, to those that occur in the wider *communities* formed by various designers and non-designers who cooperate in the realization of designed things, to those that permeate broad *societies* of people affected in one way or another by designed things. Implications are proposed for the role of designers in society, in light of this cybernetic framing of design processes. The chapter concludes by synthesizing these insights to demonstrate the potential of cybernetic perspectives in articulating the intrinsically political nature of design.

Keywords Design process · Conversation Theory · Designing-with-others · Design conversations · Design artifacts

---

T. Jachna (✉)
College of Design, Architecture, Art and Planning, University of Cincinnati, Cincinnati, OH, USA
e-mail: timothy.jachna@uc.edu

T. Fischer, C. M. Herr (eds.), *Design Cybernetics*, Design Research Foundations,
https://doi.org/10.1007/978-3-030-18557-2_12

12.1 Introduction

Even in its most elementary manifestation, involving a single designer and an individual client, designing is a process of interaction between people with different bodies of knowledge, who approach the design process from different perspectives and with different expectations. Most design processes involve a much wider range of stakeholders and expertise than this one-on-one relationship. Mobilizing this varied cast of characters to work towards a common goal requires an ongoing web of interactions and exchanges through conversations.

Increasing efforts towards more inclusive and informed design processes with approaches such as co-creation and collaborative and participatory design underscore the importance given by designers to more effective modes of engaging non-designers in the conversations of design [10]. Growing attention is being paid to the processes of design being undertaken by communities of heterogeneous individuals (not necessarily involving designers) in addressing issues in their own lives [21]. This broadens the meaning of design to include processes involving the confluence of the efforts and intentions of diverse others, in practices that may be broadly seen as designing but which transcend the understanding of designing as a special purview of professionals operating in controlled teams.

The impacts and implications of design processes and the designed things that they put out into the world, though, are felt by others even beyond this wider perspective on the communities of design, to include a wide swathe of members of a society, who are also drawn into the conversations of design. Thus, this chapter aims to explore what a cybernetic perspective can contribute to our understanding of communal processes of design in society very broadly construed.

12.2 Conversations and Design

Pask's Conversation Theory [27] describes a cybernetic mechanism by which multiple participants construct understanding of shared concepts, elaborating and developing these concepts through conversation. As this idea has been addressed at length in Chap. 8 in this volume, I will not repeat that explanation here.

Expanding upon Pask's concept, Dubberly and Pangaro [8] distinguish "conversation" from "communication." The latter term refers to the transmission of messages from senders to receivers, whereas the former involves the development of new concepts and understandings based on an iterative exchange (through which the conversing individuals also change/learn/evolve). Communication involves shared protocols for encoding and decoding messages, and a circumscribed realm of possible significances of statements (as described in Shannon's communication model [32], discussed in Chap. 3 in this volume). Conversation, on the other hand, begins with a statement introducing a new concept for which no ready-made and mutually agreed code is available, initiating an exchange of statements as participants in the conversation seek to achieve a feeling of having a shared understanding.

Both communication and conversation rely on a medium through which utterances are made, but they make very different use of this medium. Communication functions through the denotative and prosaic facet of language(s), seeking to minimize ambiguity and maximize precision. While conversation certainly draws on this aspect of language, it also mobilizes the fuzzy, multivalent, connotative and poetic capacities of (often the same) language(s) to seek to give expression to concepts for which there are no pre-existing constructs available.

Pangaro has argued that conversation and design are analogous processes, through which goals and understandings are negotiated through interaction [25]. There is thus no designing that is not co-designing. If design is conversation and conversation is design, then designing requires participants who are not only multiple but also multifarious.[1] Conversations in the cybernetic sense are initiated and sustained from a gap in understanding, and a mutual will to bridge that gap.

12.3 Designing from Teams to Communities

Starting with Pask's model of the conversation as a communal process of meaning-making, and Pangaro's assertion of the isomorphism of conversation and design, I proceed here to enquire how these characteristics manifest themselves in designing-as-actually-done, involving a large variety of different individuals and interactions. These cybernetic principles provide a way of drawing together ideas from current design discourse, as well as a framework for articulating the ways in which designing takes place in conversations within design teams, as well as between designers and the broader network of stakeholders that collude in envisioning and manifesting designed things.

12.3.1 The Conversations of the Design Process

Different perspectives on the conversational nature of design may be discerned in the writings of a number of pre-eminent design theorists of recent decades.

Nigel Cross' "Design Thinking" [5] contains a presentation of design as a conversation-like activity within groups or teams, in the context of the professional design office. For Cross, the fact that different members of a design team may have different understandings of a problem is considered as problematic and leading to conflict, and the resolution of such conflicts (driven by a shared interest in reaching an "acceptable conclusion" to the design task) is seen as a principal preoccupation of

[1]Even in Glanville's [14, p. 1178] model of design as conversation with oneself, the designer externalizes concepts in sketches, models and other media such that they may be subjected to scrutiny by other aspects of the designer's intellect. See page 33 as well as Fig. 1.5 in this volume.

design teams. The ideal, for Cross, is to make a complex composite behave as a single organism, with an aligned sense of purpose and a common goal. This can be pursued in multiple ways, including command-and-control regimes in which members are expected to align with directives from the team leader as well as mechanisms of consensus-seeking in the team. In practice, there are typically elements of both of these in the professional practice of design.

However, such regimes have a limited purview of relevance in design, if design is conceived as a multi-participant process, not constrained to the interactions that happen within the design office or team. A design team, be it a single individual or a group of dozens of people, is only one of many participants in the design process, and indeed the easiest of these participants to bring under a regime of control, camaraderie and organization optimized around designer-centric values, motivating factors and performance criteria.

This constraint is not merely a practical limitation that has to do with limits to the reach and scope of corporate organizations. As Buchanan [4, p.13] has pointed out, different participants in the design process (designers, engineers and marketers, in his example) have completely different "modes of argumentation," meaning that understandings about the content or aim of a conversation and indeed the very criteria for validity of an argument are not necessarily shared.[2] Kees Dorst [7, p.149] refers to the "battle for the user" between marketing and design (driven by the former's conception of what the user *wants* versus the latter's convictions about what the user *needs*), noting also that designers do not completely share the goals of their clients, seeing a project not just as a matter of satisfying the client's brief, but also as part of their own creative development. Dorst also refers to some others with whom designers must work to (he uses the example of the head of production in the factory that will produce the designed product) as "natural enemies" of the designer, who perceive changes entailed by designers' plans as threats to the ways of doing things that they have established within the realms under their control. Rittel and Webber's [29] very definition of the wicked problems with which design grapples points out that problems of this type involve "many clients and decision makers with conflicting values." Each participant in the design conversation can be said to be led and limited by the cognitive models and "myths" that they bring to the conversation [20, p.183].

If you and I collaborate in a design process, and our roles in knowledge construction are not redundant in that we don't stand in an asymmetrical control relationship to one another and we do not represent substantially congruent perspectives, bodies of knowledge and intentions, then the perpetuation of the design process will likely benefit from our *not* articulating the goal of the design process in the same way, such that each of us may operate within the system of values and goals that makes the process meaningful to us. Consequently, the conversation that carries this design process forward should maintain a degree of openness such that each of us can continue to project our own meaning onto it.

[2]As per Buchanan's example, industrial designers argue based on what is possible, engineers about what is necessary and marketers about the contingencies of consumer attitudes.

12.3.2 Design Artifacts as Statements

Because I am interested in *design* conversations in particular, the network of stakeholders involved in the myriad conversations of designing must be conceived as being linked not just by an exchange of words, but also by the creation and dissemination of artifacts and representations. It is not difficult to perceive this character in the types of artifacts (seen as statements or "arguments") used by designers to communicate their ideas, in which "every designer's sketch, blueprint, flow chart, graph, three-dimensional model, or other product proposal is an example of such an argument"[3] [4, p. 18].

Each statement in a conversation is a designed thing in its own right, fashioned using a language and put out into the world with the intent of having a desired effect. I am proposing here, as I have elsewhere [17], that we further generalize our understanding of statements in the conversations of design to include the full range of artifacts produced in the course of design processes, as well as the final products that are the *telos* of these conversations. In the words of Krippendorff,

> Artifacts are not only instrumental to users (operational context) and constitutive of social realities (sociolinguistic context), but they are also created, produced, marketed, consumed, retired or recycled, and experiences with them inform a subsequent generation of artifacts. This process forms a grand cycle, oversimplifyingly called the production-consumption cycle, which knits designers, engineers, producers, suppliers, distributors, advertisers, salespersons, consumers, users, waste managers, applied scientists, researchers, and regulatory agencies into an ongoing process... These participants have a stake in maintaining this process and can therefore be called stakeholders. [20, p.173]

This invites expansion of the notion of statements in design conversations to include not just literal verbal utterances, but also the plans, models and prototypes generated in the design process, the products, services, buildings and other things produced following designers' directives, the marketing materials and messages, and texts and media surrounding designed things, the practices of use of these objects, and the waste or recycled material that the products eventually become. These artifacts are "messages in a circuit... continuously created, articulated, interpreted and translated into other messages," and the various stakeholders who participate in producing and receiving these artifacts become "communicators of organized matter that make a difference in their lives" [20, p.175].

These artifacts can thus all be conceived as messages in an extended and distributed design conversation, to the extent that they are all produced by one or more of the stakeholders/conversants, perhaps "sent" to another stakeholder (construction drawings sent to a contractor, a product distributed to a retailer), perhaps projected into the conversation at large (a public space inserted into the urban fabric, open source software released into the public domain) but, in any case subjected to the

---

[3] Buchanan uses the term "argument" in the context of his thesis that design is a liberal art without its own subject matter, but which can serve as a platform for bringing together the different forms of argument that enter into the design discussion.

scrutiny and further action of other stakeholders (ideally also inviting and requiring this scrutiny and further action, so that the conversation may continue), each through the lens of their particular values, roles and expectations.

12.3.3 Design Conversations in Detail

Having argued for the conception of what might be called economies (in the sense of systems of exchange) or ecosystems (in the sense of contexts of interdependent and interacting entities) of design – taking in all of the participants, artifacts and interconnections that designing entails – as a series of interlinked conversations (or indeed one very large, distributed, multi-channel conversation), I will seek to give more detailed articulation to the workings of these design conversations, appealing to an anatomy of conversations proposed by Dubberly and Pangaro [8].

In this model, a participant (1) *Opens a channel* by making a statement that establishes the possibility for conversation, following which the/an other participant (2) *Commits to engage* by paying attention to that message and (3) *Constructs meaning* from that message. Steps 2 and 3 must be reciprocated continually by each participant, in a back-and-forth exchange of statements, in order for the conversation to continue. All participants (4) *Evolve* through this interaction, changing their beliefs, relationships or behavior in a lasting fashion, thereby (5) *Converging on agreement*, as this evolution brings participants towards alignment in their (belief that they are approaching) understanding of the concept around which (each believes) the conversation revolves. Finally, participants may (6) *Act or transact* by taking action as a consequence of the conversation, but in a realm with implications beyond the conversation itself, such as making a purchase decision or agreeing to enter into a relationship.

The above sequence describes a conversation as a primarily verbal exchange, but such exchanges can also involve different forms of "messages." For instance, taking Krippendorff's understanding, the models and sketches generated by designers in the design process are messages in a conversation between designer and client, beginning with designer and client (1) *Opening a channel* with a contract for design services, progressing through stages (2) to (5) and ending by (6) *Acting/transacting* by agreeing on the final form of the thing to be made. This is what Dubberly and Pangaro call "conversation for agreement" [8, p. 3].

This transaction in turn (1) *Opens a(nother) channel* for other conversations within which, likewise, a similar role can be discerned in the plans and prototypes through which the designer communicates the form of the thing to be produced to the manufacturer, contractor or programmer who will fabricate it, leading to the (6) *Action/transaction* of manufacturing or building the designed thing. This is a "conversation to coordinate" in Dubberly and Pangaro's terms, leading to "conversations to collaborate," in which different contributors to the process of manifesting a designed thing work together towards this shared goal [8, pp. 4–5].

It is worth reiterating that the plans and prototypes used in design processes function as multivalent messages, simultaneously or sequentially playing roles in several conversations, such as designers' conversations with clients and users, with regulating authorities, quantity surveyors, engineers, publishers, and so forth. In the conversation, each conversation partner "reads" and (3) *Constructs meaning* from the plans in a different way, depending on their roles, values, expectations and modes of argumentation. These objects are not strictly linguistic statements, but they nonetheless can be invested with meaning and significance, both by those who create them and by those at whom they are directed, allowing them to enter multiple contexts of semiotics, use and encounter, and to be imbued with a different meaning by each conversant who elects to engage in the conversation.

This level of design conversation is exemplified by the clusters of stakeholders in conventional design practice, as detailed above, and also in alternative constellations of collaborators such as the communities within which Manzini [22] discerns the emergence of experiments in alternative ways of making together in groups within larger society ("disruptive normalities") (cf. Foucault's [11] heterotopias). What draws together the participants in the design conversations at this level is a shared concern with "the conception and planning of the artificial," through exchanges in which. . .

> Communication is possible at such meetings because the results of research and discussion, despite wider differences in intellectual and practical perspectives, are always connected by this theme and, therefore are supplemental. This is only possible, of course, if individuals have the wit to discover what is useful in each other's work and can cast the material in terms of their own vision of design thinking [4, p. 12].

The language used in these conversations needs to be careful and open in order to allow diverse stakeholders to project their own expectations, modes of understanding and systems of meaning onto the endeavor [7].

12.4 Designing from Communities to Societies

The design conversations discussed up to this point are all nested neatly within the "design process," conventionally and narrowly defined, within which things are conceived, articulated conceptually and physically through iterative cycles of refinement and precision, and produced as designed "products." It is my ambition, though, to pursue this line of argument further to expand the notion of "design conversations" to encompass less controlled and consensual ways in which designing interfaces with society at large. In doing this, I conceive of the purportedly "final" results of the conversations of design delineated above, the designed and manufactured "products," as initiating statements of another level of conversation – the conversations through which design engages society.

12.4.1 Design Conversations Beyond the Design Process

To demonstrate the parallels between this process and those already discussed, I will return to Dubberly and Pangaro's schema. If we take the designed artifact that is put into the world as (1) *Opening a channel* for conversation, a stakeholder[4] (2) *Commits to engage* by establishing a relationship with the artifact by purchasing the product, using the website, entering the building, reading the poster... The decision to engage a designed artifact may be motivated by any number of factors – expediency, aesthetics, curiosity, need, desire, utility, chance, ethics (as in decisions to purchase "green" or "fair trade" products), social norms, self-image, "lifestyle" aspirations, an intention to critique, subvert, adapt or misuse.

And from this initial engagement, people begin to (3) *Construct meaning*. They find their engagement with the thing to be positive or negative, it conforms to or deviates from the expectations that motivated them to engage it, possibilities for action or understanding emerge or don't, things are learned or they aren't. And based on the experience from this first engagement with the thing, they will decide whether to continue this conversation (and in what way) or whether to abandon it.

If we take the designed thing as an initiating statement in a conversation, and if we see the decision of a person (variously framed as user, consumer, occupant or stakeholder) to engage this thing as a commitment to enter this conversation, this establishes a foundation on which conversation can proceed. However, in most cases this nascent conversation between designers and others in the world at large is immediately truncated, in that there are scant channels through which people's reactions to their first engagement with designed things flow back to the designers of those things, who then reply with new artifacts/statements and so forth.

On the one hand, some design conversations involve a sustained exchange of statements-as-physical-designed-artifacts and consumer feedback, but such conversations are rightly criticized for their "unsustainability." Examples include any designed product that feeds an economy that relies on rampant desire-driven consumption, based on trend, fashion and novelty for its own sake. Conspicuous examples can be found in fashion and personal electronics, in which new things are put out into the world at a predetermined rapid pace, based on equally rapid feedback on consumer preferences, technological possibilities and trend forecasts.

On the other hand, although such designed things can be accommodated within the conversation model (as will be demonstrated in an example below), if we bring the normative ethos of "sustainability"[5] to bear, these examples should be seen as pathological rather than normal or desirable, in that each supply-side "statement" in the conversation is a new commodity that must be purchased, above and beyond being an offering in a process of seeking understanding, requiring profligate investment of material, labor and energy, necessitating the obsolescence of the previous iteration of the product and the premature wastage of the material and energy that went into making it.

[4]A person becomes a "stakeholder" by making this commitment to engage.

[5]Remaining well aware that this concept is potentially problematic in its own right.

12.4.2 Evolving Things

Seen in the broader perspective, the end goal of the narrowly-defined design process is the production of things with the potential to operate as a class of conversants in the world at large – things that are capable of carrying on (quasi-) conversations. Though the telos of these conversations is the (imagined) designed object, the ways in which participants in this example assess the value of that artifact have to do not just with its qualities as an object for its own sake (however those may be construed), but in terms of its anticipated performance in the world. Will it be desirable in the market? Will it fulfill its intended functions? Will it meet with the approval of other designers? Will it encourage users to act and think in a desired way? In one sense, these things become emissaries charged with pursuing the ambitions of the design team out in the world. However, by the same token, these things are not merely instruments for enacting change on the world, but entities that will interact and (4) *Evolve* in unintended and unforeseen ways.

Such evolution may be understood in terms of changing roles and positions of these things within the contexts of meaning and use in which they are embedded such that, understood relationally, they continue to change. Evolution may also sometimes involve physical reconstitution, as exemplified in the continuous renovation, re-use and adaptation of buildings over time. In architecture, this is reflected in Stewart Brand's[6] thesis that certain buildings are more able than others to "learn" from their history of use and habitation, and to be physically adapted to accommodate and facilitate the evolving uses to which they are put, and the evolving socio-cultural and technical milieus within which they are embedded [1].

Designed artifacts must be understood not only as things but as ongoing processes, or more precisely as evolving participants in processes of conversation. This recalls a point that Pask himself made about buildings, but which I would propose can be generalized to include all designed things – that they only attain meaning in their interactions with humans, both influencing human behavior and becoming meaningful through the ways in which they are used by people [26].

A consumer electronics artifact that relies on rolling obsolescence and perennial demand for new versions (an iconic example of the pathological manifestation of the design conversation to which I refer above), should be understood not in terms of the pocket-sized object of desire, but rather in terms of the sum of flows of material, energy and messages through which its subsequent versions are constituted and re-constituted. This artifact is engaged in multiple conversations of different natures in its evolution. There is the conversation that constitutes the brand to which the artifact contributes and on which it draws, seeking and (in the case of a successful brand) receiving affirmation from the "brand loyal" that the new offering maintains the core hallmarks that constitute the brand. Each new proposed iteration of the artifact

[6] A countercultural icon since the 1960s and editor of the Whole Earth Catalog and CoEvolution Quarterly, Brand played a significant role in bringing cybernetics into the counterculture and ecological movements (see [19, p. 198]).

initiates a conversation with the manufacturers who must maintain conditions under which the item can be produced within the required parameters of speed, volume and cost.

The subsequent stage of (5) *Converging on an agreement* could be seen as somewhat problematic, if we understand design conversations as not ending with a "product," but spreading out via these products into society at large. A project culminates in an artifact, but the engagement of the designer, and the design profession, with society is an ongoing process of co-evolution. There is no "stopping rule," to cite another of Rittel and Webber's [29, p. 162] characteristics of wicked problems. Indeed the purpose of this conversation could be seen as its own perpetuation, rather than the attainment of a final state.[7] This conversation requires that intermediate agreements be reached, in order that the conversation may continue and the participants may evolve, but these agreements are not end-states.[8]

Likewise, conversants in these conversations constantly (6) *Act or transact* as a consequence of the conversations. Users adjust their life patterns to accommodate the designed artifacts, factories retool and train their workforce to produce them, brands change their marketing campaigns... These are the first ripples in the wave pattern through which design continuously designs the world.

12.4.3 Design That Designs

This evokes the maxim that "design keeps designing" [12]. That is, designed things, once put out into the world, continue to exert influences on the world, in ways both intended and unintended, foreseen and unforeseen by the designer and others involved in the thing's genesis. Designed things become constitutive elements of a world populated by a far larger and more diverse group of people than the particular clients, users or stakeholders at which they are aimed, and filled with a vast array of other designed and non-designed things.

The design conversation, beyond the cozy confines of a design team, is a more adversarial and competitive process, such that by nature there can be no discussion of "perfection" in its products, subjected as they are to multiple conflicting forces in their genesis and equally various perspectives in their appraisal. The spats and differences of perspective among the professions involved in the design process cited above by Dorst [7] and Buchanan [4] are benign compared to the differences among members of society at large. In the former cases, all participants are united by their focus on achieving the same goal or output, though this artifact may be perceived

---

[7]This perspective is reflected in the model of a "service and flow" economy, the third principle of Natural Capitalism [16, p. 125].

[8]Pask's later Interaction of Actors model [28], which is in part built on Conversation Theory, did away with the assumption that these interactions seek a consensus, after which the participants disengage.

differently from within their respective "object worlds" [3]. These participants have a common project and aim – the production of an artifact – after which the conversation is terminated. The processes that constitute society at large have no shared concrete final object or goal, no "stopping rule."

Rather than claiming that this puts these conversations beyond the reasonable concern of design, this is precisely the level of conversations within which design must demonstrate its relevance and importance to society, at which design has a potential to achieve meaningful change in the world, proceeding beyond the individual "project" to an ongoing engagement with society. This recalls Branzi's [2, p. 55] statement that the mission of design in the contemporary world is to create a "new ecology of the artificial universe," by taking as its subject the totality of the relationship of humanity with the synthetic world that it created.

In this level of conversation, the designed thing is not the end goal and the center of attention of a conversation or set of conversations, but rather one participant among many in a collection of intersecting and colliding conversations.

The understanding of the conversations of design as processes of consensus-seeking within groups with a common goal resonates with the philosophical position of "universal pragmatics" [15], which posits that the *telos* (final goal) of all speech is the attainment of mutual understanding, grounded in a faith in rationality as a shared human capability. The perspective of "agonistic pluralism," on the contrary, posits that the presence of incommensurable positions, and the conflict that arises from them, is not just unavoidable, but even necessary in contemporary democratic societies [24], and there are suggestions that design should intentionally seek to raise contested issues in order to open up the adversarial public discourses that sustain such democracies [6]. This position evokes the incongruent and even conflicting values and intentions of the participants in the design conversations at the societal level, and points to the value of the multivalent nature of designed artifacts as messages in these conversations, allowing conversations to progress and participants to evolve, even as these differences are sustained.

12.5 The Designer's Vantage

Is this perspective empowering or demeaning of the designer's role in society? On the one hand, it becomes clear that the conversations within which the designer is engaged in their professional practice, over which they are accustomed to exerting direct influence, are a very limited subset of the conversations within which design is implicated. On the other hand, the recognition that designed things have a potential to exert influence through many channels and upon many members of a society broadens the perspective on designers' efficacy (and responsibility).

Designers may think of the things they put out into the world as emissaries that will engage people in ongoing relationships. At one level, this can be done in the interest of encouraging emotional attachment to the product and loyalty to the brand. On another level, some designers see designed things as participants inserted into a context to achieve more idealistic goals, such as encouraging a certain way of living or behaving, facilitating actions seen as ethically desirable, or influencing the way people perceive certain issues.

While a designer is but one of many participants in the conversations of design, the role of designers is different from that of many other participants in that part of their role is to think and act on behalf of others [33]. This is implicit in even the most conventional designer-client relationship. Some designers seek to initiate and sustain conversations beyond the conventional ones discussed in this paper, as in "participatory design" approaches, in which designers engage end users and other stakeholders in increasingly substantive ways in the conversations around problem-finding and other foundational phases of the design process.

Designers sometimes use "design probes" [23] in the design process, to evoke responses through which they can better understand the situation for which they are designing. These probes are designed artifacts in their own right, not intended as products for purchase and consumption, but rather to elicit and facilitate responses. Anything that a designer designs may serve as a design probe, if the designer establishes channels for "feedback" on their designed things, on which they can react in decisions that they make in future designs. A number of such feedback loops exist in conventional practice. How well did my design sell? Was it received favorably by other designers? Did it win awards? Designers with ambitions beyond market success and prestige may pursue research into whether a given design is achieving its intended aims in society. However, it is more often than not academics and researchers who take on such critical assessments of the consequences of designed things in the world, raising the issue of the efficacy of the conversations, if any, that take place between such researchers and design professionals, such that these insights might inform future practice.

12.6 Conclusion

My ambitions in this chapter have been threefold. Firstly, I have appealed to cybernetic principles to articulate a progression of different levels of design conversations – those within *teams* of designers under organizational regimes designed to streamline efforts toward a prescribed goal, those within *communities* of heterogeneous participants with common interests working towards a shared goal, and those within *societies* of individuals with non-congruent goals, understandings and values. Secondly, I have sought to demonstrate a way in which such cybernetic principles can contribute to elucidating in more detail the inner workings of the third of these "design ecology" types, that of *societies*, in which there can be no assumption of an overarching control and organization (as in design teams), or a shared purpose among diverse participants (as in design *communities*). Thirdly, I have endeavored to show how such an understanding can provide insights into the role and position of designers in society.

All three levels of conversations are reflected in current trends in design discourse and practice, with "design thinking" [5, 30] for instance being concerned with the thought processes of designers and design *teams*, "participatory design" and "co-design" [9, 31] dealing with methods for designers to involve non-designer members of design *communities* in design processes, and "strategic design" [18] addressing the anticipation and accommodation of contextual forces at the level of *societies* on design processes (and, in some cases, the potential of design to enact change in its societal context as well), beyond the design of products and services to the design of companies and organizations.

The limits of our designing are delineated in large part by the range of others who we are able or willing to engage in design conversations. With increasing calls for design to take on a more explicitly political role in addressing the big issues of society [13, 21], it becomes increasingly imperative that designers hone their skills as gregarious design conversationalists, in engaging a broad spectrum of others in the design conversation, in committing to sustained engagement with open-ended, non-teleological conversations that transcend the individual project in time-frame, scope, scale and ambition (projects should be thought of as being contained within the conversation rather than the conversation being contained within the project), and in conceiving the things they put out into the world not just as the results of design conversations, but as initiators and participants in design conversations of a more extended scope and more profound nature.

References

1. Brand, S. (1994). *How buildings learn: What happens after they're built.* New York, NY: Viking.
2. Branzi, A. (1988). *Learning from Milan: Design and the second modernity.* Cambridge, MA: MIT Press.
3. Bucciarelli, L. L. (1994). *Designing engineers.* Cambridge, MA: MIT Press.
4. Buchanan, R. (1996). Wicked problems in design thinking. In V. Margolin & R. Buchanan (Eds.), *The idea of design* (pp. 3–20). Cambridge, MA: MIT Press.
5. Cross, N. (2011). *Design thinking: Understanding how designers think and work.* Oxford: Berg Publishers.
6. DiSalvo, C. (2012). *Adversarial design.* Cambridge, MA: MIT Press.
7. Dorst, K. (2006). *Understanding design* (revised edition). Amsterdam: BIS Publishers.
8. Dubberly, H., & Pangaro, P. (2009). What is conversation? How can we design for effective conversation? *Interactions, XVI*(4), July + August 2009.
9. Ehn, P., & Kyng, M. (1987). The collective resource approach to systems design. In G. Bjerknes, P. Ehn, & M. Kyng (Eds.), *Computers and democracy. A Scandinavian challenge* (pp. 17–58). Aldershot: Avebury.
10. Floyd, C., Mehl, W-M., Reisin, F-M., Schmidt, G., & Wolf, G. (1989). Out of Scandinavia: Alternative approaches to software design and system development. *Human-Computer Interaction, 4*(4), 253–350.
11. Foucault, M. (1970). *The order of things: An archaeology of the human sciences* (English edition). New York, NY: Pantheon Books.
12. Fry, T. (2009). *Design futuring: Sustainability, ethics and new practice.* Sydney: UNSW Press.
13. Fry, T. (2010). *Design as politics.* London: Bloomsbury Academic.

14. Glanville, R. (2007). Try again. Fail again. Fail better. The cybernetics in design and the design in cybernetics. *Kybernetes, 36*(9/10), 1173–1206.
15. Habermas, J. (1979). *Communication and the evolution of society*. Toronto: Beacon Press.
16. Hawken, P., Hunter Lovins, L., & Lovins, A. (1999). *Natural capitalism: Creating the next industrial revolution*. New York, NY: Little, Brown and Co.
17. Jachna, T. (2012). Reclaiming the cyber(netic) city. *Cybernetics and Human Knowing, 19*(3/4), 67–81.
18. Kelley, T., & Littman, J. (2005). *The ten faces of innovation: IDEO's strategies for beating the devil's advocate and driving creativity throughout your organization*. New York, NY: Currency/Doubleday.
19. Kline, R. R. (2015). *The cybernetics moment: Or why we call our age the information age*. Baltimore, MD: Johns Hopkins University Press.
20. Krippendorff, K. (1996). On the essential contexts of artifacts or on the proposition that "design is making sense (of things)". In V. Margolin & R. Buchanan (Eds.), *The idea of design*. Cambridge, MA: MIT Press.
21. Manzini, E. (2015). *Design, when everyone designs*. Cambridge, MA: MIT Press.
22. Manzini, E. (no date). *Design as everyday life politics*. Available from DESIS: https://www.desisnetwork.org/2016/09/27/design-as-everyday-life-politics. Accessed January 19, 2019.
23. Mattelmäki, T. (2006). *Design Probes*. Helsinki: Aalto ARTS Books.
24. Mouffe, C. (1999). Deliberative democracy or agonistic pluralism? *Social Research, 66*(3), 745–758.
25. Pangaro, P. (2008). Instructions for design and designs for conversation. In R. Luppicini (Ed.), *Handbook of conversation design for instructional applications* (pp. 35–48). Hershey, PA: ICI Global Publishers.
26. Pask, G. (1969). The architectural relevance of cybernetics. *Architectural Design, 7*(6), 494–496.
27. Pask, G. (1975). *Conversation, cognition and learning*. Amsterdam: Elsevier.
28. Pask, G., & de Zeeuw, G. (1992). *Interactions of actors, theory and some applications* (manuscript). Amsterdam: OOC/CICT.
29. Rittel, H. W. J., & Webber, M. M. (1973). Dilemmas in a general theory of planning. *Policy Sciences, 4*(2), 155–169.
30. Rowe, G. P. (1987). *Design thinking*. Cambridge, MA: MIT Press.
31. Sanders, E. B. N., & Jan Stappers, P. (2008). Co-creation and the new landscapes of design. *CoDesign, 4*(1), 5–18.
32. Shannon, C. E. (1948). A mathematical theory of communication. *The Bell System Technical Journal, 27*, 379–423, 623–656.
33. Sweeting, B. (2015). The implicit ethics of designing. In A. Ryan & P. Jones (Eds.), *Relating systems thinking and design (RSD4) 2015 symposium*. Banff, AB, Canada: The Banff Centre.

Timothy Jachna is Dean of the School of Design, Architecture, Art and Planning (DAAP) at the University of Cincinnati. He earned degrees from the University of Illinois at Chicago (BArch), the Architectural Association, London (AADip) and RMIT University, Melbourne (PhD). He has held academic and professional posts in architecture, design and urbanism in Hong Kong, Berlin and Chicago. Jachna is currently vice-president of the American Society for Cybernetics, and his recent research and publications apply principles of second-order cybernetics – including processes of conversation and learning, metabolic metaphors and the dynamics of control and choice – to understand societal processes and practices, in particular as they apply to the constitution and evolution of cities.

Chapter 13
A Poetics of Designing

Claudia Westermann

Abstract The chapter considers second-order cybernetics as a framework that is accurately described as a poetics. An overview is provided on what it means to be in a world that is uncertain, e.g., how under conditions of limited understanding any activity is an activity that designs and constructs, and how designing objects, spaces, and situations relates to the (designed) meta-world of second-order cybernetics. If it cannot be determined whether the world is complex or not, to assume that the world is complex is a matter of choice linked to an attitude of generosity. The chapter highlights that it is this attitude, which makes designing an ethical challenge. Designers require a framework that is open, but one that supplies ethical guidance when 'constructing' something new. Relating second-order design thinking to insights in philosophy and aesthetics, the chapter argues that second-order cybernetics provides a response to this ethical challenge and essentially it entails a poetics of designing.

Keywords Poetics · Second-order cybernetics · Design · Architecture · Aesthetics

13.1 Introduction

> And in these operations the person "I," whether explicit or implicit, splits into a number of different figures: into an "I" who is writing and an "I" who is written, into an empirical "I" who looks over the shoulder of the "I" who is writing and into a mythical "I" who serves as a model for the "I" who is written. The "I" of the author is dissolved in the writing. Italo Calvino, 1967, *Cybernetics and Ghosts* [2]

When Italo Calvino wrote the above in a lecture entitled *Cybernetics and Ghosts* that he held in several Italian cities in 1967 [2, p. 1], he gave expression to a

C. Westermann (✉)
Department of Architecture, Xi'an Jiaotong-Liverpool University, Suzhou, Jiangsu Province, China
e-mail: claudia.westermann@xjtlu.edu.cn

T. Fischer, C. M. Herr (eds.), *Design Cybernetics*, Design Research Foundations,
https://doi.org/10.1007/978-3-030-18557-2_13

discomfort that had been lingering for some time already within a community of researchers from a wide area of disciplines and with a common interest in the relation between technology and living beings. This discomfort was generated by questions about the objectivity and relevance of scientific research that is in general based on observation but excludes the act of observation from reflection (see [13, pp. 176–178]). Calvino's text from 1967 – a reflection on the reflective observer author – is significant. It precedes the official birth of the meta-level enquiry that is today referred to as second-order cybernetics, and whose concern is with the development of a new language appropriate for a dimensional shift in thinking (see [11, p. 1156]). Calvino's writing may be viewed as an account of a cultural disposition that contributed to the development of second-order research and practice. The above quote by Calvino introduces the explorations of the relationship between second-order thinking, design, and poetic forms of discourse and enquiry that are of key interest to this chapter. These are generally understood as in opposition to scientific forms of discourse and enquiry, as they are structurally – in a radical sense of the term – open.

Reviewing design theory literature, a specific interest in the relation of poetry, or the poetic, and design can be detected, particularly in the area of architectural theory. For example, in their writings, Dalibor Vesely and Alberto Pérez-Gómez [35, 41] enquire into situations from a phenomenological point of view. Foundational in this context are the writings of German philosopher Martin Heidegger. His essays *Poetically, Man dwells ...* and *Dwelling Building Thinking* [18, 19] are among the most cited texts in architectural theory. In the same context, the above quoted writer Italo Calvino is drawn upon frequently because one of his best known writings – the publication *Invisible Cities* [1] – explicates a poetic view of architecture and urban design.

The relation of writing, poetry, and design has been theorised but mostly from a point of view that tends to be in discomfort with all things *cyber*. Cybernetics is often erroneously associated with a concept of control that is imposed from elsewhere – a *Matrix* scenario [49] – and that restricts the potential of living beings to choose, to define, and essentially to design. The term cybernetics, however, derives from the Greek steersman/helmsman, and as Heinz von Foerster pointed out: steersmanship is not dictatorship [44, p. 2]. There is generally a lack of awareness that the shift in thinking from first- to second-order cybernetics is not simply a minor adjustment. There is a *cyber* – a reflective *cyber* – that is radically different from the common understanding of the term. Within the framework of the reflective *cyber* the idea of power through imposed technological control generates as much discomfort as within any framework of phenomenological leaning.

One of the most extensive overviews of the development of second-order cybernetics is given in the seminal text *Second Order Cybernetics* by Ranulph Glanville [13]. The same author has provided us with an outline of the relationship of design and second-order cybernetics in his publication *Try again. Fail again. Fail better: the cybernetics in design and the design in cybernetics* [12], which is included in this book. In the following, I will elaborate on key thoughts that may serve as a bridge between a practice of designing and an aesthetics of design, or – to emphasise the activity of designing rather than the outcome – a poetics of designing. The chapter focusses on the philosophical underpinnings of second-order cybernetics, and as such, there is a close link to the philosophical school of thought known as radical constructivism, which was developed primarily by Ernst von Glasersfeld, a close friend of Heinz von Foerster considered one of the principal initiators of second-order cybernetics. While the following explorations evolved from my specific point of view that is informed by an education, research and practice in art and architecture, there is no reason why the outlined thoughts could not also apply in other areas of design, such as graphic design, or industrial design.

13.2 Unknown Worlds

In a lecture entitled *On Constructing a Reality* [43] given in 1973 at the fourth International Conference on Environmental Design Research at the Virginia Polytechnic Institute in Blacksburg, Virginia, Heinz von Foerster stated:

> The environment as we perceive it is our invention. [43]

He was careful to pacify the audience by adding the label "outrageous claim" to the statement, before outlining several scientific studies, which show that there is indeed no support for the assumption that human perception grasps in a stable manner what could be considered the reality of objects and environments. At the time, the claim that our environment is an invention of our perception was outrageous from a scientific point of view. Science creates its results on the basis of its method through the observation of processes and its interpretation, but generally by excluding the act of observing from its analysis. In this way, science achieves clarity in the communication of results, and ensures that the results can be tested again and be confirmed or falsified. Thus, it ensures that the results can serve as a basis for predicting future processes. Science is essentially designed for the purpose of reliable prediction. However, how can we assume something to be reliable that is based on an observation that we just proved to be unreliable? Would we not need to include the act of observing into the analysis? These were some of the core questions that initiated the development of what is known today as second-order cybernetics. Being interested in the communicability of observations and interpretations, second-order cybernetics does not support solipsism, but is an endeavour in creating a structure and a framework – essentially a language – that includes the observer in the analysis of events and processes. Second-order cybernetics retained from first-order cybernetics its systems approach and its focus on circularity that was initiated at the earliest *Macy Conference* of 1942 on *Circular Causal and Feedback Mechanisms in Biological and Social Systems* [12, p. 1180]. The relationship between the first and the second-order approach has been described by Ranulph Glanville as being similar to the relationship between Newton's and Einstein's physics (see [12, p. 1182]). Second-order cybernetics is not a science as commonly defined, but a meta-enquiry that assists us in maintaining a critical view of the processes involved in creating understandings of the world, including scientific truths. Essentially, it provides a framework in which other views of the world remain possible. From a scientific point of view, this is a weakness. I will argue below, that from a design point of view, it is a strength.

If we take designing seriously, we do not need to be concerned with questions that relate to whether or not scientific truths can be confirmed as true in an external reality. The outcomes that the activity of design produces are not a basis for prediction but a basis for imagination. Design is not required to produce truth in a scientific sense. On the contrary, the outcome of a design activity constitutes an opportunity to actualise a multiplicity of truths. In line with the above mentioned arguments, the activity of designing is not primarily an activity of problem solving.

I would like to return to Heinz von Foerster's lecture *On Constructing a Reality* [43]. Let us assume that Heinz von Foerster had not given this lecture to scientists, but to philosophers. Had he mentioned in the context of a conference attended primarily by philosophers, rather than scientists, that our perception constructs our environment, he would not have needed to claim outrageousness to prevent an outcry. There is nothing outrageous about this claim from the point of view of someone familiar with the history of philosophical thought. The issue was raised already more than 2000 years ago in one of the most famous passages of Plato's writings known today as the *Allegory of the Cave* [38, 514a–520a]. The question of how we interpret reality is one of the oldest philosophical questions, and the insight that there is an intrinsic paradox to the notion that we live in a world that we might not be able to grasp is one of the oldest philosophical insights. Throughout the centuries, philosophy addressed this problem from different points of views. In second-order cybernetics, the solipsist view is rejected on the basis that other thinking entities external to the 'I' cannot be explained from a solipsist viewpoint [15, p. 83]; [43, p. 227]. Heinz von Foerster was well aware of philosophical questions. *On Constructing a Reality* could be seen to re-narrate the *Allegory of the Cave* albeit through the presentation of the results of scientific experiments. In this light, the text constitutes an anecdote for philosophers; but as an anecdote, most likely, it would have been told differently.

On Constructing a Reality performs in a manner that bears some similarities to another proof of the incompleteness of science. The proof was published in a paper with the title *On Formally Undecidable Propositions of the Principia Mathematica and Related Systems* and later became known as Kurt Gödel's *Incompleteness Theorem* [14]. The *Principia Mathematica*, developed between 1910 and 1913 by Bertrand Russell and Alfred North Whitehead [52], and mentioned in the title of Gödel's paper, had formalised all methods of proof that were used in Mathematics until then [14, p. 38]. Contrary to the thesis of his time, Gödel was able to prove that such a formal system with its defined axioms is unable to decide every question arising within it, that every consistent system must always be incomplete. A consistent system contains statements than cannot be proven by using the axioms of the system itself. Gödel's paper had a significant impact, as it proposed that its results are not only valid for mathematics but for every science operating with consistent logic. In essence, Gödel's proof of incompleteness, i.e. of undecidability, can be considered a variation of the liar paradox that is formulated in sentences such as: "I am lying" (see

[20, p. 25]). The question whether the statement is true is undecidable. It is impossible to prove the statement as either true or false. If the statement is considered true and I am lying, then the statement that I am lying must be a lie, and thus the statement cannot be true. However, if the statement is considered false, then I would need to be considered as not lying while I am lying, and again a paradox remains.

In the context of Gödel's *Theorem*, a proof is a demonstration within a system of propositions that is finite and thus fixed [14, p. 38]; [20, pp. 26–32]. Gödel demonstrated via mathematical proof that a consistent system, such as defined by the *Principia Mathematica*, contains propositions, which are not provable from within the system. They are provable only from outside, from a meta-systemic point of view. Yet, proving statements from a meta-systemic point of view is only possible if the system is broadened to a meta-system, and one is again confronted with a system in which propositions exist that are not provable from within. Gödel's *Theorem* implies that every consistent formal system must be incomplete.

Second-order cybernetics can be seen as an attempt to respond to the problematics of incompleteness. The inclusion of the reflective observer into the second-order system essentially transcends classical logic, i.e. the binary logic that Western reasoning is generally based on, at least since Aristotle [15]. While this had been recognised by von Foerster, key steps towards the development of a trans-classical logic were made when Gotthard Günther, a philosopher with an expertise on German Idealism, became a member of von Foerster's Biological Computer Laboratory (BCL) in Illinois in 1960 [45]. There is some evidence Gödel's thought has influenced the development of second-order cybernetics – albeit via Günther, who had been in correspondence with Gödel between 1953 and 1959 [16]. Günther's contributions in trans-classical logic to the research conducted at the BCL are important for the development of second-order thinking. He assisted in eliminating the gap that is logically created by the incompleteness of any first-order approach [45].

While this chapter does not detail the history and development of trans-classical logic and philosophy, a short account of Günther's insights is given to assist better understanding. It is generally recognised that the seventeenth century French philosopher René Descartes marks a culmination in the development of Western philosophy, which is essentially a dualist philosophy. In the Cartesian "I think, therefore I am" [5, p. 5] being is confirmed in the activity of reflecting. Body and mind become separated. Up to Descartes, the basic philosophical model conceives objects and subjects within the world in communication with each other through the intermediary of an absolute objective being – typically called God. Descartes' reflective I achieves independence from the absolute objective being, but at the same time the reflective I pulls itself out of the world. One could say that there is no need for communication when being is dependent on thinking alone. According to Günther, the philosophers of German Idealism had discovered a logic gap when they realised that the reflective I in this construction essentially dissolves itself in infinite reflection. To counter the dissolution of the subject, they maintained – as Descartes before – an objective being as a mediator between the subject and the world [15, pp. 74–83]. Günther made an important step in the development towards a trans-classical logic when he recognised that only in the thinking I-subject, thinking can be conceived as reflection. Other subjects – You-subjects – appear from the position of the thinking I also as pulling themselves out of the world, however, what is at the basis of this process in the You-subject appears not as reflection but as will (see [50]).

> The You is an "object of second order" that is capable to offset itself both from me (the I) and from the world – the objects of first order. It is thus "a Third, *free from both*". [15, p. 83]

The You-subjects – we could also call them Others – cannot be conceived in binary, first-order logic as having agency. If they are conceived as having agency, they must be conceived as a Third in a second-order logic. The response of second-order cybernetics to the insight that first-order approaches essentially leave us alone with our selves – as other beings cannot be thought of as having agency – is the construction of a structure that allows for the possibility of agency of others while at the same time acknowledging that this agency can never be defined (see [51]). Gordon Pask's development of Conversation Theory is such a response and it is crucial in this respect [9, 32]. Through conversation that involves circularity, feedback and recursive action, each participant creates understandings. Whether the other understands what I understand can never be proven, but if living rather than life is the focus of our attention – if thus, the *how* is considered more important than the *what*, then this proof is of no importance. It would, anyway, make limited sense. There is no meaning in proof. Second-order thinking is the response to a situation that acknowledges logical undecidability of what the world is we live in. To assume the possibility of a world that is different from our understanding, and to assume with it the possibility of agency of other living beings, remains a matter of choice (see [10]). Making this choice could be seen as an act of generosity, and as such, second-order cybernetics combines both an epistemology and an ethics. With the unknown at its basis it grants agency to others.

13.3 On Delight

The nexus of second-order cybernetics is generally considered to be in the United States where the *Macy Conferences* took place beginning in the early 1940s, and where von Foerster directed the Biological Computer Laboratory (BCL) at the University of Illinois from 1958 to 1975. However, in Britain cybernetics was also developed and engaged in from early on. The so-called *Ratio Club* organised meetings in cybernetics from 1949 to 1958. Membership was limited to those who "had Wiener's ideas before Wiener's book appeared" [21, p. 101]. Ross Ashby was part of the *Ratio Club*, as was Alan Turing and other notable figures. While participants on both sides of the ocean exchanged ideas and influenced each other, it must be noted that there is something distinct about "what can be loosely called the British cybernetics movement" [21, p. 91]. This distinctness is owed to a great extent to Gordon Pask who actively fostered the links between cybernetics and art as well as design. Pask's career in cybernetics started in the early 1950s when he was still an undergraduate student at the University of Cambridge. He was a pioneer in interaction and built interactive machines since the early 1950s [9, p. 656]. The best known of these is *The Colloquy of Mobiles*. It was exhibited in the influential *Cybernetic Serendipity – the computer and the arts* [39] exhibition of 1968, generally considered as the first media art exhibition. Gordon Pask notably was directing the cybernetic committee for Joan Littlewood's and Cedric Price's *Fun Palace* [24, 25]. Although never built, within the field of architecture, the *Fun Palace* project is generally still considered the model for thinking responsive architecture. Pask taught at the *Architectural Association* [9]. He contributed to Roy Ascott's *Groundcourse* at the Ealing and Ipswich art schools [36]. He was well received in educational programmes, but notably, also in those of art and design that would be considered avantgarde today. He also wrote plays and invented new types of theatres [27, 28]. He was well ahead of his time, theorised and practiced art, design and science, and influenced many [17, 29]. He has left an indelible mark on Britain's experimental art and design scene (see [7, 8]).

As mentioned above, *Conversation Theory* [32], conceived by Pask and later developed into a theory of *Interactions of Actors* [33, 34], can be seen as bridging the gap between a thinking 'I' and an Other whose agency can only be assumed but never known in a scientific sense, as the agency of the Other is outside the realm of classical logic (see also [23]). The bridge that Conversation Theory provides is a response to the problem that emerges once one recognises that subjective experience is the basis for a judgement. If scientific reasoning is rejected for processes of living on the basis of the arguments outlined above, and thus the act of observing is included into the analysis with the observer central to enquiry, at the basis of enquiry there is subjective experience and we face the problem that communicability is basically undecidable. In summary, in second-order cybernetics we face a problematics on a general level that had been recognised in the philosophy of art centuries earlier. One could indeed conclude that the questions that we encounter when including acts of observation into the analysis of processes are basic questions of aesthetics, and they have explicitly been recognised at least since the *Critique of Judgment* of Immanuel Kant published in 1790 [22]. Kant's critique of aesthetic judgement has influenced aesthetic thought since its publication. It is notable that even Martin Heidegger – although in general dismissive of Kant's philosophy – was judging Kant's aesthetics favourably [40].

It might be helpful to look at some of the notions and terms that are used in second-order cybernetics, and specifically by Pask, and in Kant's aesthetics. The term *purposive*, for example, ranks prominently in Kant's aesthetics and so it does in cybernetics. The concept of purposiveness is so important to cybernetics that the First Annual Symposium of the American Society for Cybernetics, published in 1968, was entirely dedicated to *Purposive Systems* [42]. Purposive systems are considered to be adaptive and self-organising. All living 'things' are considered to be purposive, including human beings. Maturana and Varela introduced the term *autopoiesis* to specify in detail how living beings self-organise through purposive behaviour [26]. *Autopoiesis* is the organisation of living things.

I restrict the following passages to an outline of how human beings fit this notion. According to Pask, human beings are entities that are curious and want to learn.

They seek novelty and pleasure or delight [30]. Within this context, a learning process is a self-replicating or self-stabilising process [32, p. 151]. One could state that human beings constantly renew themselves by looking out for that which they do not know – the uncertain – initiating then a learning process that enables them to address the situation in a purposive manner. Pask speaks of *control* in this context, but the meaning of control in second-order cybernetics is enabling – not restricting. Control relates to the initiation of a self-renewal process as we attempt to address a situation for which we had no means prior to encountering the situation. It is a process through which we learn to address new situations. If we recognise the importance in the seeking of delight or pleasure in that which is new, then of specific interest to us are environments and situations that are, as Pask puts it, *aesthetically potent* [30]. We find in Kant's aesthetics very similar notions. Already with Kant, aesthetic art is related to pleasure. Interestingly, Kant differentiates between two forms of pleasure of which each belongs to one form of aesthetic art – agreeable and fine art. What Kant considers to be agreeable art can be understood to be what we would call today entertainment. The form of pleasure that Kant relates to agreeable art immediately speaks to our senses, but the pleasure that relates to fine art reaches us through "modes of cognition" [22, p. 305]. The work of art animates the mind, and it is *purposive*. Purposive, according to Kant is what suggests order without defining it. In what is purposive we recognise the possibility of order. All fine art, according to Kant, is purposive in this sense. Kant writes:

> Fine art, on the other hand, is a mode of representation which is intrinsically purposive, and which, although devoid of an end, has the effect of advancing the culture of the mental powers in the interests of social communication. [22, p. 306]

> For the ground of this pleasure is found in the universal, though subjective, condition of reflective judgements, namely the purposive harmony of an object (whether it be a product of nature or of art) with the mutual relation of the faculties of cognition (imagination and understanding) which are requisite for every empirical cognition. [22, p. 191]

What Kant calls purposive can be translated into Pask's *aesthetically potent*. In both cases the order of what we encounter is uncertain, and what "advances the culture of the mental powers" can be understood as the learning process that Pask refers to. That such a learning process serves our ability to interact with and in society is recognised by both. Both cybernetics and Kant make a distinction between purpose and purposive by referring with purposive to an order that is not definable but is possible.

There are nevertheless core differences between the reasoning in second-order cybernetics and in Kant's aesthetics. The most significant difference is that Kant relates the work of art to the living by introducing an external mediator – a kind of metaphysical stabiliser – that assists Kant in solving the problem of the communicability of understandings, and in bridging the gap that remains of what is essentially a system of first-order with a subjective observer – central to all aesthetic judgements – at the centre. Kant introduces the artist genius through whom "nature gives the rule to art." When encountering a work of art, according to Kant, while we recognise that it is art and not nature, the work appears to us as if it was nature [22, p. 308]. The work suggests an order – it is an order of the living that cybernetics deems possible, but in contrast, Kant introduces what one could possibly call restricted decidability. The genius – and only the genius – in one way or another has access to knowledge that is beyond life. What the artist genius transmits – rather unconsciously – is the universal order. It cannot be anything else. The artist genius in Kant plays a role that is very similar to Plato's muse-inspired artist (see [37]). In both cases, the artists are mediators who assist the structuring of the creation according to the heavenly or natural orders. This way, works of art are structurally linked to the heavenly or natural orders and their messages can be conceived as universally communicable. Second-order cybernetics in contrast suggests that whether there is universal order is not decidable, nor can we assume that it is accessible. By focussing on the process of how concepts are shared, Conversation Theory circumvents the problematics of the necessity of both the assumption of a universal order and a mediator. It also circumvents the problem of a detachment of art or design from lived experience. Considering the history of the philosophy of art, second-order cybernetics can be seen as following in the footsteps of John Dewey who, in his *Art as Experience*, offers concepts for a theory of art that is grounded in nothing else but experience [6].

> Because experience is the fulfilment of an organism in its struggles and achievements in a world of things, it is art in germ. Even in its rudimentary forms, it contains the promise of that delightful perception which is aesthetic experience. [6, p. 19]

For Dewey all daily life experiences carry the germ of an aesthetic experience. It is in the rhythm of life in which he recognises the basic qualities that make an experience aesthetic. An aesthetic experience has a "developing movement towards its own closure" [6, p. 41]. This closure is a consummation, as Dewey outlines, not a cessation, or a stasis [6, pp. 35, 41]. Gordon Pask recognises in conversation the very basic human activity that holds the germ for the experiences that we seek, and develops from this what one could call a theory of living. Conversations consist also of movements towards closure, sometimes only temporarily to be re-initiated at another point in time. Closure is achieved through agreement or disagreement. In both cases unity is created as the identity of the participants is generally maintained. Conversations are purposive in the Kantian sense by carrying the *germ* of *an* aesthetic experience, or – as Pask would say – they are *aesthetically potent* [30]. Within the trans-disciplinary space of second-order cybernetics questions of designing are not exclusively related to the disciplines that range from architectural to information design. They are at the core of every activity (see [9]). Yet, art and design provide the novelty and delight we seek for as they constitute for us initiations to continuously recreate ourselves, not the least in order to maintain the connections to our social and physical environments. Because experiences that are aesthetic through providing novelty and delight are at the basis of conversation, second-order cybernetics is an appropriate theory also for processes that relate to the activities that create objects, environments, and situations aiming to provide aesthetic experiences.

13.4 For Tomorrow

As Pask outlined, and Glanville elaborated on, conversation is a non-deterministic interaction [9, 31] whose intrinsic characteristic is learning. The process of designing, in a very similar manner, if related to the act of conversing, is a process that is recursive, involves feedback and constant adjustment, while at the same time maintaining openness. A principle of radical openness is at the basis of second-order cybernetics and has been referred to as *cybernetic principle* by von Glasersfeld. Indeed, the cybernetic framework reminds us that "having no fixed goal but being open to all the possibilities that come along" [48] is a strength [46, 47]. The principle of radical openness is found on various levels of hierarchy not only in the attitude of the cybernetic practitioner towards Others – as outlined above – but also in the very processes that we engage in. Second-order cybernetics locates design within an eco-system as part of our environment. Its focus of attention is always on the verbs not on the nouns – thus on designing rather than on design. This is in contrast to what is described in architectural theory treatises belonging – according to Pask – to the realm of *pure architecture* [29] – the latter constitutes a form of detachment. A similar critique can be found in Dewey's *Art as Experience* who initiates his aesthetics with a critique of the common understanding of works of art as belonging in museums and galleries and being detached from lived experience [6, p. 6]. The detachment is also created by the common forms of discourse. Second-order cybernetics provides an alternative to these forms of discourse and a framework that assist us in avoiding such detachment when engaging in activities of creating.

Based on Pask's *Conversation Theory*, Glanville conceives the process of architectural design as a conversation that the designer holds with him/herself or with others (see [12, pp. 1178–1179]). Exploration and play rank highly in such theorisation, and while the process is potentially infinite, we will at some point decide that what we have reached is either "good enough" or we will stop and start again [12, p. 1178]. This is similar to reaching an agreement or disagreement, even an agreement to disagree, in conversation. With John Dewey, we could say that what is considered "good enough" is a state that reaches a form of closure, of unity and of fulfilment [6]. Whatever is reached, however, always remains one possibility among many others. This is a strength also because the activity of designing is always oriented towards a future that we cannot yet know. Even if we assumed that the world can be defined, in designing we always face a future. In being oriented towards the future, activities of designing always face an unknown. We do not want to restrict the future, we only want to enrich the future. It is up to future inhabitants and participants to decide whether what we create is an enrichment that is *aesthetically potent*.

> La poésie ne s'impose plus, elle s'expose.
> Poetry does not impose, it exposes itself. [3, p. 181][1]

[1]The French 'plus' suggests that the correct translation of the line should be: "Poetry does not impose anymore, it exposes itself." The common translation however is the one given. It can be added that the 'not anymore' is most likely a response to Adorno's famous postulate that there can be no poetry anymore after Auschwitz.

Exposing itself could be understood as a weakness, but it is the strength of the poetic voice – of the reflected I – and the foundation of any endeavour that is open to the future because it acknowledges the agency of Others. With a radical openness at its basis, second-order cybernetics combines both an epistemology and an ethics. It provides a structure and a framework that is essentially a poetics of designing. Possibly, we can imagine the delight we would encounter if the "tomorrow" that Constant Nieuwenhuys described in 1956, became today.

It is in poetry that life will reside. [4]

References

1. Calvino, I. (1974). *Invisible cities.* New York: Harvest/HBJ Book. First published in Italian in 1972 as *Le Città Invisibili.*
2. Calvino, I. (1986). Cybernetics and ghosts. In I. Calvino (Eds.), *The uses of literature* (pp. 3–27). San Diego/New York/London: Harcourt Brace & Company. Lecture held in Italy in 1967.
3. Celan, P. (1983). *Gesammelte Werke in Fünf Bänden* (Vol. 3). Frankfurt a. M.: Suhrkamp Verlag.
4. Constant, N. (1983). Tomorrow life will reside in poetry. In M. Wigley (Ed.), *Constant's New Babylon: The hyper-architecture of desire* (p. 78). Rotterdam: 010 Publishers. First published in 1956.
5. Descartes, R. (1983). *Principles of philosophy* (V. Rodger Miller & R. P. Miller, Trans.). Dordrecht: Reidel. First published in 1644 in Latin. French expanded edition published in 1647.
6. Dewey, J. (2005). *Art as experience.* New York: Perigee Books. First published in 1934.
7. Dubberly, H., & Pangaro, P. (2015). How cybernetics connects computing, counterculture, and design. In *Hippie modernism: The struggle for utopia – exhibit catalog* (pp. 1–12). Minneapolis, MN: Walker Art Center.
8. Fernández, M. (2008). Gordon Pask: Cybernetic polymath. *Leonardo, 41*(2), 162–168.
9. Glanville, R. (2001). And he was magic. *Kybernetes, 30*(5/6), 652–673.
10. Glanville, R. (2007). Designing complexity. *Performance Improvement Quarterly, 20*(2), 75–96.
11. Glanville, R. (2007). Introduction: Special double issue on cybernetics and design. *Kybernetes, 36*(9/10), 1153–1157.
12. Glanville, R. (2007). Try again. Fail again. Fail better: The cybernetics in design and the design in cybernetics. *Kybernetes, 36*(9/10), 1173–1206.
13. Glanville, R. (2012). Second order cybernetics. *The black boox – Vol. I. Cybernetic circles* (pp. 175–207). Vienna: edition echoraum. Previously published in: Parra-Luna, F. *Encyclopedia of life support systems, systems science and cybernetics – Vol. III.* Oxford: EoLSS Publishers. Available at: http://www.eolss.net/sample-chapters/c02/e6-46-03-03.pdf. Accessed January 19, 2019.
14. Gödel, K. (1992). *On formally undecidable propositions of the principia mathematica and related systems* (Dover books on advanced mathematics). New York: Dover Publications. First published in 1931 in German in *Monatshefte für Mathematik und Physik.*
15. Günther, G. (1991). *Idee und Grundriss einer nicht-Aristotelischen Logik* (3rd ed.). Hamburg: Felix Meiner Verlag. First edition published in 1957.
16. Günther, G., & Gödel, K. (2003). Gotthard Günther – Kurt Gödel: Correspondence. In *Kurt Gödel: Collected works, volume IV: Correspondence A–G* (pp. 456–535). Oxford: Oxford University Press.
17. Haque, U. (2007). The architectural relevance of Gordon Pask. *Architectural Design, 77*(4), 54–61.

18. Heidegger, M. (1977). Dwelling building thinking. In *Basic writings from Being and time (1927) to the task of thinking (1964)*, works (pp. 323–339). New York: Harper & Row. Essay first published in German in 1951.
19. Heidegger, M. (2003). Poetically, man dwells. In M. Stassen (Ed.), *Martin Heidegger: Philosophical and political writings* (pp. 265–278). New York/London: Continuum. Essay first published in German in 1951.
20. Hofstadter, D. R. (1999). *Gödel, Escher, Bach – An eternal golden braid* (20th anniversary ed.). New York: Basic Books. First published in 1979.
21. Husbands, P., Holland, O., & Wheeler, M. (2008). The ratio club: A hub of British cybernetics. In P. Husbands (Ed.), *The mechanical mind in history* (pp. 91–48). Cambridge, MA: MIT Press.
22. Kant, I. (2007). *Critique of judgement* (Oxford world's classics, N. Walker, Trans.). Oxford: Oxford University Press. First published in German in 1790. Page numbers refer to the pagination of the original Akademie edition included in the margin of this translation.
23. Krippendorff, K. (1996). A second-order cybernetics of otherness. *Systems Research, 13*(3), 311–328.
24. Littlewood, J. (2001). Gordon Pask. *Kybernetes, 30*(5/6), 760.
25. Mathews, S. (2006). The fun palace as virtual architecture – Cedric Price and the practices of indeterminacy. *Journal of Architectural Education, 59*(3), 39–48.
26. Maturana, H. R., & Varela, F. J. (1980). *Autopoiesis and cognition: The realization of the living* (Boston studies in the philosophy of science, Vol. 42). Dordrecht: Reidel.
27. Pangaro, P. (1993). Pask as dramaturg. *Systems Research, 10*(3), 135–142.
28. Pask, G. (1964). *Proposals for a cybernetic theatre. Privately circulated monograph.* System Research Ltd and Theatre Workshop. Available via Paul Pangaro's website. http://www.pangaro.com/pask/ProposalCyberneticTheatrePask1964r.pdf. Accessed January 19, 2019.
29. Pask, G. (1969). The architectural relevance of cybernetics. *Architectural Design, 7*(6), 494–496
30. Pask, G. (1970). A comment, a case history, and a plan. In J. Reichardt (Ed.), *Cybernetics, art and ideas* (pp. 76–99). London: Studio Vista.
31. Pask, G. (1975). *Conversation, cognition and learning: A cybernetic theory and methodology*. Amsterdam/Oxford/New York: Elsevier.
32. Pask, G. (1976). *Conversation theory: Application in education and epistemology*. Amsterdam/Oxford/New York: Elsevier.
33. Pask, G. (1992). *Interactions of actors (IA): Theory and some applications, volume 1. Outline and overview*. The Cybernetics Society. Unfinished manuscript. http://www.cybsoc.org/PasksIAT.PDF. Accessed January 19, 2019.
34. Pask, G. (1996). Heinz von Foerster's self organization, the progenitor of conversation and interaction theories. *Systems Research, 13*(3), 349–362.
35. Pérez-Gómez, A. (1983). *Architecture and the crisis of modern science* (Revised English edition). Cambridge, MA: MIT Press. First published in Spanish in 1980.
36. Pethick, E. (2006). Degree zero. *Frieze Magazine, 101*. Available at: https://frieze.com/article/degree-zero. Accessed January 19, 2019.
37. Plato. (1997). Ion. In *Plato: Complete works* (pp. 937–949). Indianapolis/Cambridge: Hackett Publishing Group.
38. Plato. (1997). Republic. In *Plato: Complete works* (pp. 971–1223). Indianapolis/Cambridge: Hackett Publishing Group.
39. Reichardt, J. (Ed.). (1968). *Cybernetic serendipity: The computer and the arts*. London/New York: Studio International.

40. Torsen, I. (2016). Disinterest and truth: On Heidegger's interpretation of Kant's aesthetics. *British Journal of Aesthetics, 56*(1), 15–32.
41. Vesely, D. (2004). *Architecture in the age of divided representation: The question of creativity in the shadow of production*. Cambridge, MA: MIT Press.
42. von Foerster, H., White, J. D., Peterson, L. J., & Russell, J. K. (Eds.). (1968). *Purposive Systems. Proceedings of the First Annual Symposium of the American Society for Cybernetics*. New York/Washington: Spartan Books.
43. von Foerster, H. (2003). On constructing a reality. In *Understanding understanding* (pp. 211–227). Springer. Reprint of the abbreviated publication of the lecture held in 1973, first published in Preiser, W. F. E. (Ed.). (1973). *Environmental design research* 2.
44. von Foerster, H. et al. (1974). *Cybernetics of cybernetics, or the control of control and the communication of communication*. Urbana, IL: The Biological Computer Laboratory, University of Illinois.
45. von Foerster, H., Lorenz, K., & Grube, G. (1997). *Interview mit Heinz von Foerster*. 1–22. Available at: http://www.vordenker.de/hvf/kl_gg_hvf_interview.pdf. Accessed January 19, 2019.
46. von Glasersfeld, E. (1999). The incommensurability of scientific and poetic knowledge. *World Futures, 53*(1), 19–25. https://doi.org/10.1080/02604027.1998.9972719. Expanded translation of a talk given at the International Congress on Science, Mysticism, Poetry, and Consciousness, Instituto Piaget, Lisbon, April 1994.
47. von Glasersfeld, E. (2007). Aspects of constructivism. Vico, Berkeley, Piaget. In E. von Glasersfeld & M. Larochelle (Eds.), *Key works in radical constructivism* (pp. 91–99). Rotterdam: Sense.
48. von Glasersfeld, E. (2010). *Speech of Ernst von Glasersfeld at the C:ADM 2010 – International Conference in Troy, NY, USA*, July 30 – August 02, 2010. Video recording of the talk published online. Available via the ASC website: http://www.asc-cybernetics.org/2010. Accessed January 19, 2019.
49. Wachowski, L., & Wachowski, L. (1999). *The matrix* (Film, 136 minutes). Warner Bros.
50. Westermann, C. (2011). Resonances of the unknown. *Kybernetes, 40*(7/8), 1189–1195.
51. Westermann, C. (2018). On delight: Thoughts for tomorrow. *Technoetic Arts: A Journal of Speculative Research, 16*(1), 43–51.
52. Whitehead, A. N., & Russell, B. (1925–1927). *Principia Mathematica* (2nd ed., Vol. 1, 2, 3). Cambridge: Cambridge University Press.
53. Wiener, N. (1961). *Cybernetics – or, control and communication in the animal and the machine* (2nd ed.). New York: MIT Press. First edition published by John Wiley: New York in 1948.

Claudia Westermann is an artist and architect, licensed with the German Chamber of Architects, and a Senior Associate Professor in Architecture at Xi'an Jiaotong-Liverpool University in Suzhou, China, where she heads the Urban Ecologies research group. With a basis and postgraduate degrees in both Architecture and Media Art, and a PhD exploring the relationship of Art, Science and Technology, her research and related art/design portfolio actualise at the intersection of art/architecture, technology research and epistemology. Her work has been exhibited and presented internationally at conferences and at more than 30 international exhibitions.

Chapter 14
A Theory of (and for) Enquiry

Thomas Fischer

Abstract At the heart of much academic design research lies a paradox: An appreciation of designing requires, systemically speaking, an *inside* perspective, while scientific research requires robustness under scrutiny by *outside* criteria. This chapter develops a *theory of (and for) enquiry* from previously unrelated cybernetic models, showing how "comfortable marriages" of design and research may be achieved by concatenating and nesting multiple kinds of enquiry within the same body of work. The purpose of this theory is to describe such concatenations and nestings and to inform postgraduate and PhD-level design research and supervision, especially where they face scrutiny by scientific standards.

Keywords Epistemology · Cybernetics · Design PhD research · Science · Design

14.1 Introduction

Conducting a design PhD can be more challenging than undertaking a PhD in another discipline. This is due to multiple, in part cultural reasons. One reason is that discourse and assessment in architecture and design tend to rely more heavily on critique than in other fields. To that extent, evaluations of design PhDs can be more adversarial, lack generosity and predictability, and may be more susceptible to factionalism than those in other fields. Another reason is the imperative for originality found in architecture and design schools. Similar to studio design being expected not only to arrive at new outcomes but to arrive at them in new (yet justifiable) ways, so is design PhD research often expected to not only make "original contributions to knowledge" but to make them via original (yet robust) methodological approaches.

T. Fischer (✉)
Department of Architecture, Xi'an Jiaotong-Liverpool University, Suzhou, Jiangsu Province, China
e-mail: thomas.fischer@xjtlu.edu.cn

T. Fischer, C. M. Herr (eds.), *Design Cybernetics*, Design Research Foundations,
https://doi.org/10.1007/978-3-030-18557-2_14

Yet another challenge of the design PhD, the one addressed in this chapter, is the discrepancy between forms of rigour[1] applied in designing on the one hand, and the academic forms of rigour that are applied in PhD exams on the other hand. Design PhD candidates and their (often professionally rather than academically trained) supervisors hence find themselves in a double bind [2, p. 271]. They are bound on the one hand to do justice to the practice of design, while on the other hand also being bound to anticipate and to prepare for academic scrutiny. As academic scrutiny applies beyond PhD exams throughout academic careers – for example in competition for research funds awarded by reviewers from other disciplines – it is prudent for design PhD education to encompass "academic training".

Following previous discussions of the discrepancy between designerly and scientific approaches and standards [31, 33], this chapter develops strategies, if not to reconcile, then at least to relate and connect these two perspectives, to hopefully widen the scopes of action of postgraduate and PhD-level design researchers and their supervisors. As the disconnect between designerly enquiry and scientific scrutiny varies between contexts, the need for this is not equal in all places. The following discussion should primarily be of interest where design PhD programmes and examination panels are unlikely to accept designerly enquiry as an adequately rigorous basis for PhD-level research. In such contexts, it is desirable for our discipline as a whole to have more PhD students engage their examiners on designerly terms. For individual PhD researchers, however, the associated risk may not be desirable. The following is offered as a clarification of what academic reviewers are likely to look for, and of how it may be delivered. It is a guide for deciding whether or not to accept the risk and not a recommendation to assume overly defensive postures.

14.2 Sometimes Uncomfortable Marriages

It has been noted that design and research enter "sometimes uncomfortable marriages" [27] and the question was raised whether the term *design research* itself is an oxymoron [33]. The relationship between design and (scientific) research [23, pp. 89–91], [29, 49] has been the subject of much discussion since the middle of the twentieth century [7, p. 1]. During this time, this relationship has been portrayed in various ways. Simon [47, p. 132] called upon design to become a proper scientific discipline among others. Positioning design as a subset of a greater scientific enterprise, this conventional view reflects the accommodation of design departments among other departments within academic institutions. Archer [1] and Cross [6, p. 221] describe design and science as co-existing separately, while Jones [31, p. 10] describes design as a hybrid of science, mathematics and the arts. Farrell and Hooker [9] argue that science and design are "not different in kind" – a view

[1]Rigour, in this context, is the resolve to enquire as thoroughly and as honestly as possible within the available resources.

subsequently disputed by Galle and Kroes [20]. Design cybernetician Glanville inverts Simon's view and argues that "scientific research is a subset of design, not the other way round" [23, p. 89], [24, p. 1179].[2]

In this design-cybernetic view, scientific research is a particularly constrained form of the more general human activity of designing. The ingredients, means and goals of scientific enquiry including hypotheses, measurement systems and experimental designs are taken to originate not within the scope of scientific reasoning but in the broader creative domain. When Rittel and Webber [43] proposed their distinction between "wicked" (i.e. design) problems and "tame" problems, they implied a side-by-side relationship of two mutually-exclusive categories. In accordance with Glanville's inversion of the relationship between scientific research and design, however, Ison et al. [28, p. 113] describe "tame problems" as a subset of "wicked problems". Tame problems are tamed wicked problems. Scientific challenges, analogously, are tamed design challenges.

Glanville's inversion resolves and clarifies several contradictions by which design is (ostensibly) disqualified from scientific enquiry, including: objective measurement vs. subjective appreciation, observable evidence vs. subjective sense/inspiration, truth and correctness vs. appropriateness and viability, generalisability vs. attention to particulars [4, p. 15], reliable prediction vs. open-ended exploration, repeatability vs. spontaneity, because-of (efficient causality) vs. in-order-to (final causality) [14, p. 56], conclusive description vs. on-going search [14, p. 56], [39, pp. 17–33], and explicit description vs. tacit knowing [41], [45, p. 21]. (See [32], [33, pp. 1381–1382].)

Clarification of these contradictions notwithstanding, the challenge of defending designerly enquiry at the postgraduate and doctoral level persists where examiners continue to adhere to tenets of (natural) science such as objective measurement and description, rational inference, repeatability, and generalisability. The *theory of (and for) enquiry* presented in the following addresses this challenge – not by advocating inscrutable emulsions between the immiscible substances designerly and scientific enquiry, but by advocating enquiries of different kinds on their terms, and by concatenating and nesting them within studies that combine multiple modes of (design) research.

14.3 Constituent Parts of the Theory

The *theory of (and for) enquiry* is, for the most part, an amalgamation of several categorisations and models proposed and developed previously by others, in particular by Christopher Frayling, Ranulph Glanville, Robert Rosen, and Stuart Umpleby. This section outlines how these various contributions relate to each other and constitute the proposed theory. It unfolds in a conceptual space opened up

[2]See page 34 in this volume.

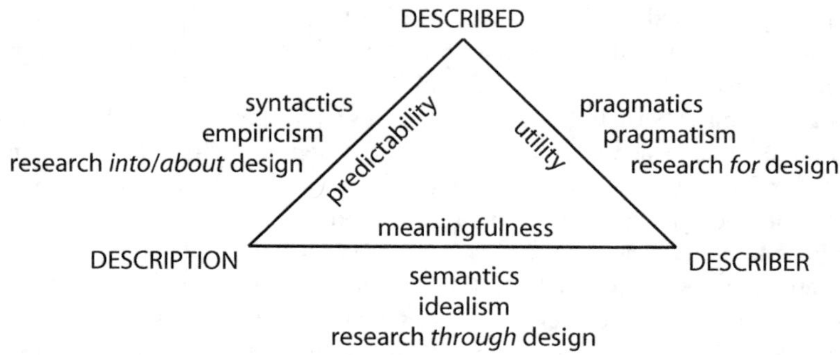

Fig. 14.1 Epistemological triangle with associated agendas

between three categories of design research proposed by Frayling [19, p. 5], and further discussed by Findeli [10, p. 2] and Downton [8, p. 2]: research *for* design, research *into/about* design, and research *through* design. Findeli [10, p. 2] describes research for design as best exemplified by "R&D" – research and development work – in support of design. He describes research into/about design as "carried out under the heading of other disciplines (sociology, semiotics, economics, history, etc. . . .) of design". Concerned with evidence-based description, research into/about design takes an empiricist approach to the processes and outcomes of design. Frayling describes research through design as "being achieved and communicated through the activities of [. . .] design" [19, p. 5]. Findeli relates the latter to what has also been referred to as "action research by project", "project-grounded research", and "practice-led research" [10, p. 2].

I [13, p. 629], [15, p. 1594] pointed out previously that Frayling's [19] design research trichotomy maps onto a diagrammatic model (Fig. 14.1) that has been referred to in the cybernetic discourse on some occasions [48, 51], the so-called epistemological triangle with roots, according to Glanville [21, p. 192], in the work of Frege.[3] The vertices of this triangle correspond to the describer, i.e. observers including you and me, the described, i.e. the observed world, and descriptions, i.e. describers' accounts of observations (see [35, p. 8]).

Since none of these three elements can be conceived of independently from the remaining two, their separation in the diagram is somewhat contrived. Ignoring the entanglement of the three elements in subjective experience and allowing structured analysis, this reductionist move of gaining the advantage of clarity at the expense of fractured and selective views is fundamental to empirical science. It is itself depicted in the diagram as the separation of description from described. This separation is in turn reflected in the etymology of the word "science", whose Indo-European root

[3]Ogden and Richards [36] propose the similar "triangle of reference", and Popper's "three worlds" follow along similar lines [42].

"skei" refers to activities such as *separating*, *distinguishing* or *taking apart*, and also forms the basis of the words *scissors*, *schism* and *schizophrenia* [3], [13, p. 629].

In response to von Foerster [51], Umpleby [48, p. 4] points out that the three edges of the epistemological triangle correspond – besides the linguistic approaches syntactics, pragmatics and semantics – to the science-philosophical perspectives of (British-originated) empiricism between description and described, (US-originated) pragmatism between describer and described, and (continental European-originated) idealism between description and describer. Each of these perspectives attends to one of the three relationships that make up the triangle while downplaying the remaining, opposite vertex. Empiricism downplays the observing describer and establishes "objective" descriptions of the observable world. The essential evaluation criterion for research along this edge is formal correspondence (or, in short, form), affording predictability. Pragmatism downplays description to establish workable ways for observers to operate in the world. The essential evaluation criterion for research along this edge, therefore, is utility. Idealism, finally, downplays the observer-independent world and establishes descriptions of explanatory value to describers. The essential evaluation criterion for research along this edge is meaningfulness.

Once any one of the three vertices of the epistemological triangle is downplayed and neglected, the relationship between the two elements remaining in focus may be examined. Every one of these three relationships is, I argue, circularly-causal in nature. Describers affect the described, and the described affects describers. Describers affect descriptions and descriptions affect describers. The described affects descriptions, which, in turn, deployed for prediction and control, affect the described. The latter relationship lies at the heart of empirical science (where the circular nature of this relationship remains largely ignored). It has been captured in the *Modelling Relation* by cybernetician Rosen [44, p. 159], which is depicted in Fig. 14.2.

This figure corresponds to the edge connecting described and description in the epistemological triangle. In Rosen's nomenclature, this is the relationship between a

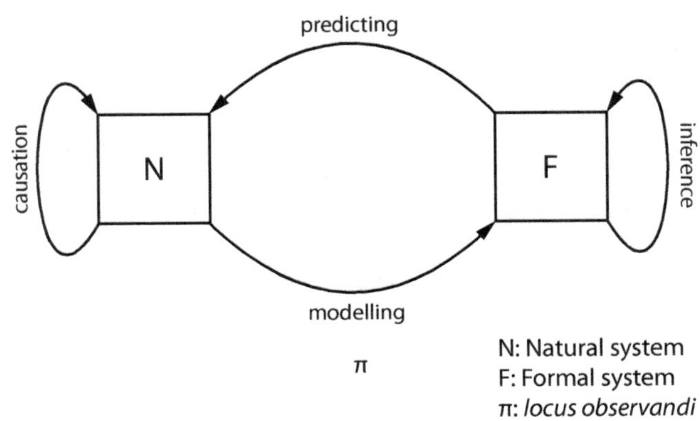

Fig. 14.2 Modelling relation based on Rosen [44, p. 159]

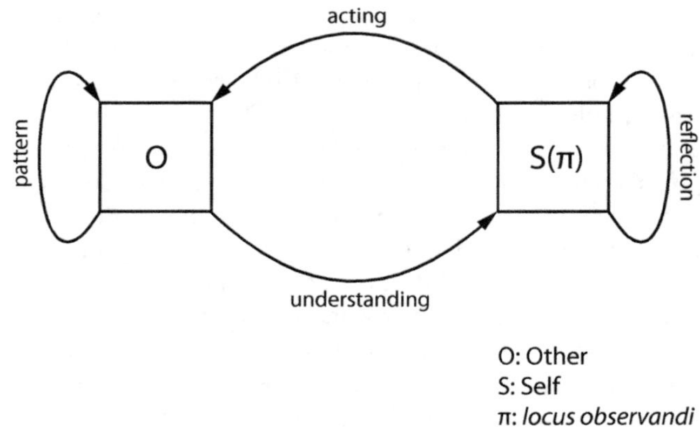

Fig. 14.3 Glanville's design conversation, illustration based on Glanville [26]

"natural system" N and a "formal system" F. The empirical investigator observes N, devises F, hypothesising that, and testing whether, F "is like" N.[4] To qualify for entry into this relation, Rosen points out, N must display causal connections. F, in turn, qualifies for entry into this relation by allowing inferences and predictive statements about not-yet-made observations of N to some satisfactory degree of reliability.

For the remaining two circularly-causal relationships in the epistemological triangle – both of which involve the subjective describer/observer – I propose an adaptation of Rosen's Modelling Relation, which reflects Glanville's design cybernetics. This structure, depicted in Fig. 14.3, shows a *self* S relating to an *other* O according to Glanville's characterisation of design as *conversation* [26] between (in the most simple scenario) a *self* and an *other*. Living as well as non-living entities qualify for entry into this relationship as an *other* by exhibiting patterns. Understanding such patterns permits reflection within *self*, allowing *self* in turn to better act vis-à-vis the *other*. Understanding and acting better over time, along these two arcs, both requires *knowledge for*, and produces *knowledge of* respectively [27, p. 17], and thus entails efficient as well as final causality [46, pp. 44–47].

The feedback relationship between *self* and *other* depicted in Fig. 14.3 differs from technical feedback loops such as thermostats (see page 36 in this volume and [25, p. 5]) with regards to the roles played by variety. In technical control relationships, on the one hand, *error* and *noise* are minimised and avoided so as to maintain requisite variety. The thermostat, with an equal and constant number of states (on and off) in both sensor and heat source, satisfies *Glanville's Corollary of Ashby's Law of Requisite Variety* [16][5] and thereby ensures effective control. The

[4]This is how I understand Gordon Pask's definition of cybernetics as "the science or the art of manipulating defensible metaphors; showing how they may be constructed and what can be inferred as a result of their existence." [38, p. 13].

[5]See footnote on page 5 in this volume.

epistemic relationship between *self* and *other*, on the other hand, is characterised by the continual renegotiation of variety on either side. Design-conversational loops harness mistakes, misunderstanding and serendipity, seeking to change (to amplify or to reduce) variety to get out-of-control, and to thereby arrive at the previously unknown. The varieties at play in the exchange are subject to the exchange itself.

Figure 14.3 depicts epistemic practice *as done*, i.e. what is meant here by the term "enquiry". Figure 14.2 depicts the structure of outcomes of empirical enquiries. Despite their similarities, these two structures differ with regards to the disposition of the observer indicated with the symbol π. In Fig. 14.2, π is located outside of the loop of enquiry to signify an external *locus observandi*, complying with the scientific requirement of objectivity. In Fig. 14.3, π is located at the position of the *self* to signify the *self*'s subjective *locus observandi*, as it is characteristic for action-based epistemic activities such as design.

Where designerly modes of enquiry are not tolerated and face academic scrutiny, PhD researchers may be well advised to commit, from early on, to work towards a defence on "robust", empirical grounds. For this purpose, as will be explained below, idealist and pragmatist design enquiries can be nested within empiricist research *into/about* designing. In this way, enquiries corresponding to Fig. 14.2 and enquiries corresponding to Fig. 14.3 can be combined, allowing design researchers to do justice to both.

Understanding cybernetics as *the study of processes in which states of affairs are adjusted with reference to other states of affairs*, and understanding systems as sets of elements with a shared goal, contained within observer-projected boundaries [18, p. 37] yields four possible dispositions (i.e. combinations of locations of observers and references relative to the boundaries of systems) [22, appendix].[6] These dispositions map onto Frayling's [19] design research trichotomy, extended by Jonas,[7] as follows:

- the observer is inside, looking outwards: research through design
- the observer is outside, looking inwards: research into/about design
- the observer is outside, looking outwards: research for design
- the observer is inside, looking inwards: research as design

These dispositions differ with regards to where investigators (observers: designers, researchers) position themselves relative to the boundaries of a given enquiry, and whether references (criteria, standards, goals) relevant to these enquiries are located

[6]See also Sect. 2.3.2.2.2 in this volume.

[7]In my 2007 thesis, I relate three of these dispositions to Frayling's three categories of design research [12, pp. 214–215]; see also: [13, p. 629], [15, p. 1594]. Having examined my thesis, Jonas [30, p. 047/6] adopted a variation of this mapping, swapping the *for* and the *about* category. This swap may be due to a conflation of the enquirer's centre of attention and the location of criteria by which results of enquiries are evaluated. In my view, the researcher-*into/about*-design ultimately aims to satisfy empiricist criteria outside observed design enquiries, whereas the researcher-*for*-design ultimately aims to satisfy designerly criteria that apply inside observed design enquiries. I therefore maintain my original mapping – with the category research *as* design added by Jonas.

within or beyond these boundaries. Where design research is to do justice to design *and* to be defended against academic (formal) scrutiny, as is the case in some design PhD enquiries, investigators must navigate with both internal references (say aesthetic or ethical aspirations) and external references (scientific standards). Designers are no strangers to navigating by both internal and external references and know the challenge of satisfying say internal creative desires as well as external resource limitations, regulatory constraints and commercial expectations. A common strategy is to neglect internal references in favour of external ones or vice versa. Navigating by both internal *and* external references, however, may be exceedingly difficult.

Recognising that enquiry extends *in time* offers a way out. It allows shifting modes of justification away from atemporal results in say statistical or logical terms (as they are encountered in *research as reported*), towards narratives that demonstrate increasingly viable processes of acting and understanding (as they are encountered in *design as done* – see pages 46ff. in this volume).[8] It also allows concatenating and nesting multiple modes of enquiry within the same body of work, as will be described in the following section.

14.4 Putting the Theory into Practice

The primary mode of design PhD research should be chosen, I suggest, in accordance with the PhD student's personal disposition towards one of the three evaluation criteria – *utility*, *meaningfulness*, and *predictability*. Methodological choices between pragmatist, idealist, and empiricist paradigms will fall into place according to Fig. 14.1. Where *predictability* and therefore an empiricist mode is chosen, defence by standards of empirical science is possible and necessary. Where utility or meaningfulness is chosen, but examinations by conventional scientific (empiricist) standards must be expected, enquiries can be nested within, and examined from overarching or subsequent empiricist perspectives.

Prior to the discussion of related strategic choices, some notes on the relationship between design and the criteria of empirical science, in particular those of reproducibility (i.e. predictability) and observability, are necessary. Conversational processes towards the previously unknown are, by definition, not determinable. That is, they are not reliably predictable or reproducible. It makes little sense, for example, to expect two designers to respond to the same brief in the same way and with the same outcomes, or to expect the same designer to design the same thing multiple times – expectations that would seem reasonable when raised analogously

[8]At some point during my PhD research with Ranulph Glanville, I remarked on the daunting challenge of fitting the entirety of my PhD research into a thesis. The gist of his response was: "When you are sent to get a medical check-up, the report will essentially state whether you're fit or not and why – without going into the details of everything the doctor did to come to that result."

towards other occupations such as accountants, nurses or engineers. Already in the 1950s, Wiener likened attempts to predict moments of creative insight to attempts to predict "the particular house in the village which would next be struck by lightning" [50, p. 25]. In this aspect, expectations of "reliability" and "robustness" in design research are likely misplaced. Spontaneity is opposed to reproducibility (and, insofar, to generalisability). Those relying on empirical methods for the sake of academic defensibility are therefore well advised to attend to aspects of design that remain largely unaffected by the spontaneity of creative insight.

The design process is furthermore limited with regards to *observability*, a fundamental assumption of empiricism [11]. In the design-conversational cycle shown in Fig. 14.3, the upper arc labelled "acting" represents the expressive and intervening output by which *self* affects the *other*, such as expressive activities (sketching, model making, verbal and written articulations, etc.). The lower "understanding" arc represents the sensory input and cognitive activities of understanding (perception, inspiration, confusion, etc.) by which the *other* affects the *self*. While the "acting" arc is largely observable, the "understanding" arc is not, as noted by Pask [37, p. 77]. Cross [5], accordingly, separates design activity into "hackwork" ("acting") and "magic" ("understanding"). Lawson points out that "[c]onducting empirical work on the design process is notoriously difficult. The design process, by definition, takes place inside our heads" [34, p. 41], and, as von Glasersfeld notes, one "can never really know what goes on in somebody else's head" [40, p. 40]. Those relying on empirical methods for the sake of academic defensibility are therefore well advised to attend to observable aspects of design.

14.5 Observer Inside, Looking Outwards: Research Through Design

The observer being inside, looking outwards corresponds to involved transcendence of what has been established previously, and hence with research *through* design. This is depicted above in Fig. 14.3. Investigators operate within their design enquiries – which entail, and may invite, error or failure – pursuing goals (meaningful resolutions of design challenges) that lie beyond these enquiries (thus potentially transcending what was previously known). In the absence of formal standards by which the attainment of these goals may be judged objectively, design research conducted in this mode tends to be difficult to defend vis-à-vis formal academic scrutiny. External approval of outcomes of this mode depends on designers' externalisation of their own criteria and standards, to hopefully convince *others* (reviewers, examiners) that an adequate degree of rigour was in effect. In other words, it depends on new shared meaning. Where this mode of justification is not entertained or unlikely to be successful, a path to defensibility may be found by concatenating/nesting this mode of enquiry within research about/into design enquiry as described in Sect. 14.6.

14.6 Observer Outside, Looking Outwards: Research About/into Design

The observer being outside, looking outwards corresponds to distanced, objective inspection, and thus to empirical scientific research *about/into* design. With this disposition, investigators identify (be it based on interest or need, or on literature review or prior research work) particular and worthwhile matters of interest pertaining to the design process, and formulate testable and falsifiable hypotheses about them. Where no suitable data sets are available to test given hypotheses, investigators may identify or devise suitable means to test the hypotheses, and carry these tests out accordingly, be it in the field, in controlled laboratory settings, or somewhere in between.[9] Taking this approach, investigators assume positions external to the design processes of interest to allow these processes to unfold with hopefully minimal bias. Observations made of design processes are captured in suitable quantitative and/or qualitative formats. Thus established, data sets are analysed to identify causal patterns which may or may not support the hypothesis at suitable degrees of reliability. Predictions regarding design processes not (yet) observed based on these causal patterns are considered justifiable according to the degrees of reliability achieved – typically by way of observing multiple design processes. This process is captured in Fig. 14.4.

The inner, investigated research through design process(es) may be conducted by one or more designers other than the investigator(s) researching into it from the outer research process. Or, both processes can be conducted by the same investigator(s), be it consecutively or in parallel. In the sequential case, the investigator(s) may first conduct the research through design process(es), and then "turn around" or "step

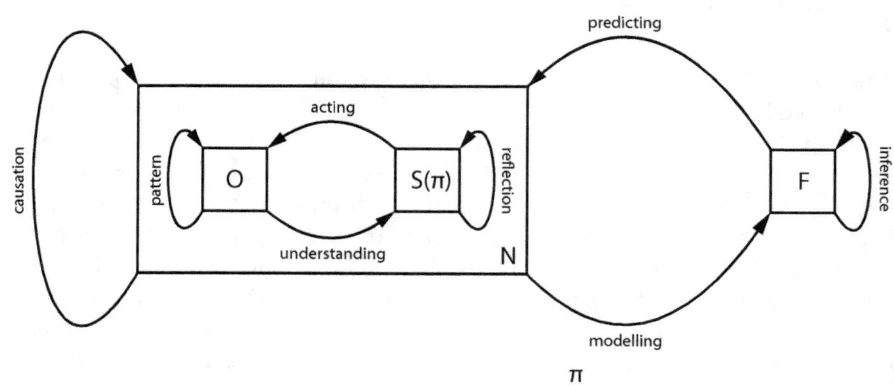

Fig. 14.4 (Outer) research about/into (inner) research through design

[9]More controlled environments are preferable with regards to the criterion *ceteris paribus*, while observations made in less controlled environments can be more naturalistic.

back" to approach that research through design activity as an observable natural system, for example by referring to records of this activity (tracks left by it) as a data set to analyse, in a separate research into/about enquiry. Findings derived in this empirical manner are, as indicated in the epistemological triangle, evaluated by the criterion of formal correspondence, i.e. the match between description and described, rather than by subjective judgement. They find acceptance where robust relationships between description and described stand up to scrutiny based on external, scientific criteria.

14.7 Observer Outside, Looking Inwards: Research for Design

The observer being outside, looking inwards aims at developing and providing *enabling resources* (such as new guidelines, tools, methods, materials, etc.) to be applied in the context of subsequent designing: research *for* design. This process is captured with the inner (nested) cascade of two enquiries shown in Fig. 14.5, the upper (enabling resource-generating) of which may be carried out in accordance with Fig. 14.2 or in accordance with Fig. 14.3.

Researchers-for-design may develop enabling resources for particular design projects of their own. This makes them competent judges of the resources' utility, but may not satisfy broader, more "objective" scrutiny that might be deemed desirable in some settings such as academic examinations. This is especially the case when the resources in question are not convincingly innovative or when their utility is

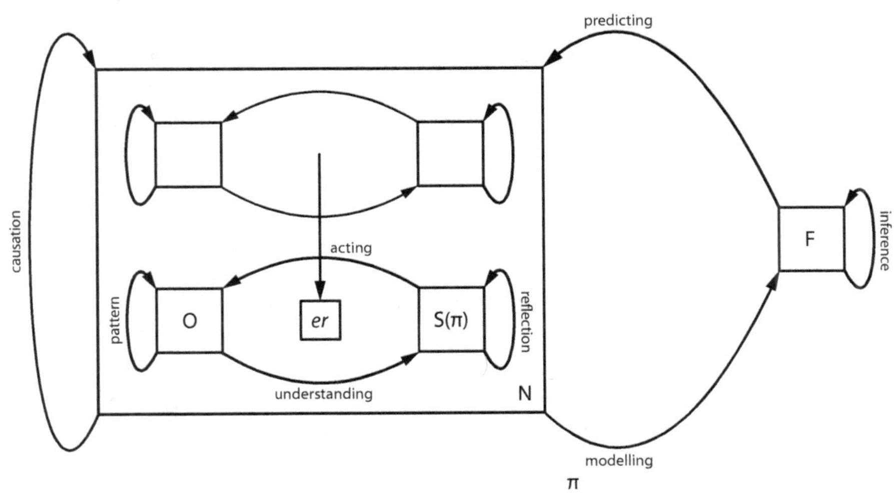

Fig. 14.5 (Outer) research about/into (inner) research for design

not entirely obvious to *others*. Alternatively, researchers-for-design may develop resources to enable design more generally, beyond the scope of their own design practice. Enabling resources produced may be passed on to other design processes, to be applied and evaluated within those contexts. Both research for design as well as the evaluation of its success may require the study of multiple design processes that are to be enabled. This approach likely involves making decisions, and embodying these decisions in enabling resources to empower *others* who have the responsibility to make those decisions within the scopes of their particular enquiries. In this way, enabling resources may have unduly restraining effects (see also [17]).

Outcomes of research-for-design are, as indicated in the epistemological triangle, subject to the criterion of utility within the context of subsequent design application. Dependent on subjective judgement and particular circumstances, these outcomes may not be robust when faced with formal, objective scrutiny. Where such robustness is desired, research for design, and the application of enabling resources so generated may be nested within research about/into design as indicated in Fig. 14.5. In this approach, the enquiry that generates the enabling resource *er*, and the design enquiry enabled by the *er* are taken as the "natural system" *N* in a third research about/into design enquiry. This concatenation and nesting of three distinct enquiries can be resource-demanding, but may be justified by the benefit of formal defensibility.

14.8 Observer Inside, Looking Inwards: Research as Design

The observer being inside, looking inwards corresponds to the investigator operating within her enquiry according to references (criteria, goals) of her own, as shown in Fig. 14.6. Jonas [30, p. 047/6] refers to this mode as research *as* design. It is the perspective from which the remaining (Frayling's) three categories of design research are navigated, chosen, nested and concatenated. In other words, this is the vantage point from which design researchers make over-arching strategic and methodological choices. Internal criteria for choices made from this perspective are, according to both Glanville [22] and Jonas [30], a matter of internal affairs, and may include delight [25, p. 8] and the increase of numbers of choices available [52, p. 282].

Design research conducted in this mode is in accord with Glanville's positioning of scientific research as one restricted subset of the more general human activity of designing. As a reversal of the commonplace academic conception of design as a subset of science, this mode requires taking careful and explicit measures to achieve robustness in the face of scrutiny, including, possibly, the use of scientific method in nested sub-enquiries to demonstrate mastery of that approach, the internalisation of external references, and the compelling enough expression of internal references. This mode may not be welcome in all places, and cybernetic design researchers

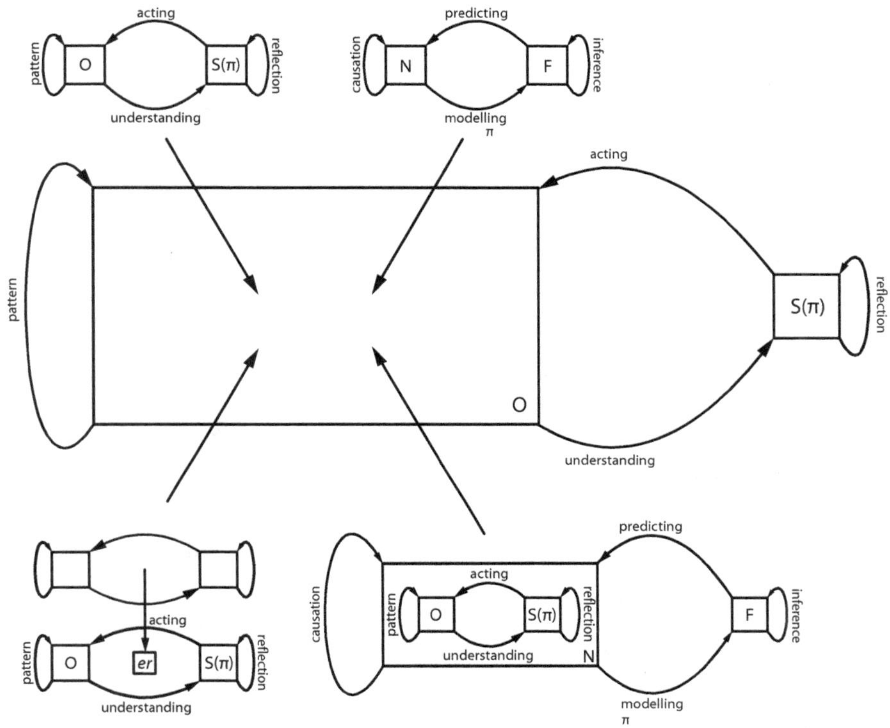

Fig. 14.6 Research as design, deploying other modes of design research as needed

engaging in this mode of enquiry would be well advised to proceed with both care and dedication to help establish it further.

14.9 Conclusion

The *theory of (and for) enquiry* developed above is offered to hopefully be of value in postgraduate and PhD-level design research and supervision. It suggests a number of ways in which design and scientific research may be concatenated and nested so as to satisfy both internal creative rigour and external formal scrutiny. These were developed diagrammatically on the basis of the epistemological triangle as described by Umpleby, Rosen's modelling relation as well as Glanville's four observer dispositions, and associated modes of research proposed by Frayling and Jonas. Several possible concatenations and nestings were discussed to hopefully inform enquiries with idealist, empiricist, and pragmatist agendas and their associated overarching evaluation criteria meaningfulness, predictability and utility.

References

1. Archer, B. (1979). Design as a discipline. *Design Studies, 1*(1), 17–20.
2. Bateson, G. (1972). *Steps to an ecology of mind*. New York: Ballantine Books.
3. Bröcker, M. (2004). The part-of-the-world position of Heinz von Foerster. *Brief Strategic and Systemic Therapy European Review, 1*, 19–26.
4. Buchanan, R. (1992). Wicked problems in design thinking. *Design Issues, 8*(2), 5–21.
5. Cross, N. (1977). *The automated architect*. London: Pion.
6. Cross, N. (1982). Designerly ways of knowing. *Design Studies, 3*(4), 221–227.
7. Cross, N. (2007). Forty years of design research. *Design Studies, 28*(1), 1–4.
8. Downton, P. (2003). *Design research*. Melbourne: RMIT University Press.
9. Farrell, R., & Hooker, C. (2012). The Simon–Kroes model of technical artifacts and the distinction between science and design. *Design Studies, 33*(5), 480–495.
10. Findeli, A. (1999). Introduction. *Design Issues, 15*(2), 1–3.
11. Fischer, T. (2008). Obstructed magic. On the myths of observing designing and of sharing design observations. In W. Nakapan et al. (Eds.), *CAADRIA 2008 Proceedings* (pp. 278–284). Chiang Mai: Pimniyom Press.
12. Fischer, T. (2008). *Designing (tools (for designing (tools (for . . .))))*. PhD Thesis. Melbourne: RMIT University. Available at: https://researchbank.rmit.edu.au/eserv/rmit:9761/Fischer.pdf. Accessed January 19, 2019.
13. Fischer, T. (2011). One-behind-the-many metaphysics and the myriad things. In C. M. Herr et al. (Eds.), *CAADRIA 2011 Proceedings* (pp. 623–632). Newcastle: School of Architecture and Built Environment, The University of Newcastle.
14. Fischer, T. (2015). Wiener's prefiguring of a cybernetic design theory. *IEEE Technology and Society Magazine, 34*(3), 52–59.
15. Fischer, T. (2017). A cybernetic perspective on determinability and design research. *Kybernetes, 46*(9), 1588–1596.
16. Fischer, T. (2019). Transcomputability, (Glanville's corollary of) Ashby's law of requisite variety, and epistemic processes. *Kybernetes, 48*(4), 793–804.
17. Fischer, T., & Herr, C. M. (2007). The designer as toolbreaker? Probing tool use in applied generative design. In G. Yu et al. (Eds.), *CAADRIA 2007 Proceedings* (pp. 367–375). Nanjing: Southeast University Press.
18. Fischer, T., & Richards, L. D. (2017). From goal-oriented to constraint-oriented design: The cybernetic intersection of design theory and systems theory. *Leonardo, 50*(1), 36–41.
19. Frayling, C. (1993/1994). Research in art and design. *Royal College of Art Research Papers, 1*(1), 1–5.
20. Galle, P., & Kroes, P. (2014). Science and design: Identical twins? *Design Studies, 35*(3), 201–231.
21. Glanville, R. (1975). *A cybernetic development of theories of epistemology and observation, with reference to space and time, as seen in architecture, also known as: The object of objects, the point of points – or something about things*. PhD Thesis (unpublished). London: Brunel University.
22. Glanville, R. (1997). A ship without a rudder. In R. Glanville & G. de Zeeuw (Eds.), *Problems of excavating cybernetics and systems* (pp. 131–142). Southsea: BKS+. Available at: https://www.univie.ac.at/constructivism/papers/glanville/glanville95-ship.pdf. Accessed January 19, 2019.
23. Glanville, R. (1999). Researching design and designing research. *Design Issues, 15*(2), 80–91.
24. Glanville, R. (2007). Try again. Fail again. Fail better: The cybernetics in design and the design in cybernetics. *Kybernetes, 36*(9/10), 1173–1206.

25. Glanville, R. (2014). How design and cybernetics reflect each other (transcript of keynote presentation). *RSD3 Relating Systems Thinking and Design 2014*. http://systemic-design.net/wp-content/uploads/2014/08/Ranulph_Glanville.pdf. Accessed January 19, 2019.
26. Glanville, R. (2014). Acting to understand and understanding to act. *Kybernetes, 43*(9/10), 1293–1300.
27. Glanville, R. (2014). The sometimes uncomfortable marriages of design and research. In P. A. Rodgers & J. Yee (Eds.), *The Routledge companion to design research* (pp. 9–22). London: Routledge.
28. Ison, R. L., Collins, K. B., & Wallis, P. J. (2015). Institutionalising social learning: Towards systemic and adaptive governance. *Environmental Science & Policy, 53*(Part B), 105–117.
29. Ito, J. (2016). Design and science. Can design advance science, and can science advance design? *Journal of Design and Science, 1*. Available at: https://jods.mitpress.mit.edu/pub/designandscience. Accessed January 19, 2019.
30. Chow, R., & Jonas, W. (2009). Beyond dualisms in methodology: An integrative design research medium "MAPS" and some reflections. In D. Durling, C. Rust, L.-L. Chen, P. Ashton, & K. Friedman (Eds.), *Undisciplined! Proceedings of the Design Research Society Conference 2008* (pp. 047/1–047/21). Sheffield: Sheffield Hallam University.
31. Jones, J. C. (Ed.). (1992). *Design methods*. New York, NY: Van Nostrand Reinhold.
32. Krippendorff, K. (2007). The cybernetics of design and the design of cybernetics. *Kybernetes, 36*(9/10), 1381–1392.
33. Krippendorff, K. (2007). Design research, an oxymoron? In (Ed.), *Design research now. Essays and selected papers* (pp. 67–79). Basel: Birkhäuser.
34. Lawson, B. (2005). *How designers think* (4th ed.). Amsterdam: Architectural Press.
35. Maturana, H. R., & Varela, F. J. (1980). *Autopoiesis and cognition. The realization of the living*. Dordrecht: D. Riedel Publishing.
36. Ogden, C. K., & Richards, I. A. (1989). *The meaning of meaning*. Orlando, FL: Harvest/HBJ. Originally published 1923.
37. Pask, G. (1971). A comment, a case history and a plan. In J. Reichardt (Ed.), *Cybernetics, art and ideas* (pp. 76–99). London: Studio Vista.
38. Pask, G. (1975). *The cybernetics of human learning and performance. A guide to theory and research*. London: Hutchinson Educational.
39. Pickering, A. (2010). *The cybernetic brain. Sketches of another future*. Chicago, IL: University of Chicago Press.
40. Pörksen, B. (2004). *The certainty of uncertainty*. Exeter: Imprint Academic.
41. Polanyi, M. (1967). *The tacit dimension*. Garden City, NY: Anchor Books.
42. Popper, K. (1978). *Three worlds*. The Tanner Lecture on Human Values – Delivered at The University of Michigan on 07 Apr 1978. Available at: https://tannerlectures.utah.edu/_documents/a-to-z/p/popper80.pdf. Accessed January 19, 2019.
43. Rittel, H. W. J., & Webber, M. M. (1973). Dilemmas in a general theory of planning. *Policy Sciences, 4*(2), 155–169.
44. Rosen, R. (1999). *Essays on life itself*. New York, NY: Columbia University Press.
45. Schön, D. (1985). *The design studio. An exploration of its traditions and potentials*. London: RIBA Publications.
46. Segal, L. (2001). *The dream of reality. Heinz von Foerster's constructivism* (2nd ed.). New York, NY: Springer.
47. Simon, H. A. (1996). *Sciences of the artificial* (3rd ed.). Cambridge, MA: MIT Press. Originally published 1969.
48. Umpleby, S. (2007). Unifying epistemologies by combining world, description and observer. Presented at the *ASC Conference*. Champaign-Urbana, IL, March 29–April 01, 2007. https://www.academia.edu/35684564/Unifying_Epistemologies_by_Combining_World_Description_and_Observer. Accessed January 19, 2019.
49. Wang, D. (2002). Design in relation to research. In L. Groat & D. Wang (Eds.), *Architectural research methods* (pp. 99–131). New York, NY: Wiley.

50. Wiener, N. (1993). *Invention: The care and feeding of ideas.* Cambridge, MA: MIT Press.
51. von Foerster, H. (1971). Computing in the semantic domain. *Annals of the New York Academy of Sciences, 184*, 239–241.
52. von Foerster, H. (2003). *Understanding understanding. Essays on cybernetics and cognition.* New York, NY: Springer.

Thomas Fischer is a design researcher, epistemologist and cybernetician. He is a Professor and Director of Research at the Department of Architecture at XJTLU in Suzhou, China. Thomas is also a Visiting Associate Professor at the School of Design at The Hong Kong Polytechnic University. He is a Fellow of the Design Research Society and received the American Society for Cybernetics' Warren McCulloch Award. Thomas holds a PhD in Education from the University of Kassel in Germany and a PhD in Architecture and Design from RMIT University in Australia. His research is focused on epistemological issues of design computing, design cybernetics, and digital media.

Chapter 15
Cybernetics and Society Redux: The Necessity of Design

Laurence D. Richards

Abstract Norbert Wiener warned us to avoid the potential application of cybernetics to the production of technologies of oppression – that is, we need to design structures and processes in which violence is not an alternative or, at least, is an alternative of last resort. This chapter presents cybernetics as a way of thinking about ways of thinking, making the way of thinking a choice. The cybernetic vocabulary of choice and autonomy provides a foundation for building a participative-dialogic approach to design (and society) that is distinct from the purposeful (goal-oriented) and hierarchical (reward-oriented) design approach of traditional engineering and management. In a participative-dialogic society, design becomes a necessity, not only to address the concerns expressed by Wiener, but also to satisfy the human need for participation in the decisions that affect our daily lives.

Keywords Goal-oriented purpose · Desires as constraints · Reward-oriented hierarchy · Networks of conversations · Relations and dynamics · Participatory design

15.1 Introduction

In 1950 (with a second edition in 1954), Norbert Wiener published his second book on cybernetics: *The Human Use of Human Beings: Cybernetics and Society* [35]. Building on his book, *Cybernetics, or Control and Communication in the Animal and the Machine*, published in 1948 (with a second edition in 1961) [36] and now considered the originating source on modern cybernetics, Wiener warned about the potential applications of ideas in cybernetics – especially robotics and artificial intelligence embedded in automated processes – to the design and production of technologies of oppression. He expressed special concern about devices that could select their own targets based on programmed criteria and act on that selection

L. D. Richards (✉)
Indiana University East, Richmond, IN, USA
e-mail: laudrich@iue.edu

T. Fischer, C. M. Herr (eds.), *Design Cybernetics*, Design Research Foundations,
https://doi.org/10.1007/978-3-030-18557-2_15

with no human intervention, the development of which had commercial value and was of particular interest to the military, irrespective of the danger such devices posed for all of humanity. While Wiener refused to participate in the development of these technologies and their commercial and military uses, he acknowledged that the interests of the ruling class would in time make them a reality; and, in fact, we now have military drones that perform this very function. Wiener also acknowledged that, once the technologies were developed, there was no turning back, just as there was no turning back on the development of nuclear weapons. It would be up to us humans then to ensure that these technologies are used to enhance our choices and alternatives rather than to limit or destroy them.

The implications of Wiener's admonition was and continues to be that we humans need to be intentional about avoiding the misuse and abuse of technology – that is, we need to design social structures and processes in which violence is not an alternative or, at least, is an alternative of last resort. Cybernetics, as a way of thinking about ways of thinking, offers an approach to design and society distinct from the purposeful (goal-oriented) and hierarchical (reward-oriented) design approach of traditional engineering and management. Cybernetic concepts of variety and constraint, time and dynamics, recursion and closure, freedom and responsibility, conversation and autonomy provide a foundation for a participative-dialogic approach for designing (a) society. In this chapter, I develop a way of thinking about the design of social systems that draws on these ideas from cybernetics, one that contrasts with conventional wisdom on design. I assume that all humans can contribute and deserve the opportunity to do so and that social systems must, therefore, be designed to maintain human autonomy and volition, as well as human interaction – that is, they must avoid oppression. This includes the design process itself. Research on this form of design becomes research on desirability – how can a design process reconcile the needs and desires of individuals with a society that designs itself?

15.2 The Uses of the Word Design

In a paper I wrote entitled "Beyond Planning: Technological Support for a Desirable Society" [21], I discuss the lexicology of the word design. I did this out of curiosity about the various uses of the word and, in particular, the use I wished to advance when talking about society. For example, a version of *The Oxford Dictionary of the English Language* lists three categories of definition for the verb "design": (1) to mark out, indicate; (2) to plan, contrive, intend; and (3) to sketch, draw, or fashion artistically. It stipulates that, in French, there are separate words for each of these three categories: *designer, desseigner,* and *dessiner,* respectively. Hence, when the English word is invoked, it could carry with it all three possible uses, including the one I wanted to advance, "to mark out, indicate".

In a conversation, Heinz von Foerster once questioned my use of the word design when talking about society and suggested I refer to *The American Heritage Dictionary*. As he had implied, the "mark out, indicate" category was not there. Listed were five definitions for the transitive verb "to design," three of which are in the "plan, contrive, intend" category, and the other two in the "sketch, draw, fashion" category. The message I think that Heinz wanted me to take from this exercise was that in the United States, if not elsewhere, the word design is strongly associated with purposeful, planning behavior, with one definition actually being: "to have as a goal or purpose". The category of definition "mark out, indicate" has been lost, undoubtedly yielding to the verb "designate". I regard this as unfortunate and agree with Ranulph Glanville [13, pp. 263–264][1] that design is a process of making distinctions, and there are many ways of doing that, of which the purposeful, goal-oriented approach is but one. I do not regard a dictionary as an authority on the use of words; rather, I relate this story as a way to highlight an issue and my desire to revive a particular use that I think is important to conserve.

That the marking out or indicating – making a distinction – aspect of design has been delegated to the word designate is an indication of how strong the goal-oriented approach to problem solving is in North America (and beyond). It is the approach explicitly taught in schools of engineering and management, as well as other professional disciplines: specify a desirable end, formulate it as a goal or objective, and then identify the most efficient and effective means to achieve it. It is so dominant that it is seldom questioned – what is important in life is what you achieve, and the only way to ensure achievement is to set goals. This has been called the "rational actor model" [1] or "rationalistic tradition" [37] of decision-making and design. It has also been labeled the "analytic paradigm" [31] and "technical rationality" [28]. Some political scientists and other students of policy decisions and social design recognize that actual policy decisions do not arise according to the rationalistic framework and that ends are not so easily separated from means. Allison [1] identifies the "organization process" and "governmental politics" models for policy decisions, relying on the ideas of "satisficing" and "bounded rationality" [29, 30] and of "disjointed incrementalism" [8] or "muddling through" [15]. In *The Intelligence of Democracy*, Lindblom [16] argues that we submit to an incremental approach to social policy and design in order to maintain democratic systems of participation. Steinbruner [31] adds a "cybernetic paradigm", relying on ideas from instrumentalism and cognitive processes, to describe how great decisions can still occasionally happen despite bureaucratic politics and incrementalism.

The outcomes of rationalistic design processes are blueprints, technical drawings and lists of specifications, which are then handed over to the builders, manufacturers and craftspeople to implement. In the design of social systems that conserve the autonomy, volition and interaction of their members, design and production merge. Blueprints, drawings and specifications are not particularly useful as they require an authority to implement them, with oppression a possible, if not likely, consequence. Yet, imagining a desirable society is a distinction-making process, with human intentions. The distinctions made constitute a design.

As an example, I like to walk a few miles every day. When I visit a city to which I have not before travelled, I need a route for my walk. I can design a route by getting

[1] See page 34 in this volume.

a map, asking some questions, collecting information, drawing the route out on the map and then taking the map with me on my walk to show me the way. I have a blueprint for my walk, and then I execute the design. Alternatively, I could start my walk with a few constraints in mind and see what happens. I know I want to walk a few miles; I know I want to end up where I started; I would prefer not to retrace my steps; and, I know I want to avoid certain obstacles and dangers along the way. I will deal with obstacles and dangers by being observant and looking ahead. While I may have to turn back and start over to avoid certain obstacles and dangers, I will have engaged in an adventure and experienced aspects of the city I would not otherwise have experienced – ends and means merge. A design for a walking route emerges as it is walked and can be adjusted during subsequent walks. This approach is particularly effective in a city for which the maps are out of date, there is limited knowledge, or the complexities of the city's streets and paths make it impossible to predict efficiencies. It is also a way for me to walk with others without dictating the route, as long as we share the desirability of the constraints. Different people can make suggestions along the way, the others disputing only whether a suggestion violates the constraints. The design that results is then a product of collaboration; designing becomes itself an end as well as a means. The latter approach could serve as a metaphor for designing a society.

15.3 Goal-Oriented Purpose and Reward-Oriented Hierarchy

The idea of teleological systems has been around for a while; the idea assumes that a system has a purpose: that is, identify the purpose of a system and the structure of the system follows. For inorganic or mechanical systems, the purpose is determined by the designer of the system. For living systems, divine intervention is required. Cybernetics questions the efficacy of this idea. In their seminal paper entitled "Behavior, Purpose and Teleology," which presaged the emergence of Wiener's cybernetics, Rosenbleuth, Wiener and Bigelow [27] demonstrate how the idea of purpose arises from simple feedback loops that maintain the value of one or more variables within limits (the constraints). Any system with constraints appears to have a purpose as there are outcomes precluded from the set of possibilities. From where do the limits/constraints come? For designed systems, it is indeed the human designers who specify the limits (raising the question of where the designers get them). For living systems, the limits are a consequence of an evolutionary process of natural selection during which the possible structures of the system become constrained by its own recursive processes of operation as the system adapts – that is, the system continually creates its own boundaries.

In the design of social systems, the word goal is often conflated with the word purpose: a goal-directed system is a purposeful system and vice versa. The words goal and purpose have also been used in the context of both natural and designed systems, the latter involving human intent arising from processes of self-consciousness. In the context of design, the word goal has become a "point" concept for formulating desires – a consciously selected end state to be pursued and achieved through the most effective and efficient means possible – the rational actor model. Gregory Bateson [5, 6] warned of the dysfunctions of this predominant way of thinking about planning and design, including the way these topics are taught in schools of management and engineering. Human consciousness, Bateson argued, focuses in on a narrow portion of a complex situation: this ability to focus is both the power and the shortcoming of conscious purposiveness. By focusing on a specific piece of a situation, the rational actor can take decisive action, but the actions taken do not and cannot account for all the ecological circularities of the situation and the unanticipated consequences inherent in taking such actions. The achievement of goals that address one aspect of an undesirable situation creates new problems elsewhere, and the new situation may be even more undesirable than the original one, even disastrous when the situation involves the biosphere.

Goal-oriented purpose as a way of thinking about human desires and intent supports and is compatible with a "reward-oriented hierarchy" way of thinking about the design of social systems [11]. Humans design social-economic organizations to facilitate the manufacture and distribution of goods and the delivery of services and, often, to create jobs and make money, functions that would not be possible without the coordination of people and technology. Hierarchy is a way of organizing a complex enterprise by subdividing the work and activity into units, with higher levels of the hierarchy coordinating the units under them to ensure the integrity of the whole. Units are given tasks (often in the form of goals) to achieve, and high achievement is rewarded with a move up the hierarchy and the associated perquisites. With the reward structure comes a power structure, where those higher in the hierarchy have more influence on specifying the goals to be achieved. Reward-oriented hierarchies are neither participatory nor dialogic. Conversation (dialogue, with conflict essential) is suppressed in favor of communication (message transmission, with conflict undesirable), and autonomy (choice of action, outcomes unknown) is suppressed in favor of control (action specified by predetermined outcomes). (See [19].) Technologies of oppression emerge if they are in the interests of the power elite, who also control the resources and the reconfiguration of resources needed for social change and transformation.

Cybernetics offers an alternative way of thinking about human desires and intentions and about the design of social systems – constraints and restraints [4]. In my "Beyond Planning" paper [21], I explore some of the implications of treating desires as constraints. A set of constraints is a "spatial" concept for formulating desires [3], in contrast to the "point" concept of goals. The resulting pattern of constraint identifies those outcomes we, individually or together, wish to avoid, leaving the remainder open as possibilities. Human intention is then realized in our efforts to avoid the undesirable outcomes, efforts we can initiate here and now; the distinction between ends and means evaporates and an alternative to the rationalistic tradition emerges.

The constraints (sometimes called values) we apply to our actions are realized in our everyday language, and the formulation, questioning and revision of those constraints happen in the conversations we have with each other. An alternative to the hierarchical way of thinking about complex systems is a dialectical process way of thinking – that is, for every idea, formulate incompatible and opposing ideas so that new ideas might emerge, along with their incompatible and opposing ideas, and so on... [24]. Such a dialectical process is realized in conversation – a particular dialogic in which a dynamics of interaction, in a language, moves from an asynchronicity toward a synchronicity, where asynchronicity takes the form of a conflict, friction, disagreement, contradiction – that is, the participants are out of sync [22]. As a conversation proceeds, new ideas may emerge to supersede the original ideas that initiated the conversation. The conversation persists as long as the participants remain interested; it will end when the participants reach agreement, including the agreement to disagree, or when they get bored or need to do something else. A network of such conversations becomes an alternative way of thinking about the structure of social organizations.[2] Desires as constraints, intention as avoidance and social structure as a network of conversations provides a foundation for thinking about and designing a participative-dialogic society.

15.4 The Cybernetics of Desire and Constraint-Oriented Design

Herbert Brün, composer and cybernetician, distinguished needs, necessities and desires [9, pp. 42–46]. The distinctions are important, as each of these words points to a different form of constraint. Unless all human needs are met unconditionally, full participation in the design of a society cannot proceed and the pursuit of desires through design is irrelevant to those whose needs are not satisfied. While I draw on Brün's distinctions among needs, necessities and desires, the descriptions of my uses of these words below are adapted for the topic of this chapter and are my own. I also add my own descriptions for the words passion, desirability and violence.

Need: when I wish to speak about a want (a lack or absence) that must be satisfied and that once satisfied will recur as a want to be satisfied again.

Necessity: when I wish to speak about the resources that satisfy a need. So, the need called hunger is satisfied by the necessity called food; the need called thirst is satisfied by the necessity called water. Humans can agree on many biological needs. However, some may resist certain needs: the recluse resists the need others have for

[2] I have chosen not to use the word anarchy in this chapter in order to avoid having to address all the emotions associated with the word, although I have used it elsewhere [23]. Suffice it to say that, if and when I use the word, I do not do so to refer to a society without a government, but rather to refer to a non-hierarchical form of governance – rules, but no rulers.

human interaction; the celibate resists the need others have for sex. Some may treat as needs what others treat as desires.

Desire: when I wish to speak about a want that once satisfied does not recur. A desire can linger; it does not require satisfaction immediately and can change with time – new ones emerge, old ones fade away or get modified. Desires are pleasant to have; without desires, we would be stuck with needs. Desires offer opportunities for conversation and provide substance for creativity. Desires can be expressed as preferences, including preferences in the ways that needs get satisfied. I may prefer to satisfy my hunger with vegetables picked from my own garden; if that is not possible, I will still satisfy my hunger in some other way, as it is a need.

Some desires may rise to the level of passions.

Passion: when I wish to speak about a desire so strongly held that I treat it as though it will not change, or that it would take something beyond my current knowledge and experience for me to imagine giving it up. Passions can serve as anchors in our lives; they can also be dangerous when we treat them as beliefs. As anchors, it is important that passions be recognized as desires and potential subjects of conversation and not as representations of some absolute or universal truth [24]. If desirable, we may wish to treat the passions of others as though they are needs, working to satisfy them in the interest of a desirable society.

Desirability: when I wish to speak of actions and designs that preclude violence, or at least treat violence as an alternative of last resort, allowing all members of a society to participate in the design of their society and pursue their (non-violent) desires within it. So, a desirable society addresses both needs and desires.

Violence: when I wish to speak of actions and designs that reduce or eliminate the participation of one or more humans as witnessed by a victim, a perpetrator and/or a third party, creating the perception of a victim with only violent alternatives as a response to the actions of the perpetrator (which can be a system).

This way of thinking and talking about needs, necessities and desires (as well as passions and desirability) supports a formulation of certain desirable human conditions in terms of needs and necessities. For example, Herbert Brün [9, pp. 91–92] formulates the condition called peace (the absence of war) as a need. The necessity that satisfies this need is non-violent conflict, the type of conflict (or disagreement) that happens in a conversation. That is, in order to have peace, we must have conflict; once satisfied, the need will recur, and new conflicts and conversations will be required (see [17]). Von Foerster [32, p. 209] spoke of education as a necessity. As a necessity, education satisfies the need for knowing and learning: specifically, the need to know and learn how to survive and grow as an individual and how to share what one has to contribute to the mitigation of human misery and the design of a desirable society. In this chapter, I speak of design as a necessity, satisfying the human need for participation in a society in which that human is a member.

In a paper entitled "Constraint-oriented vs. Goal-oriented Design: The Cybernetic Intersection of Systems Theory and Design Theory," Thomas Fischer and I [12] present a case for an approach to design that starts with the question: What is undesirable, or what do we want to avoid as consequences of our design? By treating desires as constraints, rather than as goals (desired end points, as in targets) or objectives (desired directions, as in maximize or minimize), a space of possibilities is designated within which alternative designs can be discussed. When the set of constraints precludes all possible designs, the opportunity arises for conversations on desires and desirability out of which new ideas and new ways of thinking can emerge. This is both the joy and the frustration of constraint-oriented design: the joy of conversation and working together to create the new and the frustration of delays in proceeding with designs as conflicting desires are addressed.

15.5 Time and Dynamics in Social Design

Designers design systems. These systems, including social systems, are designed to perform specific functions. The traditional notion of system is one of an entity consisting of components, elements, or variables and a set of relations among them. The pattern of relations is called the system's structure, and for systems designed to perform specific functions, the structure of the system is designed to remain relatively invariant so that the system can continue to perform the function for which it was designed. These systems are said to be state-determined. The dynamics of the system is such that I can predict the system's behavior, at least within a likelihood of outcomes. In mechanical systems, I want the states of the system to be predictable since I design it to perform a specific function. I do not want these systems doing unpredictable things, so I design the dynamics to be simple and linear, and based on a "standard clock".

For living systems and social systems, elements and relations are not sufficient to describe their behavior; the system's dynamics becomes critical to the description. I therefore extend the characteristics that all systems exhibit to five: change of state, elements, structure (pattern of relations), invariance, and mechanism of closure [22]. In a simple mechanical system, the structure is invariant and the closure that maintains the boundaries of the system is informational closure, as the structure remains impervious to new information.[3] Perturbations are responded to through regulatory mechanisms that are a part of the system's structure, a recursion in the relations among the system's elements. The structure of living and social systems, on the other hand, can change to afford the system the ability to adapt to unforeseen perturbations and is thus open to information.

Cybernetics, then, concerns itself with two separate and distinct phenomenal domains: the domain of relations (explanation) and the domain of dynamics

[3]The use of the word information here is not to be confused with its common use as a flow of data from an environment to the system. Here, information is realized by how a system and its structure respond to perturbations, either from an external medium or from its own internal operations. If the system's structure remains invariant under perturbation, it is informationally closed; if its structure changes in response to perturbations, it is informationally open.

(experience) [23]. The design of social systems needs to address both domains if the designers wish to avoid the reward-oriented hierarchy form of system structure, which reduces the choices and alternatives of the members of the system and therefore their autonomy as human participants. When the autonomy of the members disappears, the system can be said to be violent and therefore anti-social. The value of a social system is in the choices and alternatives over which the system's members have discretion, individually or collectively, that arise from the particular interactions and transactions among them. In a social system, the system's structure can change as new ideas emerge, and even the system's function(s) can change. When people are treated as mechanical components in a system, the functions and structures of the system are determined by the desires of the few who control the resources – the owners or rulers. This would be an unsocial system – a system, but not a social system.

From the perspective of the domain of relations, the designers address the causal links that are needed for the system to perform its function(s). The resulting pattern of relations (or structure) may be singular, or there may be many possibilities. The larger the set of possible structures, the greater will be the system's resilience under varying or unexpected conditions. From the perspective of the domain of dynamics, the designers address the characteristics of the interactions and transactions among the system's members or subgroups of members that will remain invariant and therefore identify the system as the same system from one moment to the next when its structure changes. The pattern of dynamics of the interactions and transactions does not change and is crucial to the ability of the system to maintain the constraints on the possible structures needed to have the system continue to perform the function(s) that its members desire. The particular interactions among the members, then, must themselves be desirable, supporting the autonomy of the members to choose from alternatives and to engage in the generation of new alternatives, while also addressing the desires for which they are maintaining the system. When the desirability of the particular dynamics of interactions conflicts with the desirability of the system's functions, the system must accommodate the possibility of new functions. When the pattern of dynamics of the interactions and transactions changes, a new system emerges. The designers of a social system need to take all of these circumstances into consideration if they are to avoid the standard reward-oriented hierarchy approach to social system design. Specifically, the design must account for the (desirable) possibility of a change of system, not just change in the system. Among other features, this distinguishes a social system from a living system.

A clock is a way of sampling a pattern of dynamics. The observer collects data on the states of the system at predetermined time intervals and from the sequence of states deduces the relations among the variables of the system being observed. A change in the sampling rate (or clock) changes the observations of system states, which can affect the conclusions about the relations. In engineering design, the assumption of a standard clock is essential for getting all the system components synched with each other, as well as potential users synched with the system being designed. The clock becomes a key device in the regulation of designed systems.

Different cultures carry different concepts of time, and, as Benjamin Whorf [34] observed, the technologies characterizing different cultures can be quite different when the concepts of time are different. Users from one culture may find the devices produced by another culture difficult, if not impossible, to use without a change of clock (heating or cooling a house, dealing with natural disasters, driving a car, flying a plane). So, the idea of a standard clock – for example, one based on the regularities of the rotation of the earth or the revolution of the earth around the sun – is not straightforward; there are many concepts of time that can be applied to the observation of and/or participation in a system, and many possible clocks for explaining and regulating the behavior of a system.

The idea of time arose with the emergence of language and human consciousness: time is a human invention created to resolve the paradoxes of self-reference and allow us to move and act with volition [26]. The clock has also become an important social tool. For us to engage in the kind of caring for each other specific to humans, to meet with particular others for conversations and to be together with others for events, we synchronize our clocks to be in the same place at the same time as others. The accepted clock or clocks get embedded in a culture as standardized and external, even though we retain the capability of alternative concepts of time and the ability to use alternative clocks. Since all technologies mediate human interaction in some way or another, and technological innovation relies on the selection (or assumption) of a clock, this concept of time and its clock gets reinforced in the culture as technology progresses. Our behavior becomes regulated by the clock we use in our everyday social interactions, including work and other economic interactions, more often than not without awareness of alternatives or choices. Without such a clock, reward-oriented hierarchies and goal-oriented purposes could not operate. The clock allows those at the top of the hierarchy, those who control resources, to regulate the behaviors of those below, and goals would have little significance without a timeline of accomplishment (hence, "time is money").

So, alternative concepts of time and alternative clocks are considerations in the design of (humane) social systems. In particular, social systems that retain the possibility of a change of system (not just a change in the system) embed the idea of alternative clocks. New systems will likely involve new concepts of time, new clocks and new technologies. The questions are: which concepts of time are desirable under which circumstances, and how can we think about a society that would embrace alternative ways of thinking about time? Cybernetics offers a way to think about making the way of thinking a choice.

15.6 Criteria for a Participative-Dialogic Approach to Design and Society

Social system (human): when I wish to speak of a set of human participants and/or groups of participants and the interactions among them where the interactions are maintained by the desires of the participants. An unsocial system would be one where the interactions are maintained by violence, by removing the choices and alternatives of some members.

Society: when I wish to speak of a particular dynamics of interactions and transactions among a set of social and/or unsocial systems. Such systems can include health care systems, educational systems, manufacturing systems, banking systems, transportation systems, etc. When the dynamics of interactions and transactions that identify a society changes, we have a new society.

The following principles of design apply to a participative-dialogic approach to social systems and society. They are proposed as topics for conversation.

(1) Full participation by all members of a social system or society is desirable. Participation happens through conversation. Conversation requires the autonomy of the participants. Autonomy implies that participants can exercise choice. (The idea of human autonomy in a social system, as the word autonomy is used here, is distinct from the idea of biological autonomy, where the word autonomy is used to indicate the self-containment and self-perpetuation of an organism. Of course, humans also exhibit self-containment and self-perpetuation, or there would be no self or self-consciousness, and therefore no choice.)
(2) All humans have desires. Desires drive our intentions once our needs are met. Desires formulated as constraints leave open the possibility of accommodating the desires of many participants in a design and help identify where conflicts exist and therefore where conversations on desirability need to happen. Overarching desires may include the desire to satisfy the desires of others, the desire for conversation, the desire to avoid violence – in short, the desire to live in a world of thinking, caring people.
(3) Greed, cruelty, abuse of power, etc., are often considered as aspects of "human nature," and as such constitute behaviors to be addressed and controlled in the design of a society. These aspects of human nature are constructs of the current society and used to place blame on individual humans rather than on the systems that reinforce, even require, those behaviors. Human nature is then used to justify systems of oppression and control. In a participative-dialogic society, humans exhibit kindness, generosity, compassion and creativity, with systems that are compatible with and support those qualities.
(4) Ashby refers to intelligence as "appropriate selection" [2, p. 272], where what is appropriate depends on the situation in which organisms or people find themselves. As such, every human being exhibits unique attributes and abilities that would be most "appropriate" in some situation. These attributes and abilities represent potentially unique contributions in some society. A participative-dialogic society seeks to use these unique contributions as sources of new ideas by creating the conditions under which they can be highlighted, rather than suppressed because they challenge the *status quo*.
(5) In second-order cybernetics – that is, when the observer and the observer's desires are accounted for explicitly in the formulation of systems – the idea of responsibility plays an important role [18]. I use the word responsibility when I wish to speak of my awareness of my likings and dislikings (my desires)

with respect to the consequences of my actions. Responsibility, and its partner freedom, are central ideas in the design of a participative-dialogic society. As an individual, I use the word freedom when I wish to speak of my awareness of my likings and dislikings of my likings and dislikings (the desirability of my desires) with respect to the consequences of my actions. Note that the idea of freedom requires the idea of responsibility. With awareness that I can change my desires and my thinking, I am free to participate in generating choices and alternatives for others (and they for me). Choices and alternatives characterize freedom in a society, and freedom is a fundamental principle of a participative-dialogic society. (See also [33].)

(6) The variety of states or structures exhibited by a system decays toward basins of stability (stable states, cycles or structures – i.e., attractors). Even when new variety (information) is introduced to a system, and the decay appears to be temporarily halted, it is done at the expense of variety lost somewhere else. A defining characteristic of living systems is their ability to retard their decay through adaptive mechanisms (changes of structure), which they do until they lose the ability and die. Beyond these adaptive instincts, self-consciousness gives humans the ability to retard, with intent, the decay of the social systems in which they live. They do this through alterations (new information) in current systems, or though the design of new systems to replace or preempt the current ones. Putting a positive spin on what otherwise might seem our inevitable fate, the decay of variety in social systems gives us humans something to do, creating significance in our social and intellectual lives. So, designing a participative-dialogic society includes retaining, and even enhancing, our ability as humans to retard our own decay through the generation, in conversation, of new ideas and designs.

(7) The ideas of knowledge, knowledge systems and knowledge processes, particularly the latter, are often associated with the idea of society. I use the word knowledge when I wish to speak of the set of all currently accepted facts, opinions, desires, theories, ideas, etc., anything that constrains human behavior based on what is accepted as possible and desirable. I use the term knowledge system when I wish to speak of the way that knowledge is structured, producing what is accepted as the currently best available knowledge [21]. Knowledge processes then refer to the dynamics by which knowledge and knowledge systems are maintained, augmented and changed. The dynamics we call society and the idea of knowledge processes are intertwined. New knowledge processes accompany a new society and therefore represent source material for designing a society.

(8) All technology mediates human interactions in some way or another. If a dialogic approach to knowledge processes is considered desirable and technology is needed to facilitate the participation of all members of a large and geographically dispersed society, new forms of technology are suggested. Computing technology has made possible connections among people from around the world. The prospect of giving all people in the world access to currently best available knowledge, anytime, anywhere, can now be imagined

[10]. While it may not yet be accepted as desirable to consider all the people of the world as a society, there are global issues (environmental, economic, military) that affect all people of the world. Conversations among people worldwide are now conceivable, even if current computing and communication technologies are not adequate for facilitating conversation, in fact, often inhibit it.

What technology could facilitate these conversations? What non-hierarchical structures could give technology access to all people (not just all people access to technology)? The intensity of the dynamics of conversation suggests that digital computing may not be sufficient. Is there a role for analog computing in capturing the dynamics of a conversation (verbal, gestural, visual, audial, kinesthetic, etc.)[4] that the digital simulation of analog phenomena cannot capture? These are design questions for social systems and society.

15.7 Research on the Design of Social Systems

For those who study design and wish to advance its practice through research, social systems present a special challenge [25]. First, researchers on design are participants in the systems being designed, and the systems include the design processes themselves. A fundamental research question is: How can researchers account for their participation in the design processes they are researching in a way that produces useful ideas (or theories) for others? Second, the questions to be asked about the design of social systems and perhaps all design processes are in the category of the undecidable question – questions that cannot be answered by the collection of evidence, questions only we can decide [33, p. 293]. These are questions of desire and desirability, not of truth and verification. Formulating hypotheses, collecting evidence and confirming or rejecting the hypotheses based on the evidence constitute a process that adds no significance for those interested in design processes for systems that do not yet exist, processes that have yet to be imagined in a society that has yet to be realized.[5]

[4]Conversations happen in a language, with asynchronicities (conflicts, disagreements, frictions, etc.) being realized in one of the two tracks of language – the descriptive track (differences in understanding of what is said, the relations in the topic at hand) or the orientative track (differences in what 'what is said' does, the dynamics of interaction). I have focused more in this chapter on the cybernetic contribution to the topic of dynamics than to the topic of relations, but they go hand in hand. Often, differences in native languages and cultures, while potential sources of asynchronicity, pose barriers to getting a conversation off the ground at all. Advancing the value of conversation for participation in spite of (or maybe even encouraged by) these differences is, I think, essential to realizing a participative-dialogic society.

[5]Horst Rittel's discussion of and approach to "wicked problems" [20] exhibit parallels to the discussion of and approach to undecidable questions. The problems of social design are certainly in the category of wicked, and Rittel's dialogic approach, including argumentation and debate (and a focus on language), is consistent with the approach here to both social design and design research.

When I know what I want and I know it is possible to achieve it, I do not need cybernetics – I just do what has to be done to achieve the outcome. However, when I only have a vague idea about what I want or do not want and I do not know how to pursue or avoid it in the current society, the vocabulary of cybernetics can be useful. Cybernetics is not about success and the achievement of goals; it is about the reconfiguration of constraints (resources) in order to make possible what was not previously possible, including the avoidance of what was previously inevitable. In other words, cybernetics is about making true what was previously false. One approach to research in this context could be the use of propositions in the form of false statements – that is, statements that are known or assumed to be currently false, but which, if true, would be desirable. The desirability of such propositions then becomes the subject of study.

Examples of currently false statements to study could include: (1) The technology of societal decision-making never discourages, preferable encourages, the participation of all members of the society in its design, including the design of technologies for decision-making; (2) The control and configuration of world-wide resources are the authority and responsibility of all humans; (3) Reconfigurations of resources are treated as preferable to maintaining the *status quo* if they would increase alternatives and/or choices for most humans (where "most" needs to be defined, but it is definitely not "the few"); and, (4) There are no social organizations in our society structured as stable hierarchies, and individuals in any temporary hierarchies receive no rewards by virtue of their positions in those hierarchies.

These are admittedly examples of grand propositions; the approach could also be used with much more specific aspects of a system. For example: A blue spruce tree, 5 ft in height, is planted 25 ft in front of the first floor window to the right of the main entrance of Building X. If determined to be desirable, the statement would likely be formulated as a goal; however, in the deliberations concerning desirability, alternative possibilities might arise with the result being formulated as a set of constraints in the form of rules or principles within which the occupants of the building would have some flexibility in the choice of tree, its size and position. The units of analysis for research on false statements are the conversations on desirability – their dynamics and facilitation. For grand propositions on designing a society, the form of the conversations becomes indistinguishable from the society being designed: What form of conversation in the current society (and its language) would lead to a society in which these conversations would be the norm rather than the outlier?

15.8 Conclusion: The Necessity of Design

For those interested in the well-being, even survival, of humanity, design is a necessity. In addition to the need to propagate the human species, design satisfies the need for participation. Even with a participatory approach to design, there are no guarantees. Some may argue that further human intervention in the biology of the world can only aggravate negatively the sustainability of that world and the human ability to survive in it: we simply need to get out of the way and let nature do what it does. Others, including me, argue that it is too late; the technologies now available for human use cannot be reversed. Using Wiener's metaphor, [35, pp. 251–254], once the genie ("djinnee") is out of the bottle she cannot be put back. The technologies we possess are a consequence of human intention; we now need to direct that attribute – human intention – toward a society in which human sustainability and well-being are conserved. This requires a different way of thinking or, more precisely, a way of thinking about ways of thinking so that all ways of thinking can be brought to bear on the design of that society, and we are not caught up, without awareness, in the prevailing or default way. That is, the way of thinking becomes a choice. Cybernetics offers a vocabulary for this way of thinking.

A participatory process of designing a society is a part of the society being designed.[6] Some might say that the process of designing a society is the society. For such a process to work in the interests of all members of the society, the uniqueness of every individual would be recognized and respected as a contribution. Some participants will have special skills in certain aspects of designing, while others will have other skills and attributes of value. When participants are called on to apply their unique skills, they would exhibit generosity toward others and the desires of others. All participants would look forward to making their needs and desires known so that they could be satisfied or revised; among those desires would be the desire for the desires of others to be satisfied. This self-referential approach toward the design of social systems, where the designers are a part of the system being designed, implies that designing a society is an ongoing process, a process not only of incremental modification but also of frequent social transformation.

The participative-dialogic (and self-referential) approach to design could apply to all types of design in a society that embraces social transformation, and the opportunities for research into such processes are many. However, experimental research in the traditional scientific sense is limited by the purposeful (goal-oriented) and hierarchical (reward-oriented) way of thinking that dominates the current society and its language, and that would be carried by the subjects of such research. Hypothetically, subjects could be taught an alternative way of thinking before participating in an experiment. Of course, this risks turning the research into a self-fulfilling prophecy – you teach people a different way of thinking about design and then they design differently. The more useful research questions are in the undecidable category, like: Would this recursive design process be desirable, not necessarily in the current society, but in a society designed by it? Is it necessary to compare the current society with an imagined one, or would our inclination to retain a *status quo* with which we have come to cope restrict the alternatives we might

[6]I do not address a specific approach to participatory design here. There are a number of possibilities. The approach I have been exploring for the past few years is Stafford Beer's team syntegrity [7]. While somewhat complicated to implement and rigid in appearance, it is non-hierarchical and facilitates conversation. I am interested in how it might be simplified, given a more flexible "feel" and adapted to large-scale application. Klaus Krippendorff's human-centered design [14], with a focus on language and culture, also deserves mention.

imagine? Or, is a new society inevitable, leaving the more important question: how can we, working together or as individuals, make a difference in what constitutes the new one?

The form of experiment for addressing these types of question might involve building into the design process the systematic collection of responses to them – that is, the design process becomes a research process (and vice versa). Furthermore, when we do not know how well a design will work until we do it, building into such designs the ability to alter them quickly, to address the research findings we uncover as we proceed, makes some sense, even if it eliminates some designs from further consideration. Whether or not most people would prefer living in (while participating in the design of) such a world remains to be seen.

15.9 Postscript

An utopia is, by definition, a state of society that cannot be achieved; if perchance an imagined utopia was to be achieved, it would no longer be utopian, as an utopia cannot be achieved and a new one would take its place. This does not preclude the desirability of seeking an utopian concept, and the approach to social design presented in this chapter has utopian intentions. In fact, I do not know why anyone would engage in imagining an alternative society with intentions other than utopian. That such an alternative might not be practical or even possible when viewed from the current society (and its language) is precisely why it is important to engage in the process. An imagined alternative society can be formulated as a false statement, a statement currently false (not possible) which, if true (possible), would be desirable. And, that's when cybernetics is needed: to reconfigure resources (constraints) to make possible that which is not currently possible – a new way of thinking. The idea of a participative-dialogic society is one such alternative, although it differs from most utopian concepts in a few fundamental ways: (1) it does not seek harmony in human relations: ongoing conflict is essential to the concept, where conflict is met by conversation rather than violence; (2) the participatory process of designing a society is a part of the society being designed – the process cannot be participative except in a participative society, a self-referential process; and, (3) the concept is not driven by an ideology, a set of beliefs about what would be desirable; rather, it is driven by the continually changing desires/passions of the participants and their interactions.

In this chapter, I have proposed that a world without violence could provide sufficient agreement on desires to serve as a starting point for conversations on desirability. Since I define participation in terms of choice and violence, and designing a society in terms of participation, a breakdown in any part of this formulation could compromise the entire approach to social design. The part about which I am most concerned is the assumption of alternatives and human choice, as this places humans separate from nature (where the idea of choice is not relevant). Human participants, capable of self-awareness and reflection, can choose to resist anti-social tendencies and treat the interests of others as their own. And, after all, there would be no concept of design without choice, and this book is about design.

References

1. Allison, G. T. (1971). *Essence of decision*. Boston: Little, Brown.
2. Ashby, W. R. (1956). *An introduction to cybernetics*. London: Chapman & Hall.
3. Ashby, W. R. (1964). Constraint analysis of many-dimensional relations. *General Systems, IX*, 99–105.
4. Bateson, G. (1972). Cybernetic explanation. In *Steps to an ecology of mind* (pp. 405–416). Chicago: University of Chicago Press.
5. Bateson, G. (1972). Conscious purpose versus nature. In *Steps to an ecology of mind* (pp. 432–445). Chicago: University of Chicago Press.
6. Bateson, G. (1972). Effects of conscious purpose on human adaption. In *Steps to an ecology of mind* (pp. 446–453). Chicago: University of Chicago Press.
7. Beer, S. (1994). *Beyond dispute: The invention of team syntegrity*. Chichester: John Wiley.
8. Braybrooke, D., & Lindblom, C. E. (1963). *A strategy of decision: Policy evaluation as a social process*. London: The Free Press.
9. Brün, H. (1990). *My words and where I want them* (2nd ed.). London: Princelet Editions.
10. Brün, M., & respondents. (1985). *Designing society*. London: Princelet Editions.
11. Brün, M. (2004). Paradigms: The inertia of language. In A. Chandra (Ed.), *When music resists meaning: The major writings of Herbert Brün* (pp. 292–300). Middletown: Wesleyan University Press.
12. Fischer, T., & Richards, L. D. (2017). From goal-oriented to constraint-oriented design: The cybernetic intersection of design theory and systems theory. *Leonardo, 50*(1), 36–41.
13. Glanville, R. (2014). Try again. Fail again. Fail better – The cybernetics in design and the design in cybernetics. In *The black boox vol. 2: Living in cybernetic circles* (pp. 253–292). Vienna: edition echoraum.
14. Krippendorff, K. (2006). *The semantic turn: A new foundation for design*. Boca Raton: Taylor and Francis.
15. Lindblom, C. E. (1959). The science of 'muddling through'. *Public Administration Review, XIX*(Spring), 79–88.
16. Lindblom, C. E. (1965). *The intelligence of democracy*. London: The Free Press.
17. Lombardi, J. (2007). *Peace is a need – Passions presentation*. Text and video available at: http://jlombardi.net/pdf/peaceisaneed_passions.pdf. Accessed 19 Jan 2019.
18. Maturana, H. (1988). Reality: The search for objectivity or the quest for a compelling argument. *Irish Journal of Psychology, 9*(1), 25–82.
19. Pask, G. (1987). *Conversation and support*. Inaugural Address presented Nov 30, 1987 at the occasion of assuming responsibility as guest professor in General Andragological Sciences. University of Amsterdam, The Netherlands.
20. Protzen, J.-P., & Harris, D. J. (2010). *The universe of design: Horst Rittel's theories of design and planning*. London: Routledge.
21. Richards, L. D. (1991). Beyond planning: Technological support for a desirable society. *Systemica, 8*(2), 113–124.
22. Richards, L. D. (2010). The anticommunication imperative. *Cybernetics and Human Knowing, 17*(1–2), 11–24.
23. Richards, L. D. (2013). Difference-making from a cybernetic perspective: The role of listening and its circularities. *Cybernetics and Human Knowing, 20*(1/2), 59–68.
24. Richards, L. D. (2013). Idea avoidance: Reflections on a conference and its language. *Kybernetes, 42*(9/10), 1464–1469.

25. Richards, L. D. (2015). Designing academic conferences in the light of second order cybernetics. *Constructivist Foundations, 11*(1), 65–73.
26. Richards, L. (2016). A history of the history of cybernetics: An agenda for an ever-changing present. *Cybernetics and Human Knowing, 23*(1), 42–49.
27. Rosenbleuth, A., Wiener, N., & Bigelow, J. (1943). Behavior, purpose, and teleology. *Philosophy of Science, 10*, 18–24.
28. Schön, D. A. (1983). *The reflective practitioner: How professionals think in action*. New York: Basic Books.
29. Simon, H. A. (1964). On the concept of organizational goal. *Administrative Science Quarterly, 9*, 1–22.
30. Simon, H. A. (1969). *The sciences of the artificial*. Cambridge, MA: The MIT Press.
31. Steinbruner, J. D. (1974). *The cybernetic theory of decision*. Princeton: Princeton University Press.
32. von Foerster, H. (2003). Perception of the future and the future of perception. In *Understanding understanding: Essays on cybernetics and cognition* (pp. 199–210). New York: Springer.
33. von Foerster, H. (2003). Ethics and second-order cybernetics. In *Understanding understanding: Essays on cybernetics and cognition* (pp. 287–304). New York: Springer.
34. Whorf, B. L. (1956). The relation of habitual thought and behavior to language. In J. B. Carroll (Ed.), *Language, thought, and reality* (pp. 134–159). Cambridge, MA: The MIT Press.
35. Wiener, N. (1954). *The human use of human beings: Cybernetics and society* (2nd ed.). New York: Avon Books.
36. Wiener, N. (1961). *Cybernetics, or control and communication in the animal and the machine* (2nd ed.). Cambridge, MA: The MIT Press.
37. Winograd, T., & Flores, F. (1986). *Understanding computers and cognition: A new foundation for design*. Norwood: Ablex Publishing.

Laurence D. Richards, Professor Emeritus of Management and Informatics at Indiana University, used his 32 years in higher education administration to experiment with ideas in systems, cybernetics and organizational design and change. Klaus Krippendorff and Shiv Gupta mentored him at the University of Pennsylvania, where he studied cybernetics and operations research. Gordon Pask and Herbert Brün introduced him to conversation theory and the role of the arts in society. His interactions with participants in the School for Designing a Society (Urbana, Illinois) further influenced his thinking.

Chapter 16
Design Cybernetics: Concluding Remarks From a Semi-external Perspective

Wolfgang Jonas

Abstract The editors of this anthology have invited me to write a synthesis, which should relate the texts to each other and discuss them with respect to the general design research discourse. Most contributions are closely leaning on Pask and Glanville. Building on Pask, Glanville conceives the design process as a conversation that the designer holds with objects, with him/herself or with others. Two basic traits of the approach become apparent that limit the approach: First, the largely personal character of the conversation; the ideal constellation consists of two people present, talking to each other. Second, the harmonic tendency towards consensus in conversations, even if the constructivist character of generating individual meaning is emphasized. My concluding essay contextualises and situates design cybernetics within the harsh and unfriendly environment of present-day digitized global capitalism, which is excessively exploiting the unlimited potential of so-called social media. Based on this and taking into account the feedback of the contributing authors I formulate some concerns regarding the deficits of current second-order cybernetics and design cybernetics. The critique can be concentrated on the missing of an advanced systemic social theory and focuses on three topics: systems, communication and evolution. Furthermore, I suggest to work out the necessarily political character of design cybernetics. In a final section I reflect on the issue of rigour and/or relevance in design cybernetics.

Keywords Second-order cybernetics · Strengths and weaknesses · Critique · Contextualization

16.1 Summary and Introduction

In 2015, a group of researchers describing themselves as "mid-career academics" decided to celebrate Ranulph Glanville's outstanding contributions to design and cybernetics with an edited collection of their own Glanville-inspired work (Thomas

W. Jonas (✉)
Braunschweig University of Art, Braunschweig, Germany
e-mail: w.jonas@hbk-bs.de

T. Fischer, C. M. Herr (eds.), *Design Cybernetics*, Design Research Foundations,
https://doi.org/10.1007/978-3-030-18557-2_16

Fischer and Christiane M. Herr, in the Preface). The contributors are dealing with "the (designed) meta-world of second-order cybernetics," as Claudia Westermann aptly denotes the joint endeavour. Nucleus and starting point, and at the same time integrating bracket for the various contributions, are the personality as well as the academic position and perspective of Ranulph Glanville. Both are inseparable.

Most of the texts are closely leaning on Pask and Glanville. The editors of the anthology have kindly invited me to write a summary, synthesis, and conclusion, which should refer to the texts, relate them to each other and discuss them with respect to the general design research discourse. This is a privileged and at the same time responsible and very challenging task. Many of the authors, as far as I know, have been students of Glanville. I have not been a student, but an almost equal-aged friend and admirer of Ranulph Glanville. In this sense, taking a "semi-external perspective" means that I allow myself some critical comments on the positions presented.

Glanville's paper "Try Again. Fail Again. Fail Better – the Cybernetics in Design and the Design in Cybernetics" [11] (see Chap. 2 in this collection) marks the position in a comprehensive manner. Building on Pask, Glanville conceives the design process as a circular conversation that the designer holds with objects, with him/herself or with others. In the most generic version, the conversation consists of making a mark with a pencil on paper (talking in a verbal conversation), and then looking at it to see what the mark suggests (listening in a verbal conversation) and, consequently, modifying the drawing (the further conversation). The process goes on and on in a potentially endless cycle. An essential characteristic is the non-representational, constructivist and thus generative character of the process [11, p. 1185]:

> No meaning, no understanding is sent from one participant to the other: the meanings we acquire as we build understandings are ours alone. This is an enormous strength of the conversational model of communication.

Despite much original substance the collection of texts lacked what I would call a rigorous, critical, self-critical and prospective element. Two basic, possibly limiting, principles of the approach become apparent: (1) The largely personal character of the conversation; the ideal constellation consists of two people present, talking to each other. (2) The harmonic tendency towards consensus in conversations, even if the social or radical constructivist character of generating individual meaning is emphasized.

Having tried to develop my reflective chapter in parallel with the authors' work, some critiques I raised in an earlier version of this chapter led the respective authors to amend their work, without entirely dispelling my concerns. Therefore, I proposed to have one more feedback cycle in order to conduct another critical discussion on design cybernetics, with an explicit view to flaws, shortcomings, blind spots, possible reservations and necessary future work. My contribution now can be seen as an attempt at a contemporary contextualisation and critique of the positions. It should not be conceived as a final evaluation from above, but as another reflection step, inspired by the texts and hopefully enriching the discussion and driving it further.

The urgent task ahead of us might be characterised as the continuous development of the delicate "plant" second-order cybernetics within the harsh and unfriendly context of digitized global capitalism. Design conversation "beyond the cozy confines of the design team, is a more adversarial and competitive process," as Timothy Jachna states on page 228 in this collection.

16.2 Big Expectations: And Emerging Doubts

The past, the present and the future development of second-order cybernetics are closely related to computing and the ubiquitous process of digitalization, not only in a technological sense, but especially in the social and cultural dimensions of the phenomenon. Dubberly and Pangaro [7] comprehensively report the close interrelations in the development of cybernetics, computing, counterculture, and design, beginning in and after the Second World War up to the present. They argue for the essential role of cybernetic thinking in overcoming the conflicts of our time and conclude, in a text from the year 2015, in a surprisingly optimistic tone [7, p. 10]:

> In the past twenty years, design has begun to catch up with cybernetics. Design practice has become enmeshed in systems and ecologies. Collaboration and transdisciplinarity have become key themes. What's more, we now recognize that the major issues the world faces – the issues that really matter – are all systems issues. They are wicked problems, which means they are essentially political in nature and cannot be 'solved' by experts. We are, in Rittel's phrase, enmeshed in a 'symmetry of ignorance'. The only way forward is through conversation. These facts make cybernetics newly relevant, because it offers tools and models, as it did at the Macy Conferences – for grappling with systems issues and the unknowable 'messes' that confront us – a *lingua franca* of design. As Pask noted: 'Human interaction is a major source of difficulties which can only be overcome by cybernetic thinking.'

Almost 20 years ago, John Chris Jones [17, p. 407] had introduced the Internet-based notion of 'creative democracy' and presented a vision of the future "in which the controlling roles and functions of modern life could be shared with everyone [. . .] a virtual planet earth [. . .] an expanded version of the internet through which 'universal despecialisation' and 'creative democracy' and other such unexpected conditions are already implicit if not active."

Glanville (no year) argues similarly, that "the computer age we now live in is the era of second order Cybernetics". Richards (Chap. 15 in this volume) refers to current social media technology and claims that "The prospect of giving access to all currently best available knowledge to all people in the world can now be imagined [. . .] Conversations among people worldwide, through the technology, are now possible."

This sounds very optimistic and promising. Richards is definitely right: current social media provide the technical infrastructure for unlimited conversation. But we have to ask: what about the risks of these fully "conversational" social media?

WIRED, a magazine that has its roots in the counterculture addressed above by Dubberly and Pangaro, but more or less changed into a technology-affirmative mainstream publication, recently published a critical article entitled "How Silicon Valley Utopianism Brought You the Dystopian Trump Presidency" [27].

> At least since the 1960s, the computer – and, beyond that, the Internet – has been a symbol and tool of personal liberation. Stewart Brand called the computer revolution 'the real legacy of the sixties' – an outgrowth of the 'counterculture's scorn for centralized authority'. The ideology was codified by WIRED alum Steven Levy in his book *Hackers* [18, pp. 39ff.], in which he summarized the Hacker Ethic:
>
> a) Access to computers should be unlimited and total.
> b) All information should be free.
> c) Mistrust authority – promote decentralization.
> d) You can create art and beauty on a computer.
> e) Computers can change your life for the better.
>
> These precepts inspired a worldview that saw institutions and middlemen as malign forces that mostly constrained human potential, and that placed unlimited faith in unshackled individuals to improve the world and their own lives. For much of the past three decades, that philosophy has borne out. It has become an unspoken truism of corporate and civic life.
>
> But Trump's inauguration provides a damning counterargument, an example of how each of those ideas can be exploited to advance the very values they were created to oppose. Universal access to computers created a greater audience for Trump's culture-jamming Twitter feed. An outpouring of free information sowed confusion and created cover for half- and untruths. Trump used anti-authoritarian rhetoric to sow mistrust of the very institutions that might have provided a firewall against his own authoritarian tendencies. Democratizing the tools of creative production created not just ennobling art but a million shitposts and Pepe memes.
>
> In designing to maximize engagement, social networks inadvertently created hives of bias-confirmation and tribalism.
>
> This is the world the tech industry now faces, a world – at least in part – of its own creation. The machinery and language of personal liberation have been colonized and subverted by the very forces they were intended to topple. By all accounts, governmental doublespeak, authoritarian intrusion, and state-sponsored surveillance promise to define the coming era. Americans may be able to resist these trends – maybe by reclaiming the technological forces that have carried the country this far. But Americans also now know that's not enough. The tech industry has achieved negative freedom. The question now is: What do people do now?

And the tech industry is being prompted to react. Mark Zuckerberg's text "Building Global Community" [29] – some euphemistically call it a 'humanitarian manifesto' – addresses the above mentioned issues and asks the big question: "are we building the world we all want?" And he continues (highlighted in the text): "In times like these, the most important thing we at Facebook can do is develop the social infrastructure to give people the power to build a global community that works for all of us." After having focused on connecting friends and families, "our next focus will be developing the social infrastructure for community – for supporting us, for keeping us safe, for informing us, for civic engagement, and for inclusion of all." Zuckerberg [29] names the problems very clearly and apparently affected, somehow:

> The two most discussed concerns this past year were about diversity of viewpoints we see (filter bubbles) and accuracy of information (fake news). I worry about these and we have

> studied them extensively, but I also worry there are even more powerful effects we must mitigate around sensationalism and polarization leading to a loss of common understanding.

And he presents the targeted countermeasures, again technology-driven, as was to be expected:

> The approach is to combine creating a large-scale democratic process to determine standards with AI to help enforce them. [. . .] It's worth noting that major advances in AI are required to understand text, photos and videos to judge whether they contain hate speech, graphic violence, sexually explicit content, and more. At our current pace of research, we hope to begin handling some of these cases in 2017, but others will not be possible for many years.

This is a frightening and at the same time naïve understanding of dealing with human individuality, stubbornness, manipulability, herd mentality and with the essentially autopoietic and chaotic nature of social dynamics and communication. In order to overcome these mentioned problems Zuckerberg introduces a kind of "3rd order cybernetics," observing the chaotic and at times destructive second-order processes in the social media. 'Smart' autonomous agents exercise control, detect and eradicate improper contributions. This sounds a bit like establishing a higher-order observer, but in fact this third-order observation collapses into another blunt first-order mechanism of control. At best one might denote it as the presumption of a benevolent, godlike position. Yet, normally, it will be plain "Big Brother" manipulation for commercial or political purposes. The *Cambridge Analytica* case [28], the deliberate manipulation of citizens' voting behaviour during the Trump campaign, appears merely as the tip of an iceberg.

By the way: Regarding 'smart' agents and their limits, see Delfina Fantini van Ditmar's Chap. 5 in this volume.

16.3 A Feedback Cycle with the Authors

Against the background of these above critical considerations, which I do not consider as transient or even zeitgeisty-fashionable, but as symptomatic of what awaits us in the near future. We see the beginning of an agonistic, if not antagonistic, confrontation of digitized neo-liberal financial market-driven global capitalism with a growing public awareness of the downsides of this development, which has long been described as having no alternatives. "Populist," reactionary and identitarian positions are merely symptoms of this confrontation. All parties use the "social" media for their own purposes, the "enlightened" public, the "seduced" public, as well as the "controllers" (*Facebook*, *Google*, etc.). Trust in consensus through conversation appears naïve in this chaotic situation, to say the least.

I decided to feed back my growing concerns to the authors, suggesting to conduct a critical discussion on design cybernetics, with special attention to flaws, shortcomings, blind spots, possible reservations and necessary future work. I asked the authors to consider the following questions:

- Which aspect(s) of your chapter do you think would be hardest for you to argue and defend if it were challenged by an outsider?
- Which aspect(s) of design cybernetics, as it stands today, do you think would be hardest for you to argue and defend if it were challenged by an outsider?
- Do you think this weakness/these weaknesses can be overcome? If so, what would be the necessary future work to do so?

The summarized answers have been as follows:

Delfina Fantini van Ditmar demonstrates in her experiment that by bringing the observer and circularity into the discussion, it became clear that users of 'smart' devices should be given responsibility for making sense of their data. Yet she sees the weakness that *design cybernetics stays in theory*, that there are not enough projects that are able to demonstrate the practical benefits of the approach. In order to overcome this deficit she makes the vague suggestion that "a systematic and constructivist culture needs to be established (this might take some time). I believe that by developing and disseminating research, design cybernetics eventually will produce a solid field."

Christiane M. Herr points to the radical constructivist epistemological basis of design cybernetics, which is focussed very much on the individual. With designing being a *social and cultural activity*, "it is perhaps strange how a seemingly individualistic epistemology could accommodate these aspects." Herr admits that the benefit of design cybernetics to practical design is not yet evident. Therefore, building on e.g. von Glasersfeld, more work is required in "analysing the ways in which humans do this, alone or in groups."

Michael Hohl refers to the (unintended) impression that "in the past everything was better," which he fears his text might provoke with his readers. He criticizes that too often underlying values remain implicit: "What are our ethics and beliefs? Did we ever make them explicit?" As the great challenge for design cybernetics he identifies "the ability to converse with people from different camps and backgrounds. [. . .] *Democracy is hard work if not a kind of battle*. Finding consensus is hard work. The ability to listen. To be able to live with states of ambiguity, unclarity, and not resolve it quickly."

Klaus Krippendorff criticizes the unclear and, in his view, sometimes inappropriate and limiting epistemological basis (cognitivist, individual, representational, descriptive) of design cybernetics and focuses on active intervention and change: "Humberto Maturana, as a biologist has no intention to design living organisms and insisted on its descriptions. Ernst von Glasersfeld was a cognitivist with minimal attention to anything social, and Heinz von Forester always talked of observers describing their observations. I hope to have shown the untenability of these conceptions for design. Design intervenes in what exists, changes observations. It needs to plan and encourage actions."

Laurence D. Richards finds it difficult to argue for the cybernetic idea that "time is a human invention and can be manipulated through design." In a capitalist society, "the employment of design cybernetics in the interest of participative democracy must be carried out behind the scenes, covertly, with the hope of a change of system motivating such an approach." But he doesn't regard this as a weakness, but as an opportunity: "Hence, in the current society *cybernetics turns design into a political activity*." And he sees the greatest opportunities in the arts and artistic activities.

Tom Scholte concedes that "ethically desirable processes of creation do not necessarily equal 'good' art." And he admits openly "that *the evangelizing tendency* that has prompted this very set of questions is one of the field's chief problems." He goes as far as stating that design cybernetics runs the risk of creating a *"straw-man-argument"*, especially in comparing design and science: "The experimental process 'as done' is already fundamentally conversational in its unfolding and does not require a body of cybernetic theory to make it so." He asks for "demonstratively different and positive results; not just in terms of ethics but also in terms of pure design functionality."

Ben Sweeting asks quite frankly "how other possible bridging theories – e.g. phenomenology, deconstruction, feminism, STS – might be more complete, or might complement each other." Its *abstraction* is second-order cybernetics' greatest strength and greatest weakness: "cybernetics explains a little about everything but never everything about anything – and where this is not kept in mind it risks deteriorating into the technocracy it should be critiquing." In order to re-introduce the human body, as opposed to the cognitivist focus of most cybernetic theory, he suggests "some bridge building between second-order cybernetics and feminism, with feminist approaches used to critique the abstraction of second-order cybernetics."

Claudia Westermann argues that design cybernetics and second-order cybernetics should be more explicitly introduced as poetics and as a way of being in the world. Because of its *anti-capitalist* character it "is too generous to be a way to 'success'. [. . .] I could also argue that this attitude is the only one that would deserve the label sustainable as it does not restrict the future." Her suggestions regarding future work to overcome the deficits are remarkable and significant: "I actually do not think it should be overcome. *The weakness is its strength*. It must be weak in the sense of a lover being weak/exposed." Surprisingly, Westermann also considers the question of how to make second-order cybernetics more fashionable, for example by recruiting advocates: "Sloterdijk, for example? [. . .] Not everyone likes Sloterdijk. On the other hand, the Habermas fans and alike would not read us anyway."

Thomas Fischer identifies a weakness in what can be interpreted as him pandering to, and as recommending to acquiescently prioritise, empiricist (i.e. realist) rather than designerly and cybernetic criteria to expedite the defensibility of postgraduate and PhD design research. He wants to promote the increasing of numbers of options to choose from, rather than lines of least resistance. For him design cybernetics is about empowering people to generate new options, which "is *immediately political*, and often not welcome due to its potential to undermine hierarchies and frameworks of control". Fischer describes his personal mission as to "build and protect islands that operate cybernetically, and show that they can be good places."

16.4 Deficits and Blind Spots of Second-Order Cybernetics

The above feedback and reflections from the authors turned out to be very productive. They confirm the discomfort with some of the texts, which I had expressed at the beginning, in particular the personal character of the conversational concept and the harmonic tendency towards consensus in conversations. At the same time they soothe my fears of doing wrong to the authors, since some of them deliberately share many of my critical assessments. They very frankly address these and other issues, such as the implicit but never explicitly formulated and justified political and social relevance, the chic but unsubstantiated anticapitalist attitude, the subliminal evangelizing tendency, the risk of creating epistemological and methodological straw-man-arguments in contrasting design and science practices, the degree of abstraction and the lack of practical relevance, etc. A further issue is the techno-affirmative, yet reflected, attitude presented by Liss C. Werner (on page 81 in this volume): "In my kind of romantic and at the same time technical understanding I envisage – and it is possible that at the time Gordon Pask did, too – a highly adaptive super-architecture, where matter in space is replaced with bits in time, and atoms amend their structural properties through absorbing bits." Which results in a bright vision, focussing on the enabling and participatory aspects of the *digital turn*: "Including the human in the loop, and integrating human feedback into "smart" digital systems will be the next step towards integrated *Design Cybernetics*" (page 80 in this volume).

My critique can be summarized as the missing of an advanced and appropriate systemic social theory. Dubberly and Pangaro's text (Chap. 4 in this volume) appears to be symptomatic in a way: they largely reduce systems thinking and systems theory to the closed, technocratic approach of *System Dynamics* and suggest, that (social) complexity is manageable in an algorithmic manner. Mikulecky's following definition of complexity seems much more adequate [20]:

> Complexity is the property of a real world system that is manifest in the inability of any one formalism being adequate to capture all its properties. It requires that we find distinctly different ways of interacting with systems. Distinctly different in the sense that when we make successful models, the formal systems needed to describe each distinct aspect are NOT derivable from each other.

Therefore, I propose to relate second-order cybernetics to Niklas Luhmann's [19] sociological systems theory, with a special focus on three topics: systems in an autopoietic understanding, communication as a process of triple selection, and evolution as the contextual condition. Furthermore, I suggest to contextualise second-order cybernetics politically, i.e. to relate it to current debates of design and the political or the social, respectively.

16.4.1 Systems Theory as Societal Theory

Glanville refers to Maturana's and Varela's concept of autopoiesis, which provides an explanation of the processes of life, as a second-order cybernetic system. However, he applies the concept of autopoiesis in a metaphorical way to the design process and to its outcome, the constant object, and not, as one might expect, to the designers or inquiring systems or social systems in general. Glanville (on page 50 of this volume) argues: “Thus, our designs are like our children, which grow to become their own persons.” The fuzziness and ambiguity of Glanville’s position with respect to autopoiesis becomes apparent in Footnote 32: “I am not yet certain, myself, whether the progress by which the autopoietic system generates itself is in a manner similar to the progress of the design process.”

Luhmann [19] argues, disturbing for many, that humans are not the basic entities of the social, but that humans consist of a hybrid conglomerate of three types of causally de-coupled autopoietic systems: bodies (living systems), consciousnesses (psychic systems) and communications (social systems). “Causally de-coupled” means that they cannot specifically influence or even control each other, but they just irritate each other, reactions being determined by the respective systemic structures. Social, psychic and living systems are operationally closed in that while they use and rely on resources from their environment, those resources do not become part of the systems’ operation. Psychic and social systems are structurally coupled by means of language. Functioning communication is unlikely, therefore consensus and harmony are rare phenomena in social situations. And one may ask: what comes after consensus? Even more disturbing in Luhmann’s very theory: societies do not consist of humans but of communications.

16.4.2 Communication Theory

Timothy Jachna (on page 228 of this collection) is one of the few contributors, who addresses these critical issues, at least to some extent. He argues that design conversation “beyond the cozy confines of the design team, is a more adversarial and competitive process”. I fully agree; and even the design team is rarely a cozy place. Second-order cybernetics describes conversation mainly as interaction between participants who are present in a situation, which is the ideal mode of mutual reciprocity. Pask [22] elaborates on “The limits of togetherness” under the conditions of unlimited communication. He differentiates conversation (concept sharing, aiming at agreement) and communication (signal transfer, aiming at true/false attributions). The possibility of communication, in the technical understanding of Shannon and Weaver [25], is undoubtedly the necessary condition for conversation, but the possibility of communication is not at all the sufficient condition for functioning conversation.

Luhmann’s [19] theory is based on the assumption that social systems consist of communications, and society is the most encompassing social system. Being the social system that comprises all (and only) communication, today’s society is a world society. Communication is characterized as a circular pattern of three basic steps, each of them a selection: information – utterance – understanding. Ego, the sender, selects a piece of information and transfers it into an utterance of his/her choice.

Alter, the receiver, is responsible for his/her understanding, i.e. s/he understands or misunderstands the utterance and eventually continues the communication. The criterion according to which information is selected and processed is meaning (in German: *Sinn*). Both social systems and psychic systems operate by processing meaning, whether based on understanding or misunderstanding. The autopoietic closure of social and psychic systems results in the delicate phenomenon of 'double contingency': ego as well as alter find themselves in the situation of contingency regarding their further acting in the communicative system. Convergence towards some stable Eigenvalue or even towards consensus is not the normal case.

Jürgen Habermas, the other great German social philosopher, with his friendly normative concept of power-free public discourse, is much more popular in the Anglo-Saxon community than Niklas Luhmann, with his "cold" descriptive theory. Habermas' position [13], however, seems more and more to be a desperate appeal to reason, rather than a realistic description of social communication. Critics argue that a public sphere as a place of purely rational independent debate never existed. Evolutionary theory elements seem to be helpful for further understanding.

16.4.3 Evolutionary Theory

Socio-cultural development may be conceived as a circular, blind, evolutionary process without any goal, consisting of the three steps variation–selection–re-stabilization. Social systems can change their own structures only by evolution. Evolution presupposes self-referential reproduction and changes the structural condition of reproduction by differentiating mechanisms for variation, selection, and re-stabilization. It feeds upon deviations from normal reproduction. Such deviations are in general accidental but in the case of social systems may be intentionally produced/designed. Yet, conscious design activities are limited episodes within this ongoing process, design interventions can be characterized as the evolutionary variations. There is only limited control over the selection- and re-stabilization processes, which means that the longer-term success of a design intervention is highly uncertain.

Evolution normally operates without a fixed goal and without foresight. It may bring about systems of higher complexity; it may in the long run transform improbable events into probable ones and an observer may see this as "progress," if his/her own self-referential procedures persuade him/her to do so. Only the theory of evolution can explain the structural transformation in history from segmentation to stratification to functional differentiation, which has led to present-day world society. And again, only observers may see this as progress. Systemic complexity, as addressed in Sects. 16.4.1 and 16.4.2 above, and evolutionary unpredictability as the basic conditions of any kind of design heavily challenge any well-intentioned and goal-directed designerly endeavours. I have formulated this fundamental reservation in various publications as the problem of control and the problem of prediction [15, 16].

16.4.4 Design Cybernetics and the Political

The above discussions question the potential of design cybernetics, at least in its current theoretical-methodological constitution. If we consider second-order cybernetics and design cybernetics as a theory and methodology and an attitude to change things in society for the better, then we have to go further and thoroughly reflect and debate design's agencies at the intersection of bottom up processes, public institutions and formalized politics. The political theory distinguishes between politics – *Politik* – *la politique* and the political – *das Politische* – *le politique*. In the German political theory discourse there is the notion of the "political difference," which explicates the distinction: *Politics* means a narrow operational concept and refers to politics as a social functional system (e.g. state, government, parties, parliamentary routines, etc.) dealing with the question of how to organize politics and how this organization can be justified. On the other hand, the broad concept of *the political* points to philosophical questions about the nature of the political and deals with the political dimension of the social. Therefore, the political is an essential category for reflection on design cybernetics.

Two tradition lines can be distinguished in the concept of the political (Mouffe [21]): the associative and the dissociative line, which can be related to Hannah Arendt and Carl Schmitt, respectively. Arendt formulates an associative theory of the political, which defines the political as a free, communicative space of co-operation, whereas Schmitt, on the other hand, emphasizes the dissociative aspect, which conceives the political as an area of power and conflict. The autonomy of the political as opposed to other areas of the social is central in the associative concept. Arendt finds this authentic character in communicative moments of 'acting in concert' and 'acting together', which can easily be related to second-order cybernetic positions in this volume. The dissociative concept (Carl Schmitt) is based on the notion of *antagonism*, which describes a struggle for dominance in a friend – enemy relation. Design thinker and critic Tony Fry [9] refers very much to Schmitt.

Building on Schmitt, Chantal Mouffe developed the concept of *agonism*: Instead of a friend-enemy relation, the relationship is formulated by the principle of the adversary or the opponent. Opponents recognize the legitimacy of the opponents, without aiming at agreement or consensus. This *agonism* is particularly evident in the struggle of incompatible *hegemonic projects*. The goal here is not the destruction of the opponents as with Carl Schmitt, but the implementation of their own projects. Since the political consists of agonisms, the hegemonic character of social order must be recognized. Obviously human societies are trapped in a perpetual dynamic of conflict and crisis, with modernization at a standstill. The deeply rooted cultural ideology of competition operates as a mode of rationality that underpins the order of domination. The concept of a domination-free discourse (Jürgen Habermas) seems naïve meanwhile. And the neo-liberal notion of the post-political, as put forward by Ulrich Beck and Anthony Giddens, appears to be equally inappropriate [21].

In their sometimes blind search for harmony and world salvation, designers often neglect or ignore the complex nature of human psyche and of social communities with all their stupidity, selfishness, hegemonial struggles and power conflicts. Reports on social design projects often show a naïve worldview in tackling the problems and a frightening triviality in the results (sharing, community, cooperation, etc. as buzzwords). Designers tend to overestimate the effects of the projects and their own contributions. They seem to take for granted that humans are good. Which they are obviously not. Human beings are good and bad and mostly mean (in both meanings of the term). And societies are complex and full of paradox and conflict.

With respect to the political in design there are two important systemic/cybernetic aspects: (1) *Boundary judgement*: how to define the design field in contrast to the context. Or: how do we determine the limits of what we think can be shaped? Which is clearly a question of power and not a question of rational reasoning. Findeli [8] calls this the *scope*, a classical topic of systemic design. (2) *Value orientation*: how to formulate a well-founded, non-trivial ethical attitude. Which is a matter of stakeholder interests and power, again. Findeli [8] speaks of the *stance* in a design project. This relates to Herbert Simons question [26]: "Who is the client?" In his famous Chapter 6 in *The Sciences of the Artificial*, entitled "Social Planning: Designing the Evolving Artifact" he argues that:

> It may seem obvious that all ambiguities should be resolved by identifying the client with the whole society. That would be a clear-cut solution in a world without conflict of interest or uncertainty in professional judgement. [. . .] The members of an organization or a society for whom plans are made are not passive instruments, but are themselves designers who are seeking to use the system to further their own goals.

One may object that in our progressive notion of design plans are not made *for* but *with* people. This simplistic notion of involvement is what Brown et al. [4] address and elaborate in their reflections on the *power relationships between the researcher and the community*. They thoroughly reflect the spectrum between complete separation and complete involvement of the observer, or between first and second order cybernetics and thus contribute to make the designers' role explicit. They distinguish six relational states, which directly affect the quality of the conversational setting in design cybernetics:

- to work *on* a community: observer, external planner
- to work *for* a community: employee
- to work *on behalf* of a community: delegate
- to work *with* a community: partnership
- to work *within* a community: sharing (their values and aims)
- to work *as* a community: belonging to the community

This opens up a continuum between the one extreme of the *Cartesian observer/expert designer* and the other extreme of the *inquiring community*, John Dewey's ideal of epistemic democracy [5]. In the first case we have design as *consultant/contractor* of politics (as in scientific policy advice), developing options, designing narratives, moderating, facilitating decision-making processes for others. Design has no decision competence here, which means that *value conflicts* are likely to occur, which is well-known in the profession. In the second case we have the individual design researcher as a politically and socially acting individual. *Role conflicts* between professional and citizen are likely to occur, which is new and has to be reflected. New role models are emerging: *the citizen designer → the designing citizen*. It seems like we are re-enacting utopias of the 1970s in the digital age? Is this the vanishing of expert cultures, what John Chris Jones [17] called 'creative democracy'? The implications for design cybernetics are unclear.

Design's unquestioned task seems to be to develop options, increase the variety of choices, cultivate the role as scout, agent provocateur, warner, jester, etc. Designing is always oriented towards a future that cannot be known, thus we do not want to restrict but we want to enrich the future. It is up to future humans to decide whether what we create is an enrichment in the sense of being aesthetically potent. It is not for us to decide. Which is – surprise! – very close to Herbert Simon, the notorious positivist [26]:

> A paradoxical, but perhaps realistic, view of design goals is that their function is to motivate activity which in turn will generate new goals. [. . .] Our essential task – a big enough one to be sure – is simply to keep open the options for the future or perhaps even to broaden them a bit by creating new variety and new niches. Our grandchildren cannot ask more of us than that we offer to them the same chance for adventure, for the pursuit of new and interesting design, that we have had.

Back to the present, back to the political. I fully agree with Carl DiSalvo [6], who relates design activity to Chantal Mouffe's [21] political theory of agonism, as described above. All of this perfectly corresponds with Horst Rittel and Melvin Webber's earlier concept of "second generation design" as an argumentative process [23]. Di Salvo [6]:

> Simply stated, the purpose of political design is to do the work of *agonism*. This means first and foremost it does the work of creating spaces for revealing and confronting power relations, i.e., it creates spaces of contest. This occurs both in and through the objects and processes of design: the objects and processes of design are both the site and means of agonistic pluralism.

Unfortunately, most of the above topics remain more or less implicit in the discourse of design cybernetics.

16.5 Design Research: Rigour and Relevance in Cybernetic Design

Discussions about the quality, validity and effectiveness of design research, especially practice-based or project-grounded design research, are frequently focussing on the topics of rigour and relevance: Are the procedures used scientifically rigorous? Are the outcomes relevant? Are these two requirements compatible? Thomas Fischer has treated these issues in a general way in this volume. The question of whether cybernetic design claims to be a scientific research approach should remain open here for the time being.

16.5.1 The Streetlight Effect

There is a story that anyone interested in human knowledge ought to know. It comes in different forms. A version of the joke appeared in the comic strip *Mutt and Jeff*, 1942: A policeman sees a drunken man searching for something under a streetlight and asks what the drunk has lost. He says he lost his keys and they both look under the streetlight together. After a few minutes the policeman asks if he is sure he lost them here, and the drunk replies, no, that he lost them two blocks down the street. The policeman asks why he is searching here, and the drunk replies: 'Because the light is better here!'

Barsky [2, p. 95] reports that Noam Chomsky has a characteristically dry and precise version of the story: "Science is a bit like the joke about the drunk who is looking under a lamppost for a key that he has lost on the other side of the street, because that's where the light is. It has no other choice." Bernstein [3, pp. 48–49] explicitly introduces the problem of *rigour or relevance* as a symptom of the Positivist view of science:

> From this perspective, we tend to see science, after the fact, as a body of established propositions derived from research. When we recognize their limited utility in practice, we experience the dilemma of rigour or relevance. But we may also consider science before the fact as a process in which scientists grapple with uncertainties and display arts of inquiry akin to the uncertainties and arts of practice.

16.5.2 The Swampy Ground

These reflections are not really new in design [14]. Donald Schön's notion of "reflection in/on action" may well be interpreted as a conversation in the sense of second-order cybernetics. Schön [24, p. 42] argues that:

> The dilemma of 'rigor or relevance' arises more acutely in some areas of practice than in others. In the varied topography of professional practice, there is a high, hard ground where practitioners can make effective use of research-based theory and technique, and there is a *swampy lowland* where situations are confusing 'messes' incapable of technical solutions.

Schön emphasizes that the relevant problems of human concern are situated in the swampy lowlands. There are professionals who "deliberately involve themselves in messy but crucially important problems and, when asked to describe their methods of inquiry, they speak of experience, trial and error, intuition, and muddling through" [24, p. 43].

16.5.3 Design as the Practice of Not-Knowing

Sociologist Dirk Baecker [1, own translation] argues that:

> Design as a practice of not-knowing may be read in reference to diverse interfaces, but the interfaces between technology, body, psyche and communication are probably dominant.

> If these 'worlds', each described by a more or less elaborate knowledge, are brought into a relationship of difference, this knowledge disappears and makes room for experiments, which are the experiments of design. [. . .] Not to take anything for granted here anymore, but to see potential of dissolution and recombination everywhere, becomes the playground of a design that eventually reaches into pedagogy, therapy, and medicine.

We conclude from the above considerations that (cybernetic) design does not seem to work "on the hard ground" or "where the light is better". The dilemma of rigour or relevance is the omnipresent condition of designerly action. Ranulph Glanville draws the elegant but controversial consequence of reversing the hierarchic relation between science and design and turning it upside down.

16.5.4 Science as a Subset of Design

Ranulph Glanville [10] argues for the most radical position: to conceive science as design. In his view, (scientific) research, whether experiment or theory, is a design activity. We design experiments and we act as designers in how we act in these experiments. We design the experiences and objects we find through experiment by finding commonalities (this is called simplification). And we design how we assemble them into patterns (leading to explanatory principles, theories). Looking at these patterns, we construct further patterns from them, the theories of our theories. He concludes:

> So the act of design, as we understand and value it, has much to offer as an example of how science and scientific research might be in a new era: an era that designer-readers will recognise as their contemporary paradigm and which is how scientists, when we talk to them, recognise and characterise their own activity. Design, being the more general case, satisfies Occam's razor for simplicity: as Einstein is to Newton, design is to science and scientific research.

Design in Glanville's view is not and should not be considered as scientific in the narrow traditional understanding. On the contrary: design in its cybernetic interpretation as a conversational process, should be regarded as the core "mechanism" of human inquiry, applicable in design as well as in the sciences.

16.5.5 Rigour as an Expression of Honesty

Design cybernetics obviously claims to operate on the relevance side of the distinction between rigour and relevance. Ranulph Glanville finally dissolves the problem of rigour easily and in an anecdotal way [12, p. 295]:

> I was a member of a panel at a conference on "Reflective Practice." We were asked how to handle rigour in reflexive research. The response was shocking: I was howled down by the larger part of the audience because, I was told, humans are not honest – which I had suggested was the key. (Whether or not we are honest has little to do with most arguments

> proposing honesty as a criterion for evaluation.) However, by the end of the session, almost everyone was talking about the need for honesty. Only a few die-hards found they could not see the central importance of honesty, their horizons limited by the overriding obsession that honesty is something humans don't always do very well. In the end my argument had the appealing side-effect that, in winning over the vast majority of the audience, a shift from the knee-jerk reaction that promoted what I think of as the unattractive view of humans-as-bad became possible.

And exactly this, at the same time naïve and liberating visionary belief in human honesty, is the great value of design cybernetics as presented in this volume. Design cybernetics as a moral stance, which cannot be overestimated (however unrealistic it may appear).

16.6 A Personal Conclusion

In a workshop with Ranulph Glanville at Hamburg University in 2004, organized by Bernhard Pörksen and dealing with the question "Is it possible to direct a closed system? Autonomy, manipulation and control in social systems." participants were asked to bring two hypotheses or questions to the discussion. Mine have been the following, which still express my humble concerns about the wonderful, delicate concept of second-order cybernetics:

1. Consciously/deliberately acting as a second-order observer (and being honest in this) weakens your position in debates, negotiations, [. . .]
2. Are there biographical influences, dispositions etc. that promote becoming a second-order observer?

My tentative answers today, about 15 years later, are as follows: (1) Yes, this assumption has been confirmed. Open self-reflection, even self-doubt that necessarily relativizes one's own position, contributes to the weakening in situations of negotiation, whether in academic, business or private contexts. It is highly dependent on the goodwill of an analogous counterpart in order to make productive progress for both parties. (2) This is very likely. It requires a big, stable self-confidence as a basis. And it requires a context, i.e. a social environment that allows non-power dominated conversation. Ranulph Glanville was a charismatic person who probably had the ability to create such productive spaces. Which explains the current book project.

As far as I see cybernetics has remained a fragile niche concept in the general design research discourse, with an exclusive and sometimes slightly esoteric touch. Maybe one may call it an ethical attitude, the practical usefulness of which remains limited. Ranulph Glanville once suggested that cybernetics might become "design's secret partner". Meanwhile I think that design cybernetics needs a strong partner for its survival. This partner might be the advancing and expanding discourse of systems thinking. The subset of cybernetics is well taken care of there.

In their preface Thomas Fischer and Christiane M. Herr express their expectations regarding this anthology: "[. . .] we hope to demonstrate the rigour, quality and potential of design cybernetics, not only in its formal manifestations, but first and foremost in its aesthetic and ethical manifestations in the wider sphere of human judgement and values." This was achieved convincingly, and precisely because it is not about the foundation of a new sub-discipline of design, but rather about a *Festschrift* (in the full and best sense of the word) for a great person.

Design cybernetics should remain an ethical attitude, an un-discipline, acting in the swampy, messy lowlands, aiming at visionary, unexpected outcomes. As Thomas Fischer puts it: Design cybernetics should exploit its "potential to undermine hierarchies and frameworks of control". Or, as Claudia Westermann gets to the point: "The weakness is its strength. It must be weak in the sense of a lover being weak/exposed."

References

1. Baecker, D. (2002). Wie steht es mit dem Willen Allahs? *Zeitschrift für Rechtssoziologie, 21*(1), 145–176.
2. Barsky, R. F. (1998). *Noam Chomsky: A life of dissent*. Cambridge, MA: MIT Press.
3. Bernstein, R. J. (1976). *The restructuring of social and political theory*. New York: Harcourt Brace Jovanovich.
4. Brown, V. A., Harris, J. A., & Russell, J. Y. (2010). *Tackling wicked problems through the transdisciplinary imagination*. London/Washington, DC: Earthscan.
5. Dewey, J. (1916). *Democracy and education*. New York: The Macmillan Company.
6. DiSalvo, C. (2012). *Adversarial design*. Cambridge MA: MIT Press.
7. Dubberly, H., & Pangaro, P. (2015). How cybernetics connects computing, counterculture, and design. In: *Hippie modernism: The struggle for utopia*. Minneapolis: Exhibition catalog, Walker Art Center
8. Findeli, A. (2010). Searching for design research questions. In R. Chow, W. Jonas, & G. Joost (Eds.), *Questions, hypotheses & conjectures. Discussions on projects by early stage and senior design researchers* (pp. 286–303). Bloomington: iUniverse.
9. Fry, T. (2010). *Design as politics*. Oxford: Berg Publishers.
10. Glanville, R. (1980). Why design research? In R. Jacques, & J. A. Powell (Eds.), *Design:science:method*. Guildford: Westbury House. Republished in Ranulph Glanville. (2014). *The black boox, volume II: Living in cybernetic circles* (pp. 111–120). Vienna: edition echoraum.
11. Glanville, R. (2007). Try again. Fail again. Fail better: The cybernetics in design and the design in cybernetics. *Kybernetes, 36*(9/10), 1173–1206.
12. Glanville, R. (2009). A (cybernetic) musing: Desirable ethics. In *The black boox vol. III. 39 steps* (pp. 293–303). Vienna: edition echoraum.
13. Habermas, J. (1981). *Theorie des kommunikativen Handelns*. Frankfurt am Main: Suhrkamp.
14. Jonas, W. (2012). Exploring the swampy ground. An inquiry into the logic of design research. In S. Grand & W. Jonas, (Eds.) *Mapping design research* (pp. 11–41). Basel: Birkhäuser.
15. Jonas, W., et al. (Eds.) (2015). *Transformation design. Perspectives on a new design attitude*. Basel: Birkhäuser.
16. Jonas, W., et al. (Eds.) (2018). *Un/certain Futures. Rollen des Designs in gesellschaftlichen Transformationsprozessen*. Bielefeld: transcript.
17. Jones, J. C. (1999). *The Internet and everyone*. London: Ellipsis.

18. Levy, S. (1984). *Hackers: Heroes of the computer revolution.* Garden City: Anchor Press/Doubleday.
19. Luhmann, N. (1995). *Social systems.* Stanford: Stanford University Press.
20. Mikulecky, D. C. (2009). *Definition of complexity.* Available at: http://www.people.vcu.edu/~mikuleck/ON%20COMPLEXITY.html. Accessed 20 May 2017.
21. Mouffe, C. (2005). *On the political.* New York: Taylor and Francis.
22. Pask, A. Gordon S. (1980). The limits of togetherness. In S. H. Lavington (Ed.), *Information processing* (Vol. 80, pp. 999–1012). Amsterdam: North Holland Publishing.
23. Rittel, H. W. J., & Webber, M. M. (1973). Dilemmas in a general theory of planning. *Policy Sciences, 4*(2), 155–169.
24. Schön, D. (1983). *The reflective practitioner. How professionals think in action.* New York: Basic Books.
25. Shannon, C. E., & Weaver, W. (1963). *The mathematical theory of communication.* Urbana: University of Illinois Press.
26. Simon, H. (1969/1981/1996). *The sciences of the artificial.* Cambridge MA: MIT Press.
27. Tanz, J. (2017). How silicon valley utopianism brought you the dystopian Trump presidency. *WIRED Magazine* Available at: https://www.wired.com/2017/01/silicon-valley-utopianism-brought-dystopian-trump-presidency. Accessed 19 Jan 2019.
28. WIRED. (2018). The Cambridge Analytica Story, Explained. Available at: Available at: https://www.wired.com/amp-stories/cambridge-analytica-explainer. Accessed 19 Jan 2019.
29. Zuckerberg, M. (2017). Building global community. *Facebook.* Available at: https://www.facebook.com/notes/mark-zuckerberg/building-global-community/10154544292806634. Accessed 19 Jan 2019.

Wolfgang Jonas holds a PhD in Naval Architecture from Berlin Technical University and the postdoctoral lecture qualification (Habilitation) for Design Theory from Wuppertal University. He has been Professor for Process Design in Halle, for Design Theory in Bremen and for System Design in Kassel. Since 2010 he is Professor for Designwissenschaft and head of the Institute for Design Research at Braunschweig University of Art, where he runs the Master in Transformation Design. His main working areas are systems thinking and methodology, futures studies and scenario approaches and the development of the concept 'Research through Design'.

Index

T. Fischer, C. M. Herr (eds.), *Design Cybernetics*, Design Research Foundations,
https://doi.org/10.1007/978-3-030-18557-2

GPSR Compliance
The European Union's (EU) General Product Safety Regulation (GPSR) is a set of rules that requires consumer products to be safe and our obligations to ensure this.

If you have any concerns about our products, you can contact us on

ProductSafety@springernature.com

In case Publisher is established outside the EU, the EU authorized representative is:

Springer Nature Customer Service Center GmbH
Europaplatz 3
69115 Heidelberg, Germany

www.ingramcontent.com/pod-product-compliance
Lightning Source LLC
Chambersburg PA
CBHW071609010626
46009CB00003B/147

* 9 7 8 3 0 3 0 1 8 5 5 6 5 *